Ancient Sources,
Modern Appropriations

Also Available from Bloomsbury

Hermeneutics between History and Philosophy, Hans-Georg Gadamer
The Beginning of Knowledge, Hans-Georg Gadamer
The Beginning of Philosophy, Hans-Georg Gadamer
A Century of Philosophy, Hans-Georg Gadamer
Truth and Method, Hans-Georg Gadamer
Ethics, Aesthetics and the Historical Dimension of Language, Hans-Georg Gadamer

Ancient Sources, Modern Appropriations

The Selected Writings of Hans-Georg Gadamer Volume III

By Hans-Georg Gadamer

Edited and translated by
Pol Vandevelde and Arun Iyer

BLOOMSBURY ACADEMIC
LONDON • NEW YORK • OXFORD • NEW DELHI • SYDNEY

BLOOMSBURY ACADEMIC
Bloomsbury Publishing Plc
50 Bedford Square, London, WC1B 3DP, UK
1385 Broadway, New York, NY 10018, USA
29 Earlsfort Terrace, Dublin 2, Ireland

BLOOMSBURY, BLOOMSBURY ACADEMIC and the Diana logo
are trademarks of Bloomsbury Publishing Plc

First published in Great Britain 2025

Copyright © Bloomsbury, 2025

Pol Vandevelde and Arun Iyer have asserted their right under the Copyright, Designs and Patents Act, 1988, to be identified as Translators of this work.

For legal purposes the Acknowledgements on p. vii constitute an extension of this copyright page.

All rights reserved. No part of this publication may be reproduced or transmitted in any form or by any means, electronic or mechanical, including photocopying, recording, or any information storage or retrieval system, without prior permission in writing from the publishers.

Bloomsbury Publishing Plc does not have any control over, or responsibility for, any third-party websites referred to or in this book. All internet addresses given in this book were correct at the time of going to press. The author and publisher regret any inconvenience caused if addresses have changed or sites have ceased to exist, but can accept no responsibility for any such changes.

A catalogue record for this book is available from the British Library.

A catalog record for this book is available from the Library of Congress.

ISBN: HB: 978-1-4411-1274-3
ePDF: 978-1-3505-1235-1
eBook: 978-1-3505-1234-4

Typeset by Integra Software Services Pvt. Ltd.
Printed and bound in Great Britain

To find out more about our authors and books visit www.bloomsbury.com and sign up for our newsletters.

Contents

Acknowledgements vii
Translators' Preface viii

Translators' Introduction 1
   I   What Do We Do When We Interpret? (by Pol Vandevelde) 1
   II   On the Art of Reading (by Arun Iyer) 19

Part I
Ancient Philosophy

1 Parmenides or Why Being Pertains to This World (1988)   43

2 Plato's Thinking through Utopias: A Lecture Addressed to Philologists (1983)   67

3 Mathematics and Dialectic in Plato (1982)   83

4 Dialectic Is not What Sophists Do: What Theaetetus Learns in the *Sophist* (1990)   101

Part II
Modern Philosophy

5 Oetinger as Philosopher (1964)   129

6 Herder and the Historical World (1967)   141

7 Schleiermacher as Platonist (1969)   157

8 Hegel and Heraclitus (1990)   165

9 Hegel and the Historical Spirit (1939)   175

10 Hegel and Heidelberg Romanticism (1961)   185

Notes	194
Appendix: Glossary of German Terms	214
Glossary of Ancient Greek Terms and Expressions	216
Glossary of Other Foreign Terms and Expressions	221
Works Cited by Gadamer	223
Index of Names	229
Index of Subjects	232

Acknowledgements

Among the many people to be thanked for the production of this edition and translation, we would like to acknowledge the work of Philip Sutherland and Jonmarc Bennett, who helped us in the preparation of the text; Frédéric Syler, who advised us on some points pertaining to the translation; James Risser and David Vessey for their continued support and their valuable recommendations. We also want to acknowledge the generous support of John Beach, who worked with the College of Arts and Sciences at Marquette University in establishing the Gadamer Translation Fund.

Translators' Preface

This third volume of *The Selected Writings of Hans-Georg Gadamer* follows the same spirit, methodology and principles as the first two volumes, *Hermeneutics between History and Philosophy* and *Ethics, Aesthetics and the Historical Dimension of Language*. The ten essays composing this volume were written between 1939 and 1990, the essays on ancient philosophy were written between 1982 and 1990 and those on eighteenth- and nineteenth-century philosophy written between 1939 and 1990. These essays expose us to Gadamer's late views on ancient philosophy, his rehabilitation of certain eighteenth-century thinkers and his lifelong contribution to our understanding of the significance of Hegel. They thus show us the transformation of his thinking on the history of philosophy over the different periods of his academic career.

The first part on ancient philosophy is made of essays written when Gadamer looks back at his own views on the pre-Socratics and Plato. They are remarkable in several respects. First, they remain quite technical, dealing with difficult passages in Parmenides and Plato, responding to the secondary literature on these texts and daring to propose consistent ways of understanding them. But second, they especially offer us the perspective of someone who himself takes a step back and provides an overall perspective on what these thinkers were after. After reading these essays we come away with the sentiment of having been brought closer to the matter of thinking when it comes to being and non-being, the relation between the one essence and the many particulars, the connection between numbers and ideas as well as the specific nature of thinking as a practice in comparison with sophistic practice.

The second part on modern philosophy comprises three essays from the 1960s on Oetinger, Herder and Schleiermacher and two essays on Hegel, one from his early period, his inaugural lecture on Hegel and the historical spirit in 1939, and the other from the later period on Hegel and Heraclitus in 1990. These texts manifest the constant interest at the heart of Gadamer's hermeneutics in the connection between thinking and history or the intrinsic historical nature of the process of thinking. These reflections bring us concretely, through specific analyses, in the presence of a way of thinking which is aware of its own situation in historical time while bringing to the fore the historical aspect of the thought interpreted. It is a remarkable demonstration and illustration of what the historical efficacy, the *Wirkungsgeschichte*, of thought is, which cannot be confined to a history of influences or reception precisely because that which is influenced or 'receives' the thought of the past is itself a 'thinking' in the active and productive sense of contributing to history.

As in the previous volumes, the pagination of the original German text of the *Gesammelte Werke* has been inserted in square brackets in the body of the translation. The bibliographical references provided by Gadamer have been completed where needed and the English translation of the works cited in German has been added when available. In the same spirit of making the translation as transparent as possible for scholars interested in close analysis, we have inserted the German words in square brackets when used technically or when Gadamer exploits the resources of the German language. These terms have been collected in a glossary of German terms in the Appendix. For facilitating the reading, we have also translated in square brackets the ancient Greek and Latin terms which Gadamer left untranslated, keeping our translation of these terms close to the manner in which Gadamer himself understands them. The same has been done for other foreign terms or expressions. These foreign terms have also been put together in a glossary in the appendix. Notes have been added to clarify some points or some allusions Gadamer is making or to provide the context of a textual reference. A list of all the works Gadamer is citing has been provided.

Translators' Introduction

I. What Do We Do When We Interpret? (by Pol Vandevelde)

Through his many studies of authors from all periods of time, Gadamer has taught us how to hear the voice of history in their philosophical texts. Against a caricature of historicism, which would make thought relative to history, as if history had a self-identity of its own over against which a particular view could be discovered to be 'relative', Gadamer shows us how the efficacy of history manifests itself in thinking, which is as much a shaping of history as it is shaped by history.

The texts translated in this volume provide additional explanations for this recasting of history by illustrating two basic positions which also underlie Gadamer's hermeneutics. The first one concerns the connection between being and thinking, which is treated in the first section of this volume, through a discussion of Parmenides' views and its reverberations in Plato's thought in the *Theaetetus* and the *Sophist* in contradistinction to the views of the sophists. The second position concerns the connection between thinking and history, which is treated in the second section of this volume through a discussion of historicism in Oetinger and the role of history in how thinking operates (in Herder and Hegel) or how interpretation is historically situated (in Schleiermacher).

These two basic positions, which have remained constant in Gadamer's thought, both with regard to the ontological power of thinking and the historical nature of thought, define his attitude towards the history of philosophy as an alternative to the history of ideas or what German scholars have called the 'history of the problem'. The 'history of ideas' tends to be blind to the linguistic flesh of the ideas which are claimed to be retrieved as well as to the historical flesh of the historians themselves who do the retrieving, as they are supposed to be ideally transparent and non-efficacious towards the 'historical ideas' unveiled. If, as Gadamer shows, interpreters are historically situated and make use of concepts, views, perspectives, methods, interests which are specific to their time period, they cannot be innocent observers or non-participating recorders. They are involved in the process of interpretation, with the consequence that the object of interpretation becomes relational. Let us examine these two basic positions held by Gadamer and then draw the consequences for how interpretation operates.

The Connection between Thinking and Being

Whether in his analysis of the pre-Socratics or of Plato, Gadamer tries to make us feel the pioneering aspect of their thinking, which attempted to liberate itself from the kind of explanations found in stories (*mūthos*) by crafting a new conceptual framework. For, in their effort to offer an intelligible account of a world order which made sense, they had to invent concepts, create tools for thinking out of the language spoken at the time. They themselves were keenly aware of this ontological connection between what their thinking was doing and the coming into being of what is particular. It is one of Gadamer's great merits to have reminded us of this conceptual construction in ancient thought and to make us feel the correlation between their ontology – what 'to be' meant to them – and the conceptualization they were inventing. He makes us realize that, if we want to understand them, we cannot just simply translate their words and concepts into ours under the assumption that these ancient thinkers thought like us.

In some of the texts of the first part, Gadamer takes the very concept of mind as an illustration and shows us the intellectual distance which exists between the ancient Greek notions of *noūs* and *noein* and our concepts of mind and thinking. For us, the mind is a very abstract thing, some apparatus supervening on a brain and providing 'representations' or 'states'. These states are assumed to be discrete entities, individuated as belonging to a specific subject, sometimes granted a 'feel' or 'first-person' aspect. These states can be described in their punctuality in terms of conditions of possibility (necessary and/or sufficient) or conditions of satisfaction. Philosophers can then examine what perception is or what a belief is, for example, by focusing on an atemporal punctual moment belonging to a specific mental state.

As Gadamer shows, the ancient word *noūs* or the verb *noein* did not name such a 'mind'. Using the research of Kurt von Fritz[1] as well as that of other philologists and philosophers, Gadamer shows that the Greek notion of 'mind' means an inner awareness of a situation in which we find ourselves and in which we are involved. Instead of a theoretical cognizance of a fact, as it is for us, thinking as 'taking in' arose from concrete experiences in which we become aware of our connections to the world. Thinking as 'taking in' makes out what is going on around us and with regard to what may happen to us. *Noūs* is thus intimately connected to one's own sense of being and to possible behaviours or actions in relation to the situation. Von Fritz connects the word *noein* (to know) to the sense of smell and gives the example of a deer sensing that something is there – 'thinking that' something is there – and suddenly running away. As von Fritz says, the deer 'smells danger' (*Wittern einer Gefahr*), and he mentions the English expression 'smelling a rat' as an analogous expression[2].

This understanding of thinking as a situation's rising to our awareness or a situation's working its way into our awareness does not fit well with our mentalistic ways of thinking, according to which we would explain the situation sequentially and ontologically: there would be, first, a situation, then the grasping of what is going on and later the behaviour in reaction to realizing what is going on, such as fleeing or attacking. By contrast to this, as Gadamer explains, using von Fritz's research,

> According to its original lexical use, *noein* seems to be something like the sense of smell possessed by deer which 'makes out' something in the sense of 'something is there'. This is the way wild animals locate danger and thereby certainly do not recognize what it is while yet sensing that something 'is' there[3].

In his explanation, von Fritz sees two fundamental meanings in the word *noein*: '"to recognize a situation" and "to plan" or "to have an intention"'. This indicates a connection between the coming into being of a fact or situation and the taking in of this situation. He mentions an example in Homer, describing someone seeing a brown spot, recognizing it as a human being and realizing that it is an enemy lying in ambush[4]. Instead of being sequential as a series of mental states subsequent to the existence of a state of affairs, the 'thinking' as 'taking in' rather posits 'being', as what matters and demands a response. Von Fritz uses the expression 'mental perception' (*geistige Wahrnehmung*) to name this non-conceptual or non-propositional act of knowing as taking in[5]. He sees a confirmation of this in the possible etymological connection mentioned by Bruno Snell between *gignōskein* (to know) and *gignesthai* (to become, to come into being). The coming into being grows on the knower, as it were, without any clear separation between knowing and being.

In order to have a contemporary sense of the belonging between thinking and being, we have to look at the phenomenologists and existentialists, who precisely rejected a strict empiricist and mentalistic framework. Sartre, for example, gives us an illustration of this knowing as taking in and being involved in this knowing. He writes: 'What I immediately grasp when I hear branches crackling behind me is not that *there is someone there* but that I am vulnerable, that I have a body which can be hurt, [...] that *I am seen*'[6]. My taking in of something being there – before my explicit knowing 'that' something is behind me – unfolds through my involvement in the situation and thanks to it. My being absorbs the being of things, which reveals itself through me.

Faced with this difference in understanding about what thinking is, we could simply use our own understanding as a standard and lament a lack of distinctions in these ancient thinkers. The alternative, Gadamer recommends, is to be mindful of the genesis of our own understanding of what thinking is and of our understanding of what 'being' means so that we may contemplate the absence of necessity in our own conception of what a mind is. In so doing, we open ourselves to being unsettled in our own views and envision an alternate way to consider the relation between thinking and being: a being which is interactive, in so far as it is of the order of a coming to be within a situation which matters to someone, who then becomes a 'knower'. In this alternate way, thinking thus pertains to being: the taking in is the ontological threshold at which something registers as being, and being is a process of 'coming to be' or a 'becoming being' in which we as knowers participate as protagonists in what becomes a disclosure of being. Of this alternate way of thinking, Gadamer says the following: 'Being is only where *noein* stumbles upon something, whether it be rendered as taking in, receiving or touching something. In any case it is clear that […] where something is taken in, something is there, being and not nothing'[7]. In Heideggerean terms, Gadamer writes that for Parmenides 'being is the there and "there" means the appearing of appearances'[8].

What the ancient meaning of *noûs* suggests to Gadamer is that to the differentiating activity of the mind there corresponds the coming into being of differentiated beings, that being and knowing are the same, as in Parmenides' famous statement[9]. It is not that this sameness would be established *after* an observer would have taken in view, sideways, that which is and that which is thought. The sameness is a resignation, so to speak, in so far as it is only through the activity of the mind, in regard to the situation and the interests of this mind, that the world reveals its layout, that, in von Fritz's Homeric example, a brown spot comes into being – discloses itself – as an enemy lying in ambush.

Gadamer sees this thread of *noûs* – knowing as taking in – in several ancient philosophers: in Democritus, who 'use[s] the word for the knowledge of the atoms', in Plato, who uses the word for 'mathematical intuition and abstraction', in Aristotle, who 'fully emphasizes that *noûs* consists in *thigganein* ["to touch"], in the immediacy of stumbling upon something and touching it, different from when we make a statement about something'[10]. It is also because of this original concrete meaning of 'taking in' and this connection to being that '*noûs* […] was thought by Anaxagoras as a most subtle material, penetrating everywhere and permeating everything. It scents everything, so to speak, because it is present in everything without ever being mixed with anything'[11]. But it is also the original sense of being which Heidegger was after, claiming to have detected a manifestation of it in the ancient Greeks as the view that being means 'entering into presence' (*Anwesenheit*).

In this regard, Gadamer's studies of the connection between being and thinking offer a clear rejoinder to Derrida's attack on the so-called 'metaphysics of presence', which he claims to see permeating the West everywhere, of which Heidegger himself is still a representative. Although Gadamer responded to Derrida elsewhere, most clearly in 'Hermeneutics on the Trail'[12], the view that thinking contributes to the coming into being or that being means 'entering into presence' is a direct refutation of such a 'metaphysics of presence', which Derrida understands exclusively 'mentally' as a presence of oneself to oneself. What Derrida misses is the 'entering' into presence or the 'coming' into being. Thinking as taking in is in fact an extended thinking, a branching out of the mind – the presence to oneself – and into the world, so that being is permeated by a becoming. Presence is thus the transient moment in being. As Gadamer shows in the case of Parmenides, coming into being or entering into presence names a collaboration between something coming to be and a taking in by someone, or it names an interaction between that which comes into presence and the one who inhabits this presence. Such an interaction between being and thinking escapes any medieval view about any '*adaequatio rei et intellectus*' or any modern match between 'mind and world', both of which appeal to a static world, which is simply laid out, whether divinely or naturally, and a static mind, which knows with its own conceptual apparatus, whether universal or socially constructed.

The view that *noûs* or the mind is not separated from the world but interacts with it forces us to revisit the *logos*, which is supposed to be the articulation of what the mind does and which has been translated as 'reason' or 'argument' or 'discourse'. For *logos* entertains a close connection both with that which it 'gathers together' (the original meaning of *legein*), and with what is supposed to be its opposite, *mūthos*, 'myth' or 'story'. Before being 'reason' or 'rational thinking', *logos* is an account of what is. As such, it cannot escape being a form of 'opinion' or *doxa*, which Gadamer sometimes translates into German as *Ansicht* or 'point of view'. The *logos* is reached by starting with 'points of view' and gathering together that which remains the same in the discussion, which will be seen as the *eidos*, the idea, the essence. Thus, the *logos* as an account has an element of a 'story' or a *mūthos* in it, and this, of necessity, as it is reached through a dialogue, through staging, characters and contextualized interactions. Gadamer points to this staging in the *Theaetetus*, when the stranger from Elea is carefully managing his handling of Theaetetus, appealing to the specific knowledge a mathematician like Theaetetus would have and tailoring his arguments to what Theaetetus is familiar with[13]. Taking into consideration the situation of the discussion partners, as is done in any genuine dialogue, belongs in part to the dimension of the *mūthos*, accompanying the production of the *logos*. As Gadamer says about Parmenides,

> Here, we are not yet in the realm of abstract conceptual formations but in a powerfully intuitive thinking in which the words of the living language are loaded with a new content of thought. It is mythical discourse, not only because of its verse form but because of its ties to intuition. It is almost like what we are familiar with in Plato as the co-existence and the togetherness of *logos* and *mūthos*[14].

This cohabitation of *mūthos* and *logos* intrinsic to the dialogue form sheds a different light on the goal of philosophy, whose pursuit is less about presenting a system of views and more about engaging and convincing those who participate in the discussion (including the readers of the dialogue). It is the purpose of the dialogue to make distinctions and elaborate definitions, either by weeding out unsatisfactory views through the elenctic method (in Plato's early period) or developing a dialectic method (in the Eleatic dialogues) or proposing big stories about the ordering of the world (in the late period). This enterprise of philosophy is unending, remaining open to debate, precisely because the *logos*, the heart of dialectic and thus of what thinking consists of, keeps this mobility of interacting with reality.

The cohabitation of *mūthos* and *logos* also points to the temporal dimension in the *logos*. Gadamer sees this dimension already in the elementary 'combination' of a noun and a verb, which together constitute a *logos*, a sentence expressing a proposition. The verb gives a temporalization to the process of 'making a statement' about something. The 'putting together' which the *logos* effectuates is a historical process. 'In this', Gadamer says,

> we find a significant hint that the sense of a statement and with it even the sense of being presupposed by a statement, depends in each case on the specific point of view from which a being is seen and addressed. Only in this connection, thus in a *pros ti* ['in relation to something'], does being at all appear and, howsoever it may be, this is only accomplished through its temporalization[15].

Using the example given by the stranger of Elea of two *logoi*, 'Theaetetus is sitting' and 'Theaetetus is flying', the first *logos* is temporal, about 'this human being in the present', and the second is false in all time in virtue of the *eidos* or being-what of a human being, who cannot fly (Arun Iyer will develop this difference in the second part of this introduction). In the *logos*, then,

> the entire amplitude of the thinking of being between the 'this here' and its 'being-what' is played out [...]. The contingency of the particular is indeed never graspable in the *logos* but the *logos* encompasses even this contingency by saying 'this'. [...] The mobility of beings, which comes through in the *logos*, and the mobility of the particular, which remains embedded in the system of movements in nature, are intertwined[16].

The intertwining between *logos* and *mūthos* is thus not a lack on the side of thinking but a requirement if thinking wants to do justice to the particular, which has its mobility, and not force it into a rigid universal. This is also why it is so difficult, as Gadamer shows, to separate clearly what sophists do from philosophy. For the former are responding to the particular, for example a specific discussion on the constitution, and think 'pragmatically', Plato being the one who drew the relativistic implications of this pragmatism, for example in the case of Protagoras[17].

The interdependence between thinking and being also changes how Plato's notion of the 'idea' is to be understood. Gadamer has relentlessly fought what he takes to be Aristotle's misrepresentation of the theory of ideas, which he presented as some mythical entities existing singly in a world separated from ours. This misrepresentation was quite influential, leading to the common and false opposition between the idealist Plato and the realist Aristotle[18]. This false view is so entrenched that we often call Plato's theory of ideas the theory of 'forms', using Aristotle's term, 'as if', Gadamer laments, 'Plato knew of matter'[19]. Here is how Gadamer presents his view on this misrepresentation:

> My thesis is [...] this: Aristotle reduces the problem of the ideas to this case which, under his ontological presuppositions, is the most promising, the case of the *phusei on* ['natural entity'], obviously with the intent on his part to show in this most promising case that here too it does not work to speak of 'ideas' being 'by themselves'[20].

Gadamer discerns two sides in Aristotle's misrepresentation. First, about the status of ideas and, second, about how participation works. Regarding the status of ideas, Gadamer takes issue with Aristotle's claim that for Plato an idea exists alone by itself in a different realm. On different occasions, Gadamer speaks about the *Diesseits* of being or the fact that being pertains to this world. Ideas may be by themselves, as Plato clearly says, but this does not entail that they are separated from the entities participating in them and countable as individuals. Gregory Vlastos confirms this view that Plato does not say that ideas, which are by themselves, are 'separated' from this world. He writes: 'The verb *chōrizein* ["to separate"] does not appear here [in the *Parmenides*] nor anywhere else in the debate, nor is it ever applied to the Forms by Plato anywhere in his corpus'[21]. The famous *chōrismos* or separation between the intelligible and the sensible world comes from Aristotle. For Plato, an idea is not a single entity existing by itself but part of a web of other ideas, so that knowledge involves many ideas, and this is why, Gadamer says, 'Plato investigates the foundations which give its form and organization to the structure of this web of ideas'[22].

If ideas are not singular ideals separated from this world, the philosophical question which Plato sees in participation is not about how a natural entity participates in an idea, which is the case Aristotle uses to defeat the theory. As Gadamer notes,

> Plato always regarded the participation of the individual in the idea as something self-evident, which is what makes the supposition that there are ideas first meaningful at all. He was, for this reason, also exceedingly loose in the linguistic characterization of this relationship, whether he calls the relation of the individual to the universal presence, community, participation, intertwining, mixture or whatever else[23].

The question Plato sees in participation is rather about how ideas participate in other ideas, making up a singular entity and allowing us to see this singular entity by recognizing its make-up in terms of the ideas 'mixed' in it, as the *Philebus* will say. '"Participation" and "taking part" do not mean here a having or a taking but a being'[24]. This is why Plato considers that

> what really *is*, is only the Idea – that is, that which makes up the unitary selfsameness of what shows itself and in view of which, alone, the change in what shows itself to the senses is understandable. Thus, that it is the 'presence' ['*Anwesenheit*'] of the idea in the individual thing that makes it exist is due to the fact that the individual thing can be understood only in view of what it always is[25].

Gadamer contends not only that Aristotle misrepresented Plato's views, although it was most likely with propaedeutic and pedagogical aims in order to bring out his own views more sharply, but that he, in fact, remained close to Plato's views. On this point, early on in his career, Gadamer took issue with Werner Jaeger who defended the view that there was a historical development in Aristotle, who, at first, was a Platonist and progressively moved away from Plato[26]. Against such a view, Gadamer contends that even when Aristotle criticizes Plato, he does so on the basis of a shared position, the one presented in the *Phaedo*. There, Socrates describes his second-best journey negatively as a rejection of the naturalistic explanations of his predecessors, the so-called 'pre-Socratics', and positively as a 'flight into the *logoi*'. This flight, Gadamer comments, 'seeks to investigate the truth as it is mirrored in the *logoi*'[27]. Aristotle is thus 'on this point a Platonist'[28]: 'When he questions the being of beings (*pōs legetai*), Aristotle begins with the question about our ways of speaking'[29]. His critique of Plato only aims at refining the understanding of the *logoi*, which will culminate in the 'schemas of the categories'. But even these categories are themselves anticipated in the *Sophist*. For in this dialogue, Gadamer notes, 'the entire amplitude of the thinking of being between the "this here" and its "being-what" is played out here, which is established in the early text on the categories and covered by the Aristotelian concepts of *dunamis* and *energeia*'[30]. The refinement Aristotle thought necessary to introduce into Plato's ideas consisted in this, Gadamer says:

> to strip the logical universality of the concept of idea from its ontological dignity and at the same time and by the same token to find a new legitimacy for the precedence of *ousia*, and doing this not in turning away from an orientation to the *logos*, but to the contrary in a clarification of the *logos* through differentiation[31].

Gadamer thus concludes that Aristotle built on Plato's views. He did not reject them.

The Connection between Thinking and History

Already in the first section of this introduction we saw how Gadamer sees the history of philosophy as pertaining to the very process of doing philosophy. The texts of the second section of this volume attempt to make a case for the historical nature of thought. This connection between thought and history was explicitly developed in the eighteenth century and gave rise to historicism. Gadamer examines some figures who elaborated this articulating role of history. Oetinger illustrates this point of tension which forced people to become mindful of their history when the modern sciences after Newton appeared more and more to challenge the views of the tradition. This requires a reform of the spirit in a century which Oetinger deplored as being 'idealist' and 'in which almost nobody knows what "life" is anymore'[32]. As Gadamer says, such a reform has to begin with the words we use: 'We are […] stuck in the mud from which we cannot dislodge ourselves if we do not begin reforming the spirit with the reform of words'[33]. 'Common sense' becomes for Oetinger a means to initiate this dual reform, reconciling Newton's physics with the world as it appears to us, that is to say, reconciling the mechanical power of forces with the traditional substance ontology. Oetinger specifically tries to transform Newton's notion of the force of attraction from a mere physical power within a mechanistic framework into a mystical power of 'liveliness', breathed into entities by the divine[34]. Science then is not only a theory of reality, but it itself comes from reality and its language originates from the language used in experience.

Herder, as the alleged promoter of historicism, also saw in Newton such a possibility of reconciling a mathematical understanding of nature with a humanistic understanding. Newton combined, in Gadamer's words, 'a physics of the earth with a physics of heavenly bodies'[35]. Concretely, Herder envisions world history in terms of how peoples experience the world specifically in their own times. In a very Gadamerian formulation, Herder writes: 'Every historical era possesses its own different horizon'[36]. This historically minded approach has become a canonical Gadamerian view, namely, that it is 'a false, unhistorical (and unreal) abstraction "to take" one's own present "for the quintessence of all times and peoples"'[37]. This view on history as living in the present is for Gadamer Herder's 'decisive insight', namely that 'history is only "disseminated" in what is national and individual, in times and peoples'[38]. History permeates the spirit of a people, manifesting itself in its political system, in its songs and folklore, in its specific language. This is the force of history which, Gadamer says, makes 'historical truth' 'the efficacy [*Wirksamkeit*] of forces'[39]. As Herder writes, 'the whole history of humanity is a pure natural history of human forces, actions and drives according to place and time'[40].

Hegel radicalizes this history as an unfolding force manifesting itself in peoples and having the efficacy of a spirit. This Hegelian view influenced Heidegger's 'history of being', developed in the 1930s, which keeps some of the Hegelian reification of history in the manner of a 'becoming'. However, Gadamer wants to take some distance from these two different Hegelian and Heideggerean views on the efficacy of history. He wants to grant it a less interventionistic power, precisely by returning to the roots of our understanding of being and thinking, as we saw in the first section. In bringing us back to the historical situation in which problems arose, questions were formulated and concepts were formed, Gadamer makes us feel the historical 'paste' of thinking, as it were, and urges us to remain mindful that we carry our own present in our investigations. These two sides of thinking – the thought to be grasped in situation and the thinking which carries its own present – render unintelligible the notion of a spirit which would materialize in the development of history.

In order to name his own views on the interaction between thinking and history or the historical nature of thinking, Gadamer coined a new term *Wirkungsgeschichte*, made of a word which means 'effect' and the other which means 'history'. Like in any compound, the grammatical connection between the two terms is not made explicit. In another context Gadamer acknowledged the temptation for philosophers writing in German to take recourse to such easy-to-make compounds and the proclivity of some to succumb to it. Including himself among them, he notes that his compound 'is perhaps a bit too ambiguous an expression' (*vielleicht etwas zu vieldeutigen*)[41]. This semantic looseness requires that we think through the expression *Wirkungsgeschichte* in order to parse it and figure out the grammatical link between the two terms composing it, just as ancient Greek readers, as Gadamer reminds us, needed to read aloud their texts which did not include a space between words, the reading aloud being the thinking necessary for parsing the sentences[42].

Normally, when we have a compound made of two nouns, the second one is the main term and the first is a complement in the genitive, as in *Problemgeschichte*, which can be translated as 'history of the problem'. In our case, the translation of *Wirkungsgeschichte* would be 'history of effect' or 'history of reception' or 'history of influence', as some translators render it. Sometimes we can consider the first term adjectivally, as in the case of *Geisteswissenschaften*, the 'spiritual' or 'human sciences'. And some scholars translate Gadamer's compound as 'effective history'. In other cases, we can invert the semantic importance of the two terms, making the first one an adjective but in the verbal sense, as in the way Dilthey's compound *Wirkungszusammenhang*, which in one sense simply means 'nexus of effects', has been sometimes translated as 'productive nexus'. The first term 'effect' becomes adjectival and active[43].

This Diltheyan compound offers a good model to translate Gadamer's own compound *Wirkungsgeschichte* by 'efficacious history' or 'the efficacy of history', which says both that history has an efficacy and that the efficacy itself is historical so that the two terms of the compound qualify each other and thus annul their own individual semantic autonomy. Gadamer himself paraphrases it by saying: 'It is the consciousness which experiences itself historically [*das geschichtlich erfahrene Bewusstsein*]'[44].

We can then respond to the different translations offered by making the following three points. First, this 'efficacy of history' cannot just be a matter of influence, as if history had some form of agency, acting upon something that would not be part of history. Second, given Gadamer's view that history is not about objects, such as a text or ideas, but that a text and ideas are themselves historical, belonging to a certain horizon, it cannot be a 'history of effects'. For this formulation would imply that there would be 'effects', for example of a text, and then afterward a history could be established of these effects, as if a work could have effects independently of any historical situation. Although we have sometimes used this translation, we need to keep in mind, as Gadamer says, that the consciousness of this 'history of effects' 'is something other than the investigation of the history of the effects [*Wirkungsgeschichte*] which a work has, like the trace which a work leaves behind'[45].

Third, because it is history that 'exerts' or produces the effect, that is to say, because the *Wirkung*-aspect belongs to history, this efficacy of history cannot be an 'effective history'. This translation may render well the '*Wirkung*' aspect of 'having efficacy', but it ambiguates the expression due to the proximity between 'effective' and 'efficient', as if history had a specific effect on something specific. In fact, history of its own has no efficacy. It is rather by being within history that works have effects which are historical. This is also why Gadamer rejects the notion of the 'history of the problem'. Such a history can certainly be useful but only as long as we do not assume that the 'problem' has remained the same in history, as if, Gadamer says, 'the problem would exist like the stars in the sky'[46], indifferent to the manners in which it has been formulated in the course of time. As he notes, 'there is truly no place outside history from which the identity of a problem could be thought in the changes of the historical efforts to solve it'[47]. A 'perennial problem' can thus only be a manner of speaking, like an umbrella term covering different issues in different time periods, which we now see retrospectively as being about the same problem. As he shows about the case of freedom, as understood by Aristotle, Plato, Christian theology and in our scientifically minded times, 'the posing of the question at each time does not become intelligible by presupposing that we are dealing with an identical problem of freedom. It is far more about seeing the real questions in the manner they pose themselves as that which needs to be understood'[48].

In sum, the two terms making up the compound *Wirkungsgeschichte*, which have a meaning as autonomous semantic entities, 'history' and 'effect', have their specific autonomous meaning annulled by the compound and become qualifiers of each other: it is a history through the effects it has and it is an effect by being historicized.

Truth and Method contains a small section titled 'The principle of the *Wirkungsgeschichte*', which is introduced by this sentence: 'A hermeneutics appropriate to the subject matter would have to exhibit in understanding itself the reality of history [*die Wirklichkeit der Geschichte*]'[49]. In the sentence which follows, he introduces the notion: 'What is required by this, I call *Wirkungsgeschichte*'. There is thus an explicit connection between the two expressions *Wirklichkeit der Geschichte* (the reality of history) and *Wirkungsgeschichte* (the efficacy of history). The English translation of *Truth and Method* even adds a word, which I italicize below, to paraphrase the first expression *Wirklichkeit der Geschichte*: 'the reality *and efficacy* of history'. Gadamer explains this connection between 'history' and 'efficacy' in the next sentence: 'Understanding is in its essence a process permeated by the efficacy of history [*ein wirkungsgeschichtlicher Vorgang*]', which the English translation renders as 'understanding is, essentially, a historically effected event'[50]. Let us examine some of Gadamer's explanations.

'When, from the historical distance which determines our hermeneutic situation in totality, we seek to understand a historical phenomenon, we are always already submitted to the effects of the efficacy of history [*den Wirkungen der Wirkungsgeschichte*]'[51], an expression which the English translation renders as 'affected by history'[52]. This efficacy of history, Gadamer continues, 'determines in advance what appears to us as worthy of questioning and as object of research'[53]. He then repeats what is well-known to his readers in a negative way: 'Understanding is never a subjective comportment towards a given "object"', and adds the positive explanation: understanding 'belongs to the efficacy of history, and this means that it belongs to the being of that which is understood'[54].

This makes clear that the efficacy of history is not meant as a new method or a new approach. It is not, Gadamer says, 'a new autonomous auxiliary discipline of the human sciences'[55]. It is rather a description of a process which incites us 'to learn and recognize that in all understanding […] the effect of the efficacy of history is at work [*die Wirkung dieser Wirkungsgschichte am Werke ist*]'[56]. Here again, the repetition of the terms *Wirkung* and *Werk*, just as before the repetition of the terms *Wirkung* and *Wirklichkeit*, shows both that reality, and thus also the work to be interpreted, is in flux, worked from the inside by a historical efficacy, and that the efficacy or the effect is the work of history itself as it is made. Gadamer can then speak of 'the power [*Macht*] of this efficacy of history'[57]. What he wants to make clear by this, he says, is that 'we cannot take ourselves out of the flow of history itself [*Geschehen*], and confront it, so to speak, with the consequence that the past would somehow become an object for us'[58]. Neither the object nor understanding can cast off their historical clothing. 'It belongs to genuine understanding', Gadamer says, '[…] to recover the concepts of a historical past in such a way that they also include our own conceptualization'[59].

Gadamer also uses the compound in its adjectival form, *wirkungsgeschichtlich* in the expression *wirkungsgeschichtliches Bewußtsein* which has been translated as 'historically effected consciousness' but we could say instead 'a consciousness permeated by the efficacy of history'. It cannot be a consciousness 'of' the effects of history or a consciousness 'of' an effective history, as we saw, as if consciousness could take such effects or such an effective history in its scope. Gadamer clearly states that 'the efficacy of history' cannot be 'the *object* [*Gegenstand*] of hermeneutic consciousness'[60]. As an adjective, *wirkungsgeschichtlich* confers on consciousness the quality of having or pertaining to the efficacy of history. Consciousness is realized historically or, as Paul Ricoeur translates it, it is 'the consciousness of being exposed to the efficacy of history' ('*la conscience d'être exposé à l'efficience de l' histoire*')[61].

This consciousness which is *wirkungsgeschichtlich*, permeated by the efficacy of history, names the fusion of horizons from within, in the manner in which it 'works' or in its operation. Gadamer himself speaks of the 'mode of enactment' [*Vollzugsweise*][62] in relation to the fusion of horizons: his presentation of the fusion of horizons, he says, 'was supposed to describe the mode of enactment pertaining to the consciousness permeated by the efficacy of history'[63]. As he explains: 'It was indeed the point of the consciousness permeated by the efficacy of history to think work and efficacy [*Werk und Wirkung*] as the unity of a sense. What I described as the fusion of horizons was the form of effectuation of this unity [*Vollzugsform dieser Einheit*]'[64].

The unsatisfactory conceptual aspect of the expression 'fusion of horizons' is due to its descriptive nature. It is a description of a process made from the outside, in a sideways manner, suggesting – against Gadamer's own intent – that there would pre-exist a native horizon of the object and a starting horizon of the interpreter. Gadamer certainly denies this: 'There is no more an isolated horizon of the present in itself than there are historical horizons which have to be acquired. Rather, understanding is always the fusion of these horizons supposedly existing by themselves'[65]. Yet, if the fusion is not between two pre-existing horizons, how does it become such a fusion other than through the initiative of the interpreter, which creates an imbalance in favour of the interpreter? And if one of the two partners in the dialogue has the initiative, is it still a genuine 'fusion'? Gadamer came to recognize this possible issue. In his 'Reflections on My Philosophical Journey', he writes: 'As I look back today, I see one point in particular where I did not achieve the theoretical consistency I strove for in *Truth and Method*, which is about 'the otherness of the Other'. He worries that he may not have shown clearly enough that this otherness of the other 'is not overcome in understanding, but rather preserved'[66]. The consciousness permeated by the efficacy of history reframes the fusion of horizons by taking the perspective of the object to be understood, which comes into being thanks to this kind of consciousness.

This is why Gadamer says that 'a consciousness permeated by the efficacy of history is [...] more being than consciousness'[67]. It is a consciousness whose 'mode of realization' or 'manner of effectuating itself' (*Vollzugsweise*) is historical and within which an object presents itself to be understood. Such a consciousness is 'first of all a consciousness of the hermeneutic situation'[68] and 'has the structure of experience [*Erfahrung*]'[69]. Because we ourselves have a 'historical being', 'being-historical [*Geschichtlichsein*] means never being wrapped up in self-knowledge'[70]. Gadamer quotes Dilthey who wrote: 'The first condition for the possibility of a science of history consists in this that I myself am a historical being, that the one who investigates history is the same as the one who makes it'[71].

Instead of a consciousness taking note of the effects of history, this consciousness which is *wirkungsgeschichtlich* is 'a moment in the effectuation [*Vollzug*] of understanding itself'[72] and is 'operative' or 'efficacious' (*wirksam*) in obtaining the right question'[73]. Gadamer also says that it is 'a consciousness of the work itself', so that this consciousness has an efficacy (*Wirkung*)[74] in turn and of its own: 'Understanding turns out to be a mode of efficacy [*Wirkung*] and knows itself to be such an efficacy'[75]. Almost in Hegelian fashion, he says that the word of the interpreter is 'the effectuation of understanding' and, as such, 'the actuality of the consciousness permeated by the efficacy of history' (*die Aktualität des wirkungsgeschichtlichen Bewusstseins*)[76]. In remarkably clear terms, he explains:

> I call this 'the consciousness permeated by the efficacy of history' because I mean by it, on the one hand, the fact that our consciousness is determined by the efficacy of history [*wirkungsgeschichtlich*], that is to say, by a real historical flow [*Geschehen*] which does not let our consciousness free in the sense of a confrontation with the past. And I mean, on the other hand, that it is important to produce in us, again and again, an awareness of this being-acted upon [*ein Bewusstsein dieses Bewirktseins*][77].

Consciousness does its work, for example in understanding, as a consciousness which is spread in the world and in history.

This connection between thinking and history, manifested by a consciousness permeated by the efficacy of history, gives interpreters a significant responsibility. They are not just discovering the meaning of past works. They contribute to the meaning of these works and these works are only meaningful and efficacious from within an interpretation. Interpretation is in this framework a performance of consciousness and the efficacy it exerts on the work consists in providing a future to the work. Interpretation as a performance is a re-enactment.

Interpretation as Re-enactment

In the reception of his scholarship, Gadamer had to contend with the dismissive attitude of some analytically trained scholars, who do not understand the historical nature of thinking and thus do not consider themselves part of the interpretation process, which they see as a neutral analysis. In this kind of 'analysis', the 'analysing' subjects remain extraordinarily oblivious of themselves, speaking in a voice or in words whose medium is assumed to be transparent – a language of thought, which is independent of any linguistic structure belonging to a natural language, whether grammatical or lexical. These analysing subjects, presenting themselves as the mind's eye which belongs to no mind in particular, know no variation in time – so that scholars belonging to this analytic school can appropriate Plato and Aristotle as fellows of their own institutions, correcting their inaccuracies and reformulating their views with the sophistication of twentieth- or twenty-first-century thinkers. Gregory Vlastos became a model for presenting Plato as the best version of an analytic philosopher by completing and correcting reasonings and arguments here and there, turning Plato into a fellow colleague. While clearly bothered with the ignoring of history and its efficacy, Gadamer remained remarkably temperate and tried and re-tried indefatigably to make a case for the fruitfulness of understanding texts in context while being mindful of our own historical situation. He writes in this regard,

> despite all the admiration I harbour for the meticulousness of the logical critique of Plato, which comes to us from England and America, I have the feeling that it is almost like something of a waste to regret the absence of rigour here and to introduce a new rigour there, where entirely different claims to be convincing were made, as they arise as 'persuasive arguments'[78] from the immediacy of the conversation[79].

Against such an attitude, Gadamer sees the history of philosophy as a way of doing philosophy and this fundamental view is at the heart of his 'philosophical hermeneutics'. As he states, his philosophical interests in Greek philosophy and hermeneutics 'have remained the two main foci of [his] work'[80] and converge on a historically minded interpretation. Already in his inaugural lecture at the University of Leipzig in 1939, he acknowledged the mediating role of history when saying that ancient philosophy is 'the basis [on] which the whole of philosophy and its history had revealed itself to me'[81].

Once we accept that there is no self-evident border between what belongs to the realm of being and what belongs to the realm of thinking, as we saw in the first section, and that thinking is historical through and through, as we saw in the second section, the consequences for interpretation, which is a form of thinking, are quite significant. If ontology and epistemology do not have their legitimacy as disciplines in a 'natural' carving out of the world and if history pertains to the very process of thinking, interpretation finds itself in a new framework both with regard to its link to its object and to its own operation.

Interpreters do not stumble on the object they will interpret as some preordained entity, lying in wait of being seized upon by interpretation. The work must speak to them, grab their attention and make a claim on them, as Gadamer says. This means that the object is dynamic. In order to do justice to the dynamics of this object, interpreters need to understand ancient authors in what is specific to their thinking. They need to be mindful that these ancient thinkers invented a conceptual apparatus to account for reality so that their writings already represent an interpretation, in the sense of an intervention in reality in order to 'cut it up' or 'carve' it, as Socrates says in the *Phaedrus*, when he recommends that our concepts 'cut at the joints' of reality and avoid 'the manners of a bad butcher'[82]. Thus, when interpreting ancient texts, we construe or re-construe this first construing, trying to recapture the performative aspect of their inventive thinking. This means that the performance is also on the side of interpretation in its operation.

Gadamer calls this dual performative aspect – on the side of interpretation and on the side of the object interpreted – the structure of question and answer, which he explains as the fact that 'to understand a question means to pose it. To understand a position [*Meinung*] means to understand it as an answer to a question'[83]. This structure is a dialogical structure, what he calls 'the original effectuation' of the dialogue[84]. He came to see more and more, he says, 'the sense of performance [*Vollzugssinn*] that a dialogue has'[85] or 'the form of effectuation belonging to a dialogue [*die Vollzugsform des Gesprächs*]'[86]. He uses the expression *Vollzugsweise*, 'mode of effectuation', for the 'hermeneutic experience'[87] itself. This element of performance, effectuation or enactment is what makes understanding an 'event' (*Geschehen*)[88] instead of a mere 'process' (*Vorgang*). Interpretation is historical in the active sense of inscribing itself – realizing itself (*Vollzug*) – in historical times and in historical terms.

On the question-side of the structure, as we saw in the second section, we are within history. It is against our background or 'horizons', that is to say, in light of our concerns and filtered by our methodologies, that something, a text or a work of art or an event, solicits us and gains an efficacy on our consciousness. It is thus within the history of the interpreters' present that the object interpreted reveals itself, that is to say, becomes an object. This is how interpretation has a historical mode of operation, which assists the coming into being of the object. This also means that, on the answer-side of the structure, the work can only 'respond' as 'a relationship in which the reality of history as well as the reality of historical understanding exist'[89]. The work interpreted is in fact a relation between what has become our question and what our response to it is.

Gadamer calls this dual performance on the side of interpretation and on the side of the work a play (*Spiel*) in so far as both authors and readers are protagonists in an event. The author is a protagonist in so far as something was meant, which is what interpreters want to understand, but this 'meaning', as being both mental (as an act of meaning something) and semiotic (as what words and sentences mean), can only be found in how interpreters are addressed, how the words are understood and received. The historical writer's intentions are only accessible through the reconstructed author's inscribed 'meanings'. And readers are protagonists in so far as they have to invest their quota of experiences in reading these words on the page if they want to make sense of them.

In this play, interpretation as a performance cannot consist in 'transposing oneself into the other'. It is not an 'immediate participation [...] in another'[90]. The goal is not 'to get inside another person and re-effectuate his experiences [*seine erlebnisse nachvollziehen*]'[91]. Yet, interpretation does not consist in what readers see in the text either and in what they make their own according to their own standards. 'Such a transposing of oneself is neither the empathy of one individual for another nor the submission of the other to one's own standards'[92]. Positively, interpretation as a performance is a 're-creation' (*Nachschaffen*)[93] or a 'new creation' (*neue Schöpfung*)[94], re-enacting a previous creation.

These performative expressions name a complex temporality, for the work actually is only in the enactment provided by interpretation. And the adverb 'actually' is quite fitting, for it also means 'in actuality'. Interpretation keeps the work 'effective' by bringing it into another present, the present of the interpreters; it re-enacts the work by providing a future to the work in the present of the interpreters. While the work has to exist first before being interpreted, it is only through interpretation that a work speaks to readers and interpreters. The re-enactment performed by interpretation is thus not second compared to the first. As Gadamer notes, 'this re-creation [*Nachschaffen*] does not follow a preceding act of creation but the figure of the work which was created'[95]. For the work as an event or an enactment cannot be simply repeated – it is 'nonsensical', Gadamer says, to view understanding as 'a second creation [*eine zweite Schöpfung*], the reproduction [*Reproduktion*] of the original production'[96]. It is also not a 'mere reproduction' (*Nachvollzug*) or a 'repetition' (*Nachreden*)[97].

This fact that the future of the work through interpretation grants a present to the work means that interpretation belongs to the life of the work. This notion of life may justify the use of a biological figure to illustrate this inversion of temporality which makes interpretation both the future and the present of the work. The biological figure is that of a cell dividing itself and giving rise to another cell which has the same 'information' while being different in its instantiation. For, like a cell dividing itself, interpretation re-enacts that which is interpreted while preserving its otherness in its singularity. Interpretation allows the work to speak from within interpretation by being turned towards the future. This is how interpretation is the future of the work, at the moment the work is considered as preceding interpretation. And interpretation is the present of the work, when the work is considered as enactment, interpretation keeping this enactment alive.

The notion of performance carries with it a social and ethical dimension. In the 'act' of re-effectuating or re-enacting the work, interpreters inscribe their interpretation in a social framework, presenting themselves as authors making claims about the truth and appropriateness of their interpretations. At the same time, given the initiative interpreters have in establishing a relation to the work and the responsibility they bear in re-enacting it, their interpretation turns them into ethical agents. Understanding is, Gadamer says, 'a moral phenomenon'[98]. I see this ethical valence of interpretation at three levels.

First, as re-enactment, interpretation treats its object as a relation and thus bears a responsibility for keeping its object relational, that is to say, relevant or alive. If interpretation makes an object exist, it can also make it not exist, for example by leaving it aside, not noticing it. The history of most countries includes the coming to terms with this responsibility for not having noticed certain events and phenomena, for having left them without a voice. And we see today in universities and in social media, works which are cast aside, dismissed or boycotted because the authors are considered 'problematic'. Or we see speakers 'cancelled' before being given the opportunity to speak. These examples confirm negatively that the relation of interpretation to an object is a relation of a process to a process, which is what the notion of 'event' is supposed to name.

Because interpretation is a re-enactment which in fact provides a presence to the work interpreted, there is no enactment in itself which the work would be and which could be re-duplicated. We always understand differently, as Gadamer famously says[99] and the difference is ethical. This difference is not to be understood in opposition to sameness, as if we could see the self-identity of what the work means before offering a 'different' interpretation of this sameness. The difference in interpretation does not lie in a distance between interpreter and object or between different interpretations. It lies in the performance of the re-enactment. As such, it is an enactment 'other' than the first one (the work), not because of the absence of a sameness – the work cannot speak before being interpreted – but because the presence of the work lies in how interpretation re-enacts it. The presence of the work lies in the process through which interpretation differentiates itself from the work and lets the work appear. Because this first enactment as an event cannot be repeated, it can only be re-enacted in what becomes 'another' event, namely, interpretation. This event-character of the work and of its interpretation belongs to the same life of the work, enacted and re-enacted. This is what the figure of a cell dividing itself while sharing the same genetic information may be fitting for the life-process of a work and thus also for the ethical responsibility of interpreters towards this life: they can provide a future to the work, keeping the work alive, or they can cancel such a future, killing the work. The prefix 're' in 're-creation' thus names this ethical relation to the object interpreted.

The second ethical aspect is linked to the first. Given the power interpreters have, it is easy and tempting for them to project themselves into the work or the past and find in it images of what they would think or do. Interpreters bring with them their present and apply it to the object to be interpreted. It is tempting for them to treat ancient authors as contemporaries, assuming, for example, that they shared the same layout of the world and organized it with the same set of concepts, so that they can be ascribed the same beliefs interpreters would have if they had been living in that time period[100]. We are certainly familiar with this in humanities departments when works of the past are read according to our present social and cultural standards, whether because they are seen as offensive or as precursors of our own views. The unethical aspect of such an attitude based on likes and dislikes is that we are not letting the otherness of the work reveal itself to us. This is why Gadamer emphasizes that interpretation is at the service of the work: 'The speech of the interpreter is thus not a text but *serves* a text'[101]. Socrates already said, quoted by Gadamer, that what is needed in order to understand arguments is 'scrutinizing them in well-meaning arguments [*en eumenesin elenchois*] and employing questions and answers without ill-will [*aneu phthonōn*]'[102]. This requires a specific attitude of benevolence on the part of the interpreters or a 'good will', as Gadamer explains in his encounter with Derrida in 1981, which Derrida dismissed.

Gadamer explains this good will of the interpreter as follows: 'We are not seeking to be right and thus to detect the weaknesses of the others. Rather, we try to make the others as strong as possible so that their statements become somewhat convincing'[103]. He says the same about texts: 'As in the dialogue, understanding must here try to make the sense of what is said stronger'[104]. This attitude was already found in Plato and Aristotle in the way they practised philosophy. Gadamer says that he 'recognized' 'in both of them the Socratic question and, with it, the primacy of *ethos* over *logos*'[105] Dialectic itself is ethical, which was already indicated in the title of Gadamer's habilitation in 1929 and which Davidson praised[106]. It 'consists in this that we do not try to meet what is said in its weakness, but we first bring it to its true force' so that it is 'the art of thinking which knows how to make stronger the objections with regard to the subject matter'[107].

Doing justice to the work means realizing the extent to which we participate in the re-enactment of the work. Because our consciousness is permeated by the efficacy of history, our norms, standards, values do not belong to the ultimate stage of moral development but inscribe us in our time and culture. Being ethical means being aware as interpreters of our own historical flesh and refraining from usurping the re-enactment by turning it into an appropriation according to our own values and standards. If we erase the distance in time, we erase the 'otherness'. Being ethical means giving a chance to these works of the past to make a claim on us.

The third ethical aspect of interpretation concerns its return effect on interpreters. By being part of the future of the work, and thus affected by its efficacy, interpreters are in fact themselves interpreted, and this means re-enacted in their own thinking. They are in a play. Their own views, values, even their concepts are susceptible to be put to the question by the work they interpret, which may not fit with what they expected, may not surrender to their conceptual grid, may make them see assumptions in the way they understand the work. This is how Gadamer makes ancient philosophers speak to us, letting them give us lessons on how we ourselves think and, through Gadamer's 'interpretations', they may teach us how to think differently by making us aware of the 'difference' between how thinking was enacted in these old works and how ours is. This acceptance to learn how to think differently is the ethical underside of understanding differently. Interpreters are those who are on the side of the difference, not the text. It is their responsibility to let themselves be transformed by the work and become different.

II. On the Art of Reading (by Arun Iyer)

Gadamer's oeuvre can be roughly divided into two kinds of texts: those in which he gives us a philosophical account of understanding where he tries to show us what is involved in the activities of reading texts, listening to others, listening to music, looking at paintings and inhabiting buildings and those in which he himself attempts to understand something, be it a text, a work of art, a piece of music or a painting. We would do well to note that the relationship between these two kinds of texts is not that of method and application. Rather the relationship between these two texts can be expressed as that between a description and a first-hand experience of the phenomenon of understanding. This needs to be shown clearly and the essays collected in this volume can help to do this if we read them in conjunction with *Truth and Method*, Gadamer's most extensive account of understanding.

Reading and Understanding in Truth and Method

In *Truth and Method*, Gadamer seems to have Schleiermacher in mind throughout, as he at various points in the book explicitly distinguishes his position from that of his nineteenth-century predecessor. In Schleiermacher, to understand the text is, on the one hand, to be able to explicate it grammatically, that is to say, to be able to place its language as a whole into the time and place that encompasses the author and its originally intended audience[108] and to grasp every word from its context[109]. On the other hand, one has to also place the text as an event in the psychic life of the author and grasp the text as the product of an embryonic decision [*Keimentschluß*] by the author[110], a decision that comes from their freedom as individuals unaffected by the time and place in which the authors find themselves. Going back and forth between these two axes – the grammatical and psychological – we have to trace the individuality of author. For it is this individuality which gives us the meaning of the text. The suppressed implication here is that every worthy literary work is an expression of the individual freedom of the author. However, Schleiermacher admits that it is not easy for authors to produce a work which expresses their individuality. This is because the expression of the author's individuality is constantly stymied by the fact that they have to resort to forms and expressions that they have to inevitably borrow from others as members of a particular civilization with particular literary traditions. Hence one can divide the author's oeuvre into occasional pieces, preparatory works and their life's work. The individuality of the author will be expressed in its fullest only in the life's work as compared to the preparatory works and not at all in the occasional works. What does this mean? It means that to grasp a work, to understand it, is nothing but grasping the individuality of the author producing the work. For the work is nothing but an expression of that individuality. Moreover, this individuality is always at the vanishing point of the work itself. For it is something that lies at the very limit of expression. Even in their life's work, despite their best efforts, authors will have to resort to forms of expression that are available to the society to which they belong. Although these forms of expression will be transformed by the individuality of the author, they will never completely disappear to give way to the pure expression of the author's individuality. But for Schleiermacher, in Gadamer's view, the very meaning of work lies in this individuality, so it lies at the point that lies outside of the work itself and to interpret is to always tend towards this point outside the work but inside the author's psyche. This is why Gadamer, maybe not all that unfairly, criticizes Schleiermacher's account of understanding as a 'mysterious communion of souls'[111].

Against Schleiermacher, Gadamer marshals Heidegger, who by showing how the hermeneutical motifs such as having a sense for the whole of text, which is not a mere sum of the parts of the text and the peculiar back-and-forth relationship between the whole and its parts, where the whole informs the parts and the parts inform the whole, imply an ontology that is radically different from the one stemming from the substance ontology of Aristotle which has dominated Western thought ever since and of which the Cartesianism of modern science is but just one variant. Whereas Heidegger tends towards a complete dissolution of substance ontology and the humanistic anthropology that goes hand in hand with it, in forging an anti-humanism grounded in the history of being (*Seynsgeschichte*), Gadamer seeks to avoid such extreme measures, wanting rather to tame the one-sidedness of such substance ontology and broadening the basis of a humanistic anthropology to challenge both the subjectivism and the naturalism that stem from it. Gadamer's project is thus situated between Schleiermacher and Heidegger. Gadamer uses Heidegger to disinfect hermeneutics of all the residual subjectivism of the Cartesian variety that continued to infect it in the nineteenth century, despite being refracted through a German Romanticism which was inspired by the Kantian account of genius.

In *Truth and Method*, Gadamer tells us that to read and understand a text is to 'be prepared for it to tell [us] something'[112] which is why a 'hermeneutically trained consciousness must be, from the start, sensitive to the alterity of the text'[113]. These statements may appear innocuous and simple. But Gadamer is telling us a lot here. To be prepared for the text to tell us something is to be convinced that the text has something to say. This is a conviction which is a necessary precondition for all reading. For Gadamer, all reading and all attempts to understand presuppose that the text has something to say, that it can tell us something that we did not know, that it can surprise us, that it can teach us something. This means that when it comes to a text, one could very well approach it with the presupposition that it has nothing at all to tell us, nothing at all to teach us. The presupposition leaves the text with only two options: at best it can confirm what we already know or at worst it can traffic in primitive ideas and regressive values that we can superciliously dismiss. In Gadamer's view, to do this is not to read at all. As Gadamer himself points out, scholarship in ancient philosophy, for example, in many instances does resort to this way of reading, betraying the lack of a hermeneutically trained consciousness. In opposition to this, all the essays included in this volume are exercises of a hermeneutically trained consciousness reading the various texts that the history of Western thought has bequeathed us.

To clarify Gadamer's positive account of understanding in *Truth and Method*, let us begin with his oft-quoted statement on understanding:

> Understanding is not, in fact, understanding better, either in the sense of superior knowledge of the subject because of clearer ideas or in the sense of fundamental superiority of consciousness over unconscious production. It is enough to say that we understand in a different way, if we understand at all[114].

As Gadamer clarifies later, what he has in mind here is Romantic hermeneutics in general and Schleiermacher in particular, who still take their point of departure from the Cartesian *ego cogito* and conceive of both the writer and the readers as Cartesian egos and so are never able to completely shed a solipsistic starting point. So, this need not be read as so obvious a statement of relativism implying that all understanding is always relative to the peculiarities of the individual subject so that everyone understands differently and there can never be a correct understanding of the text. In fact, Gadamer is quite clear that text is 'not [to be] understood as a mere expression of life but [to be] taken seriously in its claim to truth'[115]. So how does one square this claim with the palpable relativism of abandoning the idea of understanding better and settling for understanding differently? Can the same text make different claims to the truth to different readers? If that were the case, would we not be abandoning the very idea of truth, which can never be relative to the whims of the individual reader? We can attempt to answer these questions only if we can understand what Gadamer means by the historical nature of reading and understanding that he explicates in *Truth and Method* using two seemingly difficult ideas, the efficacy of the history [*Wirkungsgeschichte*] (whose provenance and meaning has already been discussed by Pol Vandevelde) of the text and the fusion of horizons [*Horizontverschmelzung*] which happens in every understanding. At the very outset, we can say that taking seriously the text's claim to the truth is to allow it to speak rather than making it say what we want to hear. When Gadamer opposes the Romantic ideal of understanding as understanding better than the author in favour of understanding in a different way, if at all, this is not a succumbing to relativism, but an attempt to grasp the meaning of the text not in terms of the psychology of the author but in terms of what the text itself says to which both the author and the reader have a common access.

Allowing the Text to Speak

The point is not to see myself as the standard of the truth upon which the text is going to be judged, nor is it the opposite, to surrender myself completely to the text, negating myself entirely by taking what the text says as the standard of truth. The text inhabits an in-between space between familiarity and strangeness. The index of the truth of the text is its ability to speak to us, by rendering our standpoint questionable. But this does not mean that the text completely demolishes our standpoint altogether, rendering us completely dumb and incapable of speaking, of questioning. In neither case of simply seeing in the text a total confirmation of our ideas or simply seeing the text as the absolute confirmation of an absolute truth does reading happen. Neither do we talk down to the text nor does the text talk down to us. The point is to undertake a conversation with the text, to put our own position into play, to expose it to the risk of being challenged. The text is as such an indicator of a truth to which it is not equal, but in which it participates along with the reader. Readers have to surrender some part of their subjectivity in order to participate in a truth that is higher than them and to which they can belong only in and through such participation.

The fabrication of the reader, their subjective imposition has to be differentiated from what the text has to say. The text has something definitive to say but it never says that thing in the same way to all interpreters. This does not mean that it is saying different things. It is telling us the same thing, but in different ways. 'To understand is to understand differently' means that the same truth has to be arrived at in different ways depending upon when and where we find ourselves as readers. It is the same truth which is expressed to us in different ways and the same truth presents itself to us in different aspects[116]. Understanding is an actualization of the truth claim made by the text in a way different from the author. Understanding is not a penetration into the recesses of the author's mind. Because the text speaks a truth about the world of which the reader and author are a part, and is not a mere expression of the author's inner being. To understand is to participate in what is common, not a mysterious communion of minds. The being of the text is not that of a scientific object. It is the manifestation of a truth in which we participate along with the author. This is how the truth of a text differs from the correctness of a scientific proposition. This truth is something to which we belong. This truth, in opposition to correctness, has the ontological structure of a situation.

Gadamer, following Heidegger's account of Dasein as being-in-the-world and Jaspers' specifically pertinent account of the concept of situation, asserts that the readers of a text are always situated. They are situated in history. Gadamer concurs with Jaspers that we can never have an overview or a comprehensive closed picture of the situation[117]. For we can never take a position outside of a situation to be able to be afforded such a view. Indeed, our awareness of the situation is always perspectival. We can have several perspectives on the situation and we try to put them together and arrive at a more comprehensive account of our situation. But the account can never be absolute and ultimately comprehensive. In fact, our awareness of our situation can only make us aware of limits of our own knowledge, making us aware of the existence of new possibilities. Gadamer develops the implications of the Jaspersian idea in his own unique way: To be situated in history is to be affected by history, to be a consciousness affected by history [*wirkungsgeschichtliches Bewusstsein*]. But the efficacy of history is not a causal efficacy. Causal efficacy presupposes a relationship between two objects, where one object produces an effect on another independent object. Instead of presupposing a relationship to an object outside of us which is causing some effects upon us, the efficacy of history is an index of our situatedness. We as readers always find ourselves situated and affected by history. The efficacy of history is therefore not at all to be understood in terms of a causal relationship between two objects. Our situatedness is what enables us to see what we can see and it can also obscure our vision. To be even clearer, following Jaspers, who understands situation as a limit on our knowability, Gadamer describes the situation as a limit on our vision. As a limit on our vision, we can understand it better as a horizon.

For Jaspers, to have an awareness of the situation in which we are, is to already be in a position to transform it. In Gadamer, similarly, to be aware of the situation in which we are is to be cognizant of our historicity. To be aware of the effect that history has on us is to be in a position to act in a way as to counter the effects of this history so that we can participate in the truth that is common to us all. The situation always affects us in a way that alienates us from the truth that is common to all. To counteract these negative effects and to allow the horizon to lead us beyond it, is to participate in the truth which is common. Indeed, this is precisely what Gadamer means when he says that we have to work out the hermeneutical situation by acquiring the right horizon, which is always to simultaneously supersede it, as we will see. To become aware of the efficacy of the history of the text is not to perform an exercise in addition to reading and understanding. To read and understand is to be aware of the history of the efficacy of the text, which is in play every time we read. The efficacy of the history [*Wirkungsgeschichte*] of a text can obscure the truth of this text. To be aware of the efficacy of this history of the text is to be aware of the biases [negative prejudices] at play in me and to articulate them as we see Gadamer explicitly do in some of his essays on ancient philosophy collected in this volume.

The Open Event of Meaning

The horizon thus is not to be understood as a wall that closes us off and secures us from everything beyond it but as a threshold that foregrounds what is close to us, establishing the right distance to it rather than disproportionately enhancing what is close to us to the utter neglect of everything else. The horizon as a threshold also indicates the provisional nature of any boundary and points beyond it, making it possible to expand our horizon. The horizon by its very definition is provisional for Gadamer and also in the process of expansion. Because we are not closed off from what is beyond the threshold, which is what the horizon actually is, the meaning of all of the objects within our purview is not just their position within an already existing nexus of relationships. If we understand the horizon historically, this means that the meaning of the past or that of the present is not to be understood as a closed system of relationships with the horizon acting as an enclosure. Meaning is not a closed system of coherence. To elicit the meaning of a text is not to outline or successfully map out this closed system of coherence, a system that can be viewed comprehensively from the outside without implicating the reader. Rather for Gadamer the past is always opening out to the present and vice versa. Understanding is nothing but this opening out and eventual merger of the past to which the text belongs but to which it is not confined and beyond which it is always reaching and the present to which the reader belongs but to which he or she is again never confined and beyond which he or she is always reaching. This is precisely what Gadamer describes as the fusion of horizons.

This is why Gadamer criticizes historical consciousness for its mistaking of a historical horizon for an enclosure. Historical consciousness encounters a transmitted text like a doctor diagnosing a patient. The doctor here seeks to properly situate the patient in the correct nosological space. They interrogate the patient accordingly so that they can arrive at the correct diagnosis. The doctor is thus interested in correctly explaining the patient's responses as expressions of the symptoms of the correct disease. The doctor who is making an initial diagnosis is not interested in the claims to the truth in the specific content of the patient's responses. In fact, the doctor's not taking the patient's statements seriously as claims to the truth is a necessity for making the correct diagnosis. According to Gadamer then, the doctor is thus not interested in understanding what the patient says because it is completely parenthetical to the task of diagnosis. But they are trying to explain the patient's responses as a sign of a certain malady or disorder. Yet, reading a transmitted text and understanding what it says are not to diagnose it like a doctor. It is not just about situating a text historically and embalming it in its own time and insulating ourselves from it. Historical consciousness is partially correct in wanting to situate the transmitted text historically. But as Gadamer points out, it treats this step, which is supposed to be a means towards an understanding of the text, as the end in itself. We take this step in order to take the right distance towards the text so that we can hear what it wants to say as clearly as possible, not in order to shut it off from us as historical consciousness does. The second step, which historical consciousness fails to take, is to now hear what the text has to say. We can do this only if we take its claim to the truth seriously. We do this by allowing the text to question us, to render us questionable.

A genuine question is an open question, which has this unique power of not closing us off from the other. For Gadamer, the meaning of a transmitted text is always that of a counter-question posed by the text to us. To ask the right question of a text is to place the text at exactly the right threshold with respect to one's present so we are in a position to listen to the text's counter-question. The meaning of a question is entirely different from that of a closed system comprising statements. It makes meaning an open event in which the reader and text are both implicated rather than a closed system which is an object of analysis or explanation for a subject. The meaning of the question always implicates the ones questioned (readers) and the one questioning (text) making them participants in a larger whole, the claim to the truth made by both. This is precisely what Gadamer means by the fusion of horizons.

The fusion of horizons cannot be understood as the imposition of one system of meaning upon another or as an artificial merger of two closed systems. The question by means of which I acquire a horizon is what allows me to set my vision properly, to take the proper approach to the text distinguishing its horizon provisionally from mine. But in asking a question, I also make myself vulnerable to a counter-question by the text and thus to the expansion of my horizon and its fusion with the horizon of the text. It is through the question and through the phenomenon of being rendered questionable that the fusion of horizons takes place. This denial of the existence of a closed system of meaning goes hand in hand with Gadamer's rejection of absolute knowledge and the absolute transparency of the self to itself. The fusion of horizons is thus Gadamer's attempt to describe the experience of understanding in a finite, historical being such as the human being. On the one hand, the transmitted text which is immediately given to us is not something ahistorical. To take it to be so is to fundamentally misunderstand it. To begin to understand the text is to recognize the mediating role of time and see the text and the reader as fundamentally historical beings. We recognize the mediating role of time by placing ourselves at the right distance from the text. This distance requires the recognition of the historical situation in which we find ourselves in contrast to that of the text. It requires us to provisionally establish the horizon of the text in contradistinction to our own. This is what allows us to maintain our mutual sovereignty in relation to each other as partners in a dialogue. But this recognition of our mutual sovereignty does not mean that we stop taking the text seriously as a claim to the truth and impose our own system of meaning upon it. It only means that we conversely don't abandon our own claim to the truth and simply surrender our selfhood to the text. For Gadamer, both of these conditions are absolutely necessary for participating in the event of understanding. In this mutual exchange of question and counter-question, we both gradually come to recognize something that goes beyond our individual being and encompasses both of us as we come to participate in the truth which transcends the text and the reader in a fusion of horizons. Let us now see how these ideas enumerated in *Truth and Method* are manifest in Gadamer's own reading of texts.

Gadamer Reading the Greeks: The Inextricable Link between Being and Non-being

Gadamer very early on in a 1939 lecture titled 'Hegel and the Historical Spirit' confesses that it was ancient Greek philosophy that acted as a portal for him towards the entirety of philosophy and its history[118]. As his late writings on ancient Greek philosophy collected in this volume confirm, Gadamer remains true to this confession throughout his long intellectual life as we will see how it is ancient Greek philosophy that allows him to recognize and articulate the pressing philosophical questions of our time.

One of the abiding questions that Gadamer keeps returning to concerns the very essence of language and the implications of its essence for the very question concerning being. True to his confession, Gadamer right from his intellectual beginnings tries to comprehend the essence of language by taking the ancient Greek notion of the *logos* as his point of departure. In *Truth and Method*, we find Gadamer explicitly distinguish what he considers language [*Sprache*] from the *logos* of the Ancient Greeks and the Christian notion of *verbum*. In the late essays on ancient philosophy collected here we find Gadamer come back again to the notion of the *logos*.

In *Truth and Method*, Gadamer places his reading of Plato's *Cratylus* at the centre of his discussion of the *logos*. The central question of the *Cratylus* for

Gadamer is not whether the relationship between the name (*onoma*) and the object it signifies is natural or conventional. Rather what Plato wants to bring to light is the fundamental weakness of all language itself and how language must be overcome in the direction of the *logos* if one has to lead a rational life. The weakness of language hinges on the very seductive nature of the word itself, which more often than not obscures what it signifies rather than illuminates it. It is this ability to obscure and to garner attention to itself rather than to what it points which is exploited by the sophists to distract their audience and substitute real wisdom for a fake one. In *Truth and Method*, Gadamer argues that Plato's despair with respect to language implies a fundamental misunderstanding of its nature. As he puts it:

> Hence the critique of the correctness of names in the *Cratylus* is the first step toward modern instrumental theory of language and the ideal of a sign system of reason. Wedged in between image and sign, the being of language could only be reduced to the level of pure sign[119].

In his criticism of Plato here, Gadamer is very close to Heidegger. Heidegger criticizes Plato for transforming the concept of truth from unconcealment to the correctness of the proposition by arguing that Plato is not really able to see the way in which being is disclosed in language and is quick to move on to a *logos* in which disclosure is reduced to pure *noesis* where the *logos* corresponds transparently to the structure of reality like a true proposition. Gadamer of course painstakingly lays out the nature of the *logos*, something one does not quite see in Heidegger. *Logos* is a relationship of essences or ideas and not merely a combination of words. As a combination of ideas, it is not exactly a proposition. But it is more like a numerical series, in which every element has its perfect place, and every element is nominated purely by convention. But the order itself is pure rationality. And it is the order and the relationship of each element to what precedes and succeeds it that matters, not the individual element in itself. In this sense the *logos* has a relational structure and if the *logos* is what makes being intelligible then being too has a relational structure which is perfectly rational.

In his 1964 essay on Plato's Seventh Letter[120], Gadamer modifies his position, noting that Plato makes it clear even in the *Cratylus* that this overcoming of language has to happen within language itself, namely, that the dimension of language [*Sprachlichkeit*] cannot be entirely escaped. What this means is that there is no transcendence towards perfect rationality. Indeed, Gadamer shows us that in the Seventh Letter the *logos* as the structure of intelligibility is constituted of four means: the name or the word [*onoma*], the concept or the explanation [*logos*], the illustrative example or the figure [*eidolon*] and the insight itself. Gadamer argues that we are not speaking here of an ascent from the irrationality of the word to the perfect rationality of insight. Rather the *logos* as a combination of these four means constantly requires us to move to-and-fro between these four means without completely relinquishing any of them. Each of these means is indispensable in order for us to illuminate the structure of existence itself. Indeed, this is what it means to be finite: that our rationality is inextricably bound with irrationality and the fight against irrationality is something constant, something we have to wage all the time. The spectre of sophism is always looming upon human affairs and it has to be battled constantly.

Despite this awareness of the finitude of human reason, Gadamer continues to argue in his 1968 essay on Plato's unwritten dialectic[121] that Plato is still not able to do justice to language. For he is unable to give a proper account of falsity [*pseudos*] as it emerges in language. Indeed, all Plato can provide is a 'formal prerequisite of the actual *pseudos*'[122] without 'provid[ing] an ontological foundation for the false appearance of something and *pseudos*'[123]. This is because the essay focuses exclusively on the statement 'Theaetetus flies'. Indeed, the falseness of this statement is based on the incompatibility of the idea of the human being and the idea of flying. To use Plato's language, as Gadamer recommends, the idea of the human being does not participate in the idea of flying or vice versa. Indeed, for Gadamer, as he argues constantly in defence of Plato against Aristotle, participation is never an attempt to explain the relationship between universals and particulars. But it is rather an attempt to simply describe something obvious that Plato uses as the starting point of his investigation, namely that ideas are never in isolation from another. An idea always points to another idea. In pointing to another idea, it points away from certain other ideas. Ideas are always found in relation to one another. What one needs to grasp is the way in which ideas are always combining with other ideas and so doing how they separate themselves from certain other ideas. But ideas are not sensible appearances. Language for Gadamer is essentially about sensible appearances which are defined by temporality. That is why he argues that Plato is unable to explain 'falsity as it emerges in language' as Plato is confined to the formality of the relationship between ideas, which is more like the relationship between numbers.

But in the very late long essay of 1990 on Plato's *Sophist* translated in this volume, where he goes through the whole dialogue with painstaking care, Gadamer migrates away from Heidegger, in whose vicinity he remained in his overall assessment of Plato in the 1960s, to his own independent position. Gadamer's careful reading finds that the account of the *logos* in this dialogue is not really just about the relationship between ideas. The text is not to be read as a treatise on ontology but rather as a dialogue on the difference between what the philosopher and the sophist do. The latter is not a mere pretext or framing device for the former. As readers, we are required, as a consequence, to pay attention to the characters in the dialogue. Theaetetus, who is the central character, is a mathematician by training and as a result is inclined to seeing the structure of the *logos* along the lines of numerical relationships. Gadamer is careful in pointing out (something he never does in the 1968 essay) that the statement 'Theaetetus flies' is called 'your statement', namely, the statement of Theaetetus, by his interlocutor, the Eleatic stranger. Indeed, this statement is explicitly differentiated from another statement 'Theaetetus sits' also provided by the Eleatic stranger but whose truth or falsity cannot be indicated on the basis of just the compatibility or incompatibility of ideas. It is clear that 'Theaetetus flies' is something easier to grasp for the mathematician Theaetetus as it deals with necessary relationships between ideas. By contrast the statement 'Theaetetus sits' is quite different. For it involves not a necessary relationship between ideas, but a contingent relationship between two sensible appearances, this human being Theaetetus present here and now and the activity of sitting expressed by the verb 'sit' which is a temporal word and includes the flow of time and the end of such an activity in time. The confirmation of the state of affairs expressed by this statement is a matter of sensible perception and the very temporality of existence is implicated here. We find being temporalized in this relationship. This is different from the Aristotelian relationship of substance and attributes, where the attributes inhere in the substance. In Plato it is the opposite. Here in Plato, 'whatever "being" may mean, in any case *ousia* ["being," "essence," "substance"] must be something that can inhere in everything that is and can be there, together with it'[124]. Temporalization in the Aristotelian framework is understood in terms of a change of attributes. But in Plato, the relationship between the noun and the verb shows us how substance inheres in its attributes, mixes with the temporality of the attribute, and is thus temporalized. The relationship then between the noun (*onoma*) and the verb (*rhema*) is not the same as the relationship between numbers. It is of a fundamentally different kind. But at the same time, Gadamer argues that the relationship described here is not the Aristotelian one of attributes inhering in a substance. And yet, it is still a mixing, a participation of the kind Plato has been taking as his starting point in all of his discussions of the ideas. Mixture or participation is the basic structure of existence itself, from where we have to begin all of our attempts to comprehend it. This is precisely what Theaetetus was unable to realize as Gadamer shows in his long essay on the dialogue *Theaetetus* written eight years before in 1982, which is again a part of this volume.

In his reading of the *Theaetetus*, Gadamer again shows us how the central meaning of the text will not be grasped if we simply view it as a treatise on epistemology. Rather the question which really brings the text to speak to us is why the two mathematicians in this dialogue show such familiarity with the doctrines of Protagoras and are so comfortable with his relativism which is completely at odds with the discipline of mathematics and despite even Protagoras's own established dislike for mathematics. Why does Plato make mathematicians the mouthpieces of Protagorean relativism? It is only when we see how mathematics can also appear to be grounded in the same kind of relativism that Plato attributes to Protagoras that it dawns on us as to how the foundations of a certain discipline need not be clear to the practitioners of that discipline and the mere exercise of seeking mathematical knowledge does not grant us any clarity into the nature of knowledge itself. The reflections necessitated by the question concerning the essence of knowledge are of a unique kind and cannot be expected from those who are in the business of procuring knowledge through the practice of the methodologies prevalent in their respective disciplines. The *Theaetetus*, more than anything, wants us readers to realize this. For if we don't, pseudo-arguments having the *imprimatur* of an established discipline can go around masquerading as genuine knowledge as the tragicomic scene of the two mathematicians unwittingly embracing relativism shows us.

In this essay on the *Sophist*, in contrast to the one written in 1968, Gadamer argues that Plato's account of the *logos* shows us that being is subject to temporality.

This subjection to temporality cannot be accounted for just in terms of a relationship between ideas. The relationship between being and not-being is not just a relationship between two ideas with non-being conceived as the different or the *heteron*, as Gadamer had argued previously. The relationship between being and non-being is understood rather as the temporalization of being. It is this unavoidable subjection of being to temporality that makes it so difficult to ascertain the truth and falsity of utterances about beings. The truth and falsity of our utterances cannot be methodologically ascertained by assessing the rigour and strength of the arguments made in support of the utterances. This is why it is so difficult to distinguish between the dialectician and the sophist. Just as being and non-being are so inscrutably intertwined such that there is always a bit of non-being in being and being in non-being, in the same way there is always a bit of a dialectician in the sophist and a sophist in the dialectician if we try to understand them as merely formal categories. Rather the sophist can be distinguished from the dialectician only existentially. 'The difference does not lie in arguments but in the intention of the one who argues. In this alone can philosophers and sophists be distinguished'[125]. Here Gadamer shows how Plato and Aristotle agree. What do we take from this? We take from this an insight into the very nature of being itself. Non-being cannot be distinguished and expelled from the realm of being once and for all by means of a method alone. '[T]he nothingness of seeming belongs to being and [one] no longer thinks that one can ward it off with the help of "science", as if it were a mere confusion'[126]. This insight shows us at once the limitations of science and how science and its technological augments cannot be seen as a panacea for all of our problems.

It has taken Gadamer a long time to do complete justice to the *Sophist* as a dialogue. Indeed, his earlier takes on Plato's *Sophist* are characterized by the very immediacy that he criticizes in *Truth and Method*, which makes us forget the efficacy of the history of the text. This history of the text makes us see Plato's thought being perfected in Aristotle and so one has the tendency to read Plato backwards from Aristotle. The tendency is to then read Plato's texts as treatises and their plurivocity is overlooked. So, the two statements 'Theaetetus flies' and 'Theaetetus sits' are then attributed to a single voice, as so many examples illustrating the nature of the *logos*. But when Gadamer notices the plurivocity inherent here by emphasizing the dialogical nature of the text, he realizes how the two statements are attributed to two different voices. The statement 'Theaetetus flies' is actually a statement preferred by Theaetetus, a statement with a structure familiar to Theaetetus the mathematician. But the statement 'Theaetetus sits' explicitly chosen by the stranger to show the nature of language, which is never just a combination of ideas. The distinction between the sophist and the philosopher, as we have pointed before, is not a mere framing device, which can be overlooked for the meat of the text, the discussion of being. Rather one can grasp the meaning of being in Plato only if we are able to see it through the relationship between the dialectician and the sophist. Only then can the text become an open event of meaning in which we come to participate rather than a closed outdated system, which can be explained away without having anything to really say to us. The text is finally made to speak. What we can see is how difficult it is to get it to do so.

Gadamer characterizes the thought of the *logos* articulated in the *Sophist* as an advance over Parmenides. But the precise nature of this advance requires that we come to grips with the teaching of Parmenides. Here again we must be cognizant of the efficacy of a history that begins with Plato and Aristotle and not allow it to obscure the meaning of Parmenides' poem by projecting back into it the distinction between *noēsis* and *aesthēsis* or between the intelligible and the sensible, which Gadamer shows is simply not to be found in the poem. The projection of this distinction into the poem goes hand in hand with equating the doctrine of being which is encountered in *noēsis*, a rather small part of the poem, with Parmenides's philosophy. As a consequence of this, the views of the mortals and their reason, which form the bulk of the poem and of which only fragments are available to us, are treated either as an outdated cosmogony which has no real link to the philosophy of Parmenides or following Aristotle it is seen as a belated change of view on the part of Parmenides who had to concede to the undeniability of certain facts. The efficacy of the poem's history has again obscured the proximity of the larger section of the poem to Ionian physics, although the nature of this proximity needs to be clarified, which is precisely what Gadamer does in his essay.

For Gadamer, it is this larger section on mortals, their rationality and their points of view which is of paramount importance and it is not inconsistent with the doctrine of being proclaimed by the goddess. While for the gods there is only being and non-being simply does not exist, mortals cannot have the privilege of this view. For us mortal beings on the other hand non-being does exist and we have to learn to avoid it. We have to learn to distinguish being from non-being and avoid non-being altogether. Why does non-being exist for us human beings? Mortal lives and their view of the world are governed by the distinction between light and night. It is this distinction that determines our encounter with all beings. It is this distinction between night and light that defines how beings emerge into mortal view. For mortals, being has always to take the form of appearance. We therefore speak of 'coming to be' and 'changing of place', which even if they do not just refer to non-being still contain non-being as one of their connotations. But we have to avoid using such words and treat them as mere words that do not refer to anything if we do not want to succumb to the vacuous thought of non-being. Gadamer argues through a careful textual analysis of Fragment 8, line 54 that light and night do not correspond to being and non-being. Both light and night are beings with markedly different qualities. Night is not to be taken as a non-being. It is a being, dark, obscure and heavy as the goddess tells us. The goddess in this way shows us mortals how to avoid positing non-being, how not to succumb to the temptation of positing non-being. But it is always very hard for us mortals to avoid speaking in this way. As a result, we mortals are always in the danger of falling for the vacuous thought of the non-being. That is why we need the goddess to teach us how to avoid this vacuous thought and stay on the course of being. It is for this reason that this section of the poem contains signposts that can help steer clear of non-being and stick to the course of being. The point here is that mortals too, can follow the doctrine of being by avoiding the thought of non-being. But being never shows itself to us as a complete sphere but only in multiple appearances, each of which is different from the other. This former is only given to gods, not us mortals. To avoid non-being, we need to recognize the most faithful sign of being. This most faithful sign is *noein*, which Gadamer argues is to be understood more along the lines of recognizing, making something out, stumbling upon, taking something in, which 'means to be completely absorbed in being, to be nothing for oneself other than just the openness for that which is'[127]. In 'coming to be' and 'passing away' we are taking nothing in. Hence, we have to avoid these words if we do not want to open ourselves up in vain to a vacuum, to sheer emptiness. Although Parmenides agrees that for us human beings, non-being remains a reality and that being is always accompanied by non-being, it is still possible to distinguish between being and non-being and avoid the latter altogether. This is what Gadamer means when he tells us that being in Parmenides is not just something otherworldly but rather belongs to this world too. Now, Plato also accepts this Parmenidean contention but what he rejects is that non-being can be simply avoided altogether and he diligently expands upon the Parmenidean concept of *noein* and *eon*. Plato shows us that being is always mixed with non-being for being always implies a difference from some other being. To be a being is not to be the same as another being. As a result, for Plato *noein* is not just a taking-in, a self-negation in openness to being, but also a self-possession in distinguishing what is taken in from that which is not taken in. Or to put it better, opening oneself to a being is always already also closing oneself from another being. To think or to take in for Plato always implies distinguishing.

Gadamer's reading of Plato's *Republic* is again a pushback against the illusory immediacy which is created by reading it as a policy document outlining the formation of a totalitarian state. Gadamer strives to create the right distance towards this text by showing us that our approach to the text should be mediated by the genre to which this text belongs, that of a literary utopia, not a policy document. Once again, we should resist the temptation to think the invocation of its genre as an adoption of historical consciousness. For Gadamer is not closing the text off by locking it up in its time and place. On the contrary, only if we recognize its genre can the text acquire the power to question us. The text fundamentally questions our conception of political rationality. Gadamer continues what he has already pursued in his prior readings of the *Republic*, where he shows how political rationality in Plato is tied very closely to education and the cultivation of a citizenry who are able to see the common good in which they all must share. In Gadamer's reading then, political rationality is not tied to the legal and administrative infrastructure of the state. He takes up those passages which are seen as evidence of Plato's advocacy of eugenics and reads them to show us clearly that they, on the contrary, depict the finitude of human reason. Gadamer brings to the fore the irony with which these passages are laced. Plato, according to Gadamer, is rather making it clear to us that a rationality which strives to escape irrationality once and for all by resorting to calculating itself out of contingency is the most extreme form of irrationality. For as human beings we simply cannot ensure that legislation will somehow account for all the contingency life is going to throw at us. To say that human reason is finite is to say that human rationality cannot escape the irrationality inherent to the perspective but is intrinsically linked to it. In living our lives as political beings, we cannot, as it were, account for all contingency once and for all. On the other hand, our education must prepare us to recognize contingency and work through it together by way of dialogue and collective action.

We now see that the open event of meaning in which we come to participate through Gadamer's late readings of these ancient Greek texts is manifest in this theme of the inextricable relationship between being and non-being – a theme which strikes us in its contemporary relevance and points to the future. What follows from this is the realization that rationality and irrationality, truth and opinion, can also not be separated once and for all by some methodological intervention. In fact, being is given to us in terms of non-being, rationality in terms of irrationality, truth in terms of opinion. To grasp the being of something, to arrive at its truth, to think and act rationally in relation to it cannot mean the complete escape from non-being, from irrationality, from opinion. It is also to not succumb to the temptation of just equating being with non-being, irrationality with rationality and truth with opinion, but to realize that truth has to arrive only through the careful parsing of true from false opinions and can only take the form of a differentiated and nuanced synthesis of opinions, to recognize that rationality can become so extreme as to turn into irrationality, to know that non-being is not just confusion but what gives being its very definition.

Gadamer Reading the Moderns: The Inextricable Link between Historicity and Finitude

In *Truth and Method*, Gadamer sees Schleiermacher and Hegel as philosophical mirror images of each other. Both of these thinkers, Gadamer argues, are besieged by a sense of loss in relation to the past. Both thinkers are interested in trying to redeem this loss by way of their respective philosophical projects. In Schleiermacher, we see the emergence of historical consciousness, which culminates in the work of Wilhelm Dilthey. Gadamer lays out for us how historical consciousness is in a certain sense unable to do justice to the dimension of history, for it is unable to overcome the Cartesian starting point of the individual subject which relates to everything as an object of observation. Historical reality is not reducible to an object. Thus, the standpoint of individual subjectivity, so prevalent in the natural sciences for its effectiveness in producing an account of nature that helps us explain and thereby dominate it, is somehow ineffective in coming to grips with historical reality. The consequence of this starting point is that historical consciousness is able to see the past only as an object, which can be described with complete objectivity only when this description is done in the terms of that very past. This is what Gadamer describes as the method of reconstruction. The past is reconstructed as accurately as possible by excluding the imposition of any prejudices coming from the present in which we, the possessors of historical consciousness, find ourselves. But Gadamer argues that this gesture of wanting to do justice to the past, to history, also in the same breath cuts off the present from the past. It encloses the past upon itself completely separating it from the present. The past in this perspective is no longer relevant to the present, it can no longer speak to the present and be taken seriously. In not wanting to assess it in terms of the present, in wanting to allow its strangeness to stand on its own without being invalidated by the standards which govern our present, we divest the past of truth altogether. We also ensure that the past can never question our standards, our convictions in any way. But this simply fails to understand the nature of historical reality, where the past is always connected to the present in such a way that it can question us; it can challenge us as if it were contemporaneous with us.

On the other side of this, we have the absolute consciousness of Hegel, whose full import for Gadamer is seen in the section on 'Manifest Religion' in *Phenomenology of Spirit*. Unlike Schleiermacher, the strength of Hegel lies, according to Gadamer, in grasping historical reality as the connection between the past and present in which the past is not merely an object of reconstruction but something that is to be integrated with the present. Hegel, according to Gadamer, is making a theoretical point here. For even a reconstructed past is not the same as the original past. It is a past which is refracted through the lens of a consciousness finding itself in the present. For Hegel therefore history is not about the reconstruction of the material substance of the past but its spiritualization in and through the consciousness which comes later. In this process the past is always integrated into the present. In seeing the task of absolute consciousness as that of integrating all of the past into the present, Hegel, according to Gadamer, shows a recognition that the past is in some sense always contemporaneous with the present. But this recognition is also accompanied by the permanent disruption of history itself. For Hegel, to spiritualize the past is to conceptualize it, to transform the experience of the past in its connection to the present, to transform the very experience of history into conceptual knowledge, whose paradigmatic case is natural science. While Hegel does not mute the past into a reconstructed totality as historical consciousness does, he does ventriloquize it by making it speak in his beloved language of concepts. In doing so, he deprives the past of essential non-conceptual resources to communicate with us, severely maiming the reality of history. This is brought out very vividly in the 1990 essay 'Hegel and Heraclitus' which is part of this volume, where Gadamer despite his lavish praise of Hegel who showed us the relevance of pre-Socratic thought once and for all, especially the enigmatic utterances of Heraclitus, is equally critical of Hegel for turning those enigmatic utterances into propositions expressing conceptual relations and unwittingly reading them exactly like Aristotle did, who was a trenchant critic of Heraclitus the obscure. In opposition to this Gadamer shows us that such a conceptualization of Heraclitus does not do complete justice to the profundity and the inexhaustibility of the truth of those enigmatic utterances.

In this sense, in Gadamer's view, both historical consciousness and absolute consciousness deny the inextricable link between consciousness and human finitude and in this way, they end up denying the very historicity of history.

Gadamer's reading of the moderns is thus directed towards the discovery of those thinkers and those elements within those thinkers which pose a challenge to historical consciousness, on the one hand, and absolute consciousness on the other, and thereby reveal this inextricable link between historicity and finitude, which is the very basis of hermeneutic experience. By exposing these elements, Gadamer effects two goals: one is bringing out the abiding relevance of the texts those thinkers are engaged with, Plato's dialogues, the wisdom of Solomon, pre-Homeric myth; the second is to bring out the abiding relevance of the thinker engaging in those exegeses.

Already in *Truth and Method*, we find a critique of the Kantian conception of the *sensus communis*. Gadamer shows how the pre-Kantian conception of common sense originates in Stoic thought, is explicitly marshalled by Vico against the Jansenists and Descartes, and culminates in the work of Hutcheson and Shaftesbury, with Oetinger being its only German proponent. Gadamer opposes this pre-Kantian notion of common sense to the Kantian one, which shorn of its content and its intrinsic civic dimension is formalized into an intellectual faculty. Gadamer's 1967 essay on Oetinger is an extension of his reflection on Oetinger in *Truth and Method*. Common sense in Oetinger, which is not an intellectual faculty of the individual subject but a wisdom, is a kind of knowledge which undergirds both the scientific experience of the universe and of the experience of ourselves and the other as members of a human community, pointing to something that cannot be accounted for by modern science alone. Common sense is what Oetinger sees manifested in the wisdom of Solomon. Against a historical reading of that text by the Jesuit theologians, who try to understand it in terms of its age and thereby do not see how it can say anything relevant about our knowledge that stems from the methodological rigour of modern science, Gadamer shows us how Oetinger himself goes against this historical consciousness which had become dominant at the time in the interpretation of the Bible. Gadamer is also revealing to us the relevance of Oetinger himself for contemporary thinking. In Oetinger, common sense is not opposed to the scientific experience of the world. But the latter, as we have already noted, is grounded in the former. Newton, seen by Oetinger as the prime representative of the scientific experience of the world, is seen as a counter to the Leibnizian abstractions of monadic representation and sufficient reason, which are excessively intellectual and do not do justice to the essential liveliness and the concreteness of experience. What Oetinger finds in the Newtonian conception of gravitational force is precisely the experience of the liveliness and concreteness of existence which is for him captured in common sense, manifest in the wisdom literature of the Bible. In going beyond Newton and trying to find a metaphysical basis of the Newtonian conception of a central force, Oetinger postulates the basis of gravity, the force by which everything is drawn towards its own centre, in the tendency towards simplification and integration, which is the basis of inwardness and the inner sense that comes with life. In this sense, among living beings, human beings are the simplest and the most integrated, second only to the angels. This force which draws everything towards its centre connects all of life and shows the ultimate and deep-seated unity of the material and the immaterial, the animate and the inanimate. Oetinger argues that gravity is something prior to all pressure and impact. If we take pressure and impact to be fundamental modes by which discrete objects influence each other, then gravity cannot be understood as simply an influence of one object upon another. Gravity is something that permeates all existence and in so doing we inhabit gravity. In this way Oetinger presages the notions of world and situation developed by Gadamer to elucidate the relationship between historicity and finitude. Gadamer's appreciation for Oetinger lies precisely in the latter's emphasis on concreteness and the liveliness inherent in experience, as well as his intuition for this deep-seated unity and continuity tying all of existence together. This points towards the belongingness of all individuals to a whole which cannot be objectified in an explanatory thinking, all too quick to offer abstractions. It points to a thinking which seeks to understand and is open to what is concrete and unobjectifiable.

Despite Schleiermacher's incorrect ordering of the Platonic dialogues (Schleiermacher sees the *Parmenides* as the first dialogue and the *Republic* as the final one), Gadamer notices in his 1969 essay 'Schleiermacher as Platonist' how this nineteenth-century interpreter is able to see better than Gadamer's own contemporaries that the fundamental problem of the one and the many in Plato is not about the relationship between the one individual idea as a universal and the many particulars which participate in it. Rather this problem is about the relationship between ideas and it is about the unity and multiplicity of the ideas themselves, which is what even an early dialogue like the *Protagoras* illustrates. Plato's starting point is never the individual ideas but always a multiplicity of ideas, like the four virtues, for example, and how they relate to each other to form a unified whole. Schleiermacher argues correctly in Gadamer's view for an account of dialectic as dialogue in Plato rather than as a 'formal logical discipline'[128]. Knowledge, the unity of thought and being cannot be accomplished deductively as a unity of all the sciences as Hegel proposes. For this does not heed the finitude of the human being. In Schleiermacher there is a recognition of such a finitude. For this ideal can never be accomplished in human experience but only approximated. Knowledge can thus only be arrived at through the concrete process of a dialogue in which we 'advance towards knowledge by overcoming doubt and conflict'[129]. Gadamer defends Schleiermacher's interpretation of Plato against Dilthey's criticism of some of its radical motifs, namely, Schleiermacher's interpretation of matter in Plato and his interpretation of the soul and body in Plato, as ahistorical. Schleiermacher, taking his lead from Plato's *Timaeus*, very ingeniously sees matter or materiality not as an independent principle, but rather simply as the difference between the original and the copy. As such a difference, matter when conceived on its terms in its raw nature, so to speak, always tends to vanish because the copy is always tending towards the original and is thus, in a sense, the same as the original. Yet, as the bearer of the copy, it is something that endures permanently as that which distinguishes the original from the copy. Schleiermacher, following the same text, does not see the soul and the body as two independent substances in Plato. Indeed, for Schleiermacher, the soul and the body are inextricable in Plato. Even if the soul is separated from the body, it continues to remain connected to a body in a manner similar to the world-soul. Likewise, the body in the process of the emergence of the world-body becomes linked to a soul and in the process transforms from an individual to a universal. Against Dilthey, Gadamer finds Schleiermacher's ingenious interpretations of some of the fundamental Platonic themes as truly historical. This is something that Schleiermacher himself was unable to see as he was only interested in casting Plato as a systematic philosopher, whose starting point is the individual subject, but who advances beyond Spinoza and Fichte in showing us the true ground which underlies physics and ethics. By showing us how Schleiermacher's interpretation of matter, soul and body in Plato's dialogues cannot be subsumed in a Judeo-Christian metaphysics, Gadamer again unearths the relevance of Schleiermacher himself for contemporary thought. In the process, he makes it clear that philological research with its dazzling technological prowess is no match for the intuitive power of Schleiermacher's reading of Plato, which is able to see through the obscurity produced by the efficacy of history of the Judeo-Christianity on our reading of Plato. It is able to show how Plato's texts reach beyond their time and speak to us as contemporaries, offering us insights which strike us even today as true and not as merely something quaint and interesting.

If Gadamer is able to uncover resources in Schleiermacher which speak against the latter's own conception of historical consciousness, in his 1939 address as a professor of philosophy in the University of Leipzig under the title 'Hegel and the Historical Spirit' he is similarly able to unearth resources in Hegel which challenge Hegel's own account of absolute consciousness. He also points to the impoverishment of history which is produced by the standard static interpretations of the Hegelian concept of absolute knowledge and the end of history, where history is seen as a negation of human freedom. Gadamer does this by taking recourse to the then recently published theological early writings of Hegel and by reading the *Phenomenology of Spirit* as a development of these early writings, rather than as a work which is to be absorbed into the systematic dialectics of *Logic*, the *Encyclopaedia* and the Berlin Lectures. Gadamer shows us in broad outlines how the concept of Spirit in the *Phenomenology* must be seen as development of the concept of love which Hegel articulates in these theological early writings. Here love is understood as a living unity in which the concrete individuality of the I and the You remains but the estrangement between the I and the You is overcome. This is a living unity rather than an abstract unity in which the concrete individuality of the individuals is sacrificed to the abstract universality of the law or reason, as we see in Kant. Gadamer sees this as the first instance of a concrete universality. Love as a living unity of the I and the thou should not be seen as a mere opposition to the 'positivity of what is given'. Hegel opposes Jesus' own conception of love as a passive relationship in which one flees the outer world, its institutions and other forms into an untouched interiority represented by love. For Hegel, love, as an overcoming of estrangement, is essentially a stepping into the outer world and a transformation of it from a dead reality of abstract relationships into a living reality of concrete relationships. It is this overcoming of estrangement which developed further in the Hegelian conception of the Spirit and its historicity. Here the historicity of the spirit is the process of the overcoming of estrangement, an estrangement that separates us from others, that turns all human institutions into static, passive, dead relationships, which thereby renders us completely unfree, trapped in the cage of an interiority of our own making. Rather than negating the freedom of the individual, the historicity of the spirit is what grants us our freedom in the first place through the overcoming of the estrangement that is antithetical to freedom. The historicity of the spirit is what does real justice to human freedom by showing us how such freedom is gained in the first place. History is not the site where freedom is absent. It is the site where we become free. In this relationship between historicity and freedom, which Gadamer finds in Hegel, we see the makings of his own postulation of the relationship between historicity and finitude.

In his 1961 essay 'Hegel and Heidelberg Romanticism' written at the time of *Truth and Method*, Gadamer finds the spirit of Heidelberg Romanticism at play within the work of Hegel, especially in his work on aesthetics. Contrary to the conventional view of Hegel as an arch-enemy of the Romantics, Gadamer shows us how we must distinguish the romanticism of Heidelberg from that of Jena, with the former enjoying an abiding presence in the work of Hegel, especially through the mediation of Friedrich Creuzer and his work on symbolism in art. This ineradicable presence of Romanticism in Hegel's work acts as an internal challenge to it, even destabilizing it to a certain extent. Creuzer argues that in pre-classical art thinking happens in pictures, where the picture, which is a finite visible phenomenon, stands in and points towards that which is 'invisible and infinite'.[130] Unlike in *Truth and Method*, Gadamer in this essay does not emphasize the difference between the symbol and allegory but is more interested in what they have in common, namely the opposition between the finite and the infinite. Gadamer shows us how Hegel, taking his point of departure in Creuzer's work, is able to go beyond Creuzer by overcoming the enlightenment thinking in which even Creuzer remains trapped. While Creuzer recognizes that pre-classical art, which is characterized by symbolism, is different from the classical, he does not grasp the implications of his work on the symbolic. Gadamer reveals how it is Hegel, who, in his aesthetics lectures, liberates these implications for the first time. To think in pictures is not something that happens after conceptual thinking. The peoples of the pre-classical world of myth did not first think conceptually and then substitute those concepts for pictures. The priests and poets, as it were, did not mask their real conceptual thought in symbols to hide it from the masses. Hegel rejects this enlightenment prejudice found even in Creuzer and argues that these people, poets and priests lived in the world of poesy and their thoughts flowed out as pictures, even if these pictures were symbols of some intangible ideas or concepts and thus remained tied to abstract ideas which never quite occurred to them. Symbolism and symbolic thinking, in this sense, is directed against enlightenment thinking and its conceptual prejudice. The symbol or the allegory thus stands in opposition to the concept. Of course, in the Hegelian history of art, art comes to an end when the concept absorbs the image into itself without remainder and renders it superfluous. Yet, the symbol does enjoy an autonomous existence in the Hegelian conception of the history of art. This parallels Gadamer's own distinction between the word and the concept, where the concept cannot absorb the word into itself. The word always emerges in a world just like the picture emerges in a world. Unlike the concept, the word and the picture are not interested in giving us an overview of an object outside of us, but a perspective upon the world we inhabit and of which we have no view from the outside. The word and the picture attest to our finitude and the inalienable link between our historicity and finitude. For Gadamer this thinking in images and words cannot be subsumed under the absolute standpoint of conceptual thinking, despite Hegel's valiant attempt to do so, and forever remains an eternal challenge to such conceptual thinking.

In his 1967 essay 'Herder and the Historical World', Gadamer again discovers in Herder a view of history different from and superior to that of historical consciousness. We see how Herder's approach to the human condition in general and history in particular is inspired by Newton. Like Oetinger, what Herder finds refreshing in Newton is the concreteness of his account of the unity of things, which does not rely on abstract and sclerotic divisions which have no basis in concrete reality, what Herder calls 'shadow images'[131]. Disregarding the 'mathematical ideal of method in Newtonian science'[132], Herder is inspired by the novel sensitivity to the balance of the universe, a balance of which the human being is a part, a balance which points to a whole of which they are no longer the centre. This is a balance of forces which penetrates and underlies both the processes of the inanimate universe and the behaviour of human beings. It is this newfound sensitivity which tries to understand the universe from within, as it were, from within its changing horizons, that Herder wants to bring to his understanding of the human condition by trying to grasp history as a play of forces. Although enlightenment prejudices do take hold of some of his reflections on human history despite his persistent attempt to overcome them, Herder, in Gadamer's view, does arrive at a view of history which does not merely objectify human history by drawing its meaning from the absolute standpoint of God, for whom there is only simultaneity and no moving through history. The meaning of history comes from the belief that there is God in history. One could say that in this conception of history, God himself puts his trust in history and becomes historical, trusting that his wisdom will be confirmed in nature through history. This is very similar to the goddess in Parmenides' poem who trusts in the mortal point of view. Just as there is no immortal way out of mortality, so is there no ahistorical way out of history. We can no longer understand history as an ahistorical plan of an otherworldly God who oversees the process of history and intervenes with miracles. Like the Derridean '*Il n'y a pas de hors-Texte*' one could say that there is nothing outside of history. The meaning of history remains in Herder a belief and his intellectual efforts are directed towards showing why this belief remains valid despite evidence to the contrary. This is unlike Hegel for whom the belief in history should be transformed into a science of history, a science which shows how history moves through contradiction and negation. Since there is no standpoint outside of history, one cannot, as it were, judge history from the outside. This also implies that we cannot judge the past from outside the past, on the basis of the present. History is also not to be understood intellectually in terms of the development of ideas, which hardly manifest history. History for

Herder is manifested in 'heart, warmth, blood, humanity, life!'[133]. This is why Herder is interested in documenting folk songs and folk practices and becomes the forefather of cultural history. For it is here that he sees the genuine dynamic of history. Hence his distrust of political institutions and the nation-state, which are simply cut off from the life of the people. If there is nothing outside of history, then there can be no end of history. There can be no culmination or insurmountable maximum in history. For this would mean completely 'annihilating the essence of time and destroying the whole nature of finitude'[134]. In recognizing in his own way this link between history and finitude, Herder, in Gadamer's view, develops a view of history which is superior to that of the enlightenment and its adversaries. In refusing any attempt to understand history as a science, it may even be superior to Hegel.

The Gadamerian Art of Reading

The Gadamerian art of reading, as we have seen from the many essays collected in this volume, is all about making the text speak to us as a contemporary. It is based on the experience of the inexhaustibility of the text. Gadamer's reading of the ancients and the moderns reveals to us how their texts continue to have an abiding relevance for the most pertinent questions of philosophy which arise in our time. His reading is not an application of a method which is articulated elsewhere in his works. Rather his readings show us the existential transformation to which the reader must be open, if they want to genuinely understand the text. A transformation which demands that we shed our attachment to the present, in order to experience the event of being questioned by the text by allowing the right questions that we need to put to the text to also occur to us at the same time. What his readings also show us is the ethical responsibility that lies at the basis of any reading. The ethical responsibility to avoid the temptation to treat the text neither like a ventriloquist's dummy nor like some cultish authority to which one surrenders one's self altogether. In Gadamer, like in Heidegger, the engagement with the history of philosophy is not just an ancillary business of philosophy. Rather, to engage in the history of philosophy is to philosophize in the deepest sense of that term.

Part I
Ancient Philosophy

1

Parmenides or Why Being Pertains to This World (1988)

[3] There is no question that Hegel and Schleiermacher form the starting point of the philosophical research and appropriation of the pre-Socratics. Both agree on the necessity of admitting the dimension of history into the work of philosophical thought. Both have exercised a decisive influence on subsequent historical research, although Hegel not so much from a historical and philological perspective. Schleiermacher's school notably achieved much in this direction. Yet, when it comes to philosophical interest, Hegel deserves first place. This interest is in no way curbed by the well-known violence, which resides in the application of the dialectic schema to history and to the history of philosophy.

The philosophy of the pre-Socratics plays a determining role in Hegel. In his *Logic*, he was the first to integrate the pre-Socratics into transcendental philosophy. He questioned back to the point that lay behind the tradition of the theory of categories, which had been shaped by Aristotle for all posterity. In this theory, the category of substance occupied the uncontested first place. In the early projects of Hegel, the being-what, i.e. the category of substance, which Aristotle had developed out of the Socratic-Platonic question, still holds primacy. With the composition of the *Logic*, however, something new comes into play in Hegel. The first chapter, the beginning of *The Science of Logic*, begins with the great simplicities of being, nothing and becoming. Here one immediately recognizes Parmenides and Heraclitus. In fact, the whole of Hegel's *Logic* reads like a dialectical organization and thorough review of the entire field of pre-Socratic philosophy. It is only after the pre-Socratics that there follows, in the second volume of his *Logic*, the logic of essence, which treats the philosophy of Plato and Aristotle.

Unfortunately, the two volumes on Hegel's lectures on the history of philosophy have been redacted and edited in a truly unfortunate manner. Nonetheless, they still present the best commentary on Hegel's *Logic* as well as on the *Phenomenology of Spirit*, of the 'history of [4] the spirit as it appears'. Gabler's well-known book[1] attests to this through a detailed illustration of the dialectic of consciousness from

---

'Parmenides oder das Diesseits des Seins (1988)' originated from a lecture given at a congress in Velia in 1988. It was first published in *La parola del passato* 43 (1988): pp. 143–76 and is now in *Gesammelte Werke*, vol. 7. Tübingen: J. C. B. Mehr (Paul Siebeck), 1991, pp. 3–31.

ancient sources, as well as the recent book of Wilhelm Purpus[2], which at the time reinvigorated the understanding of Hegel in the age of neo-Kantianism.

It belonged to Hegel's fierce power of abstraction to mirror metaphysics in his *Logic* and the history of metaphysics in the *Phenomenology of Spirit* in such an intricate manner that historical-philosophical research subsequently has remained constantly preoccupied with deciphering both these mirror-like writings.

This research was aided by the fact that Friedrich Schleiermacher, despite all his closeness to Fichte and to German idealism, could call upon his unusual philological competence and a genuine historical sensibility. Schleiermacher thus became productive in both directions. It was his merit to lead historical thinking to victory over the dogmatic 'doxographical' methods of the eighteenth century. In the other direction he also loosened up the schematic dogmatism of Hegel's dialectic. It is not by accident that Dilthey, the true founder of intellectual history, had a particular connection to Schleiermacher.

Furthermore, the philosophical presence of the pre-Socratics in Germany remained largely within the framework of the so-called 'history of the problem', of this reappropriation of Kant permeated by the late form of German idealism, which is called neo-Kantianism and belongs to the history of Hegel's influence. From the quarry that is Hegel's *Logic,* posterity has mined all that it could use.

Only with the turn that brought the age of liberalism to an end under the thunder of the battles for resources characterizing the First World War, was there a beginning of a new presence of the pre-Socratics. It began under the sign of the concept of life and in the spirit of historical thinking, which was especially promoted by Wilhelm Dilthey. In the long run, it was the influence of Nietzsche. It is true that Nietzsche's own first works, *The Birth of Tragedy*, but also the posthumous work *Philosophy in the Tragic Age of the Greeks*, still remained under the spell of Schopenhauer's late romanticism. Yet, it is with Nietzsche that the philosophy of life became the fundamental tenor of the twentieth century and so the late Nietzsche began to exercise his influence worldwide. Classical philology was not alone in being touched by it. It was especially Heidegger's renewal of the question of being in [5] the horizon of time, which went back behind metaphysics and connected with its Greek beginnings. How this looked becomes clear, for example, in Heidegger's studies on Anaximander, Heraclitus and Parmenides. Even in the research on Parmenides, the Nietzschean impulse continued to influence Karl Reinhardt, Kurt Riezler, Uvo Hölscher and Heidegger.

Especially in the case of Heraclitus but also in the case of Parmenides, the manner in which their work is transmitted demands the complete application of historical thinking. This is not just for the sake of securing reliable textual bases, which never consist only of the quotations. It is also and above all for the sake of being attentive to the history of the words and the concepts, which is necessary if we want to overcome the anachronistic influences of the Aristotelian and traditional conceptual language.

The research on the pre-Socratics, which owes a decisive debt above all else to Hermann Diels thanks to his editorial work, represents at the same time a specific era of research. It is the influence of the school of the history of religion, which continues to exercise an influence to this day on the arrangement of the fragments of the pre-Socratics. Even the still-ever instructive original edition of Parmenides' didactic poem by Diels[3], with its superb scholarly commentary, seeks above all the influence of religious poems everywhere. These are poems associated with the name of Epimenides and they all obviously follow in the footsteps of Hesiod. Yet, these poems also exhibited a shamanistic influence and were familiar with the Orphic myths of the transmigration of souls. This remains a great unknown, whose influence is as incontestable as it is unidentifiable.

Thus, for instance, the proemium and the depiction by Parmenides of his journey across all the cities and beyond can be led back to such precursors. Yet, Diels himself could not conceal that 'what separates Parmenides from all of this Orphic, Pythagorean, ecstatic character is his rationalism, which only lets the external form […] of mysticism influence it'[4]. Overall, this is a good description, even though there is good evidence otherwise of an authentic fundamental mood of religiosity in the *Magna Graecia* ['the greater Greece'] of the time. Obviously, we know all too little to be able to assess the role these religious movements played alongside the official cults of the Olympian gods. In any case, we will have to say that the language found in Parmenides is that of the Homeric and Hesiodic versification and it bears an Apollonian tone, just as earlier in Homer. How the scientific prose of the seventh and sixth centuries looked, we obviously do not know. [6] Nothing of it is preserved. Yet, we have from Anaximander a solemn statement which obviously struck Theophrastus as unusual (VS 12 A 9). We thus have to conclude that Anaximander's style was the sober style of a textbook. Even in Parmenides' didactic poem there is little to be detected of a religious movement. We can only exercise caution when using the uncertain information about the Orphic movement and likewise with the reference to shamanism. At any rate, in the meantime since Dodds and Uvo Hölscher, the religious historical background of the cosmogonies of the Eastern world has gained in substance[5], and from Protagoras himself there are threads which could run up to Iran, as van der Waerden had conjectured[6].

Nevertheless, our real knowledge about the history of Greek philosophy depends entirely on Aristotle. We generally begin with Thales. But even in this we only follow Aristotle. He called Thales of Miletus the first philosopher. Certainly, the Ionian school of Miletus taken as a whole – what in looking back in a pedantic fashion was later usually called a 'school' – would have to be treated by a philosophically motivated research as a first chapter, if only we knew more about this school. In fact, what has been originally transmitted from the early centuries, of the seventh and sixth, is limited to a few scattered quotations and Aristotelian accounts. The accounts which Aristotle has given, especially in the introduction to his *Physics* and his *Metaphysics*, carry special weight but they obviously do not present us what has been transmitted in an immediate and authentic manner. Aristotle never had historical objectivity in mind and he always drew upon his predecessors in Greek thinking only to introduce his own thinking. Here, the 'physiologists' of the Ionian school were for him a particular case. He saw himself as the adversary to Plato's Pythagorean-mathematical tendencies and, as the founder of physics, he must have recognized himself more in the Ionian beginnings of Greek thinking than in everything that came later. This had its grave consequences. Only with extreme difficulty can we differentiate the accounts which Aristotle gives us from that which had been actually meant in the original intentions of the Ionians.

The situation changes at the beginning of the fifth century. At this point in time, the Pythagorean tradition is taking shape and asserts itself. It took its orientation from mathematics, from the numerical relations in celestial movements and in the theoretical foundations of music. This did not correspond [7] to what Aristotle had established as the reliable ground of his philosophizing in the concept of *phusis* ['nature']. The same is also true for the leading thinkers of the incipient fifth century alongside Pythagoras, namely, Parmenides and Heraclitus above all. Thus, these thinkers and their doctrines could only appear at the margins for him. For both Parmenides and Heraclitus do not satisfy the fundamental presuppositions which guide Aristotle's own questions. These presuppositions lie in the concept of *phusis*. It is under this concept that Aristotle obviously recognized the Ionian beginnings and asserted it against Plato's Pythagoreanism. By contrast, Heraclitus' cryptic sayings and his doctrine of the fire of the soul (*pur phronimon*) do not even appear to him to be contributions to physics. It was above all the assimilation and continuation of Parmenides in Plato's Academy, to which Plato's Eleatic dialogues bear witness, which motivate Aristotle, in spite of everything, to include the topic of 'Parmenides' in the introduction to his physics lectures. In fact, it turns out to be nothing but a highly ceremonial execution. Nevertheless, we are indebted to the inclusion of the critique of Parmenides in Aristotle's *Physics* for the fact that the positions of Alexander as well as of Simplicius, which follow their commentary of Aristotle's *Physics*, have been preserved. It was a particularly fortunate circumstance that Simplicius, at the time of the dissolution of the Academy, discovered an old copy of Parmenides' didactic poem and, recognizing the peculiarity of the text, produced detailed excerpts.

With this, we have a singular instance in the whole of pre-Socratic thought. We are not just dependent on accounts, whether critical or more biographical, and not just on isolated quotations either. We possess almost the entire text of the first part of the didactic poem of Parmenides. It is significant that we are dealing with hexameters in the style of Homer and Hesiod, and even of verses of the kind which we otherwise only possess of the proximate contemporary Xenophanes.

Of Xenophanes it is said that he had been the teacher of Parmenides. This certainly sounds somewhat fantastic. For, as the preserved parts of his elegies show, he was poetically not an untalented rhapsode but certainly not the founder of Eleatic philosophy. Such a claim could only arise because Plato in his condensed and extremely helpful overview in the *Sophist* (242cff) refers the Eleatic school back to 'Xenophanes and those even before him'. If Xenophanes could have in any way been the teacher of Parmenides, it was certainly not because of his philosophy but because of his skill at composing verses. If so, he was not at all a bad teacher. Today, we recognize the verses of Parmenides' didactic poem to be poetically good verses. Xenophanes also serves as an important witness and as a confirmation of the fact that in the courts and cities of the Greater Greece of the time, [8] there was an interest in the new science, which had developed in Miletus. People were so interested that they even had poetic accounts of the universe and nature by rhapsodes like Xenophanes in their feasts. It is disputed whether Xenophanes had really written a didactic poem 'On Nature' (naturally not under this title). It is not impossible. But certainly the rhapsodic form of delivery was totally lacking in independence as it was in the charge of such professional singers, who generally only recited mythological themes and heroic sagas. In any case, it is certain that the later didactic poem 'On Xenophanes', which is covered by Aristotle, only stems from a much later time. Nonetheless, it is entirely plausible that Xenophanes in depicting the universe undertook predications of a hymnic style, which could be read as philosophical arguments in Aristotle's time. One can produce pretty good dialectical theses of an Eleatic style from such hymnic encomia.

By contrast, Parmenides' didactic poem stands on solid ground. It is only somewhat unusual that the new Ionian science at the time was communicated through the art of rhapsody and disseminated as far as Italy and Sicily. We have to realize this. Only then do we really understand why Parmenides, instead of writing in the prose of a treatise, composed such a didactic poem. It is true that these are external circumstances but even these external circumstances have a deeper meaning. Here a veneer of the mythic-heroic world of legends comes to expression through the curiosity of this new science about the world. This perhaps means that, in the case of Parmenides, mythical forms and cosmological contents could be fused with logical rationality to produce a new impactful unity. We should note that goddesses are introduced here and one is reminded of Hesiod's initiation by the muses. Here, it is a goddess who brings everything forth, admittedly, a nameless goddess. But this is also how the muse is in Homer. The divinity which inspires is precisely always something totally different from a god encountered in cultic life with all its mythical background. In Parmenides' text, there appear many other names of gods, 'Eros' above all, who in accordance to the Hesiodic model represents an all-encompassing power. The other deified powers which appear in Parmenides are *Dikē* ['Justice'], *Moira* ['Destiny'], *Anankē* ['Necessity'] and perhaps even *Alētheia* ['Truth']. In the names of such divinities, the creation of concepts and the traditions of myth seem indistinguishably to merge into one another.

We could most likely surmise religious backgrounds in the prooemium to the didactic poem, given the captivating depiction of the ascent of the poet to the divine palace in which the full truth about being will be promulgated to him. These are features similar to those of the mysteries. But then a doctrine of salvation and something [9] like a revelation would certainly have to follow in the form of a divine message. However, this journey to heaven has nothing to do with a journey to Hades, as would be fitting in the case of Orphism. One must first of all feel the contrast which exists here. On the one hand, we have the verse form, the language of the epic and the solemn ritual of the journey by chariot, the arrival and the reception by the Goddess; on the other, we have the sober logical and abstract announcement of her message. Divine powers are found in the course of the text, mentioned here and there, but they fit perfectly seamlessly into the language of the argument, which dominates the whole. What is at stake in the message of the goddess is not religious revelation but logical consistency. Manifestly, it is a consistency of a peculiar kind and of such paradoxical rigour that one would like to believe that no mortal would be in a position to abide by such consistency without divine authorization. This is a point which does not seem to me to have received its rightful recognition in the research and philosophical interpretation of the didactic poem up until this point.

The promulgating goddess is obviously insightful enough to take mortal reason into account and this is of decisive importance for understanding the whole. The part of the poem that has been handed down to us, which expounds on the doctrine of being, is in any case only the smaller part of the whole poem. We can infer this from the few preserved fragments from the later parts of the poem. Basically, we have to say that actually the historical efficacy [*Wirkungsgeschichte*] of the poem, which in fact permeates the entire history of philosophy, has virtually obscured the fundamental fact that the content of the didactic poem in its far greater parts is somehow a progression within the framework of Ionian physics. Admittedly, it comes down decisively to the 'how' [in the 'somehow']. Here we have a goddess who speaks, who, on all further matters, takes the mortals into consideration and turns towards their points of view.[7] This in no way means that the proper message of the goddess, on which she had insisted with solemn decisiveness in the beginning, the avoidance of the 'nothing', would be given up in the expansively elaborate depiction of the world order. The world-picture of the mortals, presented by the goddess, is explicitly grounded in the points of view of the mortals (their *doxai*). Yet, the goddess remains on the way to the truth in her presentation. She unambiguously announces that there is only one way which really leads to *alētheia* (Fragment 8, 1).

So, if there is to be truth in this depiction of the world-picture held by mortals, we are confronted in it with the task of avoiding the vacuous thought [*Ungedanke*] of the nothing, even if mortals otherwise let themselves be guided by what appears to the eye, which offers them their point of view about the really experienced world. When the Goddess, here in her depiction of the world-picture, takes oppositions as her basis, she in a certain sense follows what Anaximander already knew, namely that *phusis* consists in oppositions constantly [10] counterbalancing each other and sustaining the world order. When the goddess, for her part, speaks of oppositions now, it is still always with the claim to promulgate the truth, namely, to inform the chosen one of the points of view of the mortals in such a way that he is not led astray into the nothing. The steady truth of being and the world-picture grounded in appearance, in which light and night constantly counterbalance each other, must in a certain sense both hold to be true. Both adhere to the consistency of reason to exclude the nothing as totally unthinkable and unsayable[8].

It follows from all this that the elaborate depiction of the world-picture of the mortals is not some kind of supplement, a modification or a retrospective adaptation to fit human experience. One hardly understands how one could have tried again and again to interpret the connection between the two parts of the poem on the basis of a biographical development of the thinker and thus ignore the clear wording. One also hardly understands that one did not at all take seriously the fact that here a goddess speaks to a mortal about the points of view of mortals.

It indeed sounds fitting when Aristotle says that Parmenides had seen himself constrained by the vehemence of the facts[9] to modify his theory of the steady sphere of being by making it fit the reality of movement. But in all this, we are still dealing with the goddess' teaching and if it is an adaptation, then it is the goddess adapting to the human capacity to make judgements, a fact which cannot be circumvented. This can also be expressed by saying that the author Parmenides realizes that healthy reason cannot reconcile itself with the absurdity of denying all movement. In any case, what is at stake in the two cases, in the first part of the poem as well as in the larger second part, is the consistency of reason with itself, for which the Goddess vouches.

Since Karl Reinhardt, recent scholarship has placed the transition between the two parts of the didactic poem front and centre. The decisive verses of the transition (Fragment 8, 50ff) have been fortunately preserved without lacunae. Yet, it seems difficult to understand the text precisely. In my opinion, the difficulties disappear if we constantly bear in mind that it is a divine instruction which is being bestowed upon the privileged recipient. In any case, this togetherness of *alētheia* and human *doxai* is not about a demonic entanglement in being and semblance, which confuses human beings, in the manner of, for example, [11] Reinhardt's fascinating deciphering of the tragedy of King Oedipus. It is also not the problem of sophistic semblance which had challenged the Platonic Socrates. It is rather a twofold expression of divine knowledge. The goddess knows what is true, but she understands that human beings are oriented towards what appears to the eye. This is how she depicts the world-picture which, on the basis of this presupposition, proves itself to be tenable in her eyes. It is on this basis that the transition from the first part to the second is to be understood.

The decisive verse 8, 54 (*tōn mian ou chreōn estin – en hō peplanēmenoi eisin* ['one of them is not correct – in this they are in error']) is particularly controversial. Diels had already recognized in his time that the divine herald engages here with the opinions [*Meinungen*] of mortals, which in fact contained no truth for the goddess but which she elevates to their greatest possible consistency. In the announcement of the presentation of mortal points of view (Frag. 1, 32) and over and over again, the Greek word *chrēn* comes up. It means not so much 'it is necessary' but rather 'it is to be considered necessary': it is in order and correct, given how mortals are[10]. They are not in a position to insist on the steady immobility of being against what appears to their eyes. This is what is now expressed here with the same word *chrēn* and the goddess is supposed to characterize the opinions of mortals with just this same word. Then, verse 8, 54 says: according to the mortal point of view, it is not required to assume a unity and a single entity which would lie behind the duality of the two opposing forms of light and night as the one and true being. The two opposites are rather what is and what the world gives us to see.

Schwabl was right to insist[11], in adopting Diels' view, that the controversial verse cannot mean that it was really false to designate one of the two opposites, namely the night, as being because it would still be non-being. This would have read differently in Greek, not *mian* ['one'] but *heteran* ['another'][12]. In fact, the goddess speaks from a critical distance vis-à-vis what mortals think. This comes to the fore in verse 8, 54 through the fact that the goddess's critical remark is an appropriate interruption. The goddess here cannot suppress the critical remark that mortals are not capable of thinking the one in all being. What has indeed been said of them is that they have accepted a duality of opposing forms, which are mutually opposed to and mixed with one another. Now, these are [12] certainly not the pairs of opposites of which the Ionian physiologists spoke. The goddess shows that we are dealing with a single opposition, that of light and night, and this opposition is in fact for the mortals the one opposition which articulates the world that appears to the eye. The true world of being looks different. In her teaching, the goddess had always emphasized this fact over and over again that there is only being, the one being, in which there is no nothing. This is for mortals a superhuman truth.

That mortals are not in a position to adhere to the consistency of the truth of being against what appears to the eye thus signifies in the eyes of the goddess a certain departure from the truth. Mortals are forced into this departure by what appears to their eyes. Thus, when mortals accept two opposing forces and associate the multiplicity of what shows itself in the light and disappears in the night with being and non-being, it remains a retreat from the ultimate consistency of the thought of being. This is how mortals think and are unable to arrive at a greater consistency. Indeed, they would just not know how to live if they did not orient themselves in this way to the multiplicity of things. No matter how extensively this may be true of mortals, the goddess trusts that the thinker will let himself be taught to remain consistent as much as possible, despite his unavoidable adaptation to what appears to the eye, and avoid the vacuous thought of the nothing.

Thus, what the goddess promulgates as the plausible world-picture of the mortals founded on the opposition of day and night, is in fact something entirely new. There is truth in what thus appears to the eye. Nobody is thereby expected to take the nothing for being. Also, the goddess does not say, for example, that there is nothing at all that corresponds to this appearance to the eye. There are points of view offering themselves to us, which correspond to this appearance to the eye, and which we designate accordingly. Mortals cannot even demand the unchangeable truth of one single being. Yet, they are able to arrive at a world-picture which is nonetheless coherent in itself even if they follow what appears to the eye. This is not due, for example, to the fact that light and darkness, day and night are really the same. Rather, for the human experience of the world, they are fundamentally different aspects of the world which are superseded in their dominance and dispelled by one another. Certainly, Heraclitus chastises the others for being so ignorant as to not know that day and night, as mere effects of the sun's course, are one and the same (VS 22 B 57).[13] Heraclitus lampoons mythic discourse, when he mentions Hesiod, the thinking in oppositions practised by the Milesians (Hecataeus) for the superficial abundance of their knowledge, and similarly, Pythagoras and Xenophanes (B 40)[14]. He was quite right not also to add the name of Parmenides, whom he perhaps did not know at all.

The fact that Heraclitus mentions Xenophanes does not speak against this. Xenophanes was a rhapsode who had already been active there on the Ionian coasts, before he went to Sicily. By contrast, Heraclitus could have hardly named Parmenides in this [13] context, who so emphatically insisted upon the one being. In the depiction of both the aspects of the world, day and night, the staying-within-itself of both the aspects, their opposition is underlined with conspicuous emphasis. One fancies noticing a secret smirk from the goddess when she leaves mortals to their simple-mindedness of not knowing that day and night are truly the same. Or does Parmenides himself perhaps smirk when he has to invoke so many things, such as the 'oppressive darkness', only in order to think the night not simply as a nothing, as the nothingness of the day, and in order thereby to avoid the inconsistency of the being of nothing? The goddess explicitly underlines that the ethereal fire 'is totally for itself' and is not identical to the other, and the same is true of the night: it is 'in itself' something dense and fixed, a heavy and oppressive mass, and not quite a nothing. We understand why light and night are differentiated by human beings in this way and precisely in their constant intermingling they present what is true. This is how being looks to us. Therein lies the superiority of the divine teaching about 'being' over the Ionian thinkers, who think in pairs of oppositions. To become invisible is not to become just nothing. Light and night are both omnipresent and permeate everything (Frag. 1, 32: *dia pantos panta perōnta* ['all going through all things']). In their commingling there is no empty place, no nothing. Nonetheless, to what appears to the eye, they are the most radical of oppositions. They are the one primordial opposition, on which everything visible depends. This means: to make one out of these two, the one *eon* ['being'], would be something mortals would not be able to understand how to do and which the goddess must first make clear to the thinker. The world-picture of mortals is dominated by the opposition between light and darkness in whose changing appearances the manifoldness of things shows itself.

Finally, a world order plausible in its own terms emerges, a *diakosmos* ['arrangement'] in which everything is full of being and nothingness is nowhere to be found. This is how the poem subsequently proceeds with a cosmogonic depiction which describes the world of the stars. This is meant in full seriousness. It cannot be doubted that the form of presentation of everything subsequent was that of cosmogony. Nonetheless, it is totally different from Anaximander depicting his creation of the world in as much as even for him, as in any cosmogony, the abiding order of the world is described as the final result. The message of the goddess intends precisely to provide the poet Parmenides with a real superiority over Ionian science. Thus, this cosmogony of visibility and appearance to the eye may contain a rejection of the cosmogony of the Ionians. Particularly, Anaximander's teaching of the separation of worlds from the boundless and of the new creation of worlds must entangle itself in the vacuous thought of the nothing and in such a becoming of *worlds* also think the nothing as if it existed.

The much-debated passage in fragment 8 verse 54 cannot be discussed here in all [14] its details. I will only point out that in the verses in the highlighted passage we have in sequence first a mention of 'two' (*morphas duo* ['two forms']) and then a mention of 'one' (*tōn mian* ['one of them']). Here it seems to me that the highlighted opposition between two and one suggests that we must precisely understand that 'out of the two comes one', and this then would be the one, the sphere of being[15]. To think like this would be the teaching which human beings are not able precisely to accept and which has been hammered over and over again into the head of the listener of the poem (this is how Simplicius understood it in *Physics* 31, 7!). The goddess has every reason to underscore this departure from the truth from which mortals manifestly cannot refrain, even if they are otherwise capable of thinking consistently. This is why she interrupts her report: 'In this they strayed into error'. This also means positively that, if taught well, they will after all know how to avoid non-sense, the vacuous thought of the nothing. To this extent, they could remain on the way of the truth even if they follow what appears to their eye.

If I put such weight on the mythical form of discourse, which runs through the didactic poem and according to which the divine mouth makes disclosures about mortals and their points of view, whether better or worse, this is so as not to indulge myself in the conceptual language of Plato and Aristotle or even of Kant, who obeyed this message in their own way and distinguished 'noetic' being. I rather pose the question as to whether we can do justice to this inceptual thinking and thereby also to ourselves if we only see it in the light of the history of its effects, which begins with Plato and Aristotle, and not rather in the light of possibilities which have not come into effect. The history of effects certainly belongs to thought's sphere of meaning. And this history is particularly instructive in the case of Parmenides. Here we see indeed how the trajectories of his efficacy took two directions, as different as the corpuscular theory of the fifth century and the philosophy of the *logos*, arising at the same time towards the end of the fourth century and coming to its fruition in the dialectic of Plato and Aristotle. We have to keep both these directions in mind. Thus, we see how the Eleatic question in fact inaugurates the tradition of metaphysics and we find the didactic poem received by the ancient commentators who belong to this tradition quite obviously in terms of the distinction between 'noetic' and 'aesthetic' being, the intelligible and sensible world, to speak with Plotinus or Kant.

Yet, we ask the question with the contrary interest as to whether the didactic poem is closer to the subject matter of thinking than the metaphysical tradition could accept. Not to have distinguished something yet can [15] also mean seeing better what belongs together. At any rate, there is no doubt that the difference between *noēsis* ['thought'] and *aisthēsis* ['perception'] is primarily a Platonic coinage. This is the most important presupposition for understanding Parmenides, namely, that the opposition between *noēsis* and *aisthēsis* is not yet present here. One should not let oneself be deceived by the fact that in a later context (Frag. 7, 4), seeing, hearing and the tongue are explicitly rejected, and the *logos* is summoned against them. The passage proves the opposite. The expressions show that here there is no common concept like *aisthēsis*.

The tongue, the one for speaking, would really not belong to this concept of *aisthēsis*[16]. Here, in my own studies of Plato, I follow, despite all its rookie mistakes, the ground-breaking work of Hermann Langerbeck[17] on the *Theaetetus*. In this dialogue, we can very precisely identify the decisive point at which the theory of movement belonging to early Greek thinking is put into the mouth of Protagoras. As this theory fails, it opens up the new horizon of the *psuchē* ['soul'] and of the Platonic and Aristotelian orientation to the *logoi* ['arguments']. This is made clear by the fact that the Eleatic question is taken up in the *Sophist* and the *Parmenides*[18].

We can see in Aristotle that his critique of the Eleatics, which he brings up at the beginning of the *Physics*, does not really target Parmenides at all. The two chapters of the first book of the *Physics*, which contain this critique, are completely at cross-purposes to the subject matter of physics. Not once is there a mention of the second part of the didactic poem, which was after all a cosmology. Ultimately, it seems to me that Aristotle has Plato in mind. Plato is countered with the manifoldness of the meaning of 'being' and the Aristotelian theory of the categories is mobilized against him. Aristotle thus has in mind the Platonic assimilation of Parmenides' teaching through the *Sophist*. There, Plato has a less clear-cut course in mind. He suggests that in the teaching of the old Parmenides there could lie insights which were perhaps not yet available to us and not yet grasped. Obviously, in Plato's eyes it was in no way settled, in the didactic poem as well as for himself, that the Aristotelian distinction between substance and the remaining categories had to be the last word. The question has thus to be directed at the didactic poem itself: why is its teaching introduced like a revelation coming from the mouth of the goddess? [16] What is in conflict with all that appears to the eye, in such a way that there is simply no motion at all and not even the many, must be 'being' and truth!

When Heidegger enquires back into the realm of truth within which something like metaphysics could develop at all, what challenges him again and again must be Parmenides and his insistence that 'being is'. That this insistence at once concerns the vacuous thought of the nothing was path-breaking for me when it comes to the proximity of being and nothing, and already early on, since Heidegger's inaugural lecture. The elimination of the vacuous thought of the nothing conversely means: 'being' implies the thought of the 'there'. Here we need not let ourselves be misguided by Carnap's well-known objection to Heidegger's talk of the nothing[19], namely that something like this cannot be written on the board with our customary symbols. In fact, Carnap here essentially reveals himself to be a good Eleatic. Parmenides obviously expresses himself somewhat differently and he is not interested in the logical structure of propositions. It is thus totally beyond doubt that *esti* ['is'] in the didactic poem can hardly have the meaning of the copula and that *mē eon* ['non-being'] does not have the meaning of negation. That is why Parmenides is not kept from constantly making negative statements, despite the rejection of the 'nothing'. The discursive form of the didactic poem is not that of the proposition, which only connects a subject and a predicate. *Esti* and mostly also *to eon* carry the very heavy semantic burden of being-true and being-actual. This is why the guideposts which are listed on the way to the truth of being mean that the nothing must remain excluded from the thinking of being. The guideposts must protect us from going astray in this way. It is thus significant, that the argumentation begins with *agenēton* ['not born'] and *anōlethron* ['imperishable'] (Frag. 8, 3) and that this point is treated in particular detail. In both of these terms the nothing is necessarily thought. This is clear to everyone. What is not so obvious is the extension of this insight towards expressions such as 'changing place'. It means 'leaving a place empty'. But if it were 'empty', then the nothing would be there. The same goes for colour, which passes away, as we can say in German.[20] Here too the expression 'bright colour' indirectly points to the nothing in the passing away of the colour and perhaps not just of the colour. Or why do the dead hear silence?[21]

We should note that the enumeration that sums up what is rejected here stands under the keyword of 'name' (*onoma*) and of 'naming'. What is meant by these expressions is thus not a nothing and yet thinking is thrust into emptiness when it is supposed to think the coming to be. What is that from which something comes to be or into which it passes away, or what [17] is the emptiness, which one leaves behind or occupies anew, and so on? One can also think of the 'naming' of the nothing, which is said (Frag. 8, 17) to be unnameable (*anōnumon*). The other expressions are indeed mere names but not empty. They mean something but they do not cover everything that is meant in them. The nothing remains covered over and when one examines what is named, one is thrust into the void: '[…] For the sake of the gods, can you ever understand what is meant there?' (Plato, The *Sophist*, 243b).

It is thus an imprecise use of such names. However, these imprecise representations can be replaced with a more precise thinking, and this the goddess also teaches. It is the teaching of light and night. They are 'names', but the opposite which is always thought with them at the same time is itself existing [*seiend*] and is not nothing. Thus, what *noein* means in the didactic poem is positively clarified. It is most certainly not 'thinking', not even thinking in contrast to seeing 'what is given in person' [*leibhaft*] (to speak with Husserl). It is not about what can be thought. The didactic poem cannot mean a mere thinkability. This is already better, because it does not completely obscure Parmenides' intentions, to render *noein* as 'recognizing' [*Erkennen*]. At least here, the being of what is recognized, its being actual and true, is always present. In the meantime, we have learned from Kurt von Fritz's careful studies on the history of words and concepts what the original scope of application and the semantic field of *noein* actually are[22]. According to its original lexical use, *noein* seems to be something like the sense of smell possessed by deer which 'makes out' something in the sense of 'something is there'. This is the way wild animals locate danger and thereby certainly do not recognize what it is while yet sensing that something 'is' there. It is a very sensitive taking in [*Vernehmen*] so that it is totally hidden from the others. This is how Democritus, for example, can use the word for the knowledge of the atoms or Plato for mathematical intuition and abstraction, and Aristotle, in his conceptual analyses where he is so fond of going back to the original linguistic use, fully emphasizes that *noūs* consists in *thigganein* ['to touch'], in the immediacy of stumbling upon something and touching it, different from when we make a statement about something. We should also include Anaxagoras in this series and thereby make the results of Fritz's investigations emerging from the history of concepts fruitful for the way concepts are formed in philosophy. As Plato's critique in the *Phaedo* tells us, *noũs*, as is indeed well-known, was thought by Anaxagoras as a most subtle material, penetrating everywhere and permeating everything. It scents everything, so to speak, because it is present in everything without ever being mixed with anything. In any case, this conceptual history teaches us how close inceptual thinking, when it had to make the decision in thought between thinking being [18] and thinking nothing, must have been to representing being as this fully homogeneous and unchanging sphere of being, upon which one always stumbles if one stumbles upon something.

Here, we are not yet in the realm of abstract conceptual formations but in a powerfully intuitive thinking in which the words of the living language are loaded with a new content of thought. It is mythical discourse, not only because of its verse form but because of its ties to intuition. It is almost like what we are familiar with in Plato as the co-existence and the togetherness of *logos* and *mūthos*. What is placed in the trajectory of one's own thinking and thus of one's statements capable of giving an account and what then still exceeds them is spoken out and raised into the beyond of a world which is only conjured up and made present through *mūthos*, through 'narrative'. It is in this sense that the 'thinking of being' as the homogeneous sphere is like a pointing out of the unsayable insight that the nothing is not. The whole and, as it appears, seamlessly preserved text in which the thesis of being is presented as an extrapolation of thought in a describable reality, receives from this its clear principle of composition. Everything is signs, *sēmata*, which are planted on the way to the truth. One would hardly want to replace it with the genuinely attractive parallel which Walter Bröcker has provided us[23]. There is nothing in the didactic poem that speaks in favour of a holy street decked out with sayings. What is rather said is that it is difficult to stay the course and not to stray unawares into what is impassable. For this purpose, navigation in the world of that time needed signposts of the kind we are familiar with on the wintery ski slopes. Fragments 6 and 7 clearly show us that mortals are constantly at risk of straying from the way to the truth.

One would like to examine the series of signs which reliably mark this way to *alētheia*. One wonders whether there is rational order here or whether it is more of a rhapsodic enumeration. It is now clear that the strongest temptation to think the nothing is to be found when posing the question of the coming to be. Where does it come from? How has it come about and how come it is now no longer? Beginning with this argument thus confirms how the nothing always wants to creep into the process of thinking being and for this reason requires the most detailed argumentation.

In the sequence of the remaining signs, which are connected to this way, we would hardly want to speak of a clear arrangement. Just as the first refutation of the coming to be is repeated in the argument, the principle of repetition has in fact an essential function in this rhapsodic literature[24]. We must bear this in mind here too. The [19] concluding expression of the whole Fragment 8, from verse 42 to 49, definitely functions like the appropriation of the signs already described in verses 26 to 33. This is thus the only principle of composition which I can discover for the sequel: the parts which correspond to each other have the function of providing a frame. What it is that they frame requires a specific reflection on our part. It is the argument of *noein* and of being. This 'sign' also stands out in that it sounds like a summarizing conclusion (8, 38ff), which summarizes many things unlike what we see in 'unbecome' and 'unmoved' (8, 21).

We will have to come back again to this. Can the other quotations from this text help us further? Hardly. The fragments which have come down to us are really reliable in their sequence only in the place where they present the careful excerpt of Simplicius. By contrast, the position which Fragments 4 and 5 have received in our numbering is quite uncertain. Fragment 4 is a quotation from Clement of Alexandria. With the overhastiness of a Church Father intent on documenting, he sees in the first verse a depiction of the essence of faith. This just does not give us any clue as to the origin of the entire quotation. This is why Uvo Hölscher[25], in his substantial new treatment of the didactic poem, simply wants to remove the fragment from the first part of the didactic poem and sees in it the conclusion of the whole work. Now what we have in the fragment is a word of exhortation, which one expects more at the beginning. It is also not convincing when Hölscher invokes the parallel with Empedocles (VS 31 B 110), where at the end the listener is exhorted once more, as it were, to heed what has been learnt. However, the connection with fragment 2 is still fundamentally only very loosely intelligible. Both are exhortations. It is certainly correct that the fragment of Parmenides, which, according to Simplicius (Frag. 19), belongs to the conclusion of the whole, does not sound like a conclusion. We must, however, note that the quotation stems not from the commentary on the *Physics*, which lay before him, but from *De caelo*. It is far more plausible that Simplicius had not quoted along with the rest the actual conclusion, which was certainly still to follow. In any case, I would like to leave Fragment 4 roughly at the place at which it is listed.

By contrast, Fragment 3 has become outright questionable to me. The sentence is difficult to construct.

To gar auto noein estin te kai einai ['For knowing and being are the same']

'It is the same: *esti noein* ["knowing is"] and *esti einai* ["being is"], that one takes in and that something is actually there, which one takes in'. Through the *te kai* ['and also'], *noeien* and *einai* are most intimately connected and this connection is expressed by *to auto* ['the same'].

[20] Now, this text is not very well attested at all. It is again the learned Clement of Alexandria whom Plotinus and Proclus follow in this case. But both cite him only because of the difference between *aisthēsis* ['perception'] and *noein*. That is all. Thus, Agostino Marsoner's suggestion makes sense to me[26], who had doubts about the authenticity of this text. The verse is no complete verse anyway and sounds rather like a very concise summary of the teaching of Parmenides, which was available to Clement of Alexandria and, in fact, has only been developed out of Frag. 8, 34ff.

In any case, the context which connects Frag. 6, 7 and 8 is attested in a completely different way. It presents a reasonable composition. Shortly before the end of the introductory part, the most important of all the signs would be provided a frame, so to speak, by two other statements. That which is framed is the distinguished sign for being. Being is only where *noein* stumbles upon something, whether it be rendered as taking in, receiving or touching something. In any case, it is clear that the nothing cannot be taken in in this way and that where something is taken in, something is there, being and not nothing. We could almost say that being is then 'posited', for example like in the Stoic *sugkatathesis* ['approval'].

This is how one expresses oneself in a spontaneous manner, as one should not or, if need be, as one can express oneself in the transition to the second part of the didactic poem. There, 'to posit' has the good sense of fixing a lexical convention. There one can speak of 'positing'. Yet, to infer from a sign for being which excludes the nothing that there is a positing of being is to speak the language of German idealism, which does not belong here. This is how the fundamental principle 'thinking and being are the same', which we count as Frag. 3, has been received as a seal of approval on the part of the philosophy of identity in German idealism. In its later reception, this fundamental principle of identity has always been placed at the forefront as such a principle.

The probable model for Frag. 3 are the verses of Frag. 8, 34ff. This also has its difficulties, but the sense is clear. *Tauton d'esti noein te kai houneken esti noēma*: 'Both are the same: it is so that it is taken in and it is the case that what is taken in there, is'. Here the identity of taking in and being is thus expressed, and not something like the essence of identity. This, in my view, cannot be disputed.

Philological research has had a really hard time with this statement and the following verses. I have not fully followed the debate and do not want to intervene in it. However, I am of the opinion that one must first *hear* these hexameters if one wants to understand them and that one must always bear in mind [21] that this way of the truth is called the way of 'persuasive discourse', which claims for the persuasive suggestion a place alongside the right of logic. Here, essentially philosophical points of view come into play. These philosophical points of view come to the fore in so far as we have in general to pay particular attention to the formation of concepts in the didactic poem for reasons pertaining to its subject matter. This is why I have distinguished the achievement of the semantic construction *to eon* as an act of forming concepts. If I am now compelled to see *to auto* in the same light, as recently Hölscher again and naturally Jürgen Wiesner following him demand of me[27], I am, as a philologist, still astounded. Naturally, it is correct – who would not follow him in this? – to adduce the reception of the didactic poem by Melissus as a commentary. But what for? For this use of the word 'identity', a word which I do not know existed as a concept before Plato? This simply cannot be inferred from the commentary of Melissus.

Wiesner is certainly correct when he sees verses 8, 34ff against the background of Melissus' text (VS 30 B 8). But what for? Certainly, Melissus' text also comments upon the Eleatic notion of being precisely under the standpoint of the knowability of being. Yet, it is remarkable that in Melissus' text the allegedly thematic *to auto* does not appear at all, although in accordance to the subject matter, it would truly suggest itself in the rejection of change (*heteroiousthai* ['to become different'])[28]. It is worth noting how the reflective concept of identity insinuates itself everywhere into the explanation, which we still only know from the Platonic *Sophist*.

In the didactic poem, one appeals to verse 8, 29 because there too, at the beginning of the verse, *tauton t' en tautō* ['the same and in the same'] describes the unchanging abiding of being. Is this supposed to support what one would like to find in verse 8, 34? But there we are dealing with a keyword of a totally different kind, with *noein* as a sign of being. We can certainly describe the inseparability emphasized there of *noein* from being as an identity. But to see in this a reference to verse 8, 29 confuses semantic unities with grammatical and semantic functional relationships.

We are all in agreement in recognizing the concept of identity as a 'law of thinking' here, and this has for a long time been common in reference to the Eleatics, even since Plato. Yet, drawing on the linguistic usage of *to auto* here for understanding the text of the didactic poem remains a bad piece of evidence, at least when one is citing Melissus. It is not just that the word does not appear there at all but also why it does not appear. Melissus could obviously not insert the word in the series of signs for being – just as little as he could *noein*, which does not appear as a word either! [22] For a contemporary of Anaxagoras, as Melissus was, this is quite telling. Certainly, Simplicius is not guilty of having left something out here. Even Heidegger does not obviously intend to recover identity here as the 'law of thinking'. He speaks of the duality of being and approaches his own intuitions through the fact that *noein* appears in Parmenides under the sign of being.

If we focus on Melissus and Zeno, the difference becomes immediately clear. There the difference at once concerns the one and the many. *Eon* is certainly one and is called so in Fragment 8, 6, but in the company of *suneches* ['continuous']! This has nothing to do with the dialectic of the one and the many, which is thematized in Zeno and defines the concept of dialectic in the Pythagorean tradition and completely in Plato.

By contrast, Melissus clearly avoids speaking of *noein*. The only sign of being that is so specifically distinguished in Parmenides does not seem to exist. In this argument, there is still too much of a duality implied for him. This is why he is not interested at all in *noein* in the whole argument presented in Fragment 8, 24ff. What matters to him is only that there must be something else besides *eon* (*allo parex tou eontos* ['something else besides this being']). For him it all comes down only to the being-one of being. This is indeed why he is chided by Aristotle as a *phortikos* ['coarse'] because he leaves physics with no legitimacy at all and even says of the senses that they do not see and hear correctly (what Parmenides does not express in this way in the didactic poem).

The inseparability of *noein* and *einai*, which truly constitutes the argument, is also confirmed in what follows: 'You will not find *noein* without a being [*das Seiende*]'.

Manifestly, this must be a sign for a being. Being is always where there can be an actual taking in [*Vernehmen*] and where this sort of hollow nothing is not supposed to be. The construction of the argument remains difficult. In any case, *noein* is not what is actually sought. Here too we are concerned with *esti* and *eon*.

It therefore seems to me downright artificial when almost all who expound on this text translate: 'Without a being you will not find the thinking in which it is expressed'. Thinking is supposed to be that which is expressed? Is being not expressed when it is thought – and in negation (Frag. 2, 7) would non-being not be known and expressed? Is this not the necessary argument?

Absolutely, if we observe the structure of the verse. Verse 8, 35 does not indicate at all that verse 8, 36 is to be anticipated. Thus, the listener of this well-constructed hexameter inevitably understands that being is what is expressed.

The listener will understand the 'in which' (*en hō*) in an indeterminately temporal sense, which is completely common in Greek, almost in the sense of 'during' or even in the way we say: 'while' *to eon* is expressed, that is say, is there. [23] The sense is thus: where *noein* is, there being is. To this extent, *noein* and being are the same, that is to say, inseparable. The fact that being is there, this is what it all comes down to in all these signposts. This fits with the explicit continuation with *to eon*. What is spoken about is *to eon*, and not something like *noein*. It is about being, unchanging and present, which is found with the help of *noein*. Indeed, even for this reason, one finds oneself compelled, in order to make the whole thing sensible, not to translate *noein* with 'thinking' but with 'recognizing' [*Erkennen*]. I even suggest 'stumbling upon it' or 'making it out' or even 'taking in'. Where there is taking in, there being is 'perceived'. When, on the basis of other forms of discourse, we get used to speaking of being and non-being, change of place and colours passing away, there is no taking in of 'being'. We have already seen that all of this has the character of a mere *onoma* ['name'], because what is named cannot really be taken in, cannot be taken as being. For coming to be and passing away etc. necessarily carry with them the vacuous thought of the nothing and likewise that which is connected by the *te kai*, the *einai te kai ouchi* ['being and not being'].

We must realize against this view that the positing of names, with which the further continuation of the second part of the didactic poem begins its long course, is something different from such namings in which the vacuous thought of the nothing is also meant, even if it is there in a thoughtless manner. The encounter between light and night is not a going astray between being and nothing but the appearing of being, as is shown by what appears to the eye, which cannot be denied. Being is the there and 'there' means the appearing of appearances. This already sounds almost like the complete sphere of being, in the way the goddess had described true being. Obviously, this being does not appear in the points of view of mortals. This sphere of being is only the extrapolation of presence [*Anwesenheit*] in general. The fact that something is 'there' is the only appearance of being. For mortals, this appearance is differentiated in the multiplicity of appearances and their changing forms through light and darkness, day and night. Yet, this does not at all mean one determinate something and not another, but that something actually is. What is brought to appearance here through light and darkness is not one thing in opposition to the other and is not cut off from the other and even exists when it is no longer there (Frag. 4). What stands in the light here is 'being'. Here the Socratic suggestion at the beginning of the *Parmenides* comes to mind: the idea is one like the day and at the same time in many, and not divided and not separated from itself.[29] Here the Platonic dialogue obviously refers back to the didactic poem and the reader notices that the Socratic suggestion makes good sense, which Parmenides deliberately muddles during the conversation (*Parmenides* 131b) and Plato makes us aware of this.[30] Why does Parmenides confuse Socrates? Now, this is shown to us by the continuation: because the young Socrates has still to learn that *logos* is not a collection of beings in the same *eidos* but the bringing together of different ideas in one statement.

[24] If we follow the divine message in this way and maintain that in the second part of the didactic poem, the thinker Parmenides is meant to be granted a superiority over all other mortals – and not just over some predecessor – then many problems vanish. We should just not forget in this regard that it is the goddess who speaks here and who time and again characterizes human beings explicitly as the *brotoi* ['mortals']. This standpoint seems to me to be fundamental for explaining the whole didactic poem.

One can certainly see Parmenides putting what he himself has to say in the mouth of the goddess as a literary fiction. But why does he do this? This obviously still has its reasons. If he is not in the position to say it because he lacks the concepts, then it is perhaps wiser to accept that the goddess puts something in his mouth which she promulgates as the truth and the way of the truth. For to comprehend this by oneself is asking really too much of a mortal! For which human being is in a position to hold onto this teaching of an unchanging, unmoving, homogeneous being closed in itself against all that appears to the eye? This is not a way that one can find and maintain. This is how we understand it when the goddess promulgates this message about the way of the truth like a revelation and declares the way of the 'nothing' and of the *mē eon* ['non-being'] as simply untreadable. If we see through the eyes of the goddess – and this is what a reader of this poetic text should actually do – there is just one single way to the truth (Frag. 8, 1) to which the goddess points the poet and which protects him from the way into the nothing.

Here we still have to wonder about the way human beings actually take. There is after all obviously one way which is supposed to lead to *alētheia* but which does not bring us to that destination and rather always leads us astray.

The poet-thinker has obviously also taken this way and 'experienced' it on the way across all cities and beyond until this journey led him to the palace of the goddess and opened for him the door to *alētheia*. Now, should there be no other word uttered in the divine instructions about the way traversed by all who did not receive the goddess' instructions and whose ways, as the goddess says, are far away from where human beings move (Frag. 1, 27)?

Now, it is obviously an open question, which has not yet been clearly settled among researchers, as to whether Fragment 6 does not in fact contain the anticipated depiction of the way that goes astray. At first, we were indeed warned about the untreadable way over to the nothing (Frag. 2, 2f). In fact, the entire arrangement of the didactic poem in its first part is tasked with protecting human beings from straying from the right way to *alētheia*. Not a word thus is to be wasted on the way of the nothing. There is nothing to depict there (*panapeuthea atarpon* ['a narrow path on which there is ignorance everywhere'], Frag. 2, 6).

This is not a way for a human being to take, who wants to reach a destination. [25] The only way to *alētheia* which the goddess teaches is such that mortals need specific assistance for finding it. This is why the goddess gives a detailed description of the way and lists the signposts which are supposed to prevent our straying from the right way.

This still means that for the rest of the mortals the situation can only be such that one is constantly deviating from the way once more and going astray. Now, in the description of Fragment 6 one will not recognize this way constantly taken by mortals, which is meant to be a way to *alētheia* but never leads there. This was the suggestion made by Jacob Bernays[31], who assumed a polemic against Heraclitus here. He was fully convinced of this assumption. In this connection, he appeals in what is said here to an echo of the Heraclitean sayings about the unity of opposites.

It is obviously not easy to provide knockdown counterproofs against this assumption. When this part speaks of mortals as these two-headed beings, for whom being and non-being amount to the same thing and do not amount to the same thing, then one can wish to see in this the core of Heraclitus' teaching, who precisely sees true unity in opposition. Nonetheless, it seems to me a misjudgement of the style. The passage mentioned carries a profusive discourse. What is already conveyed in this discourse is that the doctrine of the unity of opposites is not a unitary doctrine. Rather, these verses characterize a comportment which describes a seesaw fluctuation. Between the thoughtlessly contradictory nature of a comportment and the thought of the unity of contradictions and oppositions, there lies a great difference. Whoever recognizes in the opposition and as its deeper ground, the one and true, the *sophon* ['wise'], and, like Heraclitus, asserts it with an almost prophetic pathos, has something completely different in mind. There is an obvious difference of style between the epigrammatic terseness of Heraclitus' sentences and this verse (6, 8f): *ois to pelein te kai ouk einai tauton nenomistai kou tauton* ['those for whom it has become customary that being and not being are the same']. However, it is not my intention to unfurl the whole controversy about the connection between Parmenides and Heraclitus anew. My own contribution is entirely grounded in the logic of the subject matter, in the particular case of the verses transmitted to us in Fragment 6 as well as the general problem of the substantive connection between the one being and the many points of view of mortals. Now, the controversial Fragment 6 does not stand alone, according to the tradition. It has a definite place which, like the next Fragment 7, is taken from Simplicius' transcription and offers a unified context. I would like to accord a new weight to these transmitted facts.

[26] The parts which are not taken from Simplicius' transcription are fragmentary in a totally different degree and, if we set the proemium aside, their arrangement and their inclusion in the original text are a dubious affair.

Now however, the position of Fragment 6 in the context of the whole is a different matter. Here the continuation of the subject matter is well attested in Simplicius' transcription. It is true that the reading of the introductory verse of Fragment 7 is itself controversial[32]. Only the second verse and its continuation in the third verse should make us pay attention. It is said there: 'But keep your thoughts far away from this way of seeking and do not let the habit formed from the many experiences compel you on this way'. It seems unmistakable to me that in Fragment 6 the third and fourth verses are constituted in a completely similar way. It says there: 'For this is the first way of seeking, from which I am keeping you away, and even from the one along which mortals, the ignorant, stroll'.

It is the style of repetition, which we have also otherwise observed and which constitutes the forcefulness of the teaching. If we focus on the continuation, which in one instance or another is found to be connected to this admonition, then we must likewise assume a correspondence. We are not dealing here with a so-called parallelism – Peter Szondi rightly warned us against the misuse of such parallelisms[33] – but with a stylistic device which can be frequently verified, repetition, to be precise, for which I have already referred to Diels in his old commentary (p. 23ff), where he observed something correct. Now, in this particular case, we have confirmation through Plato's *Sophist* (237a) that Parmenides always repeated the admonition and warning against the way of the nothing. Whether this goes back to the repetitions in the text of the didactic poem or to an oral tradition, which corresponds to it, does not affect the subject matter. In any case, there must have always been a cause for guarding against the assumption of the nothing, whether the warning was explicit or only came into play implicitly.

How does the anticipated repetition in Fragment 7 look? There it says that one should not let the aimless eye hold sway nor the ringing ear nor the tongue. Rather, one should judge the *poludēris elegchos* ['the much disputed refutation'][34] with thinking. In this context, this quite certainly does not mean [27] some philosophical doctrine of another but the going astray, which is prepared through habit and experience for the eye, the ear and the tongue which speaks. It seems striking here that we are warned against it and there is a constant effort towards not letting ourselves be led astray by what appears to the eye. It is indeed for mortals as such a constantly threatening confusion. In both cases of the passages from Fragment 6 and Fragment 7 which have been transmitted to us in that sequence, we are always warned against the way of the nothing precisely because mortals unwittingly fall into error, without noticing at first that their way does not lead to the destination but is *palintropos* ['turning backward']. This is how we are brought back again and again through different ways to the same point. The way of mortals is a perilous one. The goddess shows the thinker the right way, but also takes into reckoning the fact that mortals must follow what appears to the eye, if only they would not thereby compromise her thinking in its consistency.

We are now attempting to bring to their philosophical conclusion the implications of the so-called formation of concepts, which we have observed. In this regard, it essentially comes down today to Heidegger's question which he called 'the step back'[35]. He understood by this the step behind the difference between being and beings, and in the direction of the original sense of *alētheia*, that is to say, of unconcealment. Now, the text teaches us – and all interpreters agree on this – that in the didactic poem being is depicted as a being [*Seiendes*]. Nothing is to be found of an ontological difference, which, for example in Aristotle, is at least articulated in the form of the *hoper on* ['this determinate being'] (*Physics* A3).

What does this mean for the sense of *alētheia*? Such a construction of thought with a semantic basis can certainly not find confirmation in the use of these words and in their textual context. It is indeed precisely the semantic isolation which helps Heidegger's inspired fallback to a primordial experience, which long precedes all linguistic traditions of writing and text. In the best case, which happens occasionally, the linguistic context can indeed be a confirmation, and this then produces a deepened understanding of the text. In such cases, we learn something decisive for understanding Greek thinking. Occasionally, etymology can also be helpful in a similar way, [28] which is indeed all the more cut off from all linguistic use. But etymology will always only be a pointer and can never be something like a proof. In addition, precisely because it boldly leaves behind the living use of the language, etymology always awakens a resistance from the side of the traditional use of language, unless one eventually learns how to hear the archaic undertones of the word in the concept used. This is how everyone today – in opposition to the unsuccessful attempt by Paul Friedländer to cast doubt upon the privative sense in *alētheia* – always hears the same privative sense with Heidegger[36]. Even in the concept of *logos*, I have slowly learnt to hear the meaning of gathering together, for which Heidegger had argued.

We will especially have to pay heed to this when we come back once more to this very sign for being which the didactic poem especially distinguishes, *noein* in its argumentative role. *Noein* is always with being, with *eon*. It is for this reason that we are sure to avoid going astray into the vacuous thought of the nothing, when we keep *noein* in sight as a signpost. Here in a decisive passage, it is now made clear how the word, when it is a mere *onoma*, comes off badly against the true taking in of being, which is always *legein te kai noein* (the voicing, *onoma*, and the taking in of 'being', Frag. 6, 1). As *onoma*, the word is separated from the inseparable unity of being and *noein*, and is used as a 'posited' sign for mere aspects of being. This is how the entire second part of the didactic poem finds support in such a concept of *onoma*, which is supposed to designate what appears to the eye and is not supposed to take in true being. Likewise, in the first part, the concept *onoma* as the empty form of linguistic designation is said of everything that lacks the ontological quality [*Seinshaftigkeit*] of *noein*. This is true, as we saw, of all the conventional talk of 'becoming' and 'coming to be', of 'being and non-being', and all the others that are sometimes this way and sometimes that way, sometimes there and sometimes not there. All of this departs from *alētheia*.

Here begins the critique of Parmenides led by the Platonic *Sophist*. This critique has decisively insisted that in *onoma* itself, in the name, the duality of the naming and the named always already bursts out, and likewise in *noein*, the taking in, the duality of taking in and being bursts out. By contrast, the didactic poem is constructed upon sameness, on this duality which elevates being and taking in to an inseparable unity. In this, Parmenides directs the gaze solely to the truth of being. The thinking of that which is should just not succumb to the empty vacuous thought of the nothing. In Greek, *noein* means 'to be completely absorbed in being', to be nothing for oneself other than just the openness for that which is. [29] In his classical analysis of *noein* in *De anima* (Gamma 4, 429a15), Aristotle aptly formulates it as *dektikon tou eidous* ['receptive of the form']. Now, it is true that in any real taking in and perceiving one always already differentiates, takes in this or that and not other things. In stating his fundamental thought, Parmenides had not realized this, just as little as Zeno when, in Plato's *Parmenides*, he gives in his book, which has re-surfaced[37], forty proofs that there is no many but only one. But Plato suggests in multiple ways that one must explicitly take the step towards the implicit multiplicity of *logos*, even specifically in the situation depicted by the dialogue *Parmenides*. Parmenides and Zeno are well aware of the misuse of our dialectic ability, which arose with the Eleatics. Yet, they throughout remain well disposed towards the young Socrates and encourage him. The stranger from Elea stresses in the *Sophist* that he does not want to be a parricide even when he grants being to non-being – in the form of the *heteron* ['the other']. In Parmenides' didactic poem, the step in thinking, which Plato takes in the *Sophist*, is not taken. When we take this step back with Heidegger, from Plato to the didactic poem, we come close to the beginning which Heidegger is seeking by starting from the end. The *Sophist* teaches us that Plato himself abides by the truth of Parmenides. This is the reason why he lets the stranger from Elea say that he does not want to be a parricide. And in fact, in distancing itself from the arrogance of the know-it-all in which the sophists lose themselves, genuine philosophical dialogue remains close to being, even when it knows that to think and to take in are also always to differentiate. In the duality of being and *noein*, what is meant is ultimately the 'there' of being and not this or that correct thing. In this way, the ontological recognition of what appears to the eye, of which even the goddess too knows what is true, is already anchored in the being of the many. This is what Plato wanted to say with the particular appreciation which Parmenides enjoys in his late dialogues. In the one there already lies the many but in such a way that everything many is *to eon*. Dialectic comes to its truth in the *diairesis* ['division', 'separation'], in the inner logic of the dialogue. This is the teaching of the *Sophist*.

I am not underestimating the fact that it was a violent step of thinking when Parmenides began to speak of *to eon*. I believe I can say more clearly what this step signifies now that in the meantime Heidegger's works on Anaximander, Heraclitus and Parmenides from the 1950s have become available and philological research has sharpened our 'historical sense'. Already in the essay on Anaximander, which was not yet available at the time of my first works on the pre-Socratics[38], Heidegger drew on the Homeric use of language for interpreting *eon* and *einai*. [30] He cited the characteristic of the sage seer, of whom it is said that he knew that which is [*das Seiende*], that which becomes being [*das Seinwerdende*] and that which was [*das Gewesene*]. All this can be found there in the way the epic uses language for the multitude of the many existing things. Now Heidegger had discerned the temporal dimension not only from this characteristic of the seer but also from the linguistic form of the participle, and brought to light the temporal character of that which we call the verb (*verbum*). He thus succeeded in recognizing anew the meaning of being as the entering into presence of what is present [*Anwesenheit des Anwesenden*]. This comes to the fore fully in a clear way when Parmenides introduces the singular *to eon* in this context. We do not find something like this in any text of poetry or epic, and certainly not in the way language is used by the man who, in his heavenly ascent through all cities, experiences much. For this one rather requires directions from the goddess in order to make appear in all its power the proximity to the verb, which for mortals is being and the true. Heidegger had discerned something of this already in the singular quotation from Anaximander and extrapolated it boldly as 'the while'. It is to be found in the text of Parmenides' didactic poem.

By contrast, the text of the didactic poem does not produce evidence for the perspectives of thought which Heidegger had associated with *alētheia* and *lēthē*, concealment and sheltering. Heidegger inferred from this that this sense of *alētheia*, which he characterized as 'the event', had never been thought by the Greeks. I add: even the use of *to auto* is always predicative in Parmenides. When Heidegger discerns in it the 'duality' of being, this is not to be found in the expression for sameness but in that which is here the same: *einai* and *noein*.

Precisely because this expression never appears in real speech, *to eon* is a step towards the concept and makes 'being' arise as the entering into presence of what is present. This is why this expression, as 'being', also encompasses the entering into presence of what is absent [*Abwesenden*]. Now it is precisely this extrapolation that we really read in Parmenides' text as Fragment 4, where we are supposed to take in 'what is absent' as present so that a specific being [*das Seiende*] is inseparable from that which is [*vom Seienden*] and is present [*anwesend*] in the while of time [*in der Weile der Zeit*] as well as in the extension to all limits. ('To all limits', this is Parmenides; 'into the limitless', this is Melissus. Both mean the same even if Aristotle considers this as a doctrinal difference). *To eon*, a being [*das Seiende*], is not an entity [*ein Seiende*s] but as a being 'that which unfolds' [*das Wesende*] (as our language whispers to us). *To eon* knows no never and no nowhere.

In order to grasp Parmenides' thinking deliberately in its inceptual character, we saw ourselves sent back into the historical efficacy of his thought. This did not mean an artificial alienation of what belongs to us nor a violent escape and flight into the alien. It rather promises a new proximity to what is to come. What Heidegger [31] called the 'overcoming' or 'transformation' [*Verwindung*] of metaphysics or even the end of philosophy is in fact effectuated precisely in such a proximity.

Certainly, many things are brought close together in such a proximity, which the historical thinking of modernity pulls apart like a great epic historical narrative. Here we find the beginning of questioning, which in Thales brought a first 'clearing'. Here we find Parmenides' bold insistence on that which alone is [*seiend*] and can count as being [*Sein*]. He is followed by Plato's dialectical appropriation and elaboration of this question, which lurches back and forth behind the flurry of the metaphors of idea and participation, of *mimēsis* ['imitation'] and *methexis* ['participation'], of mixture and intertwining, of entering into presence and commonality. It is to this that Aristotle's conceptual doctrine connects itself, in his doctrine of the primary and secondary substance. And finally, in the same line of effects we find the drama of the world and the soul in the Platonism of a Plotinus and of the Christian Platonism of Augustine, which heralds the age of Christian thinking and resonates up to Hegel's world-historical synthesis. All this resonates between the parts of the didactic poem in the primordial Eleatic wisdom of the *alētheia* of being and the *alētheia* of appearing, as well as in the ontological difference between being and beings, in which all finite thinking is embedded. The beyond of being, which Plato proclaimed as 'the good' and from which the concept of transcendence was developed in the neo-Platonic appropriation of Plato, truly means the fact pondered by Plato and Aristotle that being pertains to this world[39].

2
Plato's Thinking through Utopias: A Lecture Addressed to Philologists (1983)

[270] Someone who looks back at his own work on Plato, going back decades, and has in particular also sought a fruitful way into Plato's political thought is faced with a criticism that goes all out. This is the challenge that is today associated especially with the name of Karl Popper. This challenge did not acquire a place in our philosophical consciousness for the first time just with the Popper of 1980, not even with the Popper of 1950. It goes back to an old question. To what extent is the picture of the sophists, with which we are familiar from the writings of Plato, really the result of a polemical misrepresentation and distortion, which misjudges the greatness of this intellectual movement and its influence? We can no longer assess this movement at all, it will be argued, because its opponents, the philosophy of Plato and its scholarly influence, going well beyond Aristotle and the peripatetic tradition, have remained triumphant to an overwhelming degree. The name of Democritus appears not once in Plato. As we know, even the existence of Leucippus was held to be doubtful and the thought of a Democritus has only come down to us in a very fragmented state, not to mention the figures of the great sophistic rhetoricians, who are only known through fragmentary testimonies and available if at all only through the Platonic depictions. It is thus *palaia diaphora*, an age-old quarrel, which does not just go back to the tensions of our century but fundamentally begins at least with Hobbes. He was the first to pose the problem. Hobbes was a translator of Thucydides, from whom we also know a lot about the sophistic enlightenment and its influence. The rediscovery of the sophists endures from Hobbes to Hegel and Nietzsche. We have to recognize the inherent legitimacy of the Sophists and their profound insight into the essence of the human being. In this respect, the contribution Popper made on this subject matter belongs to a great tradition which starts with Hobbes and goes through Grote, positivism, Hegel and Nietzsche, through the Viennese philologists and historians of philosophy of the calibre of a Theodor and Heinrich Gomperz (but Toynbee also belongs to the list),

---

'Platos Denken in Utopien. Ein Vortrag vor Philologen (1983)' was a lecture held before the German association of ancient philology in Mainz on 14 April 1982. It was first published in *Gymnasium. Zeitschrift für Kultur der Antike und humanistische Bildung* 90 (1983): pp. 434–55. It is now in *Gesammelte Werke*, vol. 7. Tübingen: J. C. B. Mohr (Paul Siebeck), 1991, pp. 270–89.

stretching right up to Popper. [271] Popper's book was written from 1938 to 1943 in New Zealand[1]. There, in the farthest remoteness, literally at the antipodes of the terrible events in our central Europe, he tried to come to terms with the situation by reading Plato, Hegel and Marx, and reflected upon the decline of public life into frightening barbarism, taking it all in with increasing horror from this farthest remoteness and indeed as someone belonging to the German cultural world. The book appeared first in New Zealand in 1944, was then published in the United States in 1950. The German edition dates back to 1955. Some forty years have thus passed since the appearance of this book to our day. This is a long time. It is indeed a noteworthy fact that anyone who today has something to say about Plato's political writings is expected to take a position specifically on the negative verdict represented by Popper.

One shall not expect any philological critique and a detailed refutation of Popper's errors from me. I would like to reflect on the pre-understanding on the basis of which Popper and the tradition to which he belongs have developed their way of reading Plato. I would like to attempt a critique of this pre-understanding by testing it against the texts and, as will be needed here and there, seek to interpret it.

The first point on which we must be clear is that Plato's political writings make a tremendous demand upon all of us. Plato really poses an enormous challenge to humanism, which in Plato honours one of its great heroes, as well as to the Christian and modern liberal consciousness. Now, we have been sufficiently educated in historical consciousness to be aware of the fact that we have to deal here with social formations and political relations, which had the church on their side when they were not 'secular'. I do not say 'religion' but 'church'. The sacral organization of ancient life was not familiar with any just secular *civitas* ['citizenship'], as presented by the political formation of social life understood in terms of modern political thought. It is thus clear that, from the very outset, when we follow our own intellectual tradition, we find ourselves in a peculiarly conflicted relationship to Platonic thinking. On the one hand, we have a plethora of political ideas, enhanced almost to an extreme, which is alien to us and confronts us in a challenging way. On the other hand, Plato touches us like an *anima naturaliter christiana* ['a naturally Christan soul']. This is the tension within which our own pre-understanding inevitably stands. The Socratic *docta ignorantia* ['learned ignorance'], the Socratic-Platonic requirement of an ultimate account, which is achieved in dialogue and dialectic, constitutes in part the self-understanding of the Western human being and has entered into the historical unity of the effects of Christian Platonism. [272] The power possessed by this history of effects to constitute a tradition is so intense that we at first read all the ancient texts that have ever been transmitted to us with the eyes of this Christian Platonism. In the nineteenth century, this self-evident unity of effects exerted by Christian Platonism suffered historical dissolution. We have to realize that with this the philosophical discipline of Plato interpretation also began to read Plato's works with a transformed pre-understanding. In order to make this somewhat clearer, I shall first make use of certain concepts of Popper in what follows, so that the reference to the controversial questions will become clearer in this way.

There is for a start essentialism. It is a word that Popper employs to name the conceptual realism of the medieval tradition because he rightly found the 'realism' of the theory of universals to be a somewhat obscure and misleading expression for lay people. His critique of essentialism naturally expresses his own position towards idealism in general. In fact, he understands Platonic idealism from the standpoint of its medieval pre-Kantian form. Now, this essentialism just became something else through the German idealist movement and its aftermath. Essentialism may have developed out of the tradition of scholastic conceptual realism but almost evolved into its opposite. This became clear as day in the philosophy of the nineteenth century. Thus, the Marburg school of neo-Kantianism taught that the idea is in fact nothing other than the natural law. The idea is said to represent the permanent, the persistent endurance of what abides over against all change, unlike the transitory phenomena which comply with it. Yet, the idea is said to possess only the validity of a hypothesis. This was Natorp's interpretation of Plato in the spirit of Galileo, which already went back to the young Hermann Cohen. As a matter of fact, Galileo did appeal to Plato against the ossified Aristotelianism of his century. It was naturally more obvious for neo-Kantianism to reappropriate Kant and to see Plato entirely in the light of Kant. *De mundi sensibilis atque intelligibilis forma et principiis* ['On the form and principles of the sensible and intelligible world'] is how the Platonizing title of Kant's dissertation reads. However, it was not this metaphysical neo-Platonic Platonism which Kant was reviving. Rather, if anything, his was a defence of the sensible world against the way the rationalism of the dominant scholastic metaphysics had misunderstood it. It was furthermore (as I believe I have also made plausible in my own works[2]) Hegel's great merit that even he, in returning to the Greek philosophers, went beyond scholastic 'substance metaphysics', thus beyond Popper's essentialism. He directed his efforts [273] to the task of fruitfully overcoming the concept of subjectivity and self-consciousness, which was the proper truth of modernity even in his own eyes, and showing the mediation between the universal and the particular as the path of speculative thought. Finally, we should not forget alongside Paul Natorp, to give a place of honour to Julius Stenzel, who was also the most significant historian of philosophy and Platonist of this epoch. It was Stenzel who liberated neo-Kantian interpretation from its anachronisms. All these researchers have differentiated the essentialism in the sense in which Popper speaks of it, with critical arguments, and have thereby in many respects already pulled the rug from underneath the Popperian interpretation. Only Heidegger is an exception here, whose thinking had the greatest impact on my generation and whose interpretation of Plato is closer to the essentialism of the Popperian kind in so far as Heidegger completely subordinated Plato's thought to the Aristotelian concept of metaphysics. He understood Aristotelian metaphysics as ontotheology, that is to say, as the project of a doctrine of being, which attaches the authentic experience of the reality of being and of the sense of being to the highest being, to God. All of Plato's efforts at thinking were for Heidegger nothing but a prefiguration of this metaphysics.

Yet, as we can see thanks to the new publications in Heidegger's *Complete Works*, the young Heidegger was permeated by the ancient Platonism of Plotinus and Augustine just as he was in pursuit of the concept of *alētheia* ['truth'] in his lectures on the *Theaetetus* and the *Sophist*. He shows Plato as well as Aristotle in an entirely different light from that of our medieval 'essentialism' and modern idealism.

This should be sufficient to describe the starting point of my own work and of that which to me seemed worthy of discussion. With this, I have in mind, first and foremost, the hermeneutic turn which, in my view, is unavoidably associated with the study of the Platonic dialogues. In a certain manner, this was already the requirement first laid down by German romanticism, by Schlegel and Schleiermacher, who discovered the dialogical principle as a fundamental metaphysical schema for the cognition of the truth. Nevertheless, there are good reasons why it is not easy, even for the knowers and practitioners of the conceptual trade, to have a sense at all for the living reality of the conversation and of the people involved in the conversation in the Platonic dialogue. Modern research on Plato which followed the period of Schleiermacher up until our century has thoughtlessly passed over the dramatic *mimēsis* ['imitation'] in the Platonic dialogue. The result was that the philosophical assessment did not pay any attention at all to the kind of hermeneutic paradox which was handed down to us when we place the Aristotelian analyses and working papers alongside the Platonic dialogues [274] as two similar sources; Werner Jaeger had already pointed this out in 1912[3].

It is from here that I took my first steps and they led me to my hermeneutic ideas. First, in 1926, as a submission for admission to Paul Friedländer's philological seminar in Marburg, I wrote a paper on the Aristotelian *Protrepticus*, which later appeared in *Hermes*[4] and in which I expressed doubts about Jaeger's construct of the increasing distance of Aristotle from his Platonic beginnings. I specifically advanced the hermeneutic standpoint against Jaeger's use of the three versions of the Aristotelian ethics and his appraisal of the *Protrepticus*. My thesis was that a *protreptikos* ['exhortatory'] is not an occasion for presenting the differences between schools. A text promoting philosophy in general – this is confirmed by Iamblichus' version, who transcribes Plato and Aristotle alongside each other – is not the place in which the writer can aim to bring out differences, for example between Plato's theory of ideas and its critique by Aristotle.

I am going to leave aside the question as to what extent I was right. A lot has come to light in the meantime. But this is not as important as the fact that, for me, the hermeneutic standpoint stood up to examination there for the first time. Besides this, influenced as I was by the circumstances and also essentially by Paul Friedländer's school, I had already begun to pay attention to something of the mimetic event of the Platonic dialogues and, like Friedländer himself, I had begun to utilize the influence exercised on all of us by the George Circle[5]. The dialogical character of the Platonic dialogues began to turn into the object of philosophical interpretation through my works, which I later placed under the general heading '*logos* and *ergon*' ['speech and work'][6], that is to say, under the standpoint that Platonic argumentation in the conversation between Socrates and his partners depends less on logical cogency than on the power of conviction which a human being can exercise. Despite all the admiration I harbour for the meticulousness of the logical critique of Plato, which comes to us from England and America, I have the feeling that [275] it is almost like something of a waste to regret the absence of rigour here and to introduce a new rigour there, where entirely different claims to be convincing were made, as they arise as 'persuasive arguments'[7] from the immediacy of the conversation.

Now one can certainly argue over how far this point of view extends. At the moment, I only need a certain preparation of this sort in order to lay out the topic of utopia, particularly in the *Republic* but also in a certain sense in the *Laws*. Presently, the commendable reappropriation of Léon Robin's research on Plato's unwritten doctrine, as it was developed by Krämer, Gaiser and the other members of the Tübingen school, has created a new situation in that the significance of the Platonic dialogues has diminished. I believe that I have adopted a principled position in my own works when I appealed to Porphyry[8], who was still familiar with Aristotle's transcription of the Platonic lecture 'On the Good' and nevertheless writes: 'Indeed, without the *Philebus* I would not understand this transcription'. A perfectly good maxim. Fortunately, we have the *Philebus*.

Now, very early on, in fact, already in the early 1930s, I had taken on the *Republic* in particular in following my hermeneutic impulse. What kind of literary work is it really? How is it then meant to be taken? Should we take it all so literally, as the modern biographical-political interpretation of Plato suggests, to which even Wilamowitz eventually gave his blessing? Or are there grounds for approaching things in a more hermeneutically sophisticated manner? In my essays 'Plato and the Poets'[9], 'Plato's Educational State'[10], and, later on, in a larger comprehensive essay on 'The Idea of the Good in Platonic-Aristotelian Philosophy'[11], I developed the fundamental outlines of how I had worked out Plato's thinking through utopias in the case of the *Republic*. I do not wish to repeat any of this in what follows. I would like to complement it.

The first argument I would like to employ in this context is the study of the literary genre to which the *Republic* belongs. This is still good old philological practice and it has its good old hermeneutic tradition, namely, to disclose the written work's law of composition on the basis of its literary genre.

Now, there can be no doubt that there was a genre of utopia. This is all the more so after Ferdinand Dümmler in [276] his famous work 'Prolegomena to Plato's State'[12] had laid bare the pre-history of the utopian representations of the state in Aristophanes' comedy as well as in Euripides' tragedy as the background of the Platonic text. But I think there can also be no doubt – and this seems to me to have never been heeded enough – if we ourselves only read carefully Aristotle's 'Politics' and its account of Plato's *Republic* and the other precursors. Here things are put in explicit words. What is first and foremost in question here is the *nomothetein*, legislation as 'literature'. (Only later will Aristotle discuss the legislation in already existing states (Sparta, Crete) and through real legislators in those states.) The literary legislations are discussed without regard for their implementability but purely in terms of the arguments used in them. Obviously, Aristotle pursues the critical goal of delineating the rationality of his own political theoretical constructions against these arguments.

There can be no dispute about the fact that he criticizes the form of thought pertaining to the utopia, the ideal state, as such. His way of thinking is certainly of a very different sort from the satirical-utopian constructions, which Plato undertakes in the *Republic* and the *Laws*. Yet, Aristotle's critique of these Platonic utopias of the state poses fundamentally the same question which provokes his critique of the theory of ideas. There one could still reckon with the great unknown, the Platonic theory of the ideal numbers and its indirect transmission. There one can still find a much direct reference to Plato's dialogues, which seems outright strange to us. Aristotle criticizes the theory of ideas by refuting not the philosophy of the *eidos* ['form', 'essence'] as such, but a specific interpretation of it, which concerns the *chōrismos* ['separation'] of the idea. Aristotle, I think, imputes to the Platonic thinking a meaning of *chōrismos* which is understood from the standpoint of Aristotelian metaphysics and which is ultimately an oversimplification, alien to Plato. Likewise, he also reads Plato's construction of the utopian state, despite all the explicit counter-assurances by Plato, as if it were a reform programme and criticizes or rather outdoes it through realistic proposals. Now, just as in relation to the theme of ontology, Aristotle must nevertheless be seen as a philosopher of the *eidos*, similarly it is also true here that, in the Aristotelian corpus of political treatises, the question of the best *polis* ['city state'] is always developed in different approaches based on the idea of the *polis*. Aristotle thus truly recognizes the literary genre of the utopia, which at least through Plato was elevated to a new authority.

There is a compelling argument for this, which has not been advanced so far. Aristotle claims that Plato was the first to draw the radical consequences of having women and children in common for his ideal state [277] and this, after Aristophanes had long before presented the same situation on the stage. Aristotle was naturally aware of this. This can only mean that he only had the literary genre of the *philosophical* utopia in mind, towards which Aristophanes naturally does not count. For this reason, I am simply not convinced that we should attribute what Aristotle himself says about the ideal state only to the period of his youth. The 'genre' retains for him its right.

There is still another very strong argument for the existence of the genre and that is the standard literary function which this kind of utopian state possessed in later times. We learn, for example, from Zeno, the founder of the Stoic school, that he himself still called his cosmopolitical point of view *Peri politeias* ['On the State'] and had in this regard also adopted arguments from the Platonic project of the state, precisely the question of having women and children in common, into his critical considerations. The literary genre thus seems to me unquestionably attested from what we see in subsequent history.

This holds true especially for the pre-history of thinking through utopias, which we can naturally reconstruct only in a fragmentary manner. We can still extend it far beyond the reflections found in Aristophanes and Euripides, which Dümmler adduces. Let me mention in this regard first the Anacharsis-style novel, thus the Scythian romances[13]. It belongs to the form of the utopia, if indeed the essence of a utopia is defined as being the form of something suggestive that comes from afar. In that case, what these Scythians allegedly were and all that the legend of Anacharsis reports are typical utopias, namely critical allusions to one's own circumstances. A similar suggestiveness that comes from afar should also apply to Egyptian romanticism and it certainly applies to Xenophon's *Cyropaedia*. Finally, in addition to all of this, we should not forget here the whole tradition of myth, particularly of a golden age, an age of paradisiac innocence, which also in Plato often shimmers in the background or in the Phaeacian romanticism of the *Odyssey*. These are all prefigurations of a literary genre which is richly attested for us, but of which we only really possess the political writings of Plato and, to a certain extent, those of Aristotle.

How does this literary genre look? We have good grounds for hearing in it an echo of the colonial age. There is a resonance of this even in Aristotle. Here we have a clear testimony. He cites Phaleas as a precursor, who speaks about land reform[14]. This is naturally an older topic, well-known in Greek history. Land reform strives [278] to even out the tensions which used to emerge again and again in the course of the Greek agrarian city-state in the area of land ownership. As Aristotle reports it, Phaleas writes that such a distribution, new distribution, equal distribution of land ownership is easier when it concerns the foundation of new cities than when it is supposed to be carried out in an existing city. This is an important reference to the colonial age.

There is another reference in Plato himself, in so far as Socrates refers to himself in the *Republic* as a *ktistēs*, as a founder. Naturally, it is a city in the clouds, a city in its ideal form[15]. But even in the *Laws*, a founding that is closer to reality is described in the form of a utopia[16]. This is how Plato allows the history of colonial thinking to flow immediately into the new literary form. I would like to think that it was not Plato who was the first, but that this most probably belonged to the form of these theoretical proposals of the state. This is made even more plausible by the fact that Aristotle's *Politics* does not encompass the entire field of *politika* ['affairs of the city'], but only the realm of legislation and does not deal with the problems of the judiciary or the administration. I infer from all this (which is in itself known) that 'legislation' was conceived as a specific model of thinking already in development, into which Plato inserted his own utopian state for reasons still to be explained.

Another problem consists in knowing how we are supposed to situate Plato's dialogical writings in his biography overall. This is connected to the debate over the authenticity of the Seventh Letter. In his latest work from 1981, which is in most aspects measured and reasonably presented, Gerhard Müller advances a new hypothesis in the Frankfurt treatises according to which the *Seventh Letter* was an epistolary novel, which was drafted in post-Platonic times, certainly shortly after Plato's death and obviously on the basis of excellent information, which was so good as to lead all modern historians astray, as we all know[17]. The plausibility of such a hypothesis is not difficult to attain, given that authenticity can almost never be demonstrated, particularly when we concede that the author has invented and executed his fiction in a very insightful and knowledgeable fashion. Gerhard

Müller accomplished this with unmatched success. I am reminded of the famous story by Bernard Shaw. When Shakespeare's authorship with respect to his dramas was in doubt, he allegedly said [279]: 'Yes, it is totally clear, Shakespeare, of whom we know nothing else, is certainly not the author of these dramas. It is someone else, of whom we also know nothing and who was also called Shakespeare'.

For my part, I will leave open the question of which one is correct – the theory of an epistolary novel, which accords with the facts, or the theory that we are dealing with an authentic letter. Only when Gerhard Müller wants to discover a certain crude mixture of Platonic and Isocratic thoughts in this letter, which must betray the incompetence of the author in philosophical matters, do I have to disagree with him. I have expressed my views with regard to the philosophical excursus found in the letter[18]. I consider the critique of this excursus to be completely unsatisfactory. It relies on misleading prejudices or on a lack of hermeneutic caution. The interpretation is completely wrongly burdened by the concept of epistemology[19]. If we take up this excursus with a modicum of hermeneutic awareness and realize that we have here a very simply presented introductory text, which should not be put on the same level as a dialogue as formidable as the *Sophist*, then the controversies disappear. This excursus is in harmony with Plato's most important positions, as I have sought to show in my essay.

Yet, I would like to consider the question of the authenticity of the letter as uninteresting for my purpose. Either the athetesis of the letter, which, as we know, Edelstein[20] tried to legitimate again, is correct. In that case, we should naturally no longer connect Plato's thinking through utopias with the failing political experiments in Sicily and make it responsible for this failure.

Or the athetesis is false, in which case what Kurt von Fritz in particular has shown in his earlier works[21] is true, namely that Plato's politics, whether it was fabricated or real, did not at any rate aim at implementing the programmatic proposals of his ideal city. We can thus dispense with the whole question. In fact, another problem lurks in the background, namely the problem pertaining to the subject matter of knowing the extent to which we can ever bring together in a full and satisfactory harmony the thinking in generalities and what is concrete, particularly in light of our transitory, uncertain and fluctuating reality. [280] In certain textual references of Popper, which I take to be misinterpretations, it seems to me that this question has been completely overlooked.

If I do not place much trust in the essentialism of the Popperian kind in so far as it is supposed to be about Plato, I must refer to my own works on Plato, which have picked up on certain motifs in Hegel's understanding of Plato and, as I am hoping, developed them convincingly. I would like to consider it a false interpretation to present the Platonic theory of ideas in the way the *Phaedo* develops it when it is introduced for the very first time and then to conjure up some sort of fantastic story that Plato had eventually over the course of time discovered the problem of *methexis* ['participation'] and began to have doubts about his early views. This seems to me to be as problematic as Popper's dependence on theses, already often advocated from other perspectives, that, if not Socrates himself, the Platonic figure of Socrates transforms from a genuine democratic to an authoritarian thinker and that this indicates a change of heart in Plato. In my eyes, it is amusing to assume such touching concern on the part of the writer Plato for the acumen of his modern interpreters. In fact, the historical-genetic schema, which is a reflex of the modern historicism, is unable to persuade us here on several grounds. I have tried to show how unified the Platonic proposal is in its totality and how it remains influential well into the Aristotelian aftermath of Plato and the critique of Plato.

This certainly demands a difficult engagement, which cannot be conducted in detail in this context. Here I must concede that today, on the basis of my own research into Plato, even Heidegger's interpretation of Aristotelian metaphysics as ontotheology, which had been decisive for me for a long time, does not fully convince me anymore and does not appear to me to be the last word of wisdom. In any case, this much is clear: the schema of ontotheology or metaphysics is, as the *word* 'metaphysics' already tells us, completely inappropriate for Plato. If anything, one could speak of 'metamathematics' in Plato and show that the proper world of the being of *a priori* structures emerges behind mathematics. By contrast, the course of motion pertaining to phenomena is only depicted in mythical metaphors by Plato, such as in the metaphor of the demiurge as the one who lays out the order of the world in the *Timaeus* or as the metaphor of the one who mixes the potion of life in the *Philebus*. In Plato's conceptual framework I cannot find anything of what metaphysics as ontotheology would be, according to which the divine, as a highest being-for-itself in its magical power of attraction as a first unmoved mover, crowns the *Physics*, so to speak. Where Plato comes the closest to such a metaphysics, in Book 10 of the *Laws*, everything is grounded in a 'theology' of the *psuchē* ['soul'] and for this purpose, Plato introduces the mythical way of speaking. Thus, I have reached a [281] paradoxical conclusion that the ontological *chōrismos* ['separation'] of ideas asserted by Aristotle had been imputed to Plato, who was only familiar with a methodological *chōrismos*. The ontological *chōrismos* is by contrast a doctrine of Aristotle and not of Plato[22]. He separated god from the physical world of motion in the way it is developed in Book Lambda of the *Metaphysics*. Now, these are assertions that I only mention here because the 'thinking through utopias' can be placed alongside this thinking through metaphors of 'making'. Both are 'mythical' forms in which Plato's thinking is presented.

Before I deal with some concrete examples of the thinking through utopias, I should still bring attention to the fact that the two Platonic utopias, the *Republic* and the *Laws*, belong to the most exoteric writings of Plato. Of this there can hardly be any doubt, certainly when we consider the oversized scope which they have within Plato's written work. On this basis, we must also understand certain stylistic and argumentative features of these writings, which have misled Popper and the others who do not want to recognize the mode of thinking through utopias.

There is, first of all, the provocative element in Plato's form of exposition, which has naturally been noticed by many. I do not see in this, as Popper does, an objection or even the mark of an inner uncertainty. It belongs to the style of this literary genre that it strives for such effects. How dramatic is the scene he constructs when in Book 4 of the *Republic* justice is supposed to be defined or when, in Book 5, the rule of the philosophers finally comes out like a withheld secret! These are quite clearly stylistic devices for drama. Likewise, at the beginning of Book 5, the manner in which the idea of having women and children in common is introduced and explained represents a clear form of provocative stylistic construction. To want to draw conclusions from this as to how literally we should understand that which is said is a naïve misjudgement of stylistic devices. The grotesque example of Gerhard Müller shows us the kind of difficulties this can lead to. He has to explain the conclusion to Book 7 of the *Republic* as an addendum. The prescription given there for implementing the ideal city, namely the expulsion of all those who are more than ten years old, appears even to him to be too utopian. The oldest methods for criticizing tradition must hurry to his aid. In fact, some hermeneutic schooling is in order to keep track correctly of the stylistic layering and the stylistic devices with which a great artist of language like Plato composes. In many instances, we have learned this slowly, for example what it means when Plato [282] writes an apology of Socrates (the achievement of Erwin Wolff[23]) or when he composes a speech supposed to represent an example of rhetoric or else when he puts something in the mouth of a known figure, such as Protagoras. These are examples of how we have advanced in our understanding of forms of literary style so that we no longer succumb to the naivety of wanting to satisfy our historical curiosity everywhere.

Now, let us turn from the problems of form to the problems of content in relation to the thinking through utopias. What comes to light here? I believe that, even if we do not want to recognize the testimony of the *Seventh Letter* for its biographical valuableness, we may say the following: the first great achievement of Plato was his confronting Socrates with the sophists. He devised this construal that Socrates engages in disputes with the sophists. In Xenophon there is a single case of a famous sophist appearing at all as a discussion partner, Hippias[24], and this turns out to be a highly peaceful affair.

Plato's new device obviously springs from his fundamental apologetic tendency to demonstrate that Attic society and the Attic court allowed themselves to be guilty of fatally confusing the newly fashionable character of the sophist with the effectiveness of Socrates. Without a doubt, he harmonized this with all that we know already, for example, from Thucydides' depiction of the destruction of the political *ēthos* ['mores'] in the beleaguered Athens. Processes of disintegration of a social kind drag on for a long time. The demand to know raised by Socrates and the demand to define *aretē* ['excellence', 'virtue'] as knowledge (if we tolerate for a moment the anachronism of 'definition' in the translation of what transpires here) have their grounds in the actual circumstances of society. The elenctic, critical activity of Socrates consists in disclosing the presumptive character of that which he, apparently for the first time, calls *doxa* ['opinion'] and differentiates from 'knowing', and in demonstrating to the discussion partner the hollowness of the claim to possess genuine *aretē*. This critical function, which we are directly connecting as such with the figure of the elenctic Socrates, need not occupy us here. There is certainly nothing utopian to it. It is all the more of concern to us to see how this figure is finally filled out.

The Socrates who in an hour-long conversation reproduces the account of a conversation he had the previous night with Thrasymachus and Plato's brothers, certainly looks quite different from the inconvenient admonisher and critic, whom the city got rid of with a cup of poison; and also very different from his romanticized image which Plato [283] sketched initially in his dialogues. To this extent, we can understand that an interest directed towards historical investigation would like to take this as historical truth. Yet, can we acquire historical truths from a historical novel? Here the gates to fantasy are fully open and one may be led into seeing Plato, who began as a devoted disciple of Socrates, as lapsing into his class prejudices and his antidemocratic tendencies. However, such a procedure seems to me to be an awkward example of critical realism.

By contrast, genuine critical caution demands, in so far as we want to understand Plato, that we bear in mind the unity of the figure of Socrates as Plato intended it, and wonder how the way in which the figure is newly filled out fits with its initial outline. If we inquire in this fashion, then the utopian figure of thought, which Plato constructed in the *Republic* and the *Laws*, loses its singularity and surprise. This figure stands alongside Socrates, the narrator of myths. Even in the latter a certain claim to truth is made, but not in the sense that what is so narrated is meant to be taken as true but rather that the search, which is on its way to the true through the process of giving a thoughtful account, is authenticated by the myth as if by a superior otherworldly reality. Even the thinking through utopias, which the Socratic-Platonic dialogue presumes to undertake, does not intend to offer the utopian as the real or that which is to be realized, but intends to extend the never-ending dialogue of the thinking soul with itself into the unconditional.

Our topic is utopia as a mode of thinking. That one interprets Plato's ideal state as a utopia is nothing new. This is mentioned in Plato often enough. The text explicitly rejects the view that the question of the realization of this ideal is to be taken as a decisively important question.[25] It is not the primary concern and the conditions under which the realization is then supposed to become plausible are all themselves more or less of a utopian nature. I would like to bring to light what is truly of concern here in terms of three turning points in the development of this utopia, which Popper seems to me to have missed.

There is first the discovery of *dikaiosunē* ['justice', 'righteousness'] with the aid of the theoretical construction of the becoming of a *polis*. These are the well-known matters of the second and third book, which come to a conclusion in Book 4. This conclusion in fact raises philological questions. Was there ever a four-book *Republic*? Was it supposed to be less utopian or to have even tried to influence Athenian politics directly? In any case, the question is this: what is the actual purpose of this entire exposition? It is explicitly concerned with the ordering of the classes in the *polis* and the ordering of the soul in the individual. We do not want to make excessive [284] use of the fact that it is only for the sake of the *psuchē* that there is a supposed interest being taken in the *polis*. This is certainly a case of Friedländer's 'ironic displacement of emphasis'. Nevertheless, it is a fiction that makes the *anima naturaliter christiana* ['the soul naturally Christian'] a little bit more intelligible, in so far as here the interiority of the soul and the justice holding sway in it become thematic. But we are certainly not going to miss the fact that the larger perspective in which justice is supposed to be made visible in a larger magnitude in the *polis* at the same time points to an indissoluble link between the individual soul and the *polis*. Whatever the case may be and howsoever ironic the displacement of emphasis between the political theme and the theme of justice in the individual soul may be, when one follows the derivation of the *polis* from the division of labour and the satisfaction of needs, it remains entirely clear in any case as to what is really at stake. It is this: where does *dikaiosunē* become visible? The indirect answer goes like this: only in light of the fact that there can be *adikia* ['injustice']. This point is illustrated in the unpolitical paradise of the city of pigs, in this cynically coloured form of the idyllic communal life. How Plato succeeds in showing there with the most extreme artistry the intrinsic impossibility of this unpolitical configuration, in which there can be no injustice because it includes in itself an ideal of the total satisfaction of the needs of all through all, and the necessity of its transition to the situation in which domination over human beings and the violence of weapons will play a decisive role!

The luxurious city requires the class of guardians. They have to defend this territory which expands more and more, the more its needs grow. Perhaps such a feverish city will also conduct offensive wars. This is in no way excluded. At any rate, this construction culminates in the fact that it is necessary to make the carriers of weapons the guardians; or more precisely to make the guardians carrying weapons good guardians. This is the political problem *kat' exochēn* ['par excellence']. Even the specialists in political science and political philosophy of today will hardly contradict me when I call this the central problem of politics. It is the task of preventing the misuse of power. One can strive for this by way of constitutions and institutions. This is what we today call 'political science' and which has made its way through history as Aristotelian 'politics'. However, one can also place emphasis on the fact that no constitution and political establishment can succeed without successfully educating its citizens. This is Plato's point, which even Aristotle does not deny. This is what guides the Socratic critique of the prevailing circumstances at the time. It first leads to the insistence on *aretē* as *epistēmē* ['knowledge']. This is the terrifying abstraction of the knowledge of virtue, which appears to be cut off from all foundation in *ethos* and from emotional situatedness. The ideal city is placed alongside this abstraction like a kind of counter-utopia, [285] which has at its disposal a super-*ethos*, so to speak. This does not attest to a change but is the logical complement. Plato symbolizes how the two belong together in an amusing invention, which obviously demands that we share Plato's sense of humour. What I am alluding to is the story about the 'philosophical dog'. The well-trained dog is the one which wags its tail only in the presence of its masters and even accepts blows from them, whereas it barks furiously at those it does not know, even if they want to lure it with treats. This is the way those with power in the state are supposed to be: they are immune to any bribes and remain unwaveringly faithful to their office as good guardian dogs. The comparison of the guardians of the ideal city with dogs thus illustrates the fundamental problem of all politics.

The second point concerns the discovery of justice. It figures as the last of the four so-called Platonic virtues[26]. The doctrine of the four virtues has an almost paradoxical history, which dates back to the time of my youth. At that time, the four cardinal virtues were taken for a Platonic discovery and Wilamowitz, as we know, rejected yet another verse of *The Seven against Thebes* (v. 610) as spurious because a prefiguration of the four Platonic cardinal virtues could be recognized in it. Now, in the meantime, it is hardly ever debated that the so-called cardinal virtues were from an older traditional material pertaining to Greece's moral-political 'codex of values'. It is particularly to Werner Jaeger's credit to have put this beyond all doubt. Yet, the fact that Plato in the *Republic* does something totally incredible when he turns these inherited virtues completely on their head, transforming them all, more or less explicitly, into forms of knowledge, has not received sufficient attention in my view. The leading example is courage. This is perhaps as daring and as profound a reinterpretation of an old heroic virtue as can be. It is obviously one of Plato's favourite thoughts, which we likewise find in the *Laches* and in the first book of the *Laws*. What emerges as true courage is something we would call civic courage or even non-conformism. Even this non-conformism is the right stance in the face of danger, which is in fact what courage is. Now, the danger which openly threatens and inspires resistance appears not to be as great as the hidden and unnoticed danger, with which the temptingly pleasant, here particularly corruption through flattery, wins one over. With this paradoxical reinterpretation, courage becomes an eminently political virtue with none of the one-sidedness of an education focused on Spartan rigour. This is authentic courage: that those in power – rulers or office-holders – do not let themselves be led astray by what they are all too likely to believe about themselves and by what anyone who has power in their hands would encounter in all forms of corruption by flattery.

But the reinterpretation of justice is also as daring as it is ingenious. It is neither the equitable distribution of goods – the oldest ideal of justice – [286] nor the equality of citizens before the law – the more recent ideal, which is at issue here. Rather what is at issue is the denunciation of the fundamental evil which Plato saw in Attic democracy. It is the denunciation of *polupragmosunē*, of being a busybody [*Vielgeschäftigkeit*], living from the intrusion of particular interests into politics. Here it seems to me striking how *sōphrosunē* ['prudence', 'moderation'], which is equated with the political ideal concept of harmony and homology, and *dikaiosunē* ['justice', 'righteousness'], which supports and constitutes the right order of the whole, converge with each other. Again, this no doubt was meant to be noted as a bold reinterpretation. What is clear in it is that Plato's interest lies in the political problem of power. This is manifest not least in the fact that the application of the newly acquired concept of justice to the inner state of the soul is indeed evidenced by deep psychology. People have always rightly admired the way in which the inner split of the 'parts of the soul' is depicted and with it the ideal of a civil peace in the soul is brought to light. At any rate, it seems indubitable to me that Plato here undertakes a transformation of the traditional virtues in the Socratic sense, which obviously does not entirely go with the slogans of the political enlightenment of the time or of the Popperian one today. Now, when Popper presumes equality before the law in this presentation of justice, he truly misunderstands the whole. It is a state of education which makes laws in general superfluous. This is the point, absurd in a certain sense, that through right education an agreement among all is supposed to result by itself as well as an assent of all to the actions of the rulers and to the elite among the rulers. In this way, everything will be in the right order.

The third example I would like to analyse more precisely concerns the transition to the famous decline of the ideal state. The question is the following: how does so wonderfully ideal an order, in which everything has been done to ensure that no injustice can happen, no disturbance can arise in the ideal harmony among all, actually come to ruin? How are political transformations supposed to happen at all in such an ideal state? For this, Plato devises the absurd story with the number pertaining to marriage, in which he really undertakes the most extreme form of ironic colouring. It seems hardly credible that one can be blind to this irony. Here the muses are invoked in a Homeric fashion, who are supposed to tell us how discord sets in for the first time and they would have spoken to us in tragic style as if bantering and chatting with children, yet completely serious and with lofty words. And then comes the solemn solution to the problem: In the human beings who have been so ideally educated to be wise, the calculations will one day go wrong, because, despite the infinitely complicated calculations for determining human marriages, marriages will be arranged *para kairon*, against the time: *agnoēsantes*, that is to say, unknowingly, and this obviously means: [287] by falsely applying the number. The reasons for why this happens are of an ontological nature, so to speak: human beings are human and if they want to make use of their calculation, they must do so with *aisthēsis* ['perception'], on the basis of their sensible perception of the world and not like the god, who has otherwise assigned periods of procreation for living beings, which are adapted to the course of time. Human beings will therefore make mistakes and it is from these mistakes that the first conflict within the rulers will emerge. For what is now gathered in this ruling class of guardians is no longer all pure gold.

Here the errors of Popper, who has no sense for the playfulness of the whole scene, can be easily understood if we start from his own preconceptions. He sees in Plato's ideal state the reconstruction of an early Greek collectivist tribal society which could be protected against ruin through the new rational methodology of a eugenics. But our text says the opposite. We cannot precisely have such a eugenics because mathematical calculations can be connected with reality only through *aisthēsis*. The origin of the mistake thus lies in this state of affairs which is based on something unchangeable and not on a deficiency in the education of these guardians, who had not really practised pure mathematics. The reference to the instruction of the guardians in pure mathematics[27], which Popper makes, is thus misleading. It goes completely against the context to say that the guardians were given insufficient knowledge and schooling in dialectic in the ideal city. What is rather meant is this: precisely those who are *sophoi* ['wise'] and have received this education, can still make mistakes.

Here I must undertake a small correction to my own presentation in 'Plato and the Poets'[28]: the mistakes are not mistakes in calculations. It is not that the number is too difficult, but the application of the number is too difficult. This is a primordial theme in Plato, which is to be seen everywhere: no form of rationality, not even a purely mathematical one can prevent us from missing the right moment, the *kairos*. In the *Phaedrus* (272a) Socrates also emphasizes the role of *kairos*, of the right moment, and the *Timaeus* in its mathematical cosmogony underscores in an unmistakable manner the necessary imperfection of human beings. The thought is thus this: when we are dealing with reality, even despite perfect rationality, there always emerges an uncontrollable aspect in which something can escape us. This is mentioned in the beginning, when the whole argument is being introduced, that in this realm of phenomenal reality, something else holds than [288] in the realm of rational ideas as such, where an *arithmos teleios* ['perfect number'][29] holds sway.

This is thus not a doubt. What Plato gives us to understand here are the very limits to the planning capacity of the human being. I will remind the reader in this regard that Nicholas Cusanus uses a similar argument when he calls human knowledge a knowledge which is always only comparative and never real, which is why he ascribes to it the character of *coniectura* ['conjecture']. This is good old Platonic tradition.

In support of my interpretation, let me furthermore remind the reader that the problem of the application of rationality is a central theme even in the *Timaeus* and the *Philebus*. I have said something about this in my essays 'Idea and Reality in Plato's *Timaeus*'[30] and in 'The Idea of the Good in Platonic-Aristotelian Philosophy'[31].

To summarize: thinking through utopias, this is the perspective under which I see Plato's political writings and under which we must read them. I wish to suggest that it is a matter of thinking and not only of outlining a utopia. What matters here is that even the reader is not, as happens in the naïve approach, to register and display mere assent or rejection with regard to the utopian contents of these writings. It boils down to learning to think in such forms of rational games. For the contemporary reader, this includes even a familiarity with the historical atmosphere. One must learn how to transform in thought the concepts of this bourgeois patrician class, which was transformed from an older aristocratic society, resting on half-agrarian half-commercial foundations. This patrician class found itself in a constant, almost internecine war with the aspiring middle classes, even in Athens. In this way, one grasps the essential motifs of thought which have exerted an influence on the whole of Western history, including its ecclesiastical history, in their intention and lasting significance[32]. This is what each Platonic dialogue demands, and this is also the case for political utopias, such as the *Republic*. The *Laws* too are eventually an enormous utopia if we bear in mind that the laws there are supposed to reach their efficacy essentially through the agreement in the preambles, which are to be sung beforehand. Therein lies a limitation of the character of the laws. This limitation aims at integrating them into the unity of the basic convictions of the state to be founded – fundamentally, like the *Republic*. I believe Herter has correctly shown this[33]. The *Laws* too are a [289] state of education. I will close with the following suggestion: we can understand philosophers only when we do not focus on their vocabulary and their metaphors as such, and this is completely true in the case of a philosophical writer like Plato, who chose the literary form of *mimēsis*. What is demanded here is that we must engage in thinking.

3
Mathematics and Dialectic in Plato (1982)

[290] It is well-known that Plato stood in particularly intimate relationship to the immense progress achieved by the Greek mathematical sciences of his time. This has been illustrated in multiple ways by many researchers. In this regard, whether we should assume an influence of Plato on mathematics, as is frequently done, or whether, in agreeing with recent scholars, we should doubt such an influence, is of secondary import. What is indisputable is that the existence of the science of mathematics held a particular significance for Platonic thinking, which comes through time and again in his dialogical works.

It has been investigated often enough and can be chalked up as an established finding that it was not for nothing that Plato was placed among the Pythagoreans by Aristotle. If his 'school' was supposed to be distinguished by the fact that one read the words *mēdeis ageōmetrētos eisitō* ['let no one ignorant of geometry enter'] on its entry gate, he had in this way not only placed an internal requirement for his 'school', but also formulated a fundamental principle of lasting truth, which has in the meantime become self-evident for all the ways of giving someone a scientific education. Mathematics is a pure rational science. It is thus different from all knowledge of what is actual [*Wirklichkeit*], howsoever important its application to the knowledge of what is actual may be. This is the Platonic legacy we all share, which completely independently of all philosophical disputes that may be connected with it, is even reflected in the very way we speak, when we grant the *entia rationis* ['beings of reason'], the 'mathematical objects', an 'ideal' or 'eidetic' or intelligible being.

In this regard, one should not forget that it was indeed first the achievement of Platonic thought, thanks to which we can attempt to say what mathematics is. In order to be a mathematician, one does not need to know this, and in order to know this, one does not need to be a mathematician. This is precisely the reason why we learn something about Greek mathematics from the Platonic dialogues. But we read them against the grain, so to speak, when we read them in this way. Much significance is accorded to the elaboration of Euclidean geometry in Plato's century

---

'Mathematik und Dialektik bei Plato (1982)' was first published in *Physik, Philosophie und Politik. Festschrift für Carl von Weizäcker*, ed. Klaus Michael Meyer-Abich. Munich: Hanser,1982, pp. 229–44. It was presented as a lecture in Göttingen on 6 July 1983. It is now in *Gesammelte Werke*, vol. 7. Tübingen: J. C. B. Mohr (Paul Siebeck), 1991, pp. 290–312.

and is associated with names, such as Theodorus, Theaetetus, Eudoxus [291]. The (Pythagorean) discovery of the irrational greatly influenced the geometrical representation of relations in number theory. Plato himself was accordingly greatly fascinated by the discovery of mathematical bodies in particular and assigned it a decisive role for the theory of elements in his cosmological myth in the *Timaeus*[1]. Yet, despite all this, the real philosophical problem that mathematics represented for Plato lies in the essence of the number. In the number, the essence of the universal becomes apparent to him, and thus the significance of the *logos* for knowledge [*Erkenntnis*]. Or perhaps we should say: in the number he was confronted with the unsolvable puzzle that the universal and the individual are entangled in each other: the unity of the many and the multiplicity of the one.

We have an irrefutable testimony for this in the *Hippias Major*, which is in no way unique and is thus unaffected by questions concerning its authenticity. There Socrates admits (*Hippias Major*, 302ff) to what has always confounded him in his search for what is common to all individuals. What is sought in this case is the beautiful. One can wonder here as to whether there is something to the fact that this question about what is common arises precisely in relation to the *kalon* ['beautiful']: is it not (like the *agathon* ['the good']) 'there' in a peculiar manner, so that the *monoeides* ['the singular'] which is ascribed to the beautiful in the *Symposium* has something paradoxical about it? What confounds Socrates in every instance is that there exists something common that does not belong to the individuals which compose it. Thus, each of the two of us would be one and not two. Now, it becomes clear that this is not something exceptional but holds true for the whole of the vast field of numbers and cannot be simply ignored, as Hippias wished (302b4). Is this a sophistical joke? Or a sign of the difference between enumeration [*Aufzählung*] and the specification of the essence? At any rate, the argumentation serves this purpose. The definition of the 'beautiful' under discussion, that it is what is pleasing to the eyes and ears, is in this way erroneous. It is an enumeration of what is in there, which means that it misses what is common so that we fall into contradictions, as Aristotle shows (*Topics* Zēta 7, 146a21ff).

Nevertheless, a connection presses itself here, which exists between idea and number: both are a 'unity' of a manifold. This leads to the question of the sense in which the 'essence' fits the individual. The introduction to the *Parmenides* teaches us how much Plato himself was aware of the problem represented by the separation of ideas from appearances and the 'participation' of the latter in the idea. The fact that the 'number' does not have an existence for-itself alongside what is counted and yet is something different than the togetherness of its addends means just as much for the relation of the idea to that which 'participates' in it. The number has 'its' monads, which are not 'things'; [292] they are themselves *eidos* ['idea', 'form'], just like the *genos* ['genus'] has 'its' species. Now, one could establish an infelicitous parallel between the specification of the *genos* and the number because the addends which make up the numerical count [*Anzahl*][2] do not possess a specific difference. However, there are also other universal concepts which are not specified according to species and genus. Here we have, for example, the relation of *tauton* ['the same'] and *thateron* ['the other'] to that which participates in these *eidē* ['forms', 'ideas'];

we also have 'being' and 'being-one', which are all 'formal-ontological' concepts (in Husserl's sense). They are not *koina* ['that which is common'] in the sense of the *genos*. Participating in them does not mean participating in something definite. It rather means that they are there alongside too. Just as any being is something that is one (but also identical with itself and different from everything else), so that being-one is immediately 'there' (*parousia* ['presence']), so too everything that is two is immediately 'there'.

This is precisely the argument of the *Phaedo* (101c). There one enquires into the cause of all becoming and passing away. Socrates introduces a first 'hypothesis of the *eidos*', an 'ideal' being in order to avoid the 'becoming' of the two and the paradoxes connected with it. And this applies of all things to 'the' two. To be sure, there will eventually be grounds for Plato not to assume that there are ideas of numbers, as numbers are all produced according to a rule[3]. This is how the paradox of the *Hippias* finds its final resolution: a number is not what is common to its addends. But this does not prevent the fact that in the *Phaedo*, the transcendence of that which underlies becoming and passing away is exhibited for the first time in the number. In this way, the inner proximity between number and idea at least comes into focus. Nevertheless, the *Phaedo* only thematizes the 'separation' of the idea from the 'appearances', of being from 'becoming'. The 'participation' of the individual in the universal does not lead to any fundamental clarification. Yet, as we know, there is no clarification even in the *Republic* – then where really do we find this clarification? In the *Parmenides*? In any case, the being of the number represents a model for the Platonic question about the 'what', to which the *eidos* is the answer, in so far as the number implies a relation between the multiplicity of the monads and the unity of the numerical count and this relation is completely and utterly 'mathematical', that is to say, 'eidetic'.

The *Phaedo* illustrates this point readily in a paradoxical way through the apparent contradiction between addition and division.

This is all well-trodden ground. Likewise, the *Meno* and the central sections of the *Republic* are always in the spotlight when we are dealing with Plato and mathematics. The famous class session with Meno's slave clarifies in a still half-mythical manner, as recollection from a previous life, the peculiar epistemic character belonging to mathematical truths. It is [293] a kind of insight, which every individual must gain by themselves and which, for this reason, cannot be designated as learning. In the *Republic* mathematics constitutes an important intermediary stage in the educational programme of the true politicians and 'philosophers', and functions as a preliminary stage to dialectic. Even this handful of pages and their explanations, which follow later, have become the object of extensive scholarly interpretations.

By contrast, this question has at most found only a partial consideration in one of the most difficult and profound dialogues of Plato, the *Theatetus*. It certainly stands to reason that the two partners in the dialogue, Theodorus and Theaetetus, significant figures in the development of the classical Euclidean mathematics that they are, are confronted by Socrates because of their mathematical achievements. Even the beginning of the *Theaetetus* has virtually the character of a dedication, which serves as a commemoration of the recently deceased brilliant mathematician. The achievement of Theaetetus for Greek mathematics is thus alluded to and this has obviously been appraised for the history of mathematics.

Nevertheless, I am of the opinion that this dialogue has not yet been rightfully placed at the centre of the theme 'Plato and mathematics'. It is not at all the case that its pivotal significance has been misjudged. This dialogue is rightfully read as an introduction to the *Sophist*. This is firmly established beyond any doubt by the unity of the characters in the two dialogues. In this respect, this dialogue has long been a favourite of philosophers and historians of science. One reads it like the reference book of ancient epistemology. In fact, the guiding question of the Socratic dialogue concerns the essence of knowledge. It will obviously turn out that the modern concept of epistemology, which is defined by the primacy of consciousness and self-consciousness, points in a completely different direction.

At first, we find in the *Theaetetus* the critique of a kinetic theory of sensible knowledge [*Erkenntnis*], which is developed with the aid of the relativistic proposition of Protagoras. Then, we find a refutation, just as comprehensive as it is brilliant, of the definition of knowing [*Wissen*] or knowledge [*Erkenntnis*] as 'true opinion'. Finally, we have a third part, which is again most peculiar, in which the supplementary determination 'true opinion "with *logos*", that is to say, 'with the right explanation', is also scuppered. The dialogue is composed in an extremely artful manner and rightfully famous for its excurses, parables, allusions, etc. There can be no doubt that it must be read like a sort of negative counterpart to the positive dialectical development of the two subsequent dialogues, the *Sophist* and the *Statesman*. It is thus clear that the understanding of knowledge, which is discussed there, still remains at the threshold of Platonic dialectic.

[294] That being said, nobody today anymore doubts that this dialogue stands in the middle of the Platonic works and at the gateway to the esoteric dialectic of the late dialogues and that it is not a dialogue about a definition that proceeds negatively in the well-known style of the early Platonic dialogues.

This can also be proven morphologically and through the history of the motifs at work here. Thus, one should not wonder why nothing of the theory of ideas is to be found here. The dialogue clarifies negatively what *logos* and *eidos* are. One is surprised today that a researcher of the calibre of Paul Natorp was taken in at the time by the superficial similarities to the early dialogues and stubbornly clung to an early dating of the *Theaetetus* (at least in its first version). This similarity is deceptive. It is first of all clear that the elenctic negativity of the Socratic dialectic is here elevated to a new awareness – and the consciousness of its positive efficacy. This is what is achieved by the ingenious introduction of the metaphor of maieutic, the art of midwifery which Socrates inherited from his mother. This goes hand in hand with the fact that the dialogue partner, the young Theaetetus, is evoked in the glory of his death in battle. One notices how the brilliant young man even now, when he fails the Socratic demand to provide an account, plays a highly commendable role. Even the well-known motif of the Socratic dialogues, wherein the demand for the definition is initially misunderstood by his discussion partners in the sense of an enumeration of the scope of the concept, receives here a clear modification. Theaetetus differentiates the theoretical and the practical-technical forms of knowledge not out of the thoughtlessness of a mere enumeration but because of a highly personal motivation. He thus gives an account of himself and admits to being a student of the mathematician Theodorus. And even when he does not succeed in bringing to a concept what knowledge as such is, how quickly he understands the demand and illustrates it in terms of his own mathematical insights! In addition, that Socrates must encourage the modest young man into finding his own 'knowledge' is completely different from the cases of the otherwise self-confident partners of Socrates. Theaetetus is fully aware of his inadequacy in the face of the task and does not first need to be compelled to admit to his ignorance.

That it is mathematicians who are questioned and taken up for interrogation by Socrates about the essence of knowing and knowledge is not in the least surprising. Mathematics is for the Greeks the obvious paradigm and the paragon of all science. Yet, remarkably, one has not yet rightfully asked as to why Plato puts these attempts at finding a definition of 'knowledge' in the mouth of the mathematicians with whom Socrates here converses. Is it not strange that a young mathematician, of all people, is supposed to have defined knowledge as sensible perception and that the mathematicians in this dialogue [295] are acquainted with the sophist Protagoras and show themselves to be quite familiar with his doctrines? It sounds as if they themselves advocate a sensualist and relativistic position. Can we understand how this is supposed to be compatible with mathematics? And this is not all. In addition, we also know that Protagoras, according to well-established traditional records, wrote polemical pieces against the mathematicians. How does this all fit together? These are questions that appear extraordinarily urgent to us today. We have learnt that the Platonic dialogues so far have been read far too much like treatises with their mimetic and dramatic character regarded as a mere decorative ingredient. We have instead begun, in the meantime, to employ the Doric harmony between *logos* and *ergon* ['work'] in the Platonic dialogical work as an essential key to understanding the dialogical event and thus to see even the content of the problem treated in Platonic thinking in a new light[4].

The Socratic dialectic is the art of leading a dialogue and is far more a real dialogue than it appears at first blush. It is true that in general Socrates' dialogue partners submit themselves to his guidance completely and utterly and confine themselves to assenting or doubting. Yet, howsoever arbitrary it might first appear, the choice of Socrates' dialogue partners is never so. That which is debated along the course of argumentation, as it happens, what is coherent and incoherent in it – all of that is incorporated into an event in which the partner is as much a participant as the guiding speaker – and so is the reader.

So, we all have reasons to ask ourselves what it means that here a young mathematician, whose genius has been explicitly extoled previously, defines knowledge as sensible perception. Is it really conceivable that he, of all people, embraces the relativistic theory of sensualism, especially when he is a mathematician? Now, recent investigations, which were first conducted by Hermann Langerbeck[5], have cast doubt as to whether it is even certain in the case of Protagoras that he really advocated a sensualist theory of knowledge. The picture which the dialogue *Protagoras* paints of him points in a totally different direction. There he appears as a teacher of political rhetoric, who in the eyes of the Attic youth was a true star, from whose doctrines and teaching one expected the best for one's own political future. [296] Encyclopaedic tendencies, as they were reported of many other sophists, only elicit his scorn.

Thus, it has become doubtful as to whether Protagoras belongs at all to the rank of those who propounded philosophical theories.

If we now follow the image of Protagoras sketched in the *Theaetetus*, it simply does not appear at first as if the sensualist theory has anything at all to do with the famous statement of Protagoras. There is certainly no doubt about its authenticity. 'The human being is the measure of all things, of those that are that they are and of those that are not that they are not'. However, in the Socratic treatment which this statement receives, it unfolds into consequences which even Socrates clearly does not deem to be Protagorean at all. As Socrates does, one can develop a very nice and profound universal theory of movement, according to which everything that we call knowledge is a mere reaction in the play of movements and encounters. Socrates puts this theory, endowed with great sophistication, under the name of Heraclitus and sums up the entire Greek tradition of older poetry and philosophy from Homer to Protagoras as Heraclitean. This is so obviously a construction that one is not surprised when, in the further course of the dialogue, Socrates comes to the defence of Protagoras himself against all the objections raised against the 'theory' thus construed. The universal physics and epistemology developed here, which assimilate the atomistic modes of representing reality, seem to be connected to the real position and the real interest of Protagoras by just a single thin thread.

As the *Theaetetus* continues, Protagoras comes across as the extreme case of an antidogmatic, whose political theory, if one wants to call it that at all, is a theory of a radical legal positivism: a right is what is elevated to a law by a decision. He accordingly sees his own profession as orator and teacher of rhetoric in the fact that he influences the decision-making process of the court or the popular assembly through speeches. It is naturally possible to expand such a position, which rejects all natural rights and confines itself to the application of the existing rights, into a universal philosophical theory. Such a theory may then make legal political matters appear as a special case of a universal conventionalism and relativism. But as he is depicted in the *Theaetetus*, this was certainly not Protagoras' concern to develop such a theory. It is at least doubtful whether the Platonic Socrates was even confronted with such a theory at all. It could after all be the case, and I believe we have reasons to assume so, that it was Plato who was the first to have discovered the relativistic implications of the technical and political pragmatism of the older generation of sophists. [297] It is anyway self-evident that the later doxography takes its own post-Platonic categories as a basis, completely in the style of Aristotle.

Yet, even if we completely drop this question, our starting question remains: what is it supposed to mean that a mathematician defines knowledge as sense perception?

Here, there is a simple answer, which is still not yet quite taken seriously. The Greek word *aesthēsis* does not have the meaning of 'sense perception' at all. The opposition between the sensible and the mental, the sensuous and the intelligible, is first a result of the Platonic philosophy. The Greek equivalent of 'mind' [*Geist*] and 'intellect', the word *noūs*, means nothing but the immediacy of the most acute perception. It means the immediate awareness of something. This was demonstrated by Kurt von Fritz in a fine piece of work[6]. In the same way, *aisthēsis* means the immediacy of noticing or, as we would say, 'sheer self-evidence'. This can be verified even in Aristotle's parlance[7].

With this, the answer given by the mathematician suddenly makes sense. Even if we are unable to dispel the surprise that these famous mathematicians were familiar and acquainted with a sophistical orator like Protagoras, we conversely understand very well that they eventually turned away from his job of making mere speeches and turned towards a matter as solid as mathematics. In mathematics we really have 'knowledge'. Faced with the confusing use of argumentation, which the newfangled teachers of rhetoric and discussion techniques had disseminated, one may indeed have been very well motivated to say that knowledge is something different, namely 'sheer self-evidence'. It is the well-known manner of Socrates to expose the unsatisfactory aspect of this answer through questionable arguments. He is the one who first associates this view with an extreme sensualism. This belongs to his elenctic, which often seems 'sophistical' and which is established upon the following fundamental principle: those who are unable to hold onto what they believe they know, without getting confused, do not know.

Truly speaking, we are dealing with two theses in the following discussion, which are otherwise independent of each other and put up for discussion one after the other: the definition of knowledge as *aesthēsis* is explicitly designated as the thesis of Theaetetus (160e1, 179c); the thesis [298] of the *homo-mensura* ['the human being as the measure'] is designated as the thesis of Protagoras. Here we thus really do not need to see the representatives of the mathematical sciences as adherents of the thesis of Protagoras, who, as mentioned above, explicitly went to bat against the mathematicians. The image of Protagoras in the dialogue of the same name is also in accord with this. There Protagoras spurns all these mathematical sciences with a superior self-assurance and prides himself at doing nothing other than fostering the political education of his students towards *aretē* ['excellence', 'virtue'], which was designated by the contemporary buzzword *euboulia* ['good judgment'][8].

So it remains a real question to which an answer must be found: Why is Theodorus at all introduced in our dialogue as an old friend of Protagoras and why is he, just like his student Theaetetus, so well acquainted with the book by Protagoras about *Alētheia* (*Theaetetus* 152a: he has read it often!). Even if these are simply meant to be historical facts well-known to the readers of Plato, the question which I pose still stands. We wonder on what specific grounds mathematicians can concur with the statement of Protagoras. I can only hazard a guess: could there not be a sense in which for mathematicians the 'human being' is the measure of what is if we turn our attention to the fact that the numbers and figures of mathematics can only come into being through our 'construction'? For professional mathematicians it makes perfect sense to say that 'for them' the triangles drawn there in the sand are not what they are for lay persons. 'For them', the mathematicians, those triangles are representations of real mathematical triangles, etc. Before Plato had discovered the ontological implications of mathematical science, the 'eidetic' character of its objects, the self-understanding of mathematical praxis may have overlapped a bit with the self-understanding of rhetorical praxis, which Protagoras had formulated. For mathematicians, there is something like a triangle because they see the figure drawn in the sand in this way, just as for politicians something holds as a right because it has been so decided by the *polis*.

Having said that, we perfectly understand that Theodorus eventually turned away from Protagoras' 'speeches' (See *Theaetetus* 165a). He, just like Theaetetus, practices real mathematics. It is just that they do not really know how to articulate what they are doing.

This is the dialogical event that takes place in the *Theatetus*. These mathematicians are not clear about what their objects actually are, which, at any rate, are not supposed to be just figures or quantities encountered by the senses. The young mathematician in fact reveals himself to be just conceptually helpless. This is how, the relativity of [299] numbers is explicitly subsumed under the question of the 'becoming more' in the example of the dice, and Theaetetus is divided. He sees that in fact there can be no 'becoming more', no increase (accumulation) and yet knows that such a 'becoming more' exists. The elaboration of the contradiction which is found here explicitly alludes to the experience of mathematicians with such relativities (155b6). Socrates praises the young man for the fact that such experiences always make him [Theaetetus] rightly dizzy: he is at least aware that he is missing the firm support (which only the 'ideality' of the mathematical world offers).

Let us note how artfully the young Theaetetus is entangled in his aporia. He is led astray in a painstaking engagement, so to speak, in so far as the concept 'becoming' is fixed logically, (155ab) of whose inapplicability to the relativity of magnitudes Theaetetus is only vaguely aware (154d). This is genuine maieutic: one is made conscious of the inappropriateness of the conceptuality available – which is found here in the concept 'becoming' – and in this manner a better understanding is prepared for the mathematicians of themselves and of their 'eidetic' science.

Even the refined process theory which Socrates introduces in the end serves the same purpose. Mathematicians may feel superior to the primitive materialists, as Theaetetus insinuates a little bit later (*Sophist* 246b4). But the subtle theory of the interaction, which Socrates develops here (*en de tē pros allēla homilia* ['in the mutual interaction'], *Theaetetus* 157a2), eliminates all *logos*, and this must increase the discomfort of the mathematician. He plainly wonders whether Socrates really means all this seriously (157c4) and Theodorus impatiently exhorts Socrates: 'but for God's sake, tell us now why it does not work that way' (161a6).

The Platonic expression for thinking, the 'flight into the *logoi*', clarified the pure 'noetic' character of mathematics for the first time. This becomes really visible in the presentation of the *Phaedo* as well as of the *Republic*. It is entirely this 'noetic' expression that explicitly underlies the development of the Pythagorean theory of oppositions into the 'four kinds', which is to be found in the *Philebus*[9]. It is only when we take the Platonic 'ontological' differentiation between the noetic and the aesthetic as our starting point that it becomes possible to differentiate conceptually the pseudo-mathematical specious proofs from the genuine mathematical demonstrations; and also, for example, as Aristotle does, to differentiate clearly between pseudo-mathematical proofs and false mathematical proofs, which do not affect the 'principles' anyway. I have laid this out [300] in my essay on the Seventh Letter[10]. The reflection that I have carried out there manages to explain how it is that the 'truth' of Protagoras in general, even if only in a completely vague manner, can accommodate the self-understanding of the professional mathematician. This is how Cornford[11] understood Aristotle's famous approval of Protagoras' critique of the geometers (*Metaphysics* B2, 997b35). Obviously, it is only from the standpoint of the Platonic foundation that Protagoras appears as a sensualist. The contemporary mathematicians were not all pseudo-mathematicians, even if they could hardly justify the ontological character of their objects as the young Theaetetus here.

It fits these mentions that in fact only the *homo-mensura* statement itself and its first clarification in the text are ascribed to Protagoras. For the text continues: 'Does he not roughly say this, that, as something appears to me at a time, so it is for me and again as it appears to you, so it is for you? Now, you as well as I are human beings' (152a). The 'roughly' (*pōs*, 152a6) is important. It is clearly no longer the wording of Protagoras but a paraphrase – and it is then entirely an illustration which Socrates inserts when he uses the example of the wind.

The example clearly means: 'It is cold for me, perhaps not for you. It appears cold to me but perhaps not to someone else'. Should we really take it that Protagoras meant his statement in this way? He could have very well said: 'I am a human being just as you'. But this addition would hardly claim to ground the absurd consequence: as we are both human beings, let each of us be the measure of all things. Here the allusion, I think, is supposed to be to that which is common to all human beings, to what distinguishes the human being as a human being. Plato brings this to a mythical representation in the sublime picture of Prometheus in the *Protagoras*: human beings needed a political ability to survive (*politikē technē*) and they thus received the gift of *dikē* ['justice'] and *aidōs* ['shame'], which was allotted to 'all' (*Protagoras* 322b-d). This entails that human beings are capable and in need of establishing and abiding by conventions without the existence of another ground of validity than the fact that conventions are indeed decided and so must hold as the law for all. Protagoras grounds his profession as an orator and a teacher on this pragmatic relativism. The particularizing version of the *homo-mensura* principle, which could support an extreme sensualism, can hardly be made compatible with the self-understanding of the political orator and teacher. A closer look at our text of the *Theaetetus* yields the same result.

[301] The passage in 154a indirectly confirms what was said. First, 'your' sensation of colour is compared to that of a dog or other animals. 'Your' thus primarily means: that of the human being. Then, the relativity is progressively

particularized: for you and another human being and, finally, for you by yourself. That this is a *Socratic* imputation is underscored by the fact that the statement of Protagoras is explicitly repeated and is equipped now *with* the addition *emoi* ['for me'] (160c9).

The passage at 152b is certainly not unambiguous. *Epakolouthēsōmen* ('let us follow') can mean a quotation or its consequence. There are however certain things which speak against the contention that Protagoras, who sees rhetoric as his profession, is supposed to have used being cold as an example of relativity. In this example, persuasion is really of little help! Could he have used the example of being cold in the wind as an analogy, for example in the following sense: I will speak in such a manner that you all will become warm? But this would be all too artificial. By contrast, he compared himself as an orator to a physician. The physician transforms through remedies (so that the patient finally tastes the wine again) and the 'sophist' transforms through discourses. This analogy is at any rate only meant as an analogy. Protagoras does not intend to heal a sick person with speeches. For him what is at stake is the role of rhetoric *en tē paideia* ['in education'] (167a). He is only a 'relativist' in the sense that he avoids dogmatic generalities. This fits his behaviour even otherwise: in the *Protagoras* (351d), he indicates that it is more reliable 'for his whole life' not to admit that what is pleasant as such is always good and what is painful always bad. He does not want to commit himself, obviously because he wants to leave everything open on a case-by-case basis for his art of persuasion. This is why he loathes all dogmatism.

This is consistent with the fact that even in the *Cratylus* (385f) Protagoras' statement is alluded to solely in this sense: It is said that it grounds the validity of conventions and in particular the agreement on which language rests. In all such applications, even in the well-known interest of Protagoras in the *orthoepeia* ['correct diction'], what is at stake is manifestly the constitution of conventions and norms, which comes down to our compliance with them. It is always Socrates who, through his conducting a dialogue, first leads this always collectively meant 'relativism' *ad absurdum* ['to absurdity'] by his practice of particularization.

I concede that these are just perspectives gained from Plato on what the historical Protagoras perhaps was. Fortunately, the philosophical train of thought in the *Theaetetus* does not depend on this. If we want to understand Plato, we only need to take the picture of the great sophist sketched there at its full value, even the standpoint of an unflinching pragmatism and legal positivism, to which Socrates in the end explicitly reduces the true position of Protagoras. The ontological consequences which Socrates educes out of Protagoras' statement [302] obviously have nothing to do with what Protagoras actually had in mind. Plato makes this clear indirectly in the course of the dialogue in so far as Protagoras has to be defended again and again against unfair allegations. If Protagoras was a pure pragmatist of rhetoric, then we understand how the refutation of Protagoras' thesis is ultimately focused on the justification and grounding of the true professional. Herein lies the real difference between Protagoras and his 'friends'. It may be the case that in relation to a world of undiscernible conventions, persuasive orators may think of themselves as the only true experts, in so far as they are in the position to precipitate the finalization of new conventions, precisely through passing a new resolution. Yet, such an ability is not knowledge.

The science of mathematics, by contrast, relies on real insight, which one finds in oneself like a submerged memory, which 'comes to me'. Here in mathematics, it is clear that we are dealing with insight, that is to say, that this 'memory' that 'comes to one' comes to all in just the same way. Like from a previous life which 'the soul' of everyone had. This is precisely what the myth of *anamnēsis* ['recollection'] in the *Meno* puts into words. In mathematics, experts are real knowers and precisely because of this they pull themselves away from being prejudiced by the way they are oriented towards reality in everyday life and the conventions which hold sway here. This is the true basis for the self-understanding of mathematicians. They only know too well the resistance of lay people to mathematics (see 170e). Yet, they must specifically remind themselves that, as mathematicians, they know the truth and all the others are in error.

Through his dramaturgy and staging, Plato gives powerful expression to the decisive significance of the conflict about the true specialist. It is noteworthy that the old Theodorus does not seem to be initially interested in the Socratic question about what 'knowledge' is and only enters the discussion when Protagoras' statement puts into question the legitimacy of the professional as a knower. He thus only takes part in the discussion until the difference between the knower and the layperson – against Protagoras' statement – is justified and secured.

In fact, as soon as the distinction of the knower has been reestablished, the refutation of Theaetetus' answer is no longer difficult. Even Theaetetus cannot avoid what is self-evident, that something like a number cannot be grasped only through a specific sense, like, for example, a colour through sight or a sound through hearing[12]. Numbers are something that are common, which the soul indeed grasps through the senses, yet not with the aid of a specific organ, but 'purely for itself'[13]. This [303] is how it is, and this holds true explicitly for numbers as well as for being and the good. At this point, it strikes us that this admission that the soul is here operative 'purely for itself' comes far too quickly. When the Platonic Socrates praises his partner in this manner, as it happens here, one must become suspicious. Has the partner really understood what 'the soul purely for itself' means? So that this does not appear simply like a sixth sense, to which admittedly thinking (*sullogismos*, 186d3) and calculating (*analogizesthai*, 186a10) belong, with whose help this sense procures knowledge for the 'soul'. But then knowing and knowledge [*Erkenntnis*] would still be a simple having of the truth. Knowing would remain an immediate 'opinion' [*Ansicht*] of the true, true opinion, so that the true being that is known would be 'there' for the 'soul' in the way that colours and sounds are there for the senses. The refutation of Theaetetus' thesis, that knowing is *aisthēsis*, is thereby completed. But the primitive concept of self-evidence which guides Theaetetus has not yet been overcome and is now reformulated into the thesis that knowing is 'true opinion'.

This is how this new definition of knowledge becomes the topic of discussion. Fortunately for our purposes, we do not need a minutely detailed examination of the discussion over this new definition that knowing is true opinion[14]. That something is not right with it becomes obvious in the problem of error. What is at play there? What is a false opinion, which is still an opinion? A confusion? Between what one sees 'there' before oneself and what one has in memory? Thus, a false combination? Error would then be a kind of confusion? Now, one may explain error, if need be, as a confusion between something seen and what was actually meant. But then what happens in miscalculation? Here, the confusion would have to occur only between things that are meant. Of what does one have an opinion here? Of a false pigeon in the aviary of truths, of a pigeon of the false? There would have to be something not-meant that is meant – and in fact Theaetetus takes recourse to something like this when he recommends *anepistēmosunē* ['non-science', 'ignorance'] (199e2) – a wonderful joke by Plato, which brings clarity to the problem. It should dawn on the reader that knowing does not consist in grasping what is correct but rather in differentiating what is correct from what is false – that it is in this way the *logos*. It is first the reader of the *Sophist* who will become fully aware of this in its consequences. Theaetetus will, meanwhile, continue to want simply to keep what is false at bay as if it were something of a being. That is to say, he continues to think of knowledge as true opinion [*Ansicht*], as the point of view [*Ansicht*] of his 'truths'.

So he tries in his new predicament to eliminate any commingling with what [304] is false by appending *logos* in the sense of 'additional explanation, supplementary account, re-examination, additional marker' to his attempt at defining knowledge. But is *logos* something that is added?

So begins the third and last part of the dialogue with the examination of the statement that knowledge [*Erkenntnis*] is a correctly explained opinion, 'true opinion with *logos*'. This is again a mysterious subject of fascinating interest. However, we are only submitting this much-treated section again to the question as to why it is rather a mathematician who recalls the theory vaguely as if it were a dream, which now Socrates propounds. Even the way it is introduced is strange. It sounds almost abrupt that Theatetus in connection with the rejection of the view that *alēthēs doxa* ['true opinion'], like a judgement declared by a court of law, is identical to *epistēmē* ['knowledge'], vaguely recalls what he had forgotten, namely, that someone had added 'with *logos*' and that a true opinion without *logos* (*alogon* ['without an account', 'without an explanation']) would be no knowledge (201cd). It may be the case that there is such a thing that cannot have a *logos* and of which one is not aware even when one harbours a true opinion of it (as, for example, in a trial based on circumstantial evidence in court). In fact, it is strange that the thesis that knowledge is a true opinion with *logos* occurs only now to Theaetetus. As if his job as a mathematician did not consist entirely in seeking and finding proofs! But the emphasis obviously lies on the second part of his 'recollection': there are things that one cannot know or does not know. What *ouk epistēta einai* ['are not knowable'] means is not entirely clear. It cannot really mean 'unknowable at all' and perhaps we should not rule out labelling something as *alogon* and *anepistēton* ['unknowable'] *so long as* there is no *logos* of it yet[15].

Socrates marks the first part of the thesis with ironic applause (202d). What is self-evidently illuminating in it is obviously something ridiculous in light of the problem which many wise people have sought in vain to solve for a long time. The irony here is clear: Theaetetus is supposed to have found it today! Something is not right here. Socrates at first does not explicate the difficulty which remains unnoticed in Theaetetus' thesis, but we will see where the difficulty lies. What does *logos* mean? The second part of the thesis clearly presupposes a definite understanding of *logos*, which specifically lurks in the word *alogon*. The refutation of this second part of the thesis thus also heralds the indirect discovery of where the understanding of *logos* fails.

[305] One must wonder what it is that is attractive to the young mathematician Theaetetus in this unclear lore that he remembers. The fact that it hovers before him like a dream, as Socrates expresses it, must contain a positive moment. We may presume this, given the other uses of the metaphor of the dream in Plato (and even in the religious appraisal of the dream in Greek life). Dream means something that possesses suggestive power, even if it cannot be readily linked to the settled experiences of the day. What attracts the young Theaetetus here in so dreamlike a manner? Should it not be the indirect confirmation which the theory propounded by Socrates represents for his [Theaetetus'] own aversion towards mere speeches? This would then restore a certain legitimacy to his first answer that knowledge is *aisthēsis*. For mathematicians there are often insights they cannot yet prove. Like the elements, they are so far *aloga* (202b6). This would entail that knowledge would be possible only in connection with the immediacy of *alētheuein*, and not in the empty technique of argumentation. It would be reasonable that not *logos* alone, but only *alēthēs doxa meta logou* ['true opinion with an account'] is knowledge. But it would also become understandable that *logos* for Theaetetus is secondary. What comes first for the mathematician is intuition, the search for proofs (and also the account that follows) only coming as a supplement.

This is how far we can make the introduction of the third attempt by the mathematician plausible. It is obvious that such an understanding of 'science' is insufficient even for the mathematician. Theaetetus himself had informed us about the masterpiece he had brought to fruition with the theory of the square and rectangular numbers. There, the *logos*, the kind of definitional 'subsumption' of the numbers treated individually by Theodorus, yields a genuine mathematical knowledge [*Erkenntnis*]. *Logos* is thus not at all something secondary but is knowledge itself, as Aristotle would say: that which holds *katholou* ['for all']. In fact, this becomes the theme of the discussion that follows: what is the *katholou* in its relation to *holon* ['the whole']? What kind of a 'whole' or 'all' is it, which holds for the whole and which we call 'universal' and which we also distinguish as that which holds for all and as knowing [*Wissen*]?

One thing is clear: the theory which Socrates propounds here from supposed memory and his critique of the same are directed at a false concept of *logos*, and precisely in this way prepare the correct concept, which the *Sophist* will develop. The point of the theory is that the elements of a complex are as such inexplicable (*aloga*) and can only be stated and only named. By contrast, an explanation (*logos*) is possible for a complex, for example, in the case of the syllable, by specifying its letters, but not for the individual letters. Thus, only the syllable would be knowable, and this means explicable.

[306] The question is not about identifying this theory through a historical analysis of the sources. Antisthenes has been evoked, who simply denied the possibility of a definition altogether. Antisthenes' motto, which we know from Aristotle, *oikeios logos* ['germane argument'], is indeed found in the text (202a7) as an unfulfillable demand, but the context is not one expected of a Socratic. This should hold true only for the ultimate components but not in general[16]. Much of this sounds like the great unknown, that is to say like Democritus, if it explicitly means: 'the first components out of which we and all other things are composed' (201e2). This expression, which reminds us of the 'Heraclitean' theory of *aisthēsis* in 156cff and also makes use of the word *athroisma* ['aggregate', 'sum'] (*Theaetetus* 157b9), is here clearly linked immediately to a dialectic level, in which we are concerned with *onomata* ['names'] and *logos*. And here Antisthenes seems closer! As is always the case with Plato, such a theory is more or less his own construction, which he builds for the purpose of delineating his views, but certainly with building blocks into whose origin we can enquire[17].

From the outset, the examination of the new definition is in any case linked to the concept of *stoicheion* ['letter'] in the general sense of component, which, like the letter, is 'element', ultimately something 'indivisible'. The discussion thus begins with the development of the dialectic, which lies in division, with the relationship of the whole and part. The analysis leads to the result that both belong together to such an extent that one should not differentiate the one or the knowable from the other, the part or the parts, as the *alogon*[18]. This reflects, it seems to me, the step beyond the Eleatic thesis of unity, which leads from Zeno to the Platonic dialectic.

The aporia reported by Aristotle (*Physics* A2 185b11 ff) is a clear testimony of this. There we obviously see in this aporia a particular problem. Even parts that are not *sunechē* ['continuous'], thus not 'organic', make up the whole like the members (*mērē te kai melē* ['parts and members'], *Philebus* 14e). These members are in a certain sense *diaireta* ['separated'], like the bricks from which a house is made. In one respect, these members are still 'one' with the whole or, when they are really just components, they are still one as a whole, one as all [307] together in relation to one another. We see how much the Eleatic concept of unity as homogeneity reveals the dialectic which inhabits the problem. What does *adiairheton* ['undivided']: *atmēton eidos* ['indivisible essence'] or *atomon* ['uncut', 'indivisible'] mean?[19] The same problem dominates the dialectic of the *Theaetetus*. Nowhere else is the dialectical differentiation between the All [*Allem*], which is all its parts, and the whole [*Ganzen*], which is the whole of its parts, run through in such an Eleatic scholastic manner.

In this regard, we should recall that in Aristotle not only the part is correlated to the 'whole' as its opposite concept but also what is dismembered or what has been damaged in its appearance (*to kolobon*): the whole is not only all its parts but is also at the same time the being-whole, which it does not 'share' with its parts[20]. By contrast, all species participate in the genus. But precisely because these clarifications are missing here, the whole theory collapses.

The letters are not supposed to be 'knowable' but can only be named – the syllable can be 'explained', precisely through an enumeration of the letters out of which it is composed. Here it is clear: the model of writing (and of speech) governs the concept of knowledge without the realization that there is a difference between the letters of speech and the components of the world.

The dialogue makes us indirectly aware of this abyss of thinking as the whole and its parts constitute an indissoluble unity. What immediately strikes us about this theory is that the *logos* is here illustrated through 'syllable'. We can hardly miss the intention. That which has sense – and this is what we understand under *logos*, speech, thought – is illustrated by something and thereby understood as something that in fact never has a sense. Syllables actually have no meaning. Only words and their being joined together into speech constitute meaning. How must *logos* be understood? Or better: How little must *logos* be understood when it is represented by 'syllable'?

But even the opposite question must be posed too: How do things stand with the letters, the elements? Are they really the ultimate or are they in the end still just 'syllables', that is to say, compositions?

[308] We immediately see this: Here the individual letter is not supposed to be defined and yet Theaetetus, unassumingly and naively, gives an excellent definition of sigma as one of the consonants which are formed with the tongue. What I mean is that readers must notice this and it must dawn on them that the whole paradigm of letters and syllables from the outset points to a completely different 'ideal' or 'symbolic' sphere and cannot illustrate an atomistic theory of ultimate components. We thus need to pay attention to the fact that the text introduces it explicitly as an illustration. This illustration has made a name for itself even in lexical history in the fact that *stoicheion*, letter, will become the 'element'[21].

At this point, we also need to recall the observations which Johannes Lohmann has shared from the perspective of historical linguistics and in connection with Hermann Koller: *stoicheion* (as member of a series) and *sullabē* (as the concept) have their origin in the language of music[22]. There definitely exist close relations to the rational constructivism which distinguishes the Pythagorean theory of music. In this respect, 'syllable' as the 'grasping together' [*Zusammengriff*] and 'concept' [*Begriff*] of the letters is no accidental neologism of conceptual construction. Music, language and writing are linguistically articulated in the same manner. Language anticipates the insight developed by Plato that the whole is not the sum of its parts and components. Here we should also ask ourselves right away as to where the 'number' has its true place and most refined function: in the counting of particles or in the structuring of a system of sounds or letters? The *Philebus* (17aff) gives an absolutely clear answer to this question when it makes the number responsible for the system of letters and sounds, and it really makes sense. Letters and sounds, which make up writing and language, are not simply the indeterminate mass of scribbles and noises, which can then be more or less combined in definite shapes, like those *athroismata* in the *Theaetetus* (157b). Letters and sounds are really only what they are through their fixed determinacy. Each of them is defined by its 'form' and all of them together are defined as a system. Each one is one of the twenty-four letters or phonemes.

But what then is a syllable? Surely, it is also a unity, a new unity, the complex unity of its components. Is it then not like the numerical count? Obviously, the numerical count is also a new unity, a complex unity made of ones. Here we can wonder: is this perhaps the dream which hovers before the mathematician Theaetetus – the dream of understanding the essence of knowledge [309] from the marvel of numbers, of counting and calculating? Knowing as enumerating? But is this enough? Does the Pythagorean dream not tell us more, regardless of what produces the sounds? Not numerical count but the relations between numbers are the being which needs to be known. If we reflect upon the fact that Democritus' atomism is a qualitative one[23], in so far as *thesei* ['position'], *schēmati* ['shape'], *taxei* ['order'] (*Physics* A5 188a22) are the *genē* ['genera'], then in this way even this atomism belongs rather in this series in which the *sullabē* is the knowable, not as a numerical count, but as a figuration.

So let us ask: what is 'numerical count'? Is it something new and different in relation to its components? And in what sense? In fact, as mentioned at the beginning, already in the *Hippias Major* Socrates characterizes as a true puzzle the fact that every numerical count, as the collection of ones, is indeed what is common to them and yet, this common term does not belong to any of these ones themselves. It is thus different from what is the case with the common kind, the species, for example the horse, where the horse-being belongs to all the individual horses. But does 'knowledge' not also mean knowing the numerical count? What then is the numerical count? On the one hand, it seems to be nothing other than the sum of its components, their mere sum. On the other hand, it must, as what is known, also be something different from what belongs to each of its components. Does the numerical count not have its own form [*Gestalt*], so to speak, its own *eidos*? It is well-known that the Greek 'mathematical logic' [*Logistik*] took the 'formal qualities' of numbers as its object.

We immediately see that we are confronted here with two essentially different domains, which Theaetetus does not know how to separate. When the whole is nothing but the sum of its parts, their mere sum, then the meaning of 'part' becomes completely obscure. It is explicitly said of the whole, at least for numbers, that it is only the sum (204d). Obviously, Theaetetus simply does not realize that he is dealing here with 'pure eidetic' objects, the ones and the numerical counts, and not with components of a 'being'! This readily permits the segue to the cases of designated numbers, the area of a land, distances, troops, where we have knowledge when we know the number, as if in these cases the specification of the number were a knowledge of the 'what', that is to say, of what an area, a distance, a troop is. The treatment quantifying states of affairs just abstracts itself from the whole question of what is quantified in each case. Quantification presupposes the similarity of what is counted.

In the example of the syllables and letters, things are completely different. Here we are dealing not with a sum of indifferent ones, but with a whole of disparate parts. [310] The entire art of writing and reading is based on this. One has not only to know the individual letters or, in the case of playing music, the individual notes. One must also know how the words are written or how a melody comes from the notes. This is not merely enumerating and forming a sum. The whole question of knowledge obviously lies beyond the distinction between letter and syllable. One must 'know' both and, in this sense, 'know', but the knowledge which belongs to writing, that is to say, to 'correct writing', is not the mere knowledge of what is available or even its enumeration. The 'number' of symbols, which makes writing possible (or the language of musical art, See *Philebus* 17aff) is not a sum of exchangeable ones (*sumblētai monades* ['combinable units']). It represents a whole of differentiated 'kinds' [*Arten*], forms, types. If we look at the *unity* which such a system represents, it is not a mere numerical count as sum, but an arrangement [*Gefüge*], an *arithmos* made of *asumblētoi monades* [non-combinable units'], not numerical count but *logos*. One sees that in the negative aspect of this aporia of the whole and the sum, there appears here as a vague outline the positive aspect of the proximity between idea and number, which we know from Aristotle's reports.

The text is full of funny reversals. Comparable to the definition mentioned above of the sigma, Hesiod's awareness [*Kennen*] of the one hundred timbers of a wagon is declared to be the true knowledge of what the wagon consists of. By contrast, we read that it is just a vague opinion of a wagon to be aware of the essential components of a wagon, such as the wheels, the axle and the rim and such other things! In the end, the readers who think with the text are not surprised that the completion of the definition – knowledge is true opinion with an explanation (*meta logou*) – easily fails. If it is already self-evident that the mere expression of what is known does not add anything to knowledge, it has now been shown that the enumeration of the components is in turn no real knowledge. The example of orthography also teaches this. A mere awareness of the letters is still not an ability to write.

Finally, the dialogue ends with the expression that knowledge would be right opinion with a knowledge of what differentiates. This is an elegant tautology. First through the specification of what differentiates, through marking, so to speak, through a mark, something is said to be grasped in such a manner that it is unambiguously determined by it and cannot be confused with something else, with what is not meant, with something common. In this way, even so rare a feature as a snub nose would not suffice for determining Theaetetus unambiguously. For Socrates, as is well-known, also had such a nose. One would thus have to know and to recognize the 'singular' nose of Theaetetus. In the end, the same would be true for 'everything you are composed of'. One would have to bear in mind the totality of all the 'singular' features if one wanted to have the true opinion of you (209c7). Only this would be the exact exposition of the advice: to add the distinguishing features to the correct opinion. [311] But this would mean that the features themselves would be like the components. In fact, the correct opinion of the totality of all the features already presupposes this. It would be the whole out of which something is composed.

This leads to the next tautology, which is already apparent. The correct opinion of all the features would be the correct opinion of the matter. This would mean that 'knowledge' would be nothing but the correct opinion with the addition of knowledge (the knowledge of the features). Knowledge would be defined through knowledge, which is a classical circular definition and, like all such circles, an expression of the fact that those who know do not know what it is that they know there and, for this reason, unknowingly presuppose the *definiendum* ['what is to be defined'].

Yet, there still lies something else here in thinking knowledge as the awareness of the difference and eventually defining it as the awareness of all the features. That would be a complete misapprehension of what a feature is. As if the feature were a component of the thing such that the inclusion [*Inbegriff*] of all features would represent the entire existing entity. If it were so, then the definition would once more be nothing but the sum of all the 'parts', that is to say, the definition would be a numerical count or an enumeration. Thus, the concept of feature truly points to the eidetic dimension in which something universal is further determined by being specified through *diaphorai* ['differences'], right up to the *atmēton eidos* ['indivisible essence']. The blindness towards the eidetic dimension leads to the absurdity in which Theaetetus is entangled. Thus, everything converges on this one point. Mathematicians are unable to jump over their own shadow. We can guess how what is positive in this negative aspect of knowing would have to look like. 'True opinion with *logos*': this is definitely a Socratic-Platonic definition of knowledge. But the *logos* should not just be added to the true opinion (*prosgignomenos* ['supplementary']).

This is the decisive point about which the young mathematician is not clear. To know [*Erkennen*] is not: first be aware [*Kennen*] and then, in addition, differentiate. To know is to differentiate. Furthermore, to differentiate is never just to know the one. It is also necessarily to know the other that is not it. Being is also non-being. The knowledge which knows what it is, is thus dialectic. This is what Theatetus will learn when he enters into a dialogue with the stranger from Elea, which the *Sophist* showcases.

There is yet another perspective that is delineated: we see how the 'numerical count' in its puzzling nature fascinates the thinking of the mathematician and at the same time leads him astray. Theaetetus simply does not notice how, to the question concerning the 'what', he, in fact, always gives an answer which would apply to the question concerning the 'how many' of the components. True dialectic will take the opposite route. In the content of the 'what', dialectic will recognize a different 'how many', the unity of an eidetic manifold, as it is implied, for example, in the 'system' of linguistic sounds or letters. With this insight the doctrine of the *Philebus* is added to the doctrine of the *Sophist*. The universality of the numerical count is only [312] knowledge when it is not knowledge of the sum but includes *eidos* and *genos*, and finds the unity in that which is multiple in kind. It is what differentiates and what is common at the same time that makes knowledge knowledge.

4
Dialectic Is not What Sophists Do: What Theaetetus Learns in the *Sophist* (1990)

[338] The *Sophist* belongs to the so-called Eleatic dialogues, which could equally well be called the 'dialectical' dialogues. The *Theaetetus*, the *Parmenides*, the *Sophist* and the *Statesman* represent a series which is perhaps inaugurated by the *Phaedrus*. The Platonic dialectic, which unfolds in this series, continues the Socratic art of the dialogue. But it also explicitly refers to the Eleatic mode of argumentation. Socrates refers to Parmenides in the *Theaetetus* and takes up Zeno's paradoxes in the *Parmenides*. Dialectic can precisely mean both; above all else it means the very art of conducting a dialogue, which is specifically associated with the figure of Socrates, who his whole life long ceaselessly held discussions with people on the street and in the public places in Athens. Even the last day of Socrates' life was occupied with a discussion on ultimate matters. This was depicted by Plato in the *Phaedo*.

On the other side of this, we have the Platonic dialogues which are held to be the later dialogues and in which the person of Socrates begins to take a step back. They are explicitly related to the way in which the Eleatic dialectic proceeds. The Platonic dialectic right to the very word formulates the Socratic question of the good and the Eleatic-Platonic question of 'being' as one. This is a close connection, which is often emphasized by Plato (for example, explicitly in *Republic* VII, 534b)[1]. It can hardly be explained as a biographical or intellectual development of Plato the thinker, as it has long been commonly done. To be sure, the Plato scholarship of our century has by and large reached a consensus on the chronology of the Platonic writings. Yet, the efforts to reconstruct a more precise arrangement of the writings which have come down to us or even to situate them in a biographical framework have never yielded an assured result. An effort like this could never succeed especially with a writer like Plato, who was adept at wearing masks and delighted in being playful. What can be rightly regarded as certain, besides the results of language statistics, is the role played by Socrates in the Platonic writings. First, there are the early [339] Socratic dialogues, which generally end in an *aporia*[2]. Then follow the great *mythical* compositions, such as the *Republic* first of all, in which Socrates figures as an inspired speaker. In some other writings, the

---

'Dialektik ist nicht Sophistik. Theätet lernt das im "Sophistes" (1990)' was first published in *Gesammelte Werke*, vol. 7. Tübingen: J. C. B. Mohr (Paul Siebeck), 1991, pp. 338–69.

figure of Socrates attains a particularly vivid portrayal. I have treated the question of what this means for Plato's philosophical statements, in relation to the *Phaedo* and the *Symposium*, on a given occasion, under the title 'Plato as Portraitist'[3]. In a third type of Platonic dialogues, the figure of Socrates takes such a step back in the face of the methodological consequences of thought that the task of leading the conversation goes over to someone else in the interim.

The Eleatic dialogues have been the central focus of philosophical interpretation for a long time. After the event represented by Hegel and his students, the later German Plato scholarship has also made a great contribution, first and foremost Paul Natorp, Nicolai Hartmann and Julius Stenzel, as well as the French-, Italian- and the English-speaking scholarship. In these Eleatic dialogues, not only does the figure of Socrates seem to take a step back but even the theory of ideas itself. There has literally been talk of a 'crisis in the theory of ideas', which is to have found expression in the late period, first and foremost in the *Parmenides*.

Against this, I have claimed from early on that the Platonic turn to the ideas always already includes the thought of the differentiation of the various ideas from one another. This is how the *Protagoras* is explicitly about differentiating the virtues, the *Phaedo* about the intimate connection between soul and life and the exclusion of death from the soul. In all of the discussions that Socrates conducts, the methodological precision of differentiating is at work, which Plato develops into a dialectic in the later Eleatic dialogues. It is the 'method of *diairesis*', of differentiating, which now dominates the manner in which the discussion is conducted. When Stenzel regarded the principle of *diairesis* as the turn which, after the ascent to the idea of the good, brings about the turn towards the descent, there certainly was something right about this. But what would the ascent to the idea be without the relational structure of the ideas through which the *logos* proceeds? This is true for the aporetic discussions held by the Platonic Socrates as well as for the process leading to the distinction between the sophist and the philosophical dialectician made by the Eleatic stranger in the *Sophist*.

This is how we come to realize more and more the inner unity of Platonic dialectic and the continuity [340] of its development. The world of numbers plays a special role in this, whose fundamental significance is attested to by Plato's 'unwritten doctrine'[4] and which is always in focus as the paradigm for the idea. We must also realize, what has hardly happened so far, that there is a close connection between, on the one hand, the mythically introduced doctrine of *anamnēsis*, of recollection, in the *Phaedo* (72eff) and the *Meno* (81cff) and, on the other, the dialectic of *diairesis*. Aristotle was totally right when he reckoned that *diaresis* as a mere conceptual distinction did not possess the character of a logical demonstration[5]. In fact, this is what is distinctive about *diairesis*, that it simply does not aim at being a logical demonstration but preserves its proximity to the art of discussion. *Diairesis* reflects the process of discussion itself, which progresses step by step from one agreement to the next. The logic which lies in this process is indicated in the *Meno*. There we are referred back to the kinship of all that is nature[6], that with the emergence of a memory, a whole process of questioning, seeking and recognizing is set in motion. Later, starting with the *Phaedrus* and above all in the Eleatic dialogues, the process of *diairesis* is nothing short of being demonstrated to us. What in each case leads to further understanding is always the recognition on which is based the agreement of the discussion partners on all the conceptual distinctions. The Socratic dialogue lives on in Platonic dialectic.

This has hardly played a role in the philosophical discussion of the Platonic dialectic so far. It is quite understandable that, in light of the esoteric character of these dialogues, one has paid little attention to the dialogical aspect of Platonic dialectic. One has sought to read them more like a philosophical textbook. What is more, the Aristotle of antiquity as well as the modern Platonic tradition rooted in antiquity has opened up a nexus of historical effects which the recent Plato scholarship has ultimately followed. So one has attempted a philosophical discussion with the Eleatic dialogues more from the standpoint of Aristotle and Hegel than from the standpoint of Socrates and the dialogical process.

Now, on top of everything, the recent Plato scholarship has been influenced in a decisive way – and how could it not be otherwise? – by the factual existence of the modern empirical sciences. This went to extremes when the Marburg neo-Kantian renewal of Kantian thought directly invoked Plato[7] [341] and in particular availed itself of the concept of hypothesis for the concept of the idea, with which the theory of ideas is introduced, it seems, for the first time, in the *Phaedo*. At that time (1903), building upon this concept of hypothesis, Paul Natorp interpreted the idea as a law of nature and elaborated the construct of a Plato who would have been a Kant before Kant. He found support for this from well-known passages in the *Phaedo* (100aff) in which Socrates introduces the 'hypothesis of the *eidos*'. But the Platonic Socrates did this to escape the entanglements and contradictions which come into play when we try to explain the coming to be of something and its passing away, thus also the problem of death. When he introduces the 'hypothesis' of the two, for example (101c), he wants to avoid the mind being confused by the contradiction between coming to be through addition and coming to be through division. In fact, Socrates thereby for the first time opens up the eidetic dimension, which, as a matter of fact, was something Eleatic and Pythagorean.

The true sense of this 'hypothesis', which is found in the *Phaedo*, is expressed clearly enough in the text. If we follow Aristotle's presentation in the *Nicomachean Ethics* A 4 and *Eudemian Ethics* A8, Plato did not suppose any ideas at all for numbers as such and neither could he really, as numbers can be produced by us according to the law of a series, according to the *prōton* ['first'] and *husteron* ['next']. What is thus at issue in the use of the word *hupothesis* ['supposition'] in this passage of the *Phaedo* is only the process of argumentation as it was already known even in mathematics. What follows from a supposition? This process is still completely free of the self-evident presupposition with which modern thought employs hypotheses, namely from the corroboration from experience. The neo-Kantian reinterpretation which we find in Natorp could obviously invoke the Platonic text. When we read the statement in the *Phaedo*, it says: 'If someone were to cling to the presupposition itself, would you not dismiss that person and not rather answer until you had considered whether the things you would derive from it are or are not in accord with each other?' (101d). Such a statement is ambiguous with regard to 'are in accord' (*sumphōnei ē diaphōnei* ['is in accord or in disaccord']). The statement receives a sense totally alien to what Plato thought if we understand this testing in the sense of a testing against experience, as is self-evident in the modern use of the concept of hypothesis. *Una instantia negativa* ['one negative instance'] decides the untenability of a theory. This belongs to the fundamental principles of the logic of experience, which Bacon had already formulated. By contrast, Plato or the Platonic Socrates means here, as the context indicates, a testing of a hypothesis against its consequences: whether these consequences are in accord with each other (*allēlois*). This test is supposed to prevent the fact that one may bring a supposition for discussion, whose sense, that is to say, whose logical implications, are not clear to one, with the consequence that it would be easily possible [342] to create confusion through empty artifices of argumentation in the style of the art of disputation of the time. Thus, what is identified as an explicit consequence of the hypothetical procedure is the fact that the true dialectician may only bring suppositions for further discussion at all after there is already complete and proven clarity about their implications. Whether the test should be a logical test, which guarantees the inner consistency of a line of argumentation or whether the line of argumentation should be tested in its objective content against experience, is a fundamentally different matter. The latter is in fact the self-evident presupposition which modern science makes in relation to the concept of hypothesis. This is how the Marburg neo-Kantian interpretation also appeals to Kepler in particular, who in a treatise which has become famous, refutes the well-meaning deflation by Copernicus' friends, who had undertaken to reduce the revolutionary turn in the image of the world provided by astronomy to a mere mathematical hypothesis[8]. It is now well-known that the concept of hypothesis found application for the first time exclusively in mathematics. This is reflected in Plato's *Meno* quite unambiguously (86e). But it is equally clear that, since Galileo and Kepler, the claim for something to be validated by experience and thus to be validated by reality has allowed the concept of hypothesis, which was originally only mathematical, to become the basis of modern scientific theory. This is also how Natorp, Cassirer and the Marburg School, always appealing to Kepler, have this modern concept of hypothesis in mind, and this means that they have refashioned Plato into a forerunner of the modern empirical sciences.

The neo-Kantian undertaking stands in an even more far-reaching context, which has shaped the philosophical interpretation of Plato, namely in the realm of effects belonging to German idealism, the last great attempt of modernity to reconcile the legacy of metaphysics with modern empirical science. Already Fichte and especially Schelling and Hegel were united in thinking that the deduction of fundamental concepts, of the *a priori* concepts of the understanding, in the end fully recovers the *a posteriori* of experience and consolidates its truth *a priori*, so to speak. Hermann Cohen too undertook to adapt to contemporary research in this manner in so far as he explained the construction of the object of experience by means of the infinitesimal method as the genuine distinction and verification of idealism. And Natorp read this into Plato. Transcendental idealism has had far-reaching consequences for the entire philosophical understanding of Plato[9].

[343] So misled by Aristotle, one saw the decisive problem of Plato's theory of ideas in the participation of the individual in the idea. My thesis is the following: this is not at all a Platonic problem but a Platonic presupposition. Plato always regarded the participation of the individual in the idea as something self-evident, which is what makes the supposition that there are ideas first meaningful at all. He was, for this reason, also exceedingly loose in the linguistic characterization of this relationship, whether he calls the relation of the individual to the universal presence, community, participation, intertwining, mixture or whatever else (See *Phaedrus* 100d5ff).

If we bear in mind that Plato, whom Aristotle deliberately counts among the Pythagoreans, has in mind the paradigm of mathematics, then it is the one and the many (*ta polla*, *talla*) that is the object of knowledge for him and not what is in each case an individual. It is indeed manifest that mathematical objects do not at all require a particular justification for multiplying. It is rather as Plato says, for example, in the *Sophist*, about so formal a concept as the *heteron* ['the other'] that it is divided into individuals. The expression for this is *katakekermatismenon* ['fragmented'] (258e1)[10]. Multiplicity is as original as unity, and this itself still shimmers through the Aristotelian description of the *two* principles of one and twoness. It was initially Aristotle who turned the participation of the individual in the universal into a problem through his critique of the mathematization of reality, which he saw in Plato and also in the mythical way in which the 'physics' of the *Timaeus* is described.

How little Plato did that can be seen especially from the introductory section of the *Parmenides*. There the question is posed as to how the appearance is supposed to participate in the ideas and all the answers of the young Socrates are led *ad absurdum* ['to absurdity']. By contrast, these questions are dismissed by the old Parmenides himself as patently insignificant. The sole meaning of the problem of *methexis* ['participation'] consists in the relation of the ideas to one another. This, and only this, is the true problem of participation in Plato. With this it is clear that the explanations of the Platonic dialectic attempted by neo-Kantianism – but it is not alone in this – overlook the matter on a decisive point. In a penetrating account, Nicolai Hartmann developed a theory of descending *methexis*[11]. Hartmann's secret goal was to overcome even the limit which the indivisible *eidos*, the *atomon eidos* uncontestably presented for Plato and for Aristotle, and thus [344] for dialectic and philosophy. As it is entirely clear in Natorp's famous formulation, the neo-Kantians had to reinterpret Kant in terms of post-Kantian idealism. The only sense of the 'thing in itself' that Natorp can see is in its presenting us with the infinite task of determining the object. This corresponds to the modern empirical sciences: approximating the individual to the point that empirical reality is fully determined and controlled constitutes the genuine sense of direction of knowledge. That there is truly only one *eidos*, the indivisible *eidos*, in which the process of specification necessarily comes to an end, is self-evident for anyone who takes their point of departure entirely from the dimension of speech and language, as it was for Plato and Aristotle. Under the presupposition of the modern concept of experience and science, the *idola fori* ['idols of the market place'] have, by contrast, no epistemic value because for the modern concept it is the concrete individual that is supposed to be what is genuinely known.

This is why nineteenth- and twentieth-century thought was particularly sympathetic to Plotinus' well-known question as to whether there were not ideas also of individuals (*Enneads* V7). Naturally, Plotinus did not have the modern natural sciences in the background and their concept of the principle of individuation through space and time. But this was indeed true of the whole of modernity and thus for the concept of being used in science. This has misled contemporary Plato scholarship. This is true even for Stenzel's significant treatise on *aretē* and *diairesis*, and for the general perspective which Stenzel associated with it. In his early groundbreaking work, he spends an entire chapter distinguishing the *atomon eidos* ['indivisible essence'] as the goal of *diairesis*[12] in a manner which corresponds more to the restriction of the theory of ideas to the *phusei onta* ['natural beings'] undertaken by Xenocrates and Aristotle. Contemporary scholarship also understood the relation of the *Republic* to the *Laws* in a similar way by interpreting the books on the laws as an adaptation to reality – even though this adaptation, as we can readily see, does not go quite far in its persuasiveness.

The picture composed of Aristotle's development seemed completely analogous, which is what was sketched by Hermann Usener and then Werner Jaeger. According to this picture, Aristotle was initially still a Platonist and adhered to the theory of ideas until he became more and more of an empirical researcher. This schema in fact follows the obvious analogy with the empirical sciences, which dominates the thought of modern science. Even after Jaeger's schema was given up, its fundamental inadequacy has still simply not been recognized. In my view, the *Parmenides* is an irrefutable document for the fact that Plato regards the problem of the participation of the individual in the idea as baseless. This is how he [345] declared dialectic to be the authentic medium of philosophical practice, precisely because dialectic operates in the dimension of the *eidos* and of eidetic relations, that is to say, the dimension of the relations of ideas to one another. This entails that knowing and knowledge are constituted not by the separation of the idea from the individual but only by the combination of ideas with one another. The actual sense of the *chōrismos* ['separation'] is the separation of knowledge from the contingency of uncertain experiences. Only because the idea of warmth is essentially linked with the idea of fire, can snow, as the *Phaedo* elaborates, never endure the presence of warmth and fire without disappearing. It is on this basis that the *Phaedo* draws the conclusion of the essential connection between soul and life, and grounds the exclusion of death and with it the proof of the immortality of the soul – of the soul of this person here (!). These are indeed the actual steps of knowledge. The mere supposition of an *eidos* as such is, as we already learn in the *Phaedo*, a simple matter. It is obviously a presupposition for all actual knowledge but it is itself not such knowledge. If we assess this in its complete scope, then the later turn of the Eleatic dialogues and the explicit thematization of *diairesis* are in fact only the consequence and the correct elaboration of what the turn to the *logoi* and the turn to the *eidos* in the *Phaedo* meant. In the *Meno* and the *Phaedo* the turn appears in the mythical form of *anamnēsis* ['recollection']. The introduction of *anamnēsis* in the *Meno* already shows that what is at stake in it is the defence against eristic nonsense and the defence against such spurious arguments with which the possibility of seeking, questioning and knowing is altogether denied.

Even in the *Phaedo*, the hypothesis of the *eidos*, as indicated above, aims at preserving thinking in its faithfulness to the matter at hand in opposition to all the sophistic arts of sowing confusion. Thinking is not only about viewing the many together in the unity of the *eidos*, which is found in the semantic unity of words. It is furthermore about distinguishing what is meant from the other in a definite way. This implies a reciprocal relationship between ideas. The eristic misuse of argumentation is based precisely on conscious or unconscious conceptual confusion. Thinking and the use of words entail that one sees the many together in the unity of what is meant (*sunoran eis hen eidos*). This turn to the idea, as the *Phaedo* shows, leads away from the labyrinth of the multiplicity of experience to the *logoi*, which since then is called 'dialectic'.

For modern scientific thinking, this view obviously involves a sort of limitation of knowledge. Knowledge is limited here to the relation of ideas and the structuring of what is meant, which reaches the goal of an understanding shared by all in an ultimately indivisible *eidos* in every case. This [346] is in fact the critical goal towards which we all are striving in every case in light of the commonality of the interpreted world. It lies in the essence of language. I am unable to see how we could regard the fundamental constitution of all speaking any differently than the way Plato described it as a relation of ideas. This may sound 'idealistic'. However, replacing the *eidos* or the intuitive unity of what is meant by the concept of a rule and its application, which have been championed as an alternative, seems to me to be only another way of describing the same eidetic turn which we all, in fact, accomplish as soon as we just use signs or open our mouth. In the terms of modern scientific theory, what one would like to reject as 'idealism' or 'essentialism' is conceived from the standpoint of the modern scientific concept. That which is of concern in Plato and Aristotle, however, has a fundamentally different place of value in the 'life-world'. Knowing here does not mean knowing in the sense of knowing for the sake of controlling, which dominates a field of experience. It is a knowing for the sake of ordering, which knows that in everything that happens there exists disorder and uncontrollable contingency, so that to all so-called knowledge is assigned another limit than experience. In the decisive passage in Plato's *Republic*, which discusses the descent which takes place from the presuppositionless beginning, this descent does not end in the 'this here', but ends in ideas (*teleuta eis eidē*, Republic VI, 511C2).

If we take the process by which the dialogue happens, which is presented in the *Sophist* in terms of the epistemic aim outlined above, it becomes immediately clear that the Socratic dialogic consummates in the Platonic dialectic. The *Parmenides* can be read from this perspective already as a kind of Eleatic self-critique. This self-critique resonates through the secret accord of the Eleatics with the young Socrates and with Platonic dialectic. The same is true of the situation with which the discussion in the *Sophist* between the stranger from Elea and the other participants begins. There, right at the beginning, in the greeting of the guest from Elea, the daimonic power of dialectic is made palpable[13]. As a matter of fact, people in Athens knew what had been passed on from Greater Greece, whether it was Gorgias' rhetoric or Zeno's negative dialectic operating with antitheses, which triggered the sophistic cultural revolution. In this way, right at the beginning of the *Sophist*, one is made fully aware of the gravity of the subject. Is there a difference at all between the sophist and the philosopher?

It cannot surprise us that this question is connected to that of the true politician, which was elaborated in the associated dialogue, the *Statesman*. In both cases, we can ask: are all dialecticians sophists and are all politicians demagogues? In the Greek city states, the art of oration and the art of disputation played such a fundamental political role that we [347] must really ask: are these arts concerned with truth at all? Does not Protagoras, with his pragmatic relativism, express precisely what was at play in the political life of the time? And did the ambitious young people not come to Protagoras precisely because these new arts, rhetoric and dialectic, promised them political success? This is how in Plato even the masters of rhetoric are found guilty of being ignorant and rhetoric is denounced in the *Gorgias* as the art of flattery.

One has the impression of being in a totally different world when one is dealing with actual knowledge and actual knowledge was reached in an exemplary manner in mathematics, which was flourishing at that time. The art of mere oration and empty dialectic belong to a world of semblance. In this way, one cannot arrive at any firm ground of truth because the pounding waves of oratory inundate everything. This is what those who are familiar with a science like that of mathematics must ask: Where is knowledge supposed to be in mere speeches of such a kind? This is what happened to Theaetetus. On account of this experience, he and his teacher, the mathematician Theodorus, have turned away from their friendly relations with Protagoras and from the art of mere oration in order to save themselves on the firm ground of mathematical knowledge. Even the *Parmenides* is not lacking in allusions as to how dangerous the misuse of dialectic can be when one is numbed by the waves of arguments.

The demonstration which the old Parmenides gives in the Platonic dialogue can illustrate this even today. Does this dialectic have a content at all? Readers find themselves totally helpless. We cannot seriously accept the allegorical interpretation of this dialectic which happens in late antiquity. Even modern interpreters and researchers have their doubts as to the meaning of the whole. Is this ultimately just a game?

For Plato, it must have been something different. This is already shown by the respectful way in which Parmenides and Zeno are depicted, and in particular the goodwill they display towards the young Socrates. No matter how playful the arguments Parmenides presents there look, one should certainly not doubt that what is practised in this manner is a discourse which reveals what matters. This finds explicit confirmation in the fact that the old Parmenides encourages and cautions the young Socrates that he should exclusively train in such dialectical discussions diligently, even if they seem like pure gibberish (*adoleschia*, *Parmenides* 135d5). With time, he will arrive at a better insight into the essence of the *logoi*.

This is the background for the dialectical arts against which the discussion on the sophists plays out. When Socrates, at the beginning, asks the guest from Elea about how people in Elea think about the difference between the philosopher, the sophist and the politician, the stranger reveals himself to be well prepared for this question. The art in question is obviously a dubious [348] art, which is much misused. The same question was already behind the discussion of Socrates with the young Theaetetus, when it was about the concept of knowledge. In the *Sophist*, at the end of the conversation, the extent of the proximity between the sophist and the demagogue comes through significantly enough (*Sophist*, 268b), and this leads to the subsequent dialogue on the true politician. There are yet other indications of this kind, which allow us to see the general background, for example, the question of whether tame animals can also be hunted (*Sophist* 222b). With this question, we must think of the sophists as well as of the demagogues. The distinction between the hunter and the herder puts both the false dialectician and the false politician completely in question. The structure of relations within which the distinction between the sophist and the true dialectician is made reaches far and wide. We are in fact not dealing here with empty displays of brilliance. It means something, when in the discussion with Socrates, the young Theaetetus, despite his scientific genius, did not know how to say what actual knowledge really is. Only the discussion with the stranger from Elea will lead the young Theaetetus to see clearly that there can also be actual knowledge in mere *logoi*. Obviously, one must be prepared for the fact that it will be a difficult task to make him (and us) recognize the difference between the philosopher and the sophist.

Ultimately, it will turn out that there is not a fixed distinguishing feature in the desired sense, for example, that an argument either has philosophical content (and this means a truth content) or that it produces what merely seems like actual knowledge. It will turn out that what is at stake in the distinction between the philosopher and the sophist (and also by the way the politician) are decisions and attitudes regarding how to live. It is thus advisable to distance oneself, even in the case of the *Sophist*, from the scientific theoretical interests manifested by Plato interpretation hitherto. In this, we should not underestimate the kind of progress in methodological consciousness the classificatory procedure represents, which leads to conceptual division. Paul Friedländer rightly pointed out that even the brilliant scientific achievement of the young Theaetetus (which is mentioned in *Theaetetus* 147dff) relies on the same procedure of division. It is especially true of the classificatory genius of Aristotle that his conceptual divisions belong to his masterly achievements. All this played a great role in the Hellenistic period – even if outsiders sneer at it (as comedy indicates). In fact, we must understand this procedure of conceptual division from the perspective of the natural and self-evident procedure with which anybody tries to overcome confusion, complication and false appearance. We know this from the many beginnings of the Socratic [349] dialogues written by Plato, in the way they explicitly set themselves the task of distinguishing concepts. For example, in the *Protagoras*, the discussion begins with the question of the unity and multiplicity of the virtues. We understand immediately that we are not dealing with a mere classification and not even with a method of a science with which it organizes its findings or endeavours to define its concepts. What we are dealing with here is something that lies much deeper and given the linguistic cast of all our experiences, it reaches down into the conduct of our life. This is how it is in general. Dialogue and *diairesis* are two forms in which the thinking reason of human beings and its linguistic articulation are realized. Both are called *logoi* in Plato: thinking and speaking, in which one makes one's distinctions. It is the completely vast space that is opened up in speech and language, and determines our being and behaviour. Mere naming already entails an identification and equally the semantic content which is attached to words. Every discussion takes place in the space of questions characterized by differentiating, which is manifested in the words available to us as well as in that which is said and distinguished with these words. It is striking that, in Plato, Prodicus is depicted as a sophist who revels in distinguishing lexical meanings while being treated not entirely without goodwill in Plato's dialogues and enjoying a certain ironic presence. There is certainly something of an irony also in the distinctions presented in the *Sophist*. This is true as much for the words suggested for the distinctions as for the things themselves, which become clearer through them. There is always something like a foreknowledge that is expressed in this. When one tries to define something or name it, then one must already know what that which is sought is. Behind all division of concepts and things stands the primordial relationship of question and answer, of seeking and finding, which Socrates has in mind with the concept of *anamnēsis*.

In the same manner, in the *Sophist* we must pay attention to what is anticipated, which is delineated in the attempts at definition and the conceptual divisions. That the distinction between the philosopher and the sophist would be an extremely difficult matter was clear from the very outset, and obviously there are multiple possibilities for undertaking conceptual divisions here. There are many pre-judgements and pre-concepts at play there, which indicate an imprecise and shaky pre-understanding. This is completely natural and goes with the way opinions are formed and reflected in language. The sophist is thus something difficult to grasp. However, there is one thing common to all these opinions on the sophists and that is that they constantly want to appear as the ones who know. Those who want to come to a clear idea about a confusing phenomenon, as is customary for mathematicians in their science, for example, will first of all orient themselves to external things, above all else, to the commercial aspect which is [350] part and parcel of the sophist's dealings. The clever Eleatic stranger leading the discussion knows the kind of prejudices that may already be present in his discussion partner. Even the reader does not need to be hinted that the sample definition of the angler carries an ironic tone. In the eyes of a mathematician, professional sophists are really something like anglers. They fish for human beings and sustain themselves by tutoring them, like anglers catch fish, sustaining themselves on fish. There are indeed many witty allusions to this in the dialogue. Yet, in the end, the figure of the sophist becomes clearer and clearer through these attempts at definition. A common trait stands out despite the dazzling multiplicity of guises taken on by the sophist. It is their anti-logic, their virtuoso capacity to find objections and to confuse and to refute. This trait in fact seems to be common to the sophist and the dialectician, the one who is called a philosopher.

In fact, there is an essential difference. Sophists appear and present themselves as the ones who know how to refute everything and therefore seem like they know everything. It is not without vigour that Theaetetus decisively rejects the claim to know everything, which is implied in the figure of the sophist (*Sophist* 233a). Those who possess actual knowledge always know about the limits of their knowledge. This is one of the fundamental presuppositions underlying the discussion that the Eleatic stranger conducts with the young mathematician. Theaetetus is someone who is familiar with genuine knowledge. This is precisely what grants Socrates in the *Theaetetus* and the Eleatic stranger here the opportunity not simply to expose what sophists do, as Plato so often does, but to defend dialectic as actual knowledge. What Plato called dialectic is something different from the pseudo-knowledge of those who have bamboozling counter-arguments for everything and thereby seem to know it all. The two Platonic dialogues, the *Theaetetus* and the *Sophist*, have the unitary task of making dialectic come to light as philosophy.

Our reflections have taken us closer to the real core of the dialogue. It still does not at all seem as though there should be any particular difficulty if one is certain that the sophist is distinguished from the philosopher by the fact that the former only pretends to have an apparent knowledge whereas the latter seeks true knowledge. Or is dialectic always just what sophists do? We should not think it is that simple to reject this question in a convincing manner. It is rather now that the discussion enters its serious stage. What the stranger now effects on the young Theaetetus is a true masterpiece of intellectual guidance. Both are united in the view that what the sophist flaunts cannot be true knowledge. Yet, why do sophists exercise such an effect? Theaetetus must himself wonder, who has had prior experience of this effect on himself and who could observe it all around on young people (233b). That this is not a matter of actual knowledge, [351] of this he remains absolutely certain (233c). The example of the showman who simply knows how to imitate everything makes the outrageousness of the sophistical claim clear. Is it then reasonable to assume that it is an imitative art employing speech and argumentation in the manner of showmanship which deceives the young, as long as they lack experience?

With this, we have the keyword for later discussion. Even the young Theaetetus is still lacking in the experience of reality, as he himself knows (234e). This is why the stranger from Elea wants to bring him closer to the matter at hand so that he does not fall for the jester, the showman and the imitator anymore. It is essential to come close to the matter at hand, if one wants to avoid the deceptive effects that come from being at a distance. There is a decisive difference here, namely, between an image that reflects something real and a deceptive pseudo-image. This is apparently something new for Theaetetus (235d4).

This difference between image and pseudo-image is clarified by way of what is grotesque to the eye. There are sculptures, which are dimensionally correct and then there are also other larger-than-life statues. In order for the latter to *appear* dimensionally correct and right in their effect, they have to be shaped *in opposition to* the true dimensions. The parts to be seen from afar have to be excessively enlarged. We can leave aside as to whether Plato and even just the stranger from Elea would seriously call such statues pseudo-images. Perhaps, for purposes of illustration they accept the lack of real aesthetic standards, as Plato indeed otherwise does, for example, in his famous critique of the poets. Here in fact the Eleatic stranger is demanding all sorts of things when he places all of painting with the arts of illusion (*phantastikē*) because it only appears beautiful (*dia tēn ouk ek kalou thean* ['through a view that is not favourable'] 236b4) but on closer inspection turns out to be a false impression [*Anschein*]. In any case, what we are dealing with here is a young mathematician for whom in his own dealings with figures it is self-evident that they mirror the actual mathematical states of affairs.

Anyway, it remains remarkable that it should be unclear even to the stranger from Elea as to whether sophists produce through their art images or pseudo-images in their speeches. This unclarity will necessitate all the twists and turns of the ensuing discussion, compelling a critique of 'father' Parmenides. This is what will soon transpire. Are all mere speeches not deceptive to the extent that they place before the eyes as if it were present something that is not actually before the eyes or not with the vivid self-evidence which mathematical knowledge produces? Obviously, in *logoi*, in mere speeches, it is not so easy to establish and make palpable the difference between making an image which is true to the subject matter and making an image which only seems to give us an impression of being true to the subject matter, [352] as is possible, for example, with regard to a statue. In the latter case, we only need to move closer to the statue seen from afar in order to establish irrefutably the distortion of the proportions which from a greater distance gave the illusion of being correct. This explains why the Eleatic stranger himself is not quite sure whether he should count the activity of the sophist as an argumentative art which mirrors the facts commensurately or as a mere pseudo-art. Theaetetus does not seem to know of any other images at all than the dimensionally correct kind (235e3). But even if images were only images, is every image itself not that which it mirrors?

This is the problem that constitutes the difficulty here, and this is what is emphatically characterized by the Eleatic stranger as the strongest position of the sophist. If one wants to follow the great Parmenides, there can be no non-being at all that one could sensibly assert. But Theaetetus avoids the question of what *logos* is. He does not understand – not even now – what *logos* actually is. As the Eleatic stranger demonstrates to him that one cannot be saying non-being because then one would be saying nothing at all, Theaetetus takes this to be the end (*telos*, 237e7) of all the difficulties. But now the Eleatic stranger leads him into a new, even greater difficulty. If to say non-being is a non-saying, thus no saying at all, then by doing this, which is what those from Elea still do, the saying of being is definitely not secured in an unassailable manner. As explicitly declared, it is rather here that the utmost difficulty begins (238a). To a being there indeed may still belong something else that is a being but it is certainly not the case with non-being.

This is the new theme, the *prosgignesthai* ['to be added'], in which the structure of the *logos* vaguely appears for the first time. The young Theaetetus understands this easily because he is used to assigning numbers to beings (*prospherein* ['to attribute'] 238b3). In fact, this is true not only for all beings but also for non-beings: numbers can be added to them. But what do we truly gain then with the inexpressibility of non-being? It must be repeated: Theaetetus still does not understand what '*logos*' is. The new argument is this: non-being itself must be assumed in speech if one wants to reject it. This is the most serious question, as the Eleatic stranger formulates it, because it causes all arguments against non-being to end in a complete failure (239b). Yet, with this, the sophist would again be on top and could be confident of making all of his assertions because there would be no such thing as pseudo-art and nothing like non-being at all.

The ironic appeal which the Eleatic stranger directs towards Theaetetus in this passage (239d) leads us on. To be sure, it is a naïve reply when Theaetetus seeks to demonstrate the actuality of appearance by pointing to mirror reflections which occur in nature and are a true nothing. He has thus not truly understood the radicality of the sophistic objection. [353] But now Theaetetus can no longer avoid realizing that all of these are *eidōla* and what this implies (240aff). The same goes for false speeches to whose impression one succumbs, as Theaetetus knows from experience, despite the fact that there is nothing to them (240d). Still, the point is that in the image, whatever it may be, non-being is indissolubly linked to being. The image is indeed not that which it mirrors, and yet what we call a picture [*Bild*] is really there. The sophistic objection contests precisely this fact that one can *mean* or *say* something at all that is not itself, thus non-being and therefore appearance and false opinion can simply not exist in the *logoi* (241aff). This is quite a negative obstacle and Theaetetus does not know how to go on.

At this point, the stranger from Elea wants to come to his aid (241c). With this, the main philosophical part of the dialogue begins, which is devoted to proving and overcoming Parmenides's prohibition of non-being. This main part is a self-contained section which provisionally pushes into the distance the attempt to capture the sophist. This discussion is certainly supposed to bring the young Theaetetus in close proximity to the matter at hand, but the course of this argument is exceedingly difficult. It would be presumptuous to treat such a philosophical masterpiece of instructive discussion in a few pages. One has to re-read the Platonic text again and again. Everything is full of subtle expressions and hidden allusions. We can hear Parmenides in the background and one cannot but also think of Aristotle, who will be attaining dominance, and his commentators, and finally Hegel, who brings so much to an end and grants resolution to so many matters. In this, I completely refrain from engaging with modern logic, whose shiny equipment worked out the logical problem of predication in the most subtle manner and approaches the Platonic discussion like a logical treatise. I see my task completely differently, more precisely, as developing the arguments used in the Platonic discussion from the standpoint of the persuasive force they have for someone who must first learn what a concept is – and the young Theaetetus is not the only such person. It is no easy task to follow the discussion led by the Eleatic stranger in such a way that the dialogue is understood as leading the discussion partner to the right distinction between the sophist and the philosopher. It is an *epagōgē* ['leading to', 'induction'].

Theaetetus is now supposed to be led to an understanding of what an actual philosopher is. This brings him face to face with the greatest difficulties. Admittedly, he is certain that sophists can only be pseudo-knowers but what actual philosophers are and what their knowledge is are totally unclear to the renegade student of the great sophist Protagoras and the young researcher that Theaetetus is. To him, all such arguments [of the sophist and the philosopher] sound like mere pseudo-knowledge. He must be led beyond himself and come to acknowledge that he himself does not know something that [354] is absolutely necessary for him to know. What a mere seeming is supposed to be is thus not intelligible and yet, it is indispensable to know this if we want to ward off the pseudo-knowledge of the sophists.

The composition of the dialogue is thus by and large clear. The critical question will be: what is seeming? What kind of seeming is it through which the sophists know how to move in such fatal proximity to the philosophers and dialecticians? It will be difficult to lead the young mathematician, who is entirely focused on the knowledge of immutable and unchanging relations, of numbers and figures, to a suitable conception of knowledge and to the consciousness of his own activity. The path which the Eleatic stranger must take for this cannot be simple. To understand this path, as readers, and to go along demand a cautious deconstruction of what is invariably self-evident to us. But the following point must convince Theaetetus: non-being (*to mē on*) cannot be encountered as itself (238b9, 239a9). Disregarding the sections most often treated in the scholarship, I would like to go over the lesson that Theaetetus receives.

The Eleatic stranger succeeds in making it clear to Theaetetus that he himself is caught up in difficulties (*en soi* ['in you'] 239b5). Theaetetus must realize this. If he wants to assert that sophists possess pseudo-knowledge, then he must be able to come to terms with this difficulty. He cannot avoid the fact that he is thereby going against the Eleatic prohibition which has a strong legitimacy in his own mathematical world, in which there is really no movement. This is why it seems to him quite strange (*atopon*) and yet unavoidable to interweave non-being with being [240c1]. With this, Theaetetus himself is caught in an aporia and is helpless when it comes to countering the objection of the sophist who contests that one can think non-being and *pseudos* ['false'] at all. The stranger now tries to assist Theaetetus as the sophists entrench themselves behind the impossibility of non-being and in this way brings him to reflect upon the meaning of 'being'.

The incomprehensibility of non-being is part of the essential legacy of Eleatic philosophy. This in itself is not a new topic. However, in the course of the dialogue not only the thinking of non-being, but also the thinking of being is recognized as problematic. This could already be seen in the didactic poem of Parmenides when it is claimed throughout so many verses that the many does not exist. In naming as well as in meaning, like in speaking of being as one, there is always already the many. Saying being involves self-contradiction. When spoken of, the one being becomes a many. In what follows, this is elevated into a theme. It is an ironic point that the young Theaetetus will himself of all people be required to ask what *to on*, what 'being' means (243d3).

We find ourselves at the critical highpoint where the need for the question concerning being will become unavoidable. Plato registers [355] this highpoint by having the Eleatic stranger make three requests (241cff), the third one of which is to accept the crazy (*anō – katō* ['upside down'], 242ab) argument.

This evokes the Platonic *Parmenides*. This dialogue presents a real challenge, as was obvious from its reception in antiquity and as it is for the modern scientific way of thinking. One asks what it is: Comedy? Non-sense? Mysticism? Sophistry? Or an elementary exercise in dialectic? And Hegel praised this as the greatest work of art in ancient dialectic! Now, the critique of Parmenides in the *Sophist*, which is what concerns us here, is no mysterious game like the dialogue Parmenides. Nevertheless, the argumentative style employed by the stranger from Elea is comparable, particularly in the variations on the greatest kinds (alongside 'being', concepts such as 'movement' and 'rest' and the more formal 'reflective concepts', such as 'identity' and 'difference'). We must listen to the message from Elea to learn its secret logic. There seems to be a good motivation for the discussion to have to turn to Parmenides' concept of being. In the incomprehensible relationship between being and seeming [*Scheinen*], between appearance [*Erscheinung*], seeming [*Schein*] and impression [*Anschein*], there lies hidden an intertwining of being and non-being. What lies in the background is perhaps the almost irresolvable relationship which pervades the whole didactic poem of Parmenides, namely, the relation between divine knowledge and human knowledge and opinion. Parmenides set his poem in Homeric verses. In a similar way, the Eleatic critique of the *Sophist* looks almost like a didactic work set in dialogical verses. The task will be to follow the course of the discussion and to take the step from convinced opinion, which keeps to the Eleatic *noein*, to the Platonic *logos*. The discussion takes its careful course in order to make us aware of the preconceived opinions and prejudices at work in the discussion partner and to overcome gradually his resistance[14]. Whoever tries to transform what comes to expression there into compelling arguments only understands half of what happens there and what the text gives us to understand.

One needs to see how the young mathematician is forced to reflect. Capturing the sophist seems impossible without the step towards the concept. This step was obviously not yet taken by those who came earlier, who [356] sought to differentiate *ta onta* ['beings'], howsoever many and howsoever different kinds there were (242c). The stranger even designates what was said earlier about being as *muthos* ['story', 'myth'], obviously because the sense of being is presupposed in it as something self-evident. At first glance, it indeed seems as though what we have before us here is the first doxography, that is to say, an overview of the doctrines of the others which Plato places in the mouth of his discussion leader as someone who has knowledge. We are familiar with something similar from the late treatises of Aristotle, by means of which Aristotle, since Theophrastus, dominates the entire tradition of Greek philosophy. In fact, Aristotle's doxography is something very different from this Platonic-Eleatic overview. Aristotle simply applies his doctrine of the four causes to his predecessors. He had developed this doctrine in the *Physics* and for physics (*Physics* B 7), and on this basis he endeavoured to bring the sense of being to concepts in his *Metaphysics*. Plato does not apply any doctrine. He rather lets the Eleatic stranger follow a Pythagorean schema and enquires into the number of beings. He lets the real question concerning being emerge only gradually from the critical analysis of those who came earlier. As a result, the discussion partner reveals himself to be helpless as he is simply incapable of mastering the ontological values of being and seeming. Yet, he shows himself in this context to be familiar with Parmenides' didactic poem as well as with the doctrines of the Ionian physiologists, against whom the Eleatic critique is directed. The constructive overview of the previous doctrines in fact serves to make us realize that 'being', whether one or many, must be a third (243e2).

Theaetetus certainly plays a modest role in the discussion. And yet it is not out of mere adherence to the dialogue form where a lecture would actually not be out of place[15]. The play of question and answer, which the Eleatic stranger plays with Theaetetus, might appear downright elementary. In fact, what is indicated in it is something decisively new, namely the emergence of the concept and the justification through dialectic, of which Theaetetus is still not at all capable. The problem is well known in Plato. It is about the step from opinions (*doxai*) to the *logos*. In Parmenides' didactic poem, this was only a juxtaposition and was introduced as a divine revelation, which was granted to the chosen one. In my contributions to this didactic poem[16], I have tried to show how the step towards [357] the concept is indicated in the use of the singular *to on*. I have equally underscored that there is no singular of *doxa* at all in the poem. The transition to the concept has not developed far enough as to be able to see the many together under the one. Plato is well aware of this and so it is only easy and cautious steps that the Eleatic stranger demands of the young discussion partner in order to lead him on the way to the concept.

The critical examination at first establishes that the Eleatic doctrine of 'one being' is not tenable. Theaetetus still tries to salvage the being-one as the sense of two designations for the one (244cd). But this remains equally futile as with the alleged being-whole of being. The result is that being is not something easier to grasp than non-being (246a). The way to the concept still seems rocky and yet, a first step along this way has been taken when 'being' is thought neither as *being* one [*eines seiend*] nor as two nor as whole nor as not-whole. It is not a telling of myths anymore. The concept comes into view.

A further step along this way announces itself now in the transformation of the scene when the Titanic struggle between the materialists (who can even almost be called Heracliteans) and the friends of ideas is depicted (246aff)[17]. One senses that both are extreme positions which fundamentally already imply a concept of being. This is indicated by the one-sidedness of these positions, which the discussion brings to light. It cannot well be the case that the restless change of becoming and the unassailable stability of the order of ideas and numbers constitute an irreconcilable opposition. As what we have here is a *gigantomachia* ['battle of giants'], we become anxious for a final decision. This was also the case in the mythical gigantomachy of Hesiod and its echoes in the Prometheus drama of Aeschylus, both of which aim at founding the enduring domination of the Olympian Zeus. One is expecting that not only the friends of ideas will not be defeated but also that a real reconciliation between the opponents is intended. In fact, the position of the materialists is not depicted in the crude sense upon which already in the *Theaetetus* a most sophisticated theory of movement was superimposed. Now, in the *Sophist*, the young Theaetetus is immediately ready to credit the materialists with appropriate improvements. Obviously, the lesson that Theaetetus had received from Socrates has already borne fruit. The being of movement and becoming other have gained in importance for the question concerning true being.

Besides, we can see that the friends of ideas are depicted in the we-form by Theaetetus – so much does the young mathematician belong to them. [358] We also note that, when universal kinetics is brought to its common concept, namely to the concept of *dunamis* ['potentiality'] (247e), Theaetetus only agrees with great reluctance. The same happens at 248c10. There, Theaetetus insists on his unchangeable world of ideas and when the concept of *dunamis* is demanded of him, the stranger simply cannot get his consent. He must give up the argument of *dunamis* (248e) and take refuge in an argument *ad hominem* ['directed at the person'], that being cannot really be rigid and lifeless (249a). Here, even the friend of ideas must admit to mobility because there must be life and thinking. Both positions, however, cannot be sustained.

So, the choice between the two opposing sides seems in the end to be a difficult one, when one has to choose. One would like to do what children do when they have to choose. They like 'both' the best. But becoming in movement and the unassailable order now appear to exclude each other completely. The tangibility of the experience of reality and the intangibility of the unchanging ideas contain no satisfactory answer to the question of what 'being' actually means. But this means that the sense of being lying between motion which is graspable and unchangeability which is ungraspable, can be grasped as little as non-being (250c9). If being is either moved or immovable, what sort of being should there then still be at all? In what direction should we look? Is there a third then (250c1)? This statement in fact stared Heidegger in the face at one time, when he was tackling the question of being. Here the statement introduces a step which ultimately leads to the thinking of *logos* (of being as *logos*). If being and non-being are both equally ungraspable, then this points to their belonging inseparably to each other, thus to their *relationship* to each other (251a). 'Relationship' is in fact the very structure of *logos* itself. This is the new horizon in which the legitimacy of dialectic proves itself in its objective right. Theaetetus again shows great difficulty understanding this.

We see how difficult it is to compel Theaetetus the mathematician to reflect on himself. He still does not know what *logos* is. The stranger from Elea had begun in a very ingenious manner by thematizing the relationship between being and non-being and thus introducing the concept of *logos* with which Theaetetus, on the basis of his science, is very familiar as a mathematical term (for 'proportion').

For whatever the case may be, the relation between two quantities is obviously independent of the specific quantities which are in relation to each other at any one time. That we are concerned with such a combination, thus with such a relationship, was already constantly present in the discussion[18].

[359] All the same, Theaetetus first needs an example to be shown what *logos* means here. The example of the human being (*anthrōpos*) is introduced under the formal point of view that the one is associated with many possible attributes (251ab). Here something like a Platonic doctrine of categories shines through. The one, which is many, between *poion* ['which one'] and *poson* ['how much']. More important is the fact that Plato here, besides the *auto*, the human being as such, also explicitly mentions in the same sense (*kata ton auton logon*) the other, *ta alla*, in each case as the other of the one, which is at the same time many. Besides, we indeed know from Plato the use of the 'what' (*ti*) and the 'how' (*poion*), in which *poion* means the variable and that which does not belong to the essence. But here it is made explicit that even this primordial differentiation between *ti* and *poion* is to be taken entirely as a form, and this means that they are interchangeable, so that we can ask just as much about the essence of the 'what' as about the essence of the 'how'[19]. In Plato, this is expressed as follows: whatever 'being' may mean, in any case *ousia* ['being', 'essence', 'substance'] must be something that can inhere in everything that is and can be there, together with it. This is definitely not the Aristotelian theory of the substance as *hupokeimenon*, to which everything can be attributed. Expressed in Aristotelian concepts, 'being' is rather *pros ti,* a term which is not already found in Plato like *ti, poion* and *poson* – because it is indeed omnipresent.

In this way, a universal access has been gained and this is also explicitly stated (251cd). With this, the whole discussion that follows receives its theme. It is the *dunamis koinōnias*, the possibility or capacity or however we want to call this 'ability' [*Können*] of being together, which is expressed in the *logos*. This is truly still no real insight into the essence of the *logos* and, as a matter of fact, Theaetetus remains completely resolute on one point: 'But in any case, movement and rest cannot be there at the same time' (252d). This is conceded by the Eleatic stranger with suspicious haste and emphasis: 'in accordance with the greatest necessities', this is impossible. Nevertheless, being (*to on*), which can be connected with everything, is said to abide as that which connects. Clearly, not everything can be connected with everything. This is immediately conceded by the Eleatic stranger. We see how carefully he prepares the young mathematician for the true essence of the *logos*: a seeing together and a differentiation. Very slowly, under the title of the 'greatest kinds', *kinēsis* ['movement'] and *statis* ['rest'] are brought close to each other (and with this finally physics and mathematics, what is likewise indicated in the *Philebus* (26d) in the third kind, the *genesis eis ousian* ['coming to being']). [360] The most comprehensive kinds are illustrated through the example of the vowels and their difference from the other letters of the alphabet. This reference to the alphabet is not quite an arbitrary example. The alphabetic script is indeed quite a tremendous achievement of abstraction which, like literacy and the musical theory of harmony, impresses on the concept of knowing a specific form. In both of these realms, we are obviously dealing with a professional mastery which rests on a structured multiplicity in which one is well-versed. It is striking that it is in this context that the concept of *genē*, of kinds appears for the first time in the discussion and is thereon retained. Just as in the case of these abilities in writing and music, now even in the universal field of tasks pertaining to discourse that is true to the subject matter, that is to say, in the ability with the *logoi*, the knowledge which belongs to this field is designated as the all-encompassing science which is the greatest of all and is explicitly attributed to philosophy. Of this discourse, of the dialectic, it is said to consist in *kata genē diaireisthai* ['to divide by genera'] (253d). This means that words and concepts are not merely put up for show like the *eidōla legomena* ['spoken images'] (234c6) but that in them distinctions are made, which articulate in a consistent manner and are true to the subject matter.

In whatever way we prefer to explain the details of the much-discussed description of the dialectic ability of the philosophers (253d), it describes in any case the true dialectic instead of the misuse of language for eristic tricks, characteristic of the sophist. This is emphatically underscored (254a). When striving to discover the essence of the sophist, we see how the sophist flees into the obscurity of non-being. To this difficulty of tracking down the sophist there corresponds a similar difficulty with respect to philosophers. Of them it is said that they too are difficult to spot because they stand all too much in the glaring light of being. What this means is at most hinted at. So, it is in this context that one speaks of most human beings being so unfree (253c7) that they are unable to look up to the divine (254b1). Nothing more is said about this. The task is indeed not to seek the philosopher but the sophist, who stands in the obscurity of non-being. Yet, one does not need to be clairvoyant indeed to find the separation of the theme of the sophist from the theme of the philosopher positively ironic. As if one could say what differentiates the philosopher from the sophist and what differentiates being from seeming without knowing both, seeming and being. On the way to plunging deeper into the greatest kinds of being, which make sense to Theaetetus and appear strange to us on account of their apparent heterogeneity, it becomes possible to attribute being to non-being so much so that even the reluctant partner can give his consent (256b8). This without a doubt opens a new horizon. The compatibility between movement and rest, between becoming [361] (or changeability) and being (or continued existence) becomes the decisive new insight. What this means is not pursued further but one can think of the mutual convergence of the two adversaries in the battle of giants. Here, one side would understand being as *dunamis*, on account of the ungraspable nature of *phronēsis* ['practical wisdom'], while on the other side, the friends of the ideas are compelled to acknowledge life and *noūs* ['mind', 'reason'], and thus movement. When one recognizes mobility and awareness here in the unity of life and soul, then one is also reminded that the same construction of the world-soul in the *Timaeus* determines the whole structure of the cosmogony[20].

In any case, the objection of the sophist can be overcome. But with this, the problem of differentiating the sophist from the philosopher has obviously not yet been resolved even if one finally knows how to justify the intertwining of being with non-being and seeming. It is only at the end of the discussion that we see that in this way the corrupted essence [*Unwesen*] of the sophist and also the true essence of the dialectician are still not identified. Only a pre-condition for this task has been fulfilled, namely clearing away the sophistic misuse of the Eleatic thesis, which says that one can neither think nor say non-being. In order to capture the sophist, the discussion must take yet another completely different turn, as will be shown later.

The choice of the greatest kinds (*on* ['being'], *stasis* ['rest'], *kinēsis* ['movement'], *tauton* ['the same'], *thateron* ['the different'] (255d ff)) appears somewhat arbitrary. What they are supposed to be is clear from the analogy. They are supposed to be like the vowels of being. Vowels do not mean anything by themselves, but they merely make syllables, words and sentences possible, which mean something. Vowels thus represent the bond of all speech. If they are called the greatest kinds, it seems to mean this: they can be there with everything, just as numbers can be there with everything, whatever it may be that is so and so many. The fact that these greatest kinds are there with everything thus does not mean that there is a highest universal kind, for example, the one, which is differentiated in multiple ways and becomes progressively more particularized. Here what the greatest kinds are has another kind of universality. Husserl would call this universality something like 'formal-ontological'. Plato calls it *aitia*, causes of everything. As that which can connect everything, they are what connects, like the vowels. Even being (*ousia* 250b9) is not introduced here as the highest kind. It is there with, albeit with everything, just like sameness and difference, as is shown later, are there with every being. But it should be noted that now even movement and rest, [362] changeability and unchangeability, and indeed along with being, the *on*, are accepted as something that is attributed to everything and connects everything. In this we can see again how much the Eleatic stranger takes into account the presupposition of the partner. But one wonders as to what can now move Theaetetus to agree when he had always insisted on the opposite. Obviously, in going along with the Eleatic stranger's course of thinking, he has at any rate arrived far enough to see that being can belong to everything, to the changeable as well as to the unchangeable. Obviously, what this means that being can be attributed to movement, to this non-being is, at first, certainly still not clear to him at all. Presumably, he still continues to think, in the way he had represented the friends of the ideas, that only ideas are *ontōs ousia* ['really being'] (248a11), *ēremoun* ['being at rest'] (248e4), *stasis* ['rest'] (249c1); all becoming is *allote allōs* ['different at different times'] (248a12).

What I most of the time render here with 'being there with' is paraphrased by the Eleatic stranger first as 'mixture' (*mixis*) and only gradually does he introduce the Platonic expression *methexis*, *participatio*, participation. Even the latter expression is often alternated in Plato with other expressions, such as mixture, community, existence, etc. 'Participation' and 'taking part' do not mean here a having or a taking but a being[21].

Whether it is about the being-together of a concept, of an idea with the other, or whether it is about the being-together of the idea with a being, always individual, or whether it is about the being-together of the idea with the *psuchē*, thus with the knower, these three connotations of the concept of participation have been rightly distinguished in Plato[22]. In any case, what we have here is a universal structural relation of a singular sort. It can be described neither by doing and suffering nor by imitation and the like, as if these kinds were ontological domains of their own. This is not what these kinds are. They are *aitia*. For example, it is also said of mobility that it 'is different from difference [*Verschiedenheit*]' (and similarly from sameness and *stasis*, 256c5). By contrast, everything that is is different. Each being participates in difference in so far as it is not another being. 'The nature of difference manifests itself as being cut up in multiple ways like knowledge' (*kathaper epistēmē* ['like knowledge'], 257c8). The result is that (258e) difference is nothing else than the being of what is different in its own way of being cut up. Only in this sense is difference there with everything that is different. Again, it is more than a mere comparison when difference is compared here with the sciences. Difference is thus present in all that is different and nowhere else, just as [363] knowing means that one can always distinguish [*unterscheiden*] or, as our language says, that one knows the ins and outs of something. We must insist that these 'greatest' kinds should be thought 'transcendentally', that is to say, not in accordance to the order of genus and species. They are rather supposed to be that which makes all distinction, specification, identification and thus all-knowing and knowledge possible at all, just like vowels make articulate speech possible – and even *kinēsis* and *stasis* belong here. These conclusions become significant for a further step.

The stranger shows that the *logos as such* in which all these 'greatest' kinds are intertwined, in so far as it is itself an all-encompassing 'family' [*Geschlecht*], is the greatest kind in its own right. Without it, there would be no philosophy (260a). Again, Theaetetus hardly understands what this actually means (*ouk emathon* ['I do not understand'] 260b4). It must be first shown to him that *logos* and *doxa* are formally teeming with non-being, deception and false semblance (260c8). This is explained to him by means of the differentiation between the grammatical concepts of noun (*onoma*) and verb (*rhēma*).

This grammatical structural analysis of *logos* marks the decisive step that Plato takes beyond Parmenides. The didactic poem certainly reflected the inseparability of 'being' from *noein* ['knowing']. This inseparability reinforced there what Parmenides always had in mind, namely that being is 'presence'. But now we see that naming is still no saying. Words strung together are still not speech which says and reveals something (*dēlounta*, 261de). There is a statement only when the *onoma*, the 'noun', is not lacking a *rhēma*, a verb [*Zeitwort*]. Time [*Zeit*]?[23] Just as in the Germanization of *rhēma as Zeitwort*, the flow of words was doubtlessly heard in the Greek word, thus *kinēsis* and with this even time. All this obviously appears outright unintelligible to Theaetetus, who is otherwise only used to dealing with numbers. Responses of the type: 'how?', 'I have not understood this' (*Sophist* 262ff) become frequent. Here *logos* is precisely a different sort of combination than the sequence of numbers. It is not only that *logos* includes or excludes the mutual compatibility of two ideas. What is found in the *logos* is also the temporalization of the statement itself, which in the example given means this Theaetetus here, this human being thrown into time.

When it is said 'Theaetetus flies', then there can be no doubt that this is false because Theaetetus is a human being and not a bird. The incompatibility of the idea of the human being with the idea of flying makes it clear that here something impossible is stated. It is not really something incorrect, although it is also undoubtedly incorrect. This is why 'who is sitting here' is explicitly added to 'Theaetetus flies', in order to differentiate the impossible from the incorrect, as it were. It could also be false that this Theaetetus is sitting here. He could surely also be standing in front of him. It is not for nothing, [364] it seems to me, that this statement 'Theaetetus flies' is characterized as *ho sos logos*, as 'your statement'. The impossibility of flying befits this person as much as the correctness or incorrectness of sitting or standing. It befits this person as any other. His being human with all his essential possibilities and impossibilities are his own. It is this Theaetetus who is sitting here. This is thus the function that the chosen example has for the proper train of thought belonging to the discussion, namely the guidance of Theaetetus who has become tired of empty polemics. When he cites the text by Protagoras on wrestling in this dialogue, he is visibly not enthusiastic about doing this (*Sophist* 232d). With this, the turn taken by the discussion towards *logos* as a kind acquires a peculiar significance.

The grammatical transition from the togetherness of ideas to the statement constituted by the togetherness of *onoma* and *rhēma* is in fact an important step (261d). It illustrates the self-evident nature of the participation of the individual in the idea, or better: the present of the idea in the individual. Participation is involved in all talk about ideas and thus constitutes in no way any special theme of dialectic. It is incorporated into the experience in the life-world, an experience which can never be completely captured by the knowledge that can be learned, the *mathemata*. Whether it is this Theaetetus, whether he is sitting or standing, this must be seen. This cannot be known in the way we know that a human being cannot fly, whether it is this individual or another[24].

And here we see at once the *pseudos*, which Theaetetus could not manage to explain in his discussion with Socrates (in the *Theaetetus*), demonstrated in relation to himself. He recognizes in the example involving him that the mixture of perception and opinion can indeed be false (264b2), and it is thus well and truly undeniable that a statement or a *logos* can be false. The escape of the sophist has failed. The final operation for the capture of the sophist can begin.

Let us think back to how, at the beginning of the discussion, the already clear form of the sophist seemed to escape again into the ungraspable because the differentiation between speeches which depict something and speeches which seem to depict something was completely stuck in the unsolvable puzzle of the picture [*Bild*] and mere seeming [*Schein*]. Now, after all this, the objection of the sophist which said that there cannot be any mere seeming at all, is behind us. It is thus easy to see that with the sophist we can only be dealing with false impression [*Anschein*], thus with an art of illusion (*phantastikē*). We had seen that it was actually difficult for the Stranger of Elea [365] – and not only for the young Theaetetus – to discriminate in their manner of appearance, which is so similar, the philosopher from the sophist, who are both concerned purely with *logoi*, thus to discriminate image [*Abbild*] from the semblance of an image [*Scheinbild*]. Now again, the stranger from Elea prepares Theaetetus carefully so that it makes sense to assign to the human reproductions, by contrast to the divine figurations, the status of being just false impressions. In this way, the application of the fundamental differentiation between image and the semblance of an image leads us to distinguish more precisely the art that gives us the impression of knowledge.

With this, the last, decisive turn to capture the sophist has been taken, which takes leave of the sphere of the *logoi*. About the series of further differentiations, the Eleatic stranger tells us that the designations for them are in general lacking (267d). This is an important indication that we are moving here in a direction which has still not received rightful attention, and this is not by chance. Finally, only this turn will lead to the real differentiation between the philosopher and the sophist. The fact that we do not even possess designations here reveals how widespread the mischaracterization of true dialectic and its confusion with the mere pseudo-art of eristic was. It was really a widespread confusion that led to the triumph of the sophistical movement. To clear up this confusion, we cannot rely on available concepts, which can be hierarchically organized *kata genē* ['by genera']. Distinctions are lacking here (267d5). It is even about a distinction which goes still further back behind our concepts. It is the question of whether one pretends to give an impression of knowledge knowingly or out of ignorance. In any case, we are no longer dealing here with imitation through speeches but with self-presentation. The difference does not lie in arguments but in the intention of the one who argues. In this alone can philosophers and sophists be distinguished.

Aristotle understood this point correctly when in book Gamma of the *Metaphysics* he distinguishes the sophist from the dialectician (what he so calls) only through the fundamental attitude towards life (*tou biou tē proairesei* ['in the choice of life'], *Metaphysics* Gamma 2, 1004b24). This attitude is what distinguishes the dialectician in pursuit of truth from the sophist. This is confirmed by the conclusion of the Platonic discussion. It is not through superior arguments that we arrive at this distinction. It was by going along with the discussion led by the Eleatic stranger. He brought the sceptical mathematician so close to the matter at hand that he will no longer succumb to false impressions in the future. In this way, he will also henceforth be able to give the account which he owed in the discussion with Socrates. Now he knows better what *logos* is and what actual knowledge is, and how it is different from sophistical pseudo-work.

What the text on the ideal city had thematized in broad outlines, namely, the ascent beyond mathematics towards dialectic [366] (*Republic* VI), is not only announced here but also performed in the persona of Theaetetus and before the eyes of the reader of this dialogue. The guidance of the Eleatic stranger has helped. Theaetetus like the reader understandingly lets go of the dominant prejudices about the sophist when he sees the sophist characterized as angling for human beings and hunting them down or as a trader with knowledge or as a mere trickster. He has learnt not to fall for semblance any more as if it were just a matter of argumentation skills and nothing else. This would again be confusing the sophist with an actual philosopher, who seeks truth in the twilight of question and answer. It remains the case that they continue to look similar to each other, but like wolf and dog (231a6). Eventually, Theaetetus knows this and not because he has learnt how to define the sophist, but because he has learnt how to make distinctions by going along with the discussion.

With this, a completely different dimension is opened than that of the *logoi* as such, of the letting appear of states of affairs, whether true or false. These virtuosos of oratory are not concerned with the truth at all. Plato calls them the dissimulating imitators and differentiates once again two forms of this dissimulating imitator – these ignorant ones, who present themselves as knowers, without being for this reason deceivers or liars. On one side, we have the demagogues who live on acclaim and are enraptured by it, so to speak. They fall for that which rhetoric grants to them each time. It is what the *Gorgias* (463b 501c) characterizes as the art of flattery. On the other side, there is the sophist who wants to stand victorious in discussion and argument, and wants to have the last word. Neither in fact belongs to the dimension of the *logoi*, which give a thoughtful account, in so far as their speech is an imitation of knowing and a pseudo-presentation which gives the impression of knowledge. Their speech gives merely a deceptive impression and in fact remains a nothing. On this long detour via the recognition of the 'not', the stranger from Elea points to the pretence and nothingness of what sophists do, the false semblance of true dialectic.

One still must look behind Parmenides or beyond Hegel in the direction of Nietzsche if one really wants to take seriously again with Plato the fact that the nothingness of seeming belongs to being and no longer thinks that one can ward it off with the help of 'science', as if it were a mere confusion. By reviving the radicality of Nietzsche, Heidegger tried to take a step back from this point and by the same token took a step forward. He recognized the limit of the Greek thinking of *alētheia* ['truth'] and thus also the force that issued forth from this Greek inception of thought in shaping the modern world civilization.

[367] My own interest in the *Sophist* and in the Platonic dialogues in general finds its motivation above all in the discussion which Heidegger has provoked about metaphysics and in particular under the slogan of 'overcoming metaphysics'. In his later works, the step behind Aristotelian ontology, which was long in preparation, resulted in Heidegger trying to discern and daring to think the hints and traces of the inceptual thinking of the Greeks from the rubble of the pre-Socratic legacy. As our accounts [of the pre-Socratics] have been shaped by Aristotle, this is an extraordinarily difficult task, which was perhaps to be achieved only with violence. In fact, Heidegger ventured something completely extraordinary by invoking a transmission without writing, a prehistory sketched only in the echoes it made in Greek language, in its words and primordial sayings. He probed them like a dowser seeking hidden sources of water. This makes his studies bearing on Anaximander, Parmenides and Heraclitus equally significant for his own way of thinking, which is quite relevant today and points to future avenues. His studies amaze us obviously by the boldness of his interpretation of fragmentary texts. The first firm ground that we can reach with a similar interest is offered in my view only by the Platonic dialogues. Plato's thought of the idea

does not seem to me to signal the advance towards Aristotelian metaphysics, as in Heidegger's portrayal of Plato. It also does not seem to me, that this turn towards the idea has introduced an abandonment of the thought of the *alētheia*, of truth, in favour of mere 'correctness', *orthotēs*, as Heidegger says. This 'turn towards the idea', understood by Heidegger as the preparation for Aristotelian metaphysics, is at any rate not found in the *Sophist*, which many, as we indeed know, understand as almost a disavowal of the theory of ideas. Heidegger's Marburg lecture on the *Sophist* from 1924, with which I am familiar only in the vague recollection of an immature auditor that I was, seemed in my view not to have been composed as much with a focus on this singular function as what Heidegger later presented publicly for the first time in 'Platos Lehre von der Wahrheit'. My own works on Plato had pointed me more and more in the opposite direction, that of the dialectical dialogues of the late period. My immersion in the *Sophist* appeared to me more and more as an opening of horizons within which indeed the question concerning being and the *logos* manifests itself under different lights but can hardly be seen as a mere precursor to Aristotelian physics and the metaphysics founded upon it. In Platonic dialectic, there is rather a distinctive perspective on the revival of the question of being, which does not culminate in the ontotheology of Aristotle. One need not see Plato's decisive step in taking the *eidos* as measure, as Heidegger does, but rather in the opening for the *logoi* in which relationships between the ideas are brought to light.[25]

[368] A Platonic dialogue has always many meanings but possibly none of the Platonic dialogues have as many meanings as the *Sophist*. The entire art of Plato the thinker is truly at its height here in the wealth of allusions and in the way interpretive possibilities are kept open. One can directly measure the effect of such a Platonic dialogue in the diversity that the Platonic heritage has yielded within the circle of the Academy. The overwhelming presence of Aristotle's physics and metaphysics belongs not in the least to this heritage. It seems to me neither correct nor possible to want to derive unambiguous doctrines which exhaust the impetus behind the *Sophist*, from the mere study of the *Sophist* and the other writings by Plato transmitted to us or those of Aristotle or even the doxography. What can be ascertained, however, is that even in the heritage of the Academy, the relationship between *logos* and being, which dominates the *Sophist*, features everywhere.

One can recognize the analysis of the *logos* in the *Sophist* and the closely related concept of *methexis* in all the testimonies we possess and understand them as the beginnings of a pre-history of metaphysics. Yet, it seems to me that the Platonic position on this question concerning the sense of being is not in any case to be sought in the Aristotelian concept of substance, which thinks under being what is available [*das Vorliegende*], the *subiectum*, to which predications are ascribed. It seems to me that we are pointed in the direction of deeply lying connections when the stranger from Elea seizes on the grammatical truth that a statement is only completed by the verb. In this we find a significant hint that the sense of a statement and with it even the sense of being presupposed by a statement, depends in each case on the specific point of view from which a being is seen and addressed. Only in this connection, thus in a *pros ti,* does being at all appear and, howsoever it may be, this is only accomplished through its temporalization. When this Theaetetus is sitting here, then it is this human being in the present. At the same time, what is present in this is that a human being can sit. To know this, one does not even need to know Theaetetus. The entire amplitude of the thinking of being between the 'this here' and its 'being-what' is played out here, which is established in the early text on the categories and covered by the Aristotelian concepts of *dunamis* ['potentiality'] and *energeia* ['actuality']. The contingency of the particular is indeed never graspable in the *logos* but the *logos* encompasses even this contingency by saying 'this'.

There is thus a good reason that Aristotle in his parlance differentiates 'being' in the sense of the categories and 'being' in the sense of *energeia* and *dunamis*, and yet does not separate them from each other. The mobility of beings, which comes through in the *logos*, and the mobility [369] of the particular, which remains embedded in the system of movements in nature, are intertwined.

This is clearly manifest in the analysis of Book Lambda of Aristotle's *Metaphysics*. Here, the analogical relationship between cause and causation is first presented in detail and then this is immediately superseded by the observation: provided that there must necessarily be a highest being, which sustains the entire system of movements as the unmoved mover. Aristotle's project of ontology virtually ends by complaining, in his critique of Plato's disciple, Speusippus, as a consequence, that only one can be the master[26]. This finds a certain correspondence in Plato in so far as Plato does not find the being of the factical conceivable in any other way than through a demiurge[27], as in the *Sophist* (255cf), the *Philebus* (28cff), the *Timaeus* (30dff.). Aristotle mocked this as an empty metaphor. And yet, Theophrastus must have already questioned Aristotle himself as to whether the mover, which moves by being loved, does not presuppose the soul of the lover. We could find allusions to this very point in the review of the *Sophist* above. Being [*Sein*] in its highest being [*Seiende*] is the embodiment of pure mobility and, as a being *par excellence* (*to pantelōs on*), it is *psychē* and *noūs*, and yet it is so that being always only shines through in the *logos*, which always combines one idea with another and excludes it from another. In the end it is a question here of the vital tension in our thinking itself, which I believe to have recognized more and more clearly in the course of my studies of the Greeks. The divine, which is in everything, and the god who, separated from everything, maintains the totality in motion, are two aspects of being which, as Platonism or as Aristotelianism, have gripped the entirety of the thinking of metaphysics up into modernity and beyond.

Part II
Modern Philosophy

5

Oetinger as Philosopher (1964)

[306] Within the history of Pietism, Friedrich-Christoph Oetinger (1702–82) has his own profile. This Swabian pastor was not only in a rather tense relationship with his Church leadership and with his congregations. Philosophically, he also advocated a most original position which constituted the starkest opposition to the dominant rationalism of a Christian Wolff. At the same time, as a theologian, he exerted a great influence in Swabian pietism, as the *Complete Works* of the early nineteenth century (edited from 1827 until 1852 by Karl Christian Eberhard Ehmann) show us. In fact, he also belongs to the history of philosophy and tried out many things, which then made history in German idealism[1].

The essay on common sense[2], of which there is a German variant from the same year, composed for a broader audience, dates back to 1753. Oetinger is at the pinnacle of his life and it is truly astounding how, from his remote corner, he keeps in touch with the philosophy of his century, not only German philosophy but also English and French philosophy, and how he appropriates and assimilates everything that finds an echo in his religiously tempered speculation on the living word of God. The theologians of today will not be less opposed than the ones of his time to the speculations of this brilliant man and they may be right about the fact that no stable dogmatics could be built on the basis of his scientific syncretism and arbitrary exegesis. Yet, the *philosophical* significance of the treatise on the *Sensus communis* is beyond doubt. This philosophical significance cannot be dismissed by scholastic polemics of a theological or philosophical nature against the 'famous *sensus communis*'. By appealing to the *sensus communis*, Oetinger advocates not so much an epistemological position as a plethora of substantial truths. The dogmatic and exegetical application of these truths may seem untenable from a theological perspective. His inclusion of modern natural science and his critique of the dogmatism of the [307] enlightenment may have been overshadowed by Kant's critique, which a few decades after would provide the new natural sciences with

'Oetinger als Philosophh (1964)' was published as the introduction to Friedrich Christoph Oetinger, *Inquisitio in sensum commune et rationem* [Enquiry into Common Sense and Reason], facsimile reprint of the Tübingen edition of 1753. Stuttgart: Friedrich Fromann, 1964, pp. v-xxviii. It was then published in *Kleine Schriften* III, pp. 89–100. It is now in *Gesammelte Werke*, vol. 4. Tübingen: J. C. B. Mohr (Paul Siebeck), 1987, pp. 306–17.

their lasting philosophical justification. However, Oetinger's idea of 'life', which he tries to shore up theologically as well as through insights coming from modern natural science, deserves its place in the history of modern thought. Similar to that of Leibniz, Oetinger's theory is an attempt to reconcile modern science with the older truths of tradition.

It is certainly a theological interest which motivates Oetinger's investigations into the *sensus communis* and *ratio* ['reason']. However, the title and the content of the treatise speak of the theories of philosophers, of the advantage of the Newtonian over the Leibnizian system and make references to the Holy Scripture not so much for its own sake as rather a means to evaluate the doctrines of philosophers. What the distinctive theological matter is for the sake of which Oetinger writes his book is revealed by the introductory letter. He would like to defend the view that the foundations of all true knowledge, even in the domains of physics and metaphysics, are to be found in the Holy Scripture and particularly in 'The Wisdom of Solomon'. The adversaries with whom he engages in the introductory piece are essentially Jesuit writers, such as Juan de Pineda, who advocate a completely different thesis. They reflect on the fact that 'The Wisdom of Solomon' should only be compared to the knowledge of his own time and in fact contains no metaphysical or physical knowledge at all. What Solomon craves from God, they say, was a teachable heart in order to be able to govern the people and differentiate good from evil. It was thus no universal science but a *sapientia practica (sive politica)* ['practical (or political) wisdom']. What appears in Solomon's writings in relation to the knowledge of nature and the world, they claim, only serves as metaphorical ornamentation of discourse.

To the advocates of these theses, which in the age of historical consciousness appear almost self-evident to us, Oetinger poses a series of questions. Even if in light of the great discoveries of the new science, for example, the discovery of the circulatory system, the nervous system and so on, he cannot deny that the reflections of his opponents are correct in a certain sense, he still claims the universality of Solomon's knowledge. To be sure, Solomon did not possess yet the specific skills pertaining to modern science, such as differential calculus. Yet, it can be said that he already truly grasped the idea of life and showed how life pervades all parts of the body through and through. This is the idea of life upon which Oetinger himself grounded his theology.

What a critical scientific mind must characterize as abstruse speculations are not altogether absent in Oetinger's writing. Yet, there lies an inner necessity in the fundamental principle from which Oetinger begins, despite all the uncritical [308] application of this principle. Modern science, with its rich and diverse material for experience and its mathematical and deductive constructions of theories, is not the only way to know. It is the limit of the modern age *quod hodie pretiosa experimenta nimis aestimantur, quod communia negligantur* ['that today valuable experiments are overestimated because common things are neglected'].

Oetinger is aware that he does not stand alone in seeking to limit the pretensions of the modern rational science. He appeals, for example, to Pascal's distinction between *esprit géométrique* ['geometrical spirit'] and *esprit de finesse* ['refined spirit']. He gladly appeals to Bacon's reduction of scholastic pseudo-knowledge to the simple and useful. He appeals to Fontenelle, to Chinese worldly wisdom, which was transmitted at the time by Christian Wolff and by his own countryman Bulfinger, etc. Thus, Oetinger was not alone at all. The entire age was faced with the task of reconciling the methodological principles of the new mathematical natural science with natural self-evidence, which found its philosophical expression in the traditional doctrine of the *species* ['species'] and the *forma substantialis* ['substantial form'].

If we generally see Descartes as the father of modern philosophy because his principle of the *cogito* ['I think'] provides mathematical natural science with its epistemological legitimacy, we are seeing things in a very modernistic manner. We should not forget that the principle of the *cogito* is a metaphysical one and implies the recognition of a dual substance. If alongside the world of extended things known to science, the *res extensa* ['extended thing'], there exists a *res cogitans* ['thinking thing'], a totally different 'thing', then what indeed is 'being'? Metaphysical reflections, *meditationes de prima philosophia* ['meditations on first philosophy'], thus became necessary. For Descartes, the metaphysical legitimacy of the ontological claim made by our 'subjective' ideas of things results from the equiprimordiality of the consciousness of God and the consciousness of self. Finding such a legitimacy was unavoidable once the ground of the 'natural' theory of knowledge, that is to say, the conviction of a like-for-like similarity between our knowledge and things, had been abandoned. But the new science requires decisively that we abandon it. Science broke down natural sensory qualities into measurable quantities of extension, movement, number and does not allow for the existence of any similarity between that which is measurable in such a way and the subjective aspect of what is measured, between the subjective quality of colour and light waves, between the sound heard and the sound wave.

It is necessary to take this philosophical background into consideration in all these appeals to the natural self-evidence of the *sensus communis*. Only then can we understand that such an appeal is not just a revolt of the natural understanding against the reflective attitude of philosophy, but [309] is meant to be a philosophical response which shares its problem with the philosophy it criticizes. So, Oetinger's real adversary is not quite rational natural science as such. He rather constantly appeals to its results and even takes Newton's side against Leibniz. This is astonishing enough, considering that Leibniz's theory of the original and living unities, the monads, offered not only an ingenious reconciliation of the traditional doctrine of substantial forms with the new mechanistic physics, but in so doing appealed extensively to the same experiences of a Swammerdam, a Boerhave, etc., whom Oetinger himself had in mind. With his complaints over our 'idealistic' century, 'in which almost nobody knows what "life" is anymore' (p. 5), should he not have seen in Leibniz an ally? And does he not rightly recognize the great merit of Leibniz in his critique of the Cartesian theory of motion and the derivation of force from the square of velocity so that only now is the real essence of motion grasped, this 'moment' consisting in a *vis* ['force'] pressing for change (p. 102)? Is he not in agreement with Leibniz when Leibniz teaches that the essence of the body does not lie in the mere intuition but in the *aggregatio virium simplicium infinita* ['the infinite combination of simple forces']?

As a matter of fact, Oetinger's appeal to the *sensus communis* cannot be interpreted as a rejection of modern science and of the insights found by it just as little can it be interpreted as a misunderstanding of the task of reconciliation for which Leibniz had devised his ingenious solution. But precisely the ingeniousness of this solution, the audaciousness, even the madness of the Leibnizian system (Oetinger calls him *audax temperarius* ['temperate bold individual']) is what repulses Oetinger, who orients himself towards the truth of the sensus communis. *Systema Leibnitianum mira concinnitate se pro vero et acceptabili insinuavit, cum tamen ex insufficientissimis nimium concludat datis, sancta scriptura plane posthabita* ['the Leibnizian system presents itself as true and acceptable with wonderful harmony whereas it draws too much from the most insufficient data, largely neglecting the Holy Scripture']. What Oetinger means is this: God is made all too dependent upon the coordination of the whole and the nexus of things. And it is true that Leibniz prided himself on having found a new proof for the existence of God in his system of a pre-established harmony among all monads, a harmony which ensues of necessity since no influence of one monad on another is conceivable. Can it be a surprise that the critical and Christian mind of Oetinger comments on this: *semper id, quod est in quaestione, tamquam principium adsumebatur* ['that which is in question is always assumed as a principle']; and that for the knowledge of God he prefers to find support in biblical revelation, with which the *sensus communis* is also capable of being in accord. This is how he rejects Leibniz: *demonstratione a contingentia totius universi non opus sit ad demonstrationem existentiae dei* ['let there be no need for a demonstration of the existence of God as a demonstration from the contingencies of the total universe'].

Now, it is certainly not Oetinger's concern to oppose an original counter-construction to the Leibnizian solution, which would continue to be obvious to the *sensus communis* and still reach the logical consistency of Leibniz's [310] system. His choice of taking Newton's side can at the very least help him in this matter. For what he rightly highlights time and again in Newton is precisely his cautious renunciation of all metaphysics, his readiness to recognize the limits of his knowledge and thus to leave room for the certainty of God and natural cognition, which are nurtured from other religious sources.

Oetinger is himself aware of the systematic weaknesses of his small work and justifies its unmethodical character by the fact that the *sensus communis* is not a principle to be rationally derived but something innate in all and which is what it is only in being used: *non posse regulis includi immensam eius capacitatem* ['it could not be included in rules given its immense capacity'] (p.55). His *inquisitio in sensum communen* does not aim to be a *demonstratio* ['demonstration'] (p. 19) at all. It is thus a highly unmethodical treatise, a mixture of erudite anthology and declamatory interpretation of Scripture. Oetinger hardly makes the effort to hide the arbitrariness and haphazardness of his associations in his reasonings. Even the critique of Leibniz presented above is not really laid out systematically. Obviously, Oetinger is also dependent on others here, on Fénelon and especially

Maupertuis, from whom he transcribes entire pieces into Latin and inserts them into his writing.

Yet, this plea for the *sensus communis* and his shoring it up through Bible interpretation are no mere syncretism of a popular philosophical type, which only wants to be at the service of revelation and its general reality of salvation. It is an entire philosophy that is erected upon the idea of the *sensus communis* and to be discerned from the engaged declamations of the author. The apologetic motif, which defends the indispensability of the *sensus communis* against *ratio* and which dominates the whole introduction of the theme, has naturally the consequence that the original train of thought, which Oetinger pursues, blends within the generalities of what a 'natural' thinking holds true. In this regard, they are all entirely sound arguments. It is convincing that the *sensus communis* remains indispensable for the *ars inveniendi* ['art of invention'] and that the mere exactness of calculation, the logical consistency in derivation in no way guarantee the truth of knowledge. No one can escape the argument that the application of rules as such still does not guarantee a sure footing over a matter. To the contrary, it rather carries with it an appearance of exactness, which easily captivates and obfuscates the matter. To put it differently, all applications of rules again require another capacity not guaranteed by rules, such as *tactus* ['touch'] or *gustus* ['taste']. Here Oetinger often appeals to Bacon and his critique of scholasticism. We follow him when he, for example in the 'Fables', catches sight of the *sensus communis totius antiquitatis* ['the common sense of the totality of antiquity']. Let us consider, for example, the historical revelatory value possessed by the anecdote, even if its authenticity is dubious. What becomes evident here is a limitation of the new methodological thinking and its [311] pathos for certainty. One has to acknowledge that it simply is not really commensurate with the situation of the human race to have to rediscover all the truths by oneself: *misere ageretur cum genere humano, si illis inveniendae essent demum illae veritates* (p. 31) ['the human race would be treated miserably if those truths had to be discovered only by human beings']. The *sensus communis* represents a genuine knowledge. Indeed, for practical worldly wisdom, there is less a need for a recourse to principles than for an intuitive grasp of the overall circumstances. How is something like this possible? The following definition indeed sounds like an entirely innocuous description of a capacity common to all human beings: *viva et penetrans perceptio objectorum toti humanitati obviorum, ex immediato tactu et intuitu eorum, quae sunt simplicissima, utilissima et maxime necessaria* ['a lively and penetrating perception of the objects which are obvious to the whole of humanity, from the immediate touch and sight of such objects, which are the simplest, the most useful and the most necessary'], etc. (p. 18f). But in fact, there lies in this the whole of Oetinger's philosophy of 'life', which he also places at the basis of his theology.

The question is indeed about the basis of the truth of such intuitive insights. Oetinger is certainly quick with the theological response at his fingertips: that this truth is of divine origin. And yet this certainty does not mean, even in his view, that everything would have been said by it. The self-evidence of what the *sensus communis* tells us, the subjective certainty that knowledge comes from the core and the heart (*ex centro vel corde* ['from the centre or the heart']) and enters precisely at the point where the mathematical method is not adequate, all this poses a problem. The comparison between the Leibnizian and Newtonian 'systems' serves to analyse this problem: how is such a penetrating gaze into the truth possible?

In order to answer the question, we have to begin with the preference given by Oetinger to Newton because he goes beyond the realm of mere mechanical connections with the *vis attractionis* ['force of attraction'], this mysterious 'force from a distance'. It is a *supermechanica vis* ['super-mechanical force']. When Newton rejected every explanation of this force, he enabled the speculative Swabian's attempt to look for clues about the cause of attraction in the natural self-evidence of the sensation of life. Oetinger sees the super-mechanical aspect of the attraction first of all in the fact that this attraction permeates all the pores of the body. These are immaterial forces which are here connected with material ones. This is also true of the fundamental constitution of life. Newton's concept of such a force also provides the possibility to think the idea of life conceptually.

Oetinger goes so far as to characterize this as the recovery of an old knowledge which 'our century' succeeded in recovering, namely, that the soul forms the body (p. 114). This was perhaps the decisive point for his rejection of Leibniz: that he argues against this natural self-evidence of the influence of the soul on the body through his monadology. Positively, it means that *in ipsa individuatione rei* ['in the very individuation of the thing'] we find an exercise of freedom (p. 130). Oetinger finds support for this in, among others, the depiction in *Genesis* of the darknesses which at the beginning covers everything and was called to creation by the enlightening word [312] of God. He opposes the unification of *spiritualitas* ['spirituality'] and *materialitas* ['materiality'] (p. 232) to Leibniz's monadological 'idealism'. We have to begin with the sensation of life if we want to understand Oetinger's interpretation of Newton's gravitation.

In opposition to Leibniz, who grants monads with a representational force (*vis repraesentativa*), as well as in opposition to Shaftesbury, who derives all movements of the soul from the sympathy and harmony of the universe, Oetinger asserts that one does not feel oneself to be defined either by the ideas of others or by the relations with others but feels in oneself the forces through which one can exert an effect on external reality. The vividly conscious being is not like the single tone in a tonic system but like an entire clavichord[3], a centre from which everything emanates. For this, the Newtonian concept of central forces offers him a universal ontological model. All-pervasiveness, presence everywhere that makes space the expression of the divine omnipresence grants the concept of central force a superiority over the Leibnizian principle of sufficient reason: gravitational attraction precedes all comportment of the body, consequently even the relationships of pressure and impact. The relationship of pressure and impact is not enough to explain the order of the heavenly bodies, not even magnetic phenomena, let alone the actual processes of life of which we have knowledge through our inner sense. This being the case, a hypothesis presents itself very easily to thought, which conversely thinks all beings on the model of the all-present, all-pervasive gravitation. This is how Oetinger consciously goes beyond Newton (*hypotheses non fingo* ['I do not invent hypotheses']) and develops a hypothesis about the cause of attraction, which explains how it happens that immaterial forces and material ones enter into a circle of life (*in unum vitae circulum*). We thus have the circular movement of the heavenly bodies resulting from the opposition of two forces, the centripetal and the centrifugal; in the same way, in a magnet, even when its mass is divided, there always results a pole of attraction; so, similarly the relation of the centre to its radiation in the circle, the relation of the one which manifests itself in different manners, is the foundation upon which we can also think all higher forms of multiplicity and unity, all differentiated forms of centre and periphery. In plants we have external organs and an integrated centralization of their being. They are a vegetative system. Animals and similar creatures are turned even more towards a centre and opened into the totality of their environment.

The fundamental concept under which the supra-mechanical force determining all being is thought is the *simplificatio*, simplification and unification. This manifests itself above all else in the living: Here it is seen as concentration through which something is ensouled by a unitary spirit. Without a doubt, the concept of the *simplex* ['simple'], which is meant *idealiter* ['ideally'] and not *materialiter* ['materially'] [313] (for we are dealing with *composita* ['things composed'] out of elements or atoms), is the proper key-concept of Oetinger's speculative interpretation of being. This concept appears not only at the beginning (par. 7), where it belongs to the definition of the *sensus communis*. It even appears as the essence of the central force, which is all-pervasive in the material world of bodies. This concept finds its proof in the stratified realm of organic beings, in its structural principle of increasing differentiation and increasing centralization, from plants to humans via the animal world – and for Oetinger up to the angels. Plants and animals are not yet sufficiently 'simplified', not yet sufficiently raised from the abyss of chaos to manifest the full divine idea of life. This only happens in human beings, who are the true *excellentia vitae* ['the excellence of life'] (p. 206) to which the creature elevates itself. With the divine breath permeating the creature and fulfilling it, the *spiritus rectores vitae* ['the spirits governing life'] is brought about and with this the unification in a centre, through which the intelligible functions of life, that is to say, a certain degree of consciousness (*conscientia*) becomes possible.

The liveliness [*Lebendigkeit*] which the divine breathes in is at the same time the vivid [*lebendig*] experience of the divine, the simplicity which is conferred and bestowed by God. It manifests itself in the naivety and the uncloudedness of consciousness, which gathers everything into itself and uniformly differentiates itself in all its modes of behaviour and expression. Consciousness possesses a concept of something higher, which is *supra me* ['above me']. It is not *ratio* that differentiates us truly from animals but this consciousness of a *superioritas* ['superiority'] which precedes all *ratio*, the certainty of conscience (*suneidēsis*).

We can see that it is a consistent line of thought which Oetinger develops. Animals too certainly have something analogous to *ratio* in their assured instincts. Yet, we sense in the purity of heart 'instincts, commands, rules', which come neither from experience nor from blood lines and which also do not rest on our preferences. For example, we cannot praise vice, despise virtue as virtue (p. 22cf, p. 172). This is the *sensus communis*, a consciousness of self, an awareness and inner-being, which distinguishes all human behaviour as human. It corresponds to wisdom in the sense of Solomon. It is not the free capacity to relate to oneself, which constitutes the essence of the *cogitatio* ['thought'], the Cartesian consciousness of self. It is rather a highest receptivity, an ability to assimilate that which is higher, which is *logos*, spirit and God. With this, the talk of the *sensus communis* acquires an anthropological-ontological sense, over and beyond the moral phenomenon of common convictions, which unify people of all places and all nations. This *sensus* is not something inferior compared to *ratio* when measured against the ontological standard of *simplificatio*.

This is expressed in Oetinger's views through the fact that inner sense – and [314] not *ratio* – stands closer to the highest mode of being of the creature, the angel. Angels are the highest because they are a *maximum compositum in simplicitate maxima* ['most composed in the greatest simplicity']. Their spiritual powers are so unified (*simplificatae* ['simplified']) that the bodies associated with the souls are really only tools (*vere sint instrumenta*). This obviously means that angels are not familiar with any dividedness, any disturbing needs of the body, any affect coming from the body – a remarkable combination of the biblical angelic doctrine and the doctrine of the stars as souls in Greek philosophy and astronomy. For we know from the metaphysical anthropology of the Greeks that human nature is not simple like that of the gods and that the pure intuition of the truth is refused to human nature as the abiding form of its being. In the same way, for Aristotle, the pure spiritual nature of the heavenly bodies is evidenced by the fact that they alone describe pure, simple, perfect, circular motion – and scholasticism follows him in this. According to Oetinger, the human soul is threefold. It is composed of the three spirits or forces: *ratio* ['reason'], *virtus* ['virtue'] and *sensus* ['sense']. These are unified by the *logos* and connected to the body, which may be dark and inert but is capable of exercising freedom (p. 237).

Here the *sensus*, that is to say the capacity of *transformatio* ['transformation'] in which lived body and soul come together, has a precedence over *ratio* and *virtus*. For its *facultas transformationis* ['faculty of transformation'] distinguishes it in that it assimilates what is external and is fully in everything that it receives. By contrast, understanding and virtue imply the opposition of the spiritual and the corporeal (pp. 237, 244). *Ratio*, we are told, is oriented to the simple constituents of the inferior nature, whereas the complete unity of body and soul, which distinguishes the *sensus*, as it were, anticipates and cognizes the higher *status* because the *sensus interior* ['inner sense'] represents the unifying bond (*vinculum* 244). What constitutes the sensible unity of the soul, in this view, is the fact that it *simplificat in unum* ['simplifies into one'] the multiplicity of that which it senses. In attracting different forms, the soul is still one and the same. The changing facial expression which, for example, the soul shows in pleasure and pain, love and hatred, cheerfulness and gloom comes to it in its unity and essential constitution – *formam certe fixam non habet, et nullam quoque non habet* ['it certainly has no fixed form and does not even have any'] (p. 163).

The *cogitatio*, the capacity to reflect, by contrast, is not the original essence of the soul. This is manifest in the way the *sensus communis* operates. Before rational deliberation the *sensus communis* already possesses the inexorability of its self-evidence, the assurance of its instinctual truth. That the *sensus communis* is like an instinct is decisive for the precedence of the *sensus communis* over *ratio*. Instincts are not just fleeting affects which overcome the soul (and which we can still control), but original tendencies (*radicatae tendentiae*, p. 246), which do not depend on affects. They come from the depths of the soul and are traces of the divine, so to speak, *residua* [315] *simulacra imaginis Divinae in anima* ['the residual images of the divine imprint in the soul']. It is precisely their dictatorial, inexorable violence that attests to their divine character. So, there exists an essential difference between *sensus* and *ratio*. It corresponds to the difference between nature and art. What God creates through nature grows in equal measure in all directions, whereas what is created through art begins in a definite part on a pre-established layout: *sensus naturam imitatur, ratio artem* ['sense imitates nature, reason imitates art'] (p. 248). As we can see, Oetinger teaches not only a *theologia de idea vitae deducta* ['a theology deduced from the idea of life']. He also has a philosophy which thinks the whole of metaphysics from the idea of life. He opposes a pneumatic, spiritualistic ontology to the Cartesianist determination of subjectivity through reflection. The fact that neo-Platonic mystical and theosophical influences can be detected in this changes nothing about the fact that Oetinger's concept of life is a prelude to the spiritualist metaphysics of speculative idealism and in particular to Hegel's critique of the philosophy of reflection and his theory of nature and spirit. The *sensus communis* is not only the unifying bond of all naturally living beings, which arise from atomic chaos. The union of the many also befits matter in a certain way – precisely in the manner of attraction. The *sensus communis*, in a different way, also encompasses all the common and natural truths that determine social and political life. It thus grants to natural knowledge laid down in language a right and privilege over against mathematical rational construction. Among the particularities which distinguish humans from animals (inner consciousness, the sense for the higher, the tendency towards eternity), it is significant that Oetinger mentions as the fourth the urge to express one's sensations in language. He sees this fourth particularity as being especially closely connected to the first particularity, inner consciousness, which does not exclude the fact that there exists a tension between the natural sense (*sensus communis*) and language, which confers on the *sensus communis* a proper function.

Oetinger hardly makes remarks of his own on the phenomenon of language. However, a treatise by Maupertuis, the Latin translation of which Oetinger inserts into his investigation – distributed over some passages – speaks for him (pp. 9–17; 165–6). It is the specific relation existing between the *sensus* and its expression in language which Maupertuis treats in his treatise on the origin of language. Precisely this connection would already no longer be perceptible for anybody who belongs to a linguistic community. 'Our languages are meant to express not so much original meanings as prejudgmental inventions' (p. 10). In order to find traces of the history of our spirit, the languages of primitive peoples would be more fertile.

This is because our memory cannot reach our own childhood where the spirit was not yet likewise filled with concepts and where consequently it was more fit for the cognition of the simple truth. [316] Maupertuis undertakes a thought experiment to unravel the structure of language in a stepwise manner, starting from the first sense perceptions and their designations. He shows the increasing distance of the sign from the original *sensatio* ['sensation'], the construction of signs for universal concepts and finally even for the metaphysical concepts of substance and mode, and the whole field of logical relations. It is a schematization that serves a pragmatic purpose but also recoils upon our own insights and leads to errors and prejudices.

> *Id quod appellamus scientias, tam arcte pendet a modo sensationes designandi, ut credam quaestiones et propositiones futuras fuisse plane alias, si aliae expressiones primarum sensationum fuissent positae* ['that which we call sciences depends so closely on the manner of designating sensations that I believe future questions and propositions would have been entirely otherwise, if other expressions of the primary sensations had been stipulated'].

Today we are in a much better position to realize the accuracy of this statement, precisely because we no longer share a tacit presupposition: that an ideal memory, which would preserve all originally simple sensations and their designations, would be free from all errors of human knowledge. We are so very conscious of the predicative structure of pre-predicative experience, that is to say, of the ineradicable retroactive effect of the logical and linguistic formation of our experiences on all our perceptions, that the concept *primae sensationes*, 'original' perceptions (sensations) has lost its epistemological privilege. Let us think, for example, of the critique of the protocol sentences and basic sentences in neo-positivism but also of the results of the modern psychology of perception (Goldstein). Maupertuis already comes quite close to these insights when he speaks about the constant influence exerted on all our knowledge by the mother tongue familiar to us. When he turns this natural origin of language in 'simple sensations' against the partisan quarrels among philosophers, this is all a prelude to the critique of metaphysics to be found in neo-positivism.

Oetinger draws from Maupertuis' analysis a positive implication in terms of the critique of language, which just makes clear the entire productive meaning of the *sensus communis*, including its confirmation and illumination through divine revelation. He means that we today have lost these most primitive and original words because our sense has been led away from what is naturally right by distorted and incorrect words. The *sensus communis* may be living in us as the expression of our dual spiritual and psychological life but we have been weakened by the ambiguous words of the snake. We are thus stuck in the mud from which we cannot dislodge ourselves if we do not begin reforming the spirit with the reform of words (*nisi a reformatione verborum mentem reformare incipiemus* ['if we do not begin reforming the spirit by reforming words'], p. 249). And now the theologian assures us that the Bible is essential for this beginning. The healthy words of the Sacred Scripture help us [317] to rein in our words. Yet, this is an unfinished struggle for we have been weakened till today by strange expressions invented by philosophers or the plebeian crowd. As a result, words often fail us in indicating what we feel. Oetinger invokes the model of Socrates and, above all, Melanchthon. Both understand their dialectic as the persistent pursuit of the divine traces. He also recommends Bengel, who can help us rediscover the old *gravitas* ['gravity']. In all of this, it is the *sensus communis* which, of divine origin, lets human beings become aware of what is most closely related to them (p. 25). Thus, the *sensus communis* remains a decisive guide even in all thinking and in all evaluation of thoughts. It is a sense illuminated by the Holy Scripture. There are no rules for understanding and evaluating thoughts which can be useful without this *sensus communis*. But those who entrust themselves to it and submit themselves to the word of God will make the right use of these rules with the help of the Holy Scripture. It will not be like the straight line in the sense of geometry but like a living line, which is united with God's presence (*ut linea viva cum praesentia Dei unita* ['like a living line united with the presence of God']). They will acquire all important thoughts from the divine works and writings. The pastor Oetinger appeals to his experience (which is known to all of us) of noticing whether someone is uttering empty words or speaks with real insight:

> *ut enim sensus est, ita formantur singula verba, quae quis eloquitur de talibus, et statim audio, num quis ex schola abstrahentium an experientium sit* ['For as the sense is, so are formed the individual words with which one speaks of such things, and I hear immediately whether one is from the school of abstractions or from the school of experience'].

Thus, the *sensus communis* is as much a critique of language, which corrects the empty generalities of the philosophers, as, at the same time, the highest fundamental principle of all understanding and of all interpretation. In this, the pietist theologian remains superior to the Jesuit expounder of the Bible in the same sense as an engagement with tradition which is directed at the 'matters' at stake is everywhere superior to merely taking note of historical information. Ultimately, is the principle which Oetinger opposes to his theological opponents not also *mutatis mutandis* the right principle for us? If interpreters do not recognize that the statements they want to interpret are the outpourings of the highest insight and cognition, then they are not seeking anything that is worthy of their investigative efforts:

> *si interpres non agnoscit, quod ex summa ratione et cognitione profluxerint dicta, quae interpretari vult, nil dignum sua investigatione quaeret*? ['if interpreters do not acknowledge that the words they want to be interpreted have poured out from the highest reason and knowledge, are they seeking anything worth their investigation?'].

6
Herder and the Historical World (1967)

[318] We live in an era in which new forms of rational order of an industrially and technologically developed world have let the old Europe, saturated with tradition and historical consciousness, be absorbed into a culture of evening out [*Ausgleichskultur*]. Even if these new forms may not deny their European origin, this culture still receives its legitimacy from nothing other than its rational and economic efficiency. In view of this self-propagating world culture, we may very well speak of the end of colonialism. But it belongs to the dialectic of history that it is the very form of civilization developed by colonialism which today spreads over the most diverse indigenous forms of life like a layer of techno-commercial administrative apparatus. What is pushing towards planetary domination here seems to destroy as much as to develop. This is true not only for the so-called developing countries but indeed also for the true motherland of this world civilization, Europe, in so far as there too that which came to be through history is being increasingly supplanted and a techno-pragmatic consciousness dawns, breaking away from this historical heritage.

At this hour, we no longer read the early manifesto of historicism, which Herder drafted in 1774, with the consciousness that we are getting to the bottom of something that has triumphed by going back to its beginnings. Rather, we approach this text with the question that doubts as to whether these beginnings of historicism did not already betray something of its limits, which have started to become so clear today. What in fact is this 'historicism'? If we follow the historian Friedrich Meinecke, what we have are the two fundamental ideas of 'development' and 'individuality', which, under the aegis of historicism, are asserted against the presupposition, characteristic of natural law, of an abiding human nature[1]. Yet, this redescription quite certainly does not cover the full sense of what Herder has in mind. It would at best be applicable to Ranke, whose Lutheran theology of history is essentially centred in the immediacy in which all times stand to God. When

---

'Herder und die geschichtliche Welt (1967)' was first published as the afterword to the edition of J. G. Herder: *Auch eine Philosophie der Geschichte zur Bildung der Menschheit*. Frankfurt: Suhrkamp, 1967, pp. 146–77 [English translation: *Another Philosophy of History and Selected Political Writings*, trans. Ioannis D. Evrigenis and Daniel Pellerin. Indianapolis/Cambridge: Hackett Publishing Company, 2004]. It is also in *Kleine Schriften* III, pp. 101–17. It is now in *Gesammelte Werke*, vol. 4. Tübingen: J. C. B. Mohr (Paul Siebeck), 1987, pp. 318–35.

Meinecke sees in Ranke the consummation of [319] historicism because here we arrive at a 'critical respect for tradition', what he touches upon thereby is more a general moment of a genuine scientific attitude towards history. What he does not grasp is Ranke's historicism in its true foundations, which even in Ranke lie in the theology of history, as has been recently emphasized[2]. This is even truer for Herder. When Meinecke notices 'still too much transcendence' in Herder, because Herder always had his eyes on the 'plan' of providence, he obviously applies an inappropriate standard.

We will thus have to set aside the categories of the academic problematic of historicism and rather begin with what the small text itself, with its expressive force and dynamism, wants. What it expresses is a tension of the will and what holds sway in it is a polemical acuity, which widely separates Herder's words from the romantic-historical nineteenth century. We need to understand it from the possibilities of the eighteenth century. The title of the text: 'Yet Another Philosophy of History for the Cultivation of Humanity' certainly has an ironic ring to it. With this, Herder demarcates himself in a provocative manner from the philosophy of history which, in a proud consciousness of progress typical of the triumphant Enlightenment, relates all that is past to the perfection of its own present. Yet, he calls his text just a contribution to the contributions of the century. Howsoever different a contribution it may be and howsoever much a bitter satire directed against the rational pride of the enlightenment, this text is also meant to be a contribution to the cultivation of humanity. The cultivation of humanity means something wherein the self-consciousness of the present is also present. How it has been cultivated means at the same time what it is. To this extent, the sensibility of this essay is in no way that of a romantic turning back to a transfigured past and in no way just a critique of the ideas of the enlightenment. It is a contribution to the future: 'And once all the seeds mature, to which the more noble part of our century also contributed quietly and silently, in what a blissful time my gaze loses itself!'

It was in this sense that Herder later in the introduction of his *Ideas* interpreted this small text and its title as the expression of an unpretentious modesty. This is obviously not completely justified. For we are dealing here with a provocative polemical text, which is not sparing in irony and satire, and which sets for itself the stated objective of pursuing a philosophy of history in another sense than what his contemporaries had done: Iselin[3], who made the progress of the Enlightenment so much the standard [320] that ancient times appear only as times of ridiculous superstition and cynical deception by the clergy; Voltaire[4], who adopted the attitude of a witty scepticism against the entirety of human affairs. In comparison to them, Herder's own contribution is only modest in the sense that he avoids both extremes: the presumption to feel oneself to be the zenith of all the ages, on the one hand, and the mischievous dissolution of all the expectations tied to the course of human history, on the other. His contribution confines itself to weigh gain and loss in a fair manner as they have to be assessed for all epochs of the past as well as for one's own present.

In a certain sense, historical fairness was in tune with the times. It was the abiding effect of the famous *querelle des anciens et des modernes* ['quarrel between the ancients and the moderns'], which loomed over the beginning of the eighteenth century. If this quarrel over the possibility of matching up to the ancient classics or not is also about an aesthetic quarrel, then its resolution has a profound effect on the foundation and limits of the historical self-consciousness of modernity[5]. Herder's text certainly shows no explicit traces of this. Christian self-consciousness is rooted too deeply in him for such a quarrel or a resolution of this quarrel to exist in historical scepticism. He could never be overcome by the temptation to elevate classical Greece to the canon of all that is true, good and beautiful. Yet, as little could his sensitive insight into the differences of times, peoples and cultures drive him into the arms of a relativistic historicism, however great and devastating his critique of the Enlightenment's schema of progress might have been. If we assess his text from the perspective of the problems which are of interest to a consummated historicism, then we do not do it justice. What results then is a false impression that the later exposition of this text in the *Ideas* and above all the thrust of the 'Letter on Humanity' were a fallback into the Enlightenment's ways of thinking.

It is easy to see how false this is. For today we are at the end of a development which, not without the influence of Herder's thought, has given rise to the birth of modern national states. And we are at the end of this peculiar development in central Europe, which was determined by German romanticism and the dogma of the opposition between civilization and culture. This dogma could appeal to Herder's critique of France's intellectual and aesthetic culture. In a manner [321] which becomes progressively clearer to the consciousness attuned to time, our own epoch becomes more tightly connected with that of the eighteenth century and makes Herder's ties to the ideas of the eighteenth century, as well as his inauguration and anticipation of romantic motifs, appear in a new light. We must ask ourselves as to whether the 'unsurpassed residues of transcendence', which the age of consummated historicism saw in him, are not conversely essential for a unified vision of nature and history which supports the totality of his conception.

We have two definite points which allow us to determine more closely the guiding idea of this manifesto of 1774, which is more an explosive venting than a neatly arranged treatise. The first point is the early draft of a 'history of the human soul' found in the autobiographical *Travel Diaries* of 1769. The other point is the exposition of this early program in the mature years of the Weimar period: in 1784 appeared the first volume of *Ideas on the Philosophy of the History of Humanity*. When we endeavour to determine the place of our text from these two limiting points, it loses its irritating aspect of an anticipation of the historicism of 1900. It entirely escapes being subjugated to the lineage of a history of the problem which is constructed from the standpoint of the neo-Kantian philosophy of history. It can rather be seen as the document of a spirit which plumbs the farthest reaches, looking beyond the opposition between nature and history.

Let us begin with the *Travel Diaries* (1769). How does the idea of the book on the human soul germinate here, of which our text is the first bloom and the *Ideas* the mature fruit? A soul deeply stirred, removed from all ties and influences, which an early success in life imposed upon the genial young man, admits to the limitations and restrictions of its life. Faced with the prodigious mirror which the sea, the limitless expanse and the wilderness of the elements hold against him, Herder invokes a new beginning constituted by the 'Remarks on Realities and Action'. Everything that is excited in him, the vision of the streams of peoples, which have carried the human race forward and have cultivated it into its current form, the formative power of seafaring, which feeds the imagination, the eastern homeland in the twilight of its farewell and beckoning him to turn back as if in the dawn of a great reformatory ascent, the wish to become the 'first judge of human nature' in this 'province' – all this lets him dream in the same breath of a school for humanity and of a book for human and Christian education and of himself as the reformer of Livonia on the model of Peter the Great. The enthusiasm of a sensitive soul, of an original genius of oration and of a forward-thrusting will blazes forth in everything. For this soul, the teachings of Christianity guarantee an ideal of humanity and of a spiritual [322] culture – an astonishing man, an astonishing programme of a life. We can imagine how challenging and how strange his appearance in the tiny Bückeburg must have been, this distinguished and youthful phenomenon, which occupied an indeterminate middle-ground between a Christian cosmopolitan and a cosmopolitan Christian, between a pastor and a scholar.

In sketching the great idea of a universal history of the cultivation of the world, of a history of the human soul itself 'in times and peoples', he proclaims: 'What kind of Newton belongs to these works!' This word [Newton] becomes a motto. At no point in time, not even in the latest texts which are already almost alienated from his creative intuitions, is the great model which he conjures up for himself the expression of a naturalistic violation of the historical world. Rather, Newton is for him the model of a genuine 'remark' on and experience of realities rather than 'abstract shadow images'. It is not the mathematical ideal of method in Newtonian science that inspires him. What moves him with vivid effect is the great unity of nature, which Newton made visible by combining a physics of the earth with a physics of heavenly bodies.

It is not so easy for us to conceive of the enthusiasm with which Newton's work was celebrated as the construction of a new cosmos after the collapse of the Aristotelian and scholastic geocentrism, and the response it generated. In Herder's description we hear its echoes. It is a new feel for the ordered equilibrium of all things, which also promises a new self-understanding to the human soul. The soul's place in the whole is certainly no longer the centre of the universe. But it is itself the place in which the great equilibrium of the whole comes to be felt, this interaction of all forces which determine the course of nature and human destiny. It is a feeling of life, which, from its own centre, lives through the whole, a force from far and near, as confirmed by Newton's distant forces and the great discoveries of the biology of the time. This is what a contemporary and witness to the new physics, the Swabian pietist Oetinger, perfected into an influential fusion of the idea of life with the spirit.[6]

Herder's unlimited capacity for feeling grasped the significance of Newton in its depth, without ever reaching conceptual clarity. As Newton taught us to represent the most diverse phenomena as the effects of one and the same force of attraction, avoiding any hypothetical explanation of the experience so described, Herder in the same way wanted [323] to learn how to experience the true realities of human life as facts. He, who saw himself as a bookish man overwhelmed by bookish knowledge, wanted to be 'immersed in things, not trained in words'. He who says about himself: 'I have been led somewhat too far away from the truth [...] I am in the land of hypotheses, abstractions, dreams', wished to learn 'to philosophize from nature, without books and instruments'. Even the book of a Newton, he would like to read like he says here on a ship, sitting under a mast on the vast ocean, and this means, in the vision of his whole being affected by life:

> and to guide the sparks of electricity from the impact of the waves right into the storm, and raise the pressure of water right up to the pressure of air and the wind, and follow the movement of the ship, surrounded by water, right up to the shape and movement of the stars, and rather not stop until I know everything *for myself*, because *until now* I know nothing about myself.

This new will to know, which he calls 'knowing for myself', means the new intimacy of an experience of force and living efficacy. It goes with the radical denial of his presumed knowledge until then. This leaving of the coasts behind, sailing in the open sea with the endless horizon always expanding, this is for him the breakthrough to a new way of thinking from the experience of being moved.

He realizes that only thinking in changing horizons reveals realities. In a draft, it is said: 'Philosopher, you who only see the fundamental bass of your abstraction, do you see the world? The harmony of the whole? Do you stand in the right place?' And so he asks himself: 'When will I be so far away in order to destroy everything in me that I have learnt and invent for myself what I think and learn and believe?' Even the concept of virtue becomes questionable for Herder, the pastor and educator, as an abstract name to which 'we have resigned ourselves' in language. 'Virtue is nothing other than human life and bliss; every date is action, all the rest is shadow, is reasoning'. From the very beginning, Herder, the literary critic, was already a wonderfully sensitive observer, a virtuoso of historical empathy. This is how, in opposition to Lessing, he wanted 'to feel the full force throughout the energy', for example in Homer. Now, however, this genial capacity of his acquires the self-consciousness of a new way of thinking as that of a universal task. Herder's breakthrough to a new way of thinking in realities is his entry into the historical world. He accomplishes it in the discovery of a new force in himself, which rises out of the force of historical self-reflection, out of his own life and his ownmost experiences. 'No step, no history, no experience would be in vain, I would have everything in my power, nothing would fade away, nothing would be unfruitful, everything would be a lever to push me forward'.

This is how Herder was led from the experience of his life history to the experience of the world history which is to be experienced in 'peoples and times'. [324] His strength is to develop a new sense 'to discover analogously', that is to say, to think in analogies. So it dawns on him in his experience of seafaring how every historical era possesses its own different horizon. In this living experience he recognizes the right of historical times, which had remained concealed to him up until now by the prejudices of his education. He thus grasps for instance the necessity in the despotism of all earlier times by analogy with the communal destiny of a ship on a great journey and similarly sees in the credulity of the seafaring folk and their fondness of story-telling the key to understanding the mythology of the ancients. The naïve pride that enlightened times take in their education comes to a naught once Herder learns to see in such an analogical way. As a matter of fact, the very marine world of fish gives him the opportunity to think fish in their own element and thereby to note the limits and conditioning exerted by the elements of the present in which he lives. But the first fruit of this thinking is this: 'The human race in all of its ages can be summed up by happiness, albeit only of a different kind in each age'. With this assertion, Herder overcomes not only the Enlightenment but also its opposite, Rousseauism, not only the intellectualism of the 'abstract shadow images', which pretend to be a progress, but also the revolt of sentiment: he becomes the discoverer of historical sense. The historical sense is a *sense for force*. Herder sees through the prejudices of his time all the way to the forces of the human heart, which are the same in all historical happenings. 'Humanity always remains humanity'. This means that the representations of virtue and happiness, freedom and God, which the refined, enlightened human beings of today have, are for him no useful standard for understanding history. 'We seek and weigh forces, not the shadow image of their abstractions and consequences, which perhaps change with every ray of sun'.

This is how Herder recognizes the particular form of life which dominates the early days of humanity, the age of patriarchy. This is an age that, measured against the standard of the fine and weakened sensitivity of the eighteenth century, obviously appears as a time of despotism and superstition but in fact 'breathes the healthy spirit of all childhood'. Thus, Herder makes what holds as a universal law of life fruitful for the understanding of history: in youth, maturity and old age, the whole of life appears in the same way and in the similarly necessary forms. This law of growth, in accordance with the ages of life, teaches us, for example, that the time of patriarchy lies settled under the 'silent eternal power of the paragon'. To learn through authority is as much appropriate for the childhood of humanity as its childish religious feeling. 'There our deism would be like an old person of three'.

Herder sees the schema of the ages of life more as an image for [325] understanding history. He realizes that one has to defend a time from being measured by standards coming from another time – even if it is one's own present. He thus discovers as a *first* fundamental feature of history that any time and any people, just like any age of human beings, 'has in itself the middle point of its happiness'. He realizes that it is misguided (what was then in vogue) to want to compare times or peoples in terms to their happiness. He recognizes the false arrogance of his own present lurking in this. It is a false, unhistorical (and unreal) abstraction 'to take' one's own present 'for the quintessence of all times and peoples'. 'The enlightened human being of later times does not merely wish to be the one listening to everything, but himself to be the last note humming out all the notes, the mirror of all of the past and the one representing the purpose of the composition in *all* its scenes! – The precocious child is blasphemous'. Faced with this foolishness of his century, Herder discovers the essence of history. He sees that history is no mere nexus of ideas. 'Ideas in fact only yield ideas'. There may be a progressive clarity to be found in ideas but the 'juice and the core of all history' which Herder is seeking are not to be found in the rational ideals of his century. 'Heart, warmth, blood, humanity, life!' – rather this is the core of history, which the century lacks.

> You, the entire nature of the soul, which permeates everything, which also models all the other inclinations and powers of the soul after itself, which colours even the most casual actions after itself, in order to feel it alongside, answer not in words but immerse yourself in the age, in the heavenly space, the whole history, feel yourself inside everything.

It is always about the whole element in which the times and peoples live. This, however, is the decisive insight: history is only 'disseminated' in what is national and individual, in times and peoples. This gives the problem of history its philosophical weight that in it no linear progression towards the perfection of humanity is to be found (at least not, as Herder adds the qualification, 'in the limited scholarly sense'). Only if the sense of history does not lie in the perceived end of the present or of a foreseeable future does history itself as the great continuous chain of destinies have its own specific sense in each of the links of the chain.

Secondly, to the essence of history there belongs the fact that it is a succession. This means that any 'maximum' is untenable in relation to it, that it can possess no duration, no 'natural eternity'. To require this would mean nothing other than 'annihilating the essence of time and destroying the whole nature of finitude'. With this insight, even the idea of a favourite people also becomes untenable, and Herder thereby becomes a critic of a classicist image of Greece. Against Winckelmann he finds that Egyptian culture has its own legitimacy. Against Winckelmann he recognizes, despite all his love for it, the limits of [326] ancient Greece. Even this most beautiful youth of humanity is submitted to the law of history. Every progress is at the same time a loss. 'The human race is just not capable of any perfection; it must always abandon it by moving forward'. And this is precisely the task that Herder sets for himself: to examine closely this progress, this fateful advance of history through peoples and times. And to examine it not only impartially but with the aim of perceiving God's ways in it, that is to say, to sense God as forces and effects. This is how he sees it (and anticipates in this an insight which has become familiar to us from Nietzsche's second *Untimely Meditation* 'On the Uses and Disadvantages of History for Life'): Every life has a closed horizon in order 'to give me satisfaction in the middle point which supports me and it does this in this moderation of the human vision (which results in the "loss of feeling, coldness and blindness" towards what is dissimilar and alien in the past)'. In a century taking pride in its lack of prejudices, Herder recognizes the power of prejudice in making one happy by 'huddling peoples together in their middle point'. In this,

Herder lapses as little into the self-satisfaction of the later historicism that he quite recognizes the advantage of the wider vision carried by the position of one's own present, its place, so to speak, on the finest and highest branches and forks of the great tree of humanity. Yet, he does not conceal from himself the weakness which lies in such refinement. He sees the task of the historian as that of obtaining the criteria for historical reflection in these life-supporting prejudices.

But *thirdly*, finding the proper criteria of the times does not exclude questioning the comprehensive sense of history. Herder's statements on this fundamental metaphysical problem of the philosophy of history have apparently undergone a radical transformation. In the Bückeburg text the sense of world history is only treated like a foreboding certainty, which has its guarantee only in an otherworldly plan of God. To want to know it goes beyond the fragmentary existence given to us humans. Our own fragment of life is no match for the magnitude of God's course through the times. Yet,

> even the limitedness of my earthly point, the bedazzlement of my gaze, the foundering of my purposes, the riddle of my inclinations and desires, the subjection of my powers only to the entirety of a day, of a year, of a nation, of a century – this is for me precisely a guarantee that I am nothing but that the whole is everything!

This is how Herder concludes from the impenetrability of the course of history to his own place in the whole. What appears to us as a 'bewildering labyrinth' is in fact 'the palace of God'. One should just not resort to looking for particular purposes in history or asking about the advancement of the happiness of the individual in the course of history and conceal from oneself the fact that a greater plan of God is at work in the whole. [327] Completely hidden from individual, self-interested players (for their passions keep them biased), the sense of history announces itself in the 'turning away', but not in such a way that we could so much be the spectators 'in calmly anticipating the entirety of the consequences' in order to recognize God's plan fully. The philosophy of history is only guided by this: to remain constantly certain of this advancement into what is great. Even in this limitation of our insight, history retains 'something of its harmony'.

Later, in the *Ideas*, this sounds different. But only the emphasis is placed differently. Now, armed with the analogy of nature Herder wants to venture into the labyrinth of human history. We read in volume 15 of the *Ideas* how everything strives, even if jaggedly and with many setbacks, towards a single course of development of humanity, of reason and fairness in world history. We may add how Herder, in the presentation of history, begins to align himself with this criterion of humanity and thereby eventually tries to force the great justice of the world history into his perspective. In the face of all this, one could likely think that he has fallen back into the Enlightenment's belief in providence, a belief which he himself explicitly fights to the very end. Indeed, even now his motto remains: no particular ultimate purpose, thus no patronizing schooling from God and history!

Even now he still wants to see history as the field where natural forces are at work. World history is no 'fairytale'.

This seems to be in contradiction with the belief in humanity, which Herder enthusiastically proclaims. Humanity alone, the purported goal of world history, has a sense in Herder which does not contradict his insights into the essence of history and remains close to the doctrine of the otherworldliness of the divine plan of history. We only need to ask: what is the discernible sense of history if nothing else than the advance into what is great, into the whole, is sighted in history? What is historical reality then experienced as? Obviously as a *force* and as a configuration of forces. Now it appears that even Herder's concept of humanity is not an abstract ideal concept but a concept of force. Therein lies Herder's place in the history of philosophy, that he is the one who applied the concept of force or of organic forces to the world of history.

Herder does not arbitrarily apply the concept of force to history and to the determination of its ontological rank. A look at the history of the concept of force may rather teach us that this concept is thereby thought back into its own origins. The concept of *dunamis* ['potentiality'], which was transmitted by the Stoic and neo-Platonic theory of nature and underlies the modern concept of force, is thought anthropologically in an essential way. It is not only that the word originally belongs to this field, that is to say, that it is used to speak about the capacities of the living and particularly of human beings. It rather belongs to [328] the manner in which we experience what force is: that we are aware of it in the resistance experienced by the force expressing itself, and as resistance. It is a fundamental determination of force that it has its expression only in the play of forces. All the same, force is only experienceable as the force which is accumulated and not fully expended in its expression. It thus belongs to the experience of force, to our awareness of it, that we sense possibilities, a conscious virtuality, which projects a space in the future, a breadth of variations of effects and expressions. The conceptual dialectic of force, which Hegel elaborated: soliciting, expression and accumulation, reflection into itself and finally the play of forces, extends across a purely anthropological original dimension. Above all else, the concept 'play of forces' is originally an experience of a felt alertness, obviously such that the free playing activity, for example of the senses, of the limbs, is itself only an aspect of this play in which the whole of the soul is a co-player of vanishing minuteness. The concepts of soliciting and being solicited, of self-restraint and self-expression are themselves at play across the universal constitution of being.

This is how the felt origin of force expands itself into the realm of natural order as well as into the realm of history which transcends individual consciousness and includes it into its play. Behind Herder's comprehensive vision of nature and history there is an ontological problem, which questions behind the Cartesian opposition of *res extensa* ['extended thing'] and *res cogitans* ['thinking thing']. Herder thus stands among the successors of the great Leibniz, who introduced the concept of force into the Cartesian theory of movement and took it as the basis of his metaphysical projects. The dynamic pantheism, which Herder developed in this emulation and with this intention – his highly influential re-interpretation of Spinoza – may lag behind the depth of Leibniz's ideas. Yet, the concrete sense for the forces of history, which he displays, gives his conceptually unsatisfactory attempts at a philosophy of history the powerful impact of a new world-historical truth.

Historical truth is the efficacy of forces. When Herder says that world history is God's course among peoples, this thus means that God or the force of the universe manifests itself in individual national effects of forces. It does not manifest itself in the transparent planning, which sees in peoples and times only the means towards the divine purpose of salvation for the sake of an eternal or temporal bliss. No time period is just a means, each is a purpose. 'Feeling, movement, action, even if proceeding without goal (what has an *eternal* purpose on the stage of humanity?') – this is the reality of history. 'What power! What effect! Fed on the heart, not on the head'. Already in the Bückeburg text, the concept of force rings through the decisive context of the statements about human nature [329] (*humanitas*). In relation to bliss, Herder says there: 'human nature is no receptacle of an absolute bliss. But everywhere it attracts as much bliss as it can'. There is thus a proportion between this ability of humanity as force, on the one hand, and bliss, the enjoyment of force, on the other. Every individual is 'left with forces with regard to the whole but each only with the feeling of bliss also in accordance to the magnitude of these forces'. The reality of history shows itself in this and not in connection to a purpose of salvation posited externally. Herder opposes this historical concept of force to questions originating in the Enlightenment about the advancement of virtue and bliss.

This is the place where the Weimarian conception of the *Ideas* can be linked. This conception follows the guiding thread of the analogy of nature and the approach towards the concept of humanity also lies in this guiding thread. Even where humanity becomes something like a criterion of all times, it still remains an expression for the natural creative force of history. 'History is the science of that which is there, not of that which could well be according to secret intentions of destiny'. After already wandering through some millennia of world history, Herder asks: 'What is the fundamental law that we noticed in all the great phenomena of history? That everywhere on our earth what happens is what can happen on it'. This law encompasses the history of the earth and the history of human beings. It is not a 'natural law' that could be formulated mathematically. It is the law of naturality itself, of the organic formative power of nature. Herder can thus say: 'The whole history of humanity is a pure natural history of human forces, actions and drives according to place and time'. The human race, humanity is not an abstract ideal (even though it explains itself as the ideal of reasonableness and fairness) but the paragon of human nature, that is to say, a force which has an effect on itself. Humanity is no purpose of human nature which it would have outside of itself, but the purpose that humanity itself is. This is precisely the nature of human beings: 'to cultivate oneself into a kind of humanity'. The essence of human beings is to be 'a self-efficacious nature, with a circle of free activity around itself'. Just as every creature in nature has its own element of life, so the human being has an infinite element in which to expand through strenuous action. It is the element of world history.

Herder designates humanity as the state of equilibrium of human history. He refers thereby to the sort of economic and teleological principles which in the eighteenth century one undertook to establish in the realm of mechanical nature. He himself once writes: 'Lambert, the Leibniz of our time, has established the theory of maximal state of equilibrium as a mathematical, physical and metaphysical formula'. Herder thus introduces with the word 'state of equilibrium' something known from the mechanical order of nature, into human history. Humanity [330] becomes a natural law 'on which the essence of the human race rests'. It is not the result of the construction of an ideal, neither 'through the arbitrariness of a lord' nor 'through the persuasive power of tradition'. It is the natural condition of the endurance of human-historical existence. Humanity is 'reason and fairness'. The two are based on one and the same natural law, from which even the constancy of our essence (for example, in the alternation of sleep and waking) follows, namely, on a relation of forces towards periodic rest and order. Both have the enduring symmetry of things in view. Such a symmetry of forces is that in which alone the full enjoyment of existence lies.

This is how the initial experience of the living human forces and their proportion to happiness, which also guided the Bückeburg text, is developed into a concept of humanity as a natural system of living forces. In his own way, Herder has remained true to the motto chosen by appealing to Newton. His law 'of a heavenly Adrastea'[7] in the distribution of the weight and the movement of bodies according to mass, space and time' corresponds to the order which holds sway in the whole of world history.

Now, Herder manages to give another answer to the historical question of meaning than just the reference to the otherworldliness of the divine plan. He sees in history the spread and advancement of humanity, a humanity, however, precisely in history. In the full diversity of the individualities of peoples, in the infinite variations in their sensitivities, thoughts, aspirations there still lies a striving for unity. 'It is called (I always want to repeat this) understanding, fairness, goodness, *feeling of humanity*'. Already in the *Travel Diaries*, in a significant semantic tension between the eschatological and the organic consciousness of history, it was called: 'The great theme: the human race will not pass away *until it all happens*'. Because they are the conditions for the endurance of the human order in general, reason and fairness must show themselves in an increasing magnitude as what is abiding in history. It may be that all the progress of the discoveries and of all civilizational accomplishments of humanity is questionable due to its being accompanied by an equal progress in the possibility of misuse and destruction – Herder did not hide from this hard reality of history. Yet, he still believes too much in the goodness of reason as it has proven its worth so often in the resolution of a problem individually for not also trusting the usefulness of reason 'in the infinity of things'. His belief is not a belief in the moral progress of humanity from virtue. In this, Herder remains true to himself and to Rousseau, in that he subordinates the abstraction of virtue to the efficacious force of nature. Yet, [331] it is true of nature itself that even if 'it does not prevent any power, not even excessive power in its efficacy, all things are still constrained by the rule that one opposite effect cancels out the other with only the fruitful ultimately enduring'.

This trust in history is not based on the insightful reenactment of a divine plan for history but is a belief that believes in God in history because this belief finds his wisdom confirmed in nature. What philosophy of history serves, to be sure, is not to unravel God's plan for human beings, but to counter the scepticism in light of the change and the transitoriness of everything historically great and beautiful through the insight into the unity of human history and nature. Herder's belief in history is not a reason recognized in history but a belief in the permanence of what is rational. His claim is not Hegel's claim to grasp history, that is to say, to see in the necessity of its sequence the development of something that was already laid out 'in itself'. He believes rather in accepting what is unknown to us as a whole, the infinity of history, as still something divine that is worked out in a planned manner, in which individuals have to live in their specific place. The philosophy of history is not for him, as it is for Hegel, the elevation of the belief in history to a science. It is rather just clearing away the doubt about history and finding support for the belief in history through science, in particular through the embedding of human history into the greater and structurally more convincing totality of the history of the earth. Herder does not dispute the misleading and confusing picture offered by a history of human beings, rich in collapses and setbacks. Yet, even he comes close to the principle, methodologically elaborated later by Hegel, of an antagonism in the progress of history. Whereas this principle in Hegel gives history the course of necessity, it is in Herder's model of history more an indication that we should assume the 'hopeful truth' of progress even there where the facts fail to manifest it.

Herder himself formulated his belief in history in Greek concepts: as the reign of Nemesis = Adrastea, 'the most just controller of all human destinies, who looks after us the longest and quickly overtakes us'. Herodotus is for him the model of the genuine writer of history and the true philosopher of history because he venerates the law of history in the compensation and expiation of human arrogance, thus in the reign of the 'goddess who metes out'.

It could also be held as a prejudice of the enlightenment to think that the rational is triumphant in the long run. In particular, the belief in the progress of humanity and the peacefulness of human history, 'this pleasant dream of human beings', as Herder's editor, [332] Johannes von Müller calls it, was already 'terribly shattered' immediately after Herder's death by the age of the great Napoleon. Yet, von Müller adds this: 'but the denouement of the drama is not before our eyes'. In fact, the belief in the triumph of reason and fairness may accompany not only the suffering part of humanity as a consolation. Even the 'heroes' of history will seek the legitimacy of their plans and hard decisions in this belief. What was in any case epoch-making in Herder's thought about history was that his belief was not a trust in an otherworldly divine will of salvation and did not leave everything to God's inscrutable decisions. Rather, his belief was grounded in the inner necessity, in the 'nature' of human beings and history, in the natural system of its living forces. Through this, his legacy in relation to the philosophy of history has remained alive as the whole of his fundamental theological and metaphysical convictions faded away. Just as in rejecting every supernatural theory for the origin of language, he became the inaugurator of the proper science of language, in the same way, through his philosophy of history, he paved the way to a universal and, in particular, for a cultural history. By the same token, he also gave a far-reaching impetus to the political will and thought of the subsequent times, certainly not in the immediate manner of which the young seafarer dreamt when he saw himself as a political reformer, standing under the powerful reverberations of the reforms made by Peter the Great.

Even as a political thinker, he did not say anything new or anything of singular character. In this, he was simply a student of his times and of its great and admired model, Montesquieu. Neither in political history nor in the history of the theory of the state does he have really a place. The state is for him a machine in the meaning the word had in the seventeenth and eighteenth centuries. In such a meaning, a stifling soullessness and admirable artfulness are connected together. He was also more preoccupied by the dangers of a state machine for the general quality of life and bliss than by its meaning of stability and order. States are artificial and about a false appearance of life, Trojan horses, guaranteeing each other immortality (he means through inventions of statecraft, contracts and alliances). Yet, 'without national character there is no life in them' and statecraft 'plays with peoples and human beings like with lifeless bodies'. What the state can give us are artificial tools but unfortunately it can also steal something far more essential from us, ourselves'.

Like Montesquieu, Herder indeed looks with admiration at the Greek states animated by a common living spirit: 'And so the age of the Greek republics was the first step towards the maturity of the human spirit in the important matter of how humans were to be ruled by humans'. [333] Conversely, with Montesquieu he sees the crudest despotisms at work in later Roman history. A disastrous assessment of Rome, which has burdened the German history of the last two centuries. But he is in general no friend of the state. In this regard, he does not only and not primarily have the free happiness of the individual in mind, which is threatened by the state machine. He also does not have, like Montesquieu, a political ideal of the state, which ensconces itself in the cold scientificity of a formal theory of the constitution. He sees historically. Thus, he sees with Montesquieu the danger of clinging to antiquated forms of domination up to the point of horrific revolutionary catastrophes. He sees above all with Montesquieu the whole 'genetic spirit and character of a people' as the fruit of its history, and yet also as something of almost indestructible natural endurance. Precisely for this reason is he an adversary of the theory of constitution which is oriented towards the dead letter of the law, as he is in general an adversary of the folly of building nations through an ideal legislation. He sees historically: 'such an ideal law for all times and peoples would not even be for the people for whom this law is supposed to be adopted, like its garment'. How different is the task 'of providing nourishment for the veins and sinews of one's people so that it strengthens its heart and refreshes it in bone and marrow!'

In the recognition of this task there are insights which point far beyond Herder's immediate statements about the essence of the state. We have in our possession notes from his reading of Montesquieu from the time the *Travel Diaries* were composed in Nantes. These notes show how the new kind of thinking, which he embraces when breaking away from his previous life as a reader and literary critic, sees the essence and the task of the state in a new light. Montesquieu's essay about 'the spirit of the law', he believes, was in its intent still 'a philosophical attempt to take note of all the modes of governance … ' and thus 'to arrive at the essence of the whole form of governance'. But, according to Herder, he misses the genuine universality of 'taking note', the study of the living mores and habits of peoples instead of their written laws. 'He was too little a human being, too little a *natural philosopher*'. 'A book on the *cultivation* of peoples begins with vivid examples, habits, education and ends with the shadow image of desiccated laws'.

A book on the cultivation of peoples – at the bold beginning of his life's journey, Herder everywhere sees tasks and possibilities for cultivation and formation, even in the realm of the state. It is to the laws of nature that 'I want to take recourse in the darkness of my labyrinth to see how laws for nations are to be created, that these laws in so far as they are valid for nations, become effective, bring about happiness, reach their goals'. These are therefore laws that are different from those of present-day Europe, for 'the laws of our states only exert [334] weak command and do not bring about happiness. They are content with not making us unhappy'. With this guiding thread of nature Herder offers a new standard for the politics and theory of the state of his time: 'Laws which are so natural in their essence, which have originally formed precisely this nation in this way, which have preserved it in this way as those laws (i.e. of mechanical nature) have sustained the body – this is true legislation'.

Thus, from Herder's new historical experience of reality there emerges the guiding idea of a living state constitution from the spirit of a nation. But this is the point on which Herder has come to have a wide-ranging influence even in the realm of the life of the state and the theory of the state. His blindness to the tasks of order and organization, which even the absolutist state of his time still fulfilled, makes him the visionary of a new fundamental force in the public sphere. This force is the people. Herder perceives this reality first in the voice of the peoples in songs. He recognizes the sustaining and nurturing power of the mother tongue. He senses in all this the formative force of history, which is fused with the natural conditions of blood, climate, terrain, etc. His sense for what has grown and is growing to maturity in the life of peoples continues to have an influence in the attempt by the historical school of jurisprudence to conceptualize the essence of the law completely from its source and habit. In this regard, Herder himself is free from the romantic overestimation of what has historically grown and does not underestimate the formative force which historical deeds also have. The young Herder writes in this sense: 'Against the objection of those who say that everything takes form by itself, I say, yes, but also conversely. Here a monarch must steer the flow'. The task demands of monarchs, who here become creators, that they know their people as God knows the world; that they form their people so that the laws are its nature and its nature produces these laws …

It was thus certainly false to see in Herder the forerunner of von Savigny's theory of law. Yet, without Herder, German romanticism would not be thinkable. It is only that his influence runs deep in a more secret manner. This is why he is at the same time also the forerunner of the antipode to the historical school of jurisprudence, of Hegel. Herder continues to live also in Hegel's concept of the spirit of a people. If we finally think of the influence which Herder exerted on Eastern and South-eastern Europe by helping to awaken the self-consciousness of the small nations – I am reminded of the famous chapter on slaves in the *Ideas* – then it is clear that Herder recognized an element of modern political life and brought it to self-consciousness. It might appear to him in the age of absolutism that there was still a need to defend against the violent disfiguration of life through 'statecraft'. The age of revolutions, of the bourgeois and socialist revolutions, in which we live has changed the front lines, particularly as the nineteenth-century romantic principle of a national state [335] has lost more and more of its weight. Yet, this manifesto of 'historicism' was not only, as Herder wrote, full of the future. It retains its truth even in our present, which changes everything and compares everything, in teaching us not to forget what is unchanging, what has become, the 'cultivation' of humanity.

7

Schleiermacher as Platonist (1969)

[374] If we want to assess correctly the significance which Schleiermacher's studies on Plato possessed for his own thinking, we first of all need to be clear about the enormous breadth of these studies. As we know, it was the initiative of Friedrich Schlegel, who wanted to put together a translation of Plato's work with Schleiermacher, which drew Schleiermacher to these studies. But interest in Plato was really in the air at the time. We only need to think of the influence that Hemsterhuis exerted on Schleiermacher and his contemporaries. Now, it was of the greatest significance that Schleiermacher, thanks to his own highly artistic sensibility, was receptive to the artistic moment in philosophical speculation and the poetic configuration of the Platonic dialogues. This really set this newer preoccupation with the work of Plato on its own feet. Until close to the end of the eighteenth century, there were indeed individual attempts at translating Plato's dialogues into modern languages but the real interest lay in the Platonic thoughts about the intelligible world, that is to say, in a dogmatic theory transmitted through neo-Platonism. It was a truly watershed moment when Schleiermacher obtained his picture of Plato entirely from the dialogues and pushed aside the dogmatic model of thought proper to Platonism as well as the indirect transmission to the extent that it does not show itself directly to be a positive verification of the dialogical work.

From Schleiermacher we possess the great work of the translation with its general introduction and the particular introductions to the individual dialogues. This is a remarkable linguistic and philological achievement. What the introductions convey to us is meant for a wider circle of readers, but it also remains very characteristic of Schleiermacher's own access to Plato. This was elaborated above all by Wilhelm Dilthey, who, in his biography of Schleiermacher, but in particular in the academy essay on Schleiermacher's translation of Plato of 1898, situated Schleiermacher's achievement in its time and offered an interpretation of

---

'Schleiermacher als Platoniker' was first published in France in *Archives de philosophie* 32, 1 (1969): pp. 28–39. It appeared in *Kleine Schriften* III. Tübingen: J. C. B. Mohr (Paul Siebeck), 1972, pp. 141–49. It is now in *Gesammelte Schriften*, vol. 4. Tübingen: J. C. B. Mohr (Paul Siebeck), 1987, pp. 374–83. [Translators' Note: We have consulted the French original on some occasions to clarify the sense of what Gadamer meant or correct references].

the relationship of Schleiermacher to Plato. More concentrated and more exciting than what is stated within the translation work is however the relevant chapter from Schleiermacher's notes on the lectures on the [375] history of philosophy, which Heinrich Ritter edited and which, if I understand him correctly, stem from 1812. Schleiermacher's treatment of Plato in this draft demonstrates a far deeper penetration into Platonic philosophy than he reveals in his introductions to the translations, which chronologically precede this draft. Obviously, he developed his own philosophical position during his work on the translation and in his constant engagement with Plato. It is time to investigate Schleiermacher's Platonism anew, after so many decades of Plato research have produced manifold changes to our perspective on Plato's dialogues vis-à-vis Dilthey's perspectives. New aspects of Schleiermacher's reception of Plato become visible due to this.

In some respect, Schleiermacher was the first who made use of the details of the *Seventh Letter* in the sense that he envisaged the political goals set by Plato. In fact, the *Seventh Letter*[1] offers a detail that enabled Schleiermacher to say this: 'He often came close to his fulfilling his political goals but then again he was far until he finally gave up the hope and now left behind the image of the state in writing'. This is a perspective that Schleiermacher did indeed not pursue further. Yet, in the recent German research in Plato this perspective was developed to such an extent that one has attempted to interpret a part of the Platonic dialogues directly from Plato's political intentions and tendencies – with hardly any justification.

The first problem which presents itself in this context is that of the arrangement of the dialogues. Here, Schleiermacher starts from a rigid fundamental assumption in so far as he sees in the myth a kind of provisional function vis-à-vis the *logos*. On the origin of Schleiermacher's arrangement of the dialogues, we have interesting details from the correspondence between Friedrich Schlegel and Schleiermacher, which shows the latter to be the reliable and assiduous worker. The dialogical work reveals itself slowly to the sustained efforts of the translator Schleiermacher and no systematizing conception prejudices the finally chosen arrangement. It is first of all necessary to rectify a fiction which has gained validity in the history of Plato research, according to which Schleiermacher is to have presupposed that the dialogues were fundamentally conceived in a systematic and pedagogical manner and chose this fundamental view as the foundation for his arrangement of the Platonic dialogues. In opposition to this, the philologist Karl Friedrich Herrmann in his polemic against Schleiermacher is to have justified a genetic organization. This is a fiction in so far as Schleiermacher too, greatly influenced in these matters by the instigations from Friedrich Schlegel, had no other intention than finding the natural order of the dialogues. This natural order is also in his eyes understandably genetic. [376] What is correct is only this fact that for Schleiermacher the genetic order is also concretely appropriate to the philosophical and methodological intentions of Plato's construction so that *muthos* ['story', 'myth'] generally precedes *logos* ['discourse', 'reason']. In this one sees no fundamental opposition to Herrmann, who, for his part, finds a structural idea as the basis of the order, namely, that the dialectical dialogues as 'negative' precede the positive ones, the *Phaedo* and the *Republic*, even if he otherwise relied more strongly on external indications in his arrangement, like Tennemann before him.

Friedrich Schlegel had probably taken the lead in this consequential decision made by the two friends on the dialogues to be assessed as early. What amazes us today is not so much that the *Phaedrus* is to have been the first dialogue but that the *Parmenides* and the *Protagoras* are supposed to belong to the same beginning. These two dialogues represent in the eyes of the two friends the introductions to the theoretical and the practical part of philosophy in that one brings to light the aporias belonging to the knowledge of the ideas and the other the aporias of the teachability of virtue. What is no less amazing to the contemporary reader – something of which in general Plato research has no memory – is the fact that, in Schleiermacher's eyes, the text of the *Republic* with its continuation, the *Timaeus*, is not only a kind of solution to the early puzzle but forms the capstone of the entire literary plan and work. Naturally, in the process, the *Laws* are completely overlooked, about which it was already accepted at the time that Plato had left them unfinished, as ancient testimonies assure us. Thus, from purely external circumstances we can explain why Schleiermacher went on to not include the *Timaeus* in his translation, and this is true more than anything for the *Laws*. The *Republic* and the *Timaeus* in the eyes of Schleiermacher crowned the entire structure of Plato's dialogical work.

It would be cheap to sneer at the astonishing assurance with which Schleiermacher declares his own arrangement of the dialogues as self-evident and indisputable. At times in the process, he makes it unnecessarily difficult for himself by breaking self-evident connections and making frantic efforts to justify it, for example, when he inserts the *Meno* between the *Theaetetus* and the *Sophist*. In what follows, we will be contenting ourselves with such cases in which Schleiermacher's assertions are of real interest.

Already in antiquity one advocated the view, which Schleiermacher also makes his own, that the *Phaedrus* was the first of the Platonic dialogues. Here many elements come together which make the dithyrambic description of the ascent to the intelligible world appear youthful and at the same time as the initiation rite of academic philosophizing. But Schleiermacher's own justification for dating the *Phaedrus* early is manifestly weak. Yet, the assurance with which he [377] sees the unity of the disparate contents of this work is worth admiring, namely the unity or rather the deep connection between drive and method, as he calls it, an insight which, in relation to the dominant neo-Platonic mystification of the dialogue, betrays a deep understanding of Platonic dialectic. Yet, all the conclusions that he draws from this for the early composition of the dialogue lack any force of conviction. As we know, the early dating of the *Phaedrus* has continued to be influential well into our century, for example on Paul Natorps's interpretation of Plato. However, today it may be stated that the *Phaedrus* rather introduces the late period of Plato's dialogical work.

The situation is totally different with the early dating of the *Parmenides*, as Friedrich Schlegel and Schleiermacher have together recommended. This has found no followers at all. One can find this dialogue enigmatic. One can declare it inauthentic, as Überweg, for instance, has done, which on its merits is an outlandish assertion. If this dialogue is Platonic, though, then there can be no doubt that it belongs to the late phase of Platonic creation.

Let us ask what underlies the suggestion to date it early. In so doing, we want to put aside the still understandable hypothesis which Schlegel and Schleiermacher, both true romantic friends of the fragmentary, proposed with regard to the *Parmenides*, namely that it has been transmitted to us in an incomplete form. It has to be granted that the conclusion of the dialogue is very abrupt. Modern scholarship is quite helpless in the face of the fact that, with the single exception of the *Clitophon*, whose authenticity is very much in doubt, only the *Parmenides* terminates with abrupt suddenness without its own well-rounded conclusion. One can of course bring up other reasons which speak for the fact that the work is not fragmentary (for example, the increasing sketchiness in the exposition of the hypotheses). However, whether it is complete or fragmentary, how can one come to the estimation of it as early?

The reasons are worth clarifying. They obviously lie in the fact that here Socrates is introduced as a very young man, who is instructed by the aging Parmenides. The primary reason is that the acceptance of the existence of ideas, advocated here by Socrates, is led to a series of aporias by Parmenides, who leads the real discussion. Even if one finds the first of these arguments naive, the second is all the stronger. In terms of its thought content, this dialogue distances itself in an astonishing manner from the theory of ideas as it is commonly advocated in the Platonic dialogues. One cannot even say that the conclusion which Schleiermacher draws from this finding is completely without plausibility, even if it is not true in the literal sense in which Schleiermacher draws it. He concludes that the assumption of the [378] existence of the ideas as such is not to be attributed to Plato but that this was already one of the Socratic theses which Plato found extant and by the problematization of which, he was led precisely to his dialectic.

Another explanation is generally privileged today. One sees in the dialogue the expression of a crisis in the theory of ideas. By separating the theory of ideas from the moral-philosophical context in which this theory was originally conceived and by turning it into the universal, which is very explicitly reflected at the beginning of the *Parmenides*, Plato is said to have become entangled in the problems posed by his own acceptance of it. Quite a few go so far as to believe that he gave up his theory of ideas – which is awkward enough when the *Timaeus* in fact stands alongside the dialectical dialogues of the late period and repeats the theory of ideas with the old vigour. Under the circumstances, there is much that speaks in favour of the view that the supposition of the existence of the ideas as such, and in particular the supposition of the existence of individual ideas, should not be held as what is essential to Plato's philosophy but that what is essential is the dialectical connection between unity and multiplicity which underlies the ideas. At any rate, Schleiermacher is right to the extent that the problem of the one and the many, as it emerges in the Platonic dialogues as *the* problem of dialectic, is in no way limited to the relationship of the one *eidos* ['idea'] to the many things participating in it. From the very outset, this is not what the problem is. The problem of the dialectic is the problem of the multiplicity of ideas themselves, and this is so from the very outset. Already in the *Protagoras*, whose early dating was accepted by Schlegel and Schleiermacher, as we mentioned, and which is taken to be an early dialogue even today, what is being discussed is the unity and multiplicity of 'virtues'. It is in fact a question which implies the relationship between unity and multiplicity within the ideas.

If we now examine the chapter on Plato in Schleiermacher's draft of the history of philosophy, then it is striking that he begins with the academic division of philosophy into dialectic, physics and ethics. Even if this division stems from the Academy[2], it still is patently un-Platonic. With what artistry has Plato in the *Timaeus* woven that which Aristotle called 'physics' into the great discussion about the just state! Schleiermacher obviously follows the system of contemporary philosophy, which goes back up to Aristotle. According to this system, nature and morals become the object of two philosophical sciences, erected upon completely different principles, with a formal logical and dialectical discipline preceding these two sciences. In any case, Schleiermacher puts precisely this division as the basis of a critical discussion already in his *Outlines of a Critique of all Previous Theory of Morals*, in which he distinguishes Plato alongside Spinoza, as the one who [379] satisfied the requirement which remained unfulfilled in Kant and Fichte: to derive the duality of nature and morals from a common ground, namely the infinite being [*Wesen*][3].

Now, it is remarkable how Schleiermacher completely sets aside the indirect Platonic tradition about the two principles of unity and duality and obtains the fundamental features of the Platonic dialectic only from the dialogues and their statements on the essence of dialectic. This betrays the intrusion of a concrete philosophical interest of his own. In fact, what comes out clearly in this most highly speculative interpretation which Schleiermacher gives of Platonic philosophy is the decisive appropriation of the objectively central motifs.

His starting point is obviously the thought of a systematic connection between all human forms of knowledge. One already finds this thought in Schleiermacher's first main philosophical work, *Outlines of a Critique of All Previous Theories of Morals* of 1803. But this is not, as in Fichte's theory of science and in Hegel's logically grounded science of philosophy, coupled with the claim to deduce systematically this overall interconnectedness of science. To the contrary, it is associated with the idea that human thinking must necessarily lag behind this claim and can only manage to approach this idea approximatively. This is obviously the sense of the fact that Schleiermacher explicitly appeals to the Platonic concept of dialectic. He teaches us later on in his dialectic that the unity of thinking and being underlies the possibility of knowledge but that thinking can progress towards knowledge only in dialogue, in the overcoming of doubt and conflict. Dialectic is thus no merely formal logical discipline, as it has been understood in Aristotle and in the times that follow, but it concerns the 'fundamental principles for the methodical way of conducting a dialogue in the domain of pure thinking'[4]. In the transcription of the lecture from 1818 shared by Jonas, it is explicitly said:

> I go back to the time which lies beyond the separation (of logic and metaphysics). Then the entire effort of doing philosophy has another character. It also wants science, a science which wants to become not philosophy but the science of

nature and of human beings, physics and ethics. Philosophy comes out in this view more as a method [*Kunstlehre*][5] according to which a real knowledge is supposed to be produced in these areas. This is precisely what the Platonic but also some post-Aristotelian schools which have not adhered to Aristotle, have called dialectic[6].

[380] Schleiermacher thus explicitly appeals to the Platonic dialectic and the manner in which he does this teaches us in addition the nature of the concrete interest he must have in the form of transmission of Platonic philosophy, the form of the dialogue. It is precisely the inconclusive dialogical interaction, which points to a continuation, that grants immediate expression to the production of thought. This accommodates Schleiermacher's conviction that the systematic connection of all human forms of knowledge only presents an ideal. His treatment of Plato in his draft of the 'history of philosophy' shows in addition how he grounds and delimits his position (also precisely against Fichte's claim). One might surmise that the *Meno* possessed a particular significance for him. He alludes to it when he says that teaching is 'no bringing out but a calling out of something that is already originally present'. The mythical doctrine of preexistence and recollection represents in his eyes the ancient answer to the (modern) question of the universal validity of knowledge. The foundation of the systematic connection of all forms of knowledge upon which he builds[7] sounds entirely like a quotation: 'As indeed the whole of nature is akin'[8]. The two uses of 'awakened' or 'woken up'[9] also correspond to *Meno* 86a[10], where it is said that opinions when awakened by a question (*erōtēsei epegertheisai* ['awakened by questioning'])[11] become forms of knowledge. There is no doubt that this description of knowledge corresponds to Schleiermacher's own position. The root of Schleiermacher's understanding of the mythical in Plato also lies here. It is necessary in order 'to replace the doctrinal expression of the absolute unity, an expression which is impossible without being completed from all sides'[12]. Furthermore, Schleiermacher thoroughly contrasts dialectic with the sophistic practice, and this is good Platonism.

What differentiates the Platonic dialectic from the antilogies of the sophistic practice is supposed to be above all the fact that negative statements are shown to be relative. What is meant by this is obviously the critique of Parmenides in the *Sophist*, in which non-being is shown to be a 'determinate negation', the *mē on* ['non-being'] as *to heteron* ['the other'][13]. Schleiermacher is right: this is indeed the final refutation of the antilogic of the One and the Many, as it arose out of relativity, i.e. the relativity of perceptual qualities. Schleiermacher uses here what is for our historically educated ear a somewhat peculiar expression in so far as he uses Aristotelian terms to describe Plato. He indeed speaks of the division into the *kath' auto* ['by itself'] and the *pros ti* ['in relation to something'] which Plato is supposed to have found. The distinction between the in-itself and the relative is in fact the [381] presupposition for demystifying sophistic chatter. Plato had accomplished it and Aristotle brought it to concepts. But there lies something still different in such a division 'which presents the unity of the essence in the multiplicity of relations', and here Schleiermacher becomes truly brilliant in his appropriate interpretation of the Platonic dialectic. In recognizing the relational structure of the *logos*, he in the end eliminates anew the opposition between the *kath' auto* and the *pros ti*. He says the following: this division

> at the same time sets the task of leading every *kath' auto* through all *pros ti*, which must form a complete system, so that every unity of the essence becomes again a totality of determinations – and a totality of relations, to the extent that the essence can also be considered under *tautotēs* ['identity'] and *heterotēs* ['difference']; thus as unity and totality, every unity becomes again an image of the whole[14].

I take this to be the only enlightening foundation for the explanation of the much-discussed passage in *Sophist* 253d (which Schleiermacher in his detailed annotation of this passage in his translation had not yet presented with such clarity). Only in this way can what no one had explained satisfactorily so far be explained, namely that here in the activity of the dialectician, an explicit reversal is asserted. The *kath' auto* of the *mia idea* ['one idea'] is maintained throughout all relations (*pantē diatetamenēn … diaisthanetai* ['sees clearly maintained everywhere'] d6) and in this manner becomes the totality of its relations. Conversely (*au*, d8), every relational perspective can be maintained in relation to itself and is thus for its part the *kath' auto* of all its relations. This is an enlightening application of the dialectical interconnectedness of identity and difference to the description of the dialectician. And this application arises quite consequentially from the critique of Parmenides in the *Sophist*.

It is not so convincing to say that Plato 'indisputably' sees in this 'at the same time the recognition of the individual'. This is more Leibniz than Plato (in this case, given Schleiermacher's historical self-consciousness, we would have to say Spinoza instead of Leibniz). But this is grounded in Schleiermacher's own thinking, as it can be shown. In the introduction to the *Critique of All Previous Theories of Morals*, Schleiermacher grants Plato the distinction of being the only one (besides Spinoza) to have enquired into the ground of unity, which brings together physics and ethics, and to have recognized their primacy in the derivation of the idea of absolute unity or rather of divinity. This distinction granted to Plato and his critique of the theory of postulates in the *Critique of Practical Reason* underlie Schleiermacher's re-thinking of Platonic dialectic into a metaphysics of the individual. Schleiermacher thinks the world as an artwork of the divinity and he believes to find this in Plato, probably appealing here above all to the concrete inner connection between the text of the *Republic* and the *Timaeus*. But with this he explicitly interprets [382] ideas as the thoughts of the divinity. This is certainly not to be found in Plato and became possible in the first place only centuries later, as is clear to us today[15]. But it is clear how only this re-interpretation allowed Schleiermacher to think that the divinity manifests itself in creation and thus in every individuality. To this extent, his re-interpretation of the Platonic dialectic from the perspective of the recognition of the individual is no accidental anachronism.

It would be worth pursuing the analysis of the chapter on Plato in the *History of Philosophy* still further. For even in other theorems which Schleiermacher presents, he demonstrates the same speculative sense that allows him, despite the employment of Aristotelian concepts, to grasp the authentic thinking of Plato. This is true above all for two concepts, the concept of matter, which he applies to the interpretation of the *Timaeus* and about which he rightly says: 'Matter only expresses the difference between original and copy so that as raw matter it is thought in its passing away, but, as the bearer of the copy, it is thought in its permanence'[16]. This is excellent and it reaches an understanding of the Aristotelian concept of matter shorn of all dogma. A second example is his exposition on the concept of the soul and in particular of the world soul. What is admirable in his interpretation of the concept of the soul is again the methodological proximity to Plato. He obviously sets himself the task of interpreting the *Phaedo* from the standpoint of the *Timaeus* and in so doing he arrives at a result which I would not dare to designate with Dilthey as unhistorical. Schleiermacher writes:

> Body and soul as such are not for Plato proper substances but the soul, once separated from the body, is left over as something similar to the world-soul but as necessarily in need of being attached to a body. The body for its part, as a singularity taken from the becoming of the world-body falls back into the universal. Thus, the mortal soul is not a proper substance but what is such is only that which is posited in the soul through its union with the body.

This sounds rather Averroistic. Yet, what considered from the Christian views on the soul and creation is a heresy comes much closer, as we can see today, to the philosophical theology of the Greeks than the earlier tendency to seek all over for anticipations of Christian teaching.

It is also not correct, as Dilthey did under the coercion of the systematic nature of his own typology of worldviews, to account for the position of Schleiermacher as 'objective idealism'. For Schleiermacher was not only seeking to avoid the one-sidedness of a 'subjective' idealism [383] but was striving in his interpretation of Plato to confine 'idealism' to a partial aspect of the whole of the Platonic philosophy. His appropriation of Platonic dialectic rested precisely on this. In addition, it helped him to eliminate the separation of the intelligible (ideal) world of being from the 'real' world of becoming: 'As in the original, being and knowledge are the same, and this sameness is precisely its essence, in the same way, the fundamental vision of the copy is also the being-one of the spiritual and the material in the form of life'[17]. In this manner, Schleiermacher derives the organic unity of reality from idealistic identity. Only when we see this do we understand the peculiarity to which the present study is dedicated, namely, that the discoverer of the Platonic dialogical form places the systematic construction of Platonic philosophy in the foreground and makes so big a deal of the idea of a Platonic physics, as it is offered to him by the *Timaeus*. He accepts the later division of philosophy into dialectic, physics and ethics for Plato. He takes it at face value.

8
Hegel and Heraclitus (1990)

[32] Heraclitus – the beginning, Hegel – the completion: this is how Hegel himself saw the significance of the obscure (*ho skoteinos*), as Heraclitus was already called in antiquity. 'From him the beginning of the existence of philosophy is to be dated – it is the abiding idea that is the same in all philosophy up until the present day, as it was the idea of Plato and Aristotle'[1].

When we read such a statement we are gripped in some way. This is still something different from the erudite and sensitive reconstruction which Schleiermacher was the first to grant the philosophy of Heraclitus the obscure. It is like a programme of Hegel's own philosophy, indeed of philosophy in general. How in one stroke, we see revealed in it the vision of an inner continuity of philosophical thought over and beyond the gaps and fissures, declines and renaissances, which have given its form to philosophy in the Western sense of the word. What Hegel undertakes here is not an artificial and erudite review which only accompanies his own system of philosophical sciences. This system is the last great attempt to reconcile the historical legacy of humanism and the violent upsurge of modernity through the force of thought, to reconcile it with this new period of the empirical sciences and the reshaping of nature into a single great site of production, in which the human spirit of invention and the human force of production are tested. What Hegel undertakes here is more than that.

'Here we see land. There is no statement of Heraclitus that I have not incorporated into my *Logic*', Hegel confessed. This is what not only grips us in this confession but rather astounds us: Is this meant to be the purpose towards which everything strives, the Hegelian logic, this completion of the thought of the *logos*, which found for the first time in Heraclitus its obscure and equally ambiguous expression? What is this *logos*, 'which always is and which human beings always confront with incomprehension, as much before they [33] got to hear this word as after they have heard it' (Frag. 1)? Ever since, we have wondered in relation to this first statement of Heraclitus' text as to what 'always' means here: the word in its eternally valid truth or the ever-lasting incomprehension of human beings. Aristotle, who quotes the statement for this very reason, saw in it a problem of punctuation: before the word 'always' or after it, 'eternally valid' or 'always without understanding'. But

---

'Hegel und Heraklit' was first presented as a lecture in Italian in Naples in 1988. It was first published in *Gesammelte Werke*, vol. 7. Tübingen: J. C. B. Mohr, 1991, pp. 32–42.

who would want to separate by a mere comma what inseparably belong together, truth and untruth, reason and unreason? Even the ear of the listener may not be able to separate them. It is certainly different with readers, who must articulate the unparsed signs of writing without really 'hearing' when reading. This was precisely the case of the great reader Aristotle, as he was known among his contemporaries. Like all ancient humans, he had certainly read it aloud. But he was a man for whom only the clear distinctness of thoughts mattered and not the wavering ambiguity of sonorous, enigmatic expressions in the way Heraclitus had crafted them. Hegel too, like Aristotle, was a reader and so he too separates in such a way – and for him it is clear – that it is the *logos* that always is. With his one-of-a-kind power of abstraction and with his belief in reason bordering on madness, he saw 'the logical' at work at all times and in all places. It was not only, like for the Greeks, in the ordering *logos* which permeates the universe but equally so in chaotic human affairs, with their ups and downs of fortune and misfortune. To be sure, the Greeks also held the cosmic order to be a model for human beings but always as something unreachable. By contrast, Hegel resolutely opposed the logic of history, the belief in reason in history to the truly well-founded scepticism of the moralists of all times. In the introduction to 'The Philosophy of Right' he intensified his opposition to provocative levels with the statement: 'That which is rational is real; and that which is real is rational'. Only a very high concept of reason can grant a sense at all to this statement, not the concept of the ever-limited human reasonableness, which can only with difficulty guard against the violence of our will and wishes. Only then is this statement perhaps true, but precisely *sub specie aeternitatis* ['under the aspect of eternity'], not for us and within the bounds of our temporality.

We must thus ask: Are we not speaking here of past forms of the spirit, of a Hegel whom we may admire but cannot follow, and of his first initiator, Heraclitus, whom nobody understood and nobody understands? Or do we still find in his thinking for all time and also for us, as Hegel said in his lectures, 'the abiding idea, which is the same in all philosophies up until the present day'?

The fact is that two great thinkers after Hegel, who both fought Hegel [34] without ever completely freeing themselves from him, Nietzsche and Heidegger, have quite resolutely declared themselves to be followers of Heraclitus. The young Nietzsche saw Heraclitus under the thinkers vividly carved out of stone in the tragic age of the Greeks as one who taught how to justify all becoming. Unbeknownst to him at the time, this was an anticipation of his own doctrine of the innocence of becoming and the *amor fati* ['love of one's fate']. At the same time, he saw in Heraclitus, and already when he was just starting out, the ideal of someone solitary and independent, as he himself was. And Heidegger: Above the lintel of Heidegger's cabin in the Black Forest, engraved in a bark there was Heraclitus' saying: 'Lightning steers everything' – and this means: not the eternal fire, not the highest God in Mount Olympus who thunders from on high when something might not be done according to his will; rather lightning, which for the duration of a moment tears apart the darkness all around us before we are enclosed in an even deeper darkness. With the prophesier of European nihilism, this most uncanny of all guests, as with the thinker of the oblivion of being, who in the nothing finds the veil of being left behind for us and who thinks the concealment of the divine, are we not the farthest from Hegel's idealism of the absolute spirit, a spirit which almost promises to bring about 'the annihilation of nothingness'[2] in itself?

Who then was Heraclitus? And who was Hegel, who could see in Heraclitus the true beginning of philosophy? And who are we, who do not find this beginning of philosophy, in the way Hegel undertook to think it from the standpoint of its completion, to be enough, but would like to think something more original and inceptual, in which there is still something else sheltered than this end of 'the logical' in the absolute idea? Let us question Hegel's own reference to Heraclitus. It is attested twice, in his 'Lectures on the History of Philosophy' and his 'Science of Logic'. Yet, this attestation is in fact just a single one. Hegel's appropriation of the history of philosophy is in fact not a mere historical digression but rather the immersion into the truth unfolding itself in time. 'It is in accordance with the concept of spirit that the development of history falls into time'[3] and the history of philosophy is 'the innermost aspect of world history'.

Hegel's treatment of Heraclitus in his history of philosophy introduces a new moment. Hegel formally inverts the contrast between the Eleatic [35] doctrine of the One and Heraclitus's theory of the constant flux of all things, which had been common since Plato but in fact did not fully express Plato's own insight. Hegel does not do this for reasons of historical chronology but on logical grounds. The truth of becoming is precisely for Hegel not a lesser aspect which was overcome by the profound insight which Parmenides had into the truth of being, and by Platonic thinking, which arrives at its truth in the *ontōs on* ['what is most being in being'] of the ideas.

The truth of becoming is in Hegel's view rather the higher truth, compared to the abstract identity of being without becoming, which completely excludes the nothing from itself. This is how Hegel also cites Heraclitus as a witness at this point at the beginning of his *Logic* where he defends the paradoxical statement that being and nothing are the same. This statement is in fact the greatest conceivable challenge to healthy common sense and precisely for this reason, the sharpest profile of the 'rigour of the concept' demanded of philosophical thinking. Being is not something that is and the nothing is not something that is not. Both do not mean 'something'. In both we are dealing with 'empty affairs of thought'. This is how it is called in Hegel himself. They form the beginning of Hegel's logic precisely because both say nothing yet. Whoever thinks only being thinks nothing definite and says nothing yet. Very much against his own fundamental principle to bracket out all external reflection and follow 'the things themselves' in the dialectic proper to them, Hegel defends this beginning of logic in four long remarks, which are all already to be found in the first edition of the *Logic* of 1812. This is significant. This great effort serves the purpose of conferring becoming the rank of a first truth, of a truth which is authenticated as coming into being as well as passing away – and always as both. We could indeed surmise that Heraclitus (and no one else) stands behind the transformation which Hegel made to his theory of categories developed as a 'logic' by introducing this theory with being, nothing and becoming. The beginning of logic with being and nothing instead of with something (= existence) did not in any case arise without having Heraclitus' thinking in view.

In this, Hegel takes his point of departure from the Aristotelian formulation of the Heraclitean principle: 'Being is not more than non-being' or 'being and nothing are the same'. He takes them to be original Heraclitean statements. He has no real sense for the structural principles of Heraclitean sentences. He may not, like Cicero, ascribe its obscurity to something intentional and yet he anyway follows Aristotle and his own aversion for the obscurity in Heraclitus when he sees a deficiency in it and says of Heraclitus: 'His obscurity is rather more due to the negligent use of words and unsophisticated language'. It would be more advisable for us to admire the unique Heraclitean art of arranging words and the profundity of his use of metaphors, as the whole later antiquity did anyway.

[36] However, this is no accidental misjudgement on the part of Hegel or the consequence of the fact that philological research has only become fully cognizant of the formal aspect of such texts in our century. What is shown to us here is rather Hegel's own ambivalent position between self-being and self-consciousness, between living and thinking. On the basis of self-consciousness, he attempts to discern the self-being of the living and nevertheless he wants to 'prove' the continuation of the objectively logical into the subjectively logical through a dialectical intensification of contradictions.

His speculative genius allows him to recognize in Heraclitus, as later in Plato and even in Aristotle, the deepest speculative content. This is how he was the first to bring the late Platonic dialogues and their proximity to the universal conceptual art of Aristotle back to eminence and thereby set a standard which has never been reached by classical philology despite all of its advancements. In accordance with this, he emphasizes however in his *Logic* and precisely at this point that the form of the proposition is not conducive for expressing speculative truths. As he explains, the speculative statement is in fact no real propositional judgement. Thinking does not posit any given subject, attributing predicates to it. Thinking is rather the subject itself which finds itself again in the predicate and determines itself further in terms of itself. This is how the form of the proposition is destroyed in thinking itself. Furthermore, Hegel now recognizes the right of non-speculative thinking in so far as 'the opposing movement' must also be expressed and the dialectical contradiction, the return of the concept into itself, must also be presented, posited in the 'there'. The making explicit of the implicit dialectic of the speculative is in his view just simply the form of philosophical demonstration.

The statement 'being and nothing are the same' must be complemented by the statement 'being and nothing are not the same'. Only in this way is the result, becoming, expressed in a manner recognizable in statements. This indeed explains why Hegel does not pay any attention to the linguistic skills of Heraclitus. The speculative sense of these thoughts does not elude him at all. He basically wants nothing other than to make explicit the implicit dialectic which he perceives in Heraclitus' statements. He rightly grasps the unity of the opposites, which Heraclitus detects in innumerable variations, as the inseparability of opposites, and recognizes therein the dialectical structure of movement, becoming, process. The One of Heraclitus is a speculative principle. The One, which unites the opposites, 'is not the abstract but the activity of self-differentiation; the dead infinite (that is to say, of Anaximander) is a bad abstraction against the depth which we see in Heraclitus'. Heraclitus is the first to recognize the dialectic of the whole and the parts, the unity of the whole with all its parts, which precisely for this reason are not so much parts (*merē*) as they are members (*melē*). Since Heraclitus, this has [37] been a key part of all dialectic of the concept, in Plato and Aristotle as well as in Kant or Hegel. We encounter even in Plato something like a formula: *merē te kai melē* ['parts and members']⁴. Thus, Heraclitus' fire in turn cannot be understood as a dead component or in general as something that comes first. Hegel's power of abstraction frees Heraclitus' doctrine of the fire from the Aristotelian interpretation of fire as an element. 'Heraclitus could no longer express water or air as absolute essences in the manner of something that comes first, out of which the other also emerges, in that he thought being as the same as non-being', and this means as the 'process'. This – and not a first being – is what fire is for him, 'this absolute unrest, absolute dissolution of permanence – the passing away of the other but also of itself; it is not abiding'.

Consistently sticking to this insight and prior to all the techniques of source criticism, which was only developed by modern philology, Hegel recognizes that the world conflagration, which was read out from Heraclitus' statements since Aristotle and above all by the Stoics and which was to become a particular favourite of the Christian Fathers, can simply not be a Heraclitean doctrine.

All in all, we understand what made Heraclitus so attractive for Hegel. Here, everything is speculative, a dialectic not owed to external reflection, which approaches an issue under various points of view from the outside and discloses its contradictions. It is a movement of the matter itself, its vividness, its 'reflection in itself', which unfolds itself. Certainly, this reflection also includes the thinking reflection as external, but this movement of the matter itself is 'objective'. It presents itself just as much as the in-itself of the substance as the for-itself of self-consciousness. Hegel calls this logical structure the 'concept' in so far as the concept comprehends everything in itself. It is the conceptual comprehensiveness [*Inbegriff*] of everything. The highest fulfilment which the concept presents, according to Hegel, touches and grasps even the mystery of the Trinity in itself. How in a single bound Hegel goes beyond his epoch when he links Heraclitus' deep insight into the One, which unfolds in its opposites, with the ultimate secrets of the Christian Gospel. 'That God created the world, undertook self-differentiation, produced his son, etc., all of this that is concrete is included in this determination'.

When we read this, we wonder whether Hegel has thereby not misunderstood the essence of the incarnation and the act of grace and faith in which it is experienced and whether he has not re-interpreted the Christian element into something ancient-Heraclitean. The way from the Heraclitean fire to such a bold synthesis of Christianity and philosophy is long, and not only long but hardly binding for us any longer in the goal it sets. Neither [38] do the Christian churches recognize themselves in Hegel's universal mediation nor do other religious denominations and religious experiences see themselves comprehended in it, and especially not the God-seekers at the pinnacle of modernity: Nietzsche, who disclosed the illusions of self-consciousness by radically questioning the world as will and representation, and Heidegger, who undertook to lay bare anew the question concerning being by thinking substance and subject against the horizon of time, showing them to be derived modes of being. How does Heraclitus' beginning appear to these God-seekers? What are the untrodden ways that are thinkable from this beginning?

It must be astonishing to us today that Hegel's speculative genius, which truly proves itself in Heraclitus with the full force of its recognition, at the same time sticks in principle to the so obviously inadequate Aristotelian schema of natural philosophy. Also astonishing is that he did not see the connection between Heraclitus' most profound statements about dream, sleep and waking, about death and life, about darkness and light and Heraclitus' eternally flickering fire. It is precisely this dimension of depth in Heraclitus which fascinates us today so much that we can scarcely believe that the history of philosophy once simply situated him in the series of Ionian naturalist philosophers, and many still do today. Far too overtly does this philosopher lament human beings and their lack of understanding and absentmindedly reflects upon human life which, stretched out between sleep and waking, death and life, dream and the common-to-all rationality that characterizes the day, is profoundly incomprehensible to itself – so truly exposed is this life to the abruptness of transition and the enigma of non-being. No moralist speaks like this in the style of those who admonish and issue warnings politically of the calibre of a Theognis or Simonides, who were not rare in his time, but even less a polymath or a herald of salvation, in the style of his Ionian compatriots Anaximander or Pythagoras. Most likely still related to his great opposite Parmenides, he attests to the openness and promise, which everything inceptual itself possesses in advance in contrast to what is consummated.

Nietzsche sensed something of this when he circumscribed the image of the classical Greece presented by the new humanism – the image of Apollonian serenity of the Olympian world of the gods – with the opposing power of Dionysius, indeed exalting in the end in Dionysius, the God of creation and destruction, the true core of all reality. He could have retrieved many of these insights also in Heraclitus. Heidegger absolutely had Heraclitus in view since he attempted with tireless perseverance to resist the conceptual coercion of metaphysics and to interpret being as event, thinking as being eventuating itself [*sich ereignende*]. Here Heraclitus suddenly becomes meaningful. The flux and the fire then not only symbolize the speculative [39] principle of processuality, which Hegel's dialectic elevation of the external reflection proper to 'the thinking that understands' had seen in it. Being, the One gathered in the *logos*, which human beings never understand because they chase after their waking dreams of desire and interest, after the illusion of domination and profit, is in itself discord and conflict. It gives itself and withdraws, and it is not a limitation of its being as unconcealment or disclosure that it also conceals itself. It rather shows itself as being [*seiend*] precisely by withholding itself at the same time. *Phusis kruptesthai philei* ['nature likes to conceal itself'] (Fr. 123) is like a formula of the post-Hegelian insight which

Schelling was the first to sense as the counter-position of the never to be illuminated ground of all reality [*Realität*]. Heidegger outrightly spoke of the superficiality of the Greeks because they, the ones who came later, Plato and Aristotle, understood being as that which is uttered, as *logos*, and thus took what is superficial and what is uttered for what is true. By contrast, Heidegger tries to think what is inceptual in Heraclitus by taking his point of departure from the original experience of disclosure, which at the same time includes concealing, just as the sprouting of the growing plant at the same time pushes its roots into the dark earth. Conflict and counter-conflict of war and peace, dearth and abundance, even of conflict and right, are one and the same. 'War' is the father of all; Heidegger interprets this as an expression or echo of the primordial Greek experience of being in disclosure and concealing. In this way, Heidegger came a step closer to the profundity of Heraclitus by calling him as a witness to a distant primeval time and prehistory, which can hardly be inferred from his statements but rather only from the roots of his words. Heidegger recognizes in the words 'primordial words' [*Urworte*], the primordial articulation of an experience of the world as it is accumulated in the 'lexicon' ['*Wortschatz*'][5] of a language. Heraclitus himself was admittedly rather a later thinker, at home in a fully mature, overabundant commercial and port city in the flourishing prosperity of the Greek colonial period. What he had in mind was far more human beings, their illusions and the enigmas that we are to ourselves as mortal but nevertheless thinking beings, than drawing out the primordial linguistic articulation of being in his thinking.

Let us test this by laying out before us in closing an enigmatic pronouncement of Heraclitus. It reads (in the clarification which I believe must be carried out upon it): 'In the night human beings kindle a light for themselves when the light of their eyes has been extinguished: living, they come in contact with the dead, awake they come in contact with the sleeping' (Frag. 26)[6]. We wonder what is being said in these enigmatic antitheses and analogies. Here everything is intertwined into one another, life and death, waking and sleep, night and day, light and darkness, kindling and extinguishing of lights. Everything is equivocal, fits together and does not. Is there a light kindled here or does it go on of its own? Is there a light extinguished here or does it go out on its own? [40] What goes out here? The light of the eye, which goes out? How does this fit together with the being-alive and the being-awake? Everything is obscure and rife with connotations. Only one thing seems clear: Just as the self-kindling of light is thought together with the being-by-oneself, 'being' flashes up for a moment as 'there'. Being is something of a relation to oneself in everything therein. So Hegel is not that far, his being-in-itself and being-for-itself, and Plato is definitely not far. In the *Charmides* (169a), Socrates is longing for a wonderful person who might be able to think such a self-relation in the essence of *dunamis* ['potentiality'][7]. It is a world of the Greek manner of being oneself that opens itself here. Self-movement of the living, which is not pushed and prodded, but can move from itself and by itself: in the heat, which suddenly, as if by itself, bursts into flame when the log in the fireplace catches fire; in self-perception, which is inseparable from all our sensations and perceptions, preceding them as their possibility; and finally in knowledge, which is such that it always at the same time knows its own awareness of knowing. Admittedly, what is in focus here is nothing of the new primacy of self-consciousness over against the consciousness of the world, nothing of that inversion and reversal of world consciousness and self-consciousness, which distinguishes modern thought and which gained prominence with modern scientific thought and its primacy of the method, with the primacy of certainty over truth. Precisely for this reason does Hegel recognize himself in this, he who pushed beyond 'subjective idealism', and Heidegger, who over and beyond all 'consciousness' seeks being in difference.

Even when Heraclitus speaks of the boundaries of the soul, which could never be traversed to the very end (Frag. 45), it is certainly a great step in a direction familiar to us[8]. And yet, even here what opens to the thinking gaze is not so much the labyrinths of the soul or the vast riches of interiority, the treasure houses of memory, of which the god-seeking soul of an Augustine knew how to speak so suggestively. The soul in Heraclitus ascends from dampness like a mist and dissipates itself in the brightness like the glitter in the blue of the southern sky. He says of himself: 'I sought myself' (Frag. 101). But we may have to accept that he lost himself on this search in the unfathomable. For what is this ungraspable, unfathomable, in which there seem to be no boundaries? Even we do not know how to say what this being-with-oneself is, which distinguishes the waking human life. It bears its constant thinking beyond, which knows no boundaries and for which as a result the end, death, remains something most profoundly incomprehensible.

[41] An ultimate boundary seems to be outlined here, which is not so much of the Greek feeling of life as of rational ability of all human beings to know. In all the enigmatic correspondences to be found in Heraclitus, the relation of life to death rises up like an ultimate insoluble self-resolving enigma, namely, as if there were a way back from death to life like from sleep to being awake, like from the delusion of dreams to the truth of the day. Death, *thanatos*, the crisp-sounding word for death and completion, should be encountered as a mere pole in a pulsating rhythm of life. It is just that the one direction, towards being dead, is still the compelling course of life characterizing our temporality.

It sounds different in Heraclitus. Even in the discussion dedicated to the immortality of the soul in Plato's *Phaedo*, which Socrates conducts with his friends on the day of his execution, the cycle of nature is treated like a suitable argument in order to prove the immortality of the soul. It is certainly complemented in multiple ways. Yet, even at the high point of his argument, Socrates confesses that his deepest certainty is not that of these arguments but his ties to the good. This rings through in multiple ways in Socrates' attitude and behaviour. True life is proceeding towards death. Reaching death while alive is like gaining everlastingness, whether it is reached in the immortality of fame or in the clarity of the mind or in the mythic present of heroic existence, venerated in cults. This is not incomprehensible to us. Has the same not always been expressed in the distinction of human beings that they bury their dead? To preserve the dead, in tombs, cult and memory appears like a denial of death. The transformation of the proceeding to death into the deathless sounds from this point of view like a highest wisdom.

Good, but how should there be a way back? Is Heraclitus serious about this or has Heraclitus thought beyond the limits of the Greek experience of transcendence? We have another enigmatic pronouncement by Heraclitus, which can hardly be rendered in another language: 'Immortal mortals, mortal immortals, living the death of those, dying the life of those' (Frag. 62)[9]. Whatever the solution of this enigmatic statement may be, it must still concern the inseparability of life and death like the inseparability of sleep from waking. So we ask: the *athanatoi*, the immortals, are they living at all? Do we human beings perhaps live the death of those because that which does not face death is not life and in this sense being-dead? And are we in the presence of the life of those others like the dead, because we in fact live and, as living, even deny death and yet know that we must die? In Heraclitus, this peculiar limit of the religious experience, which is proper to the Greeks, may be visible throughout, but if we dare to understand him in this way, it is an experience of the limit itself that he expresses and not only its elimination and concealment in the cycle of natural life. This limit remains [42] an enigma for our thinking as it is for Heraclitus' thinking. But there are enigmas which refuse their solution and still leave no doubt that they have a solution. Let us think, for example, of works of art, which are such enigmas, and which perhaps even permit many resolutions without still losing in the process the unity of what they say. We may thus dare to say with Hegel that Heraclitus 'up until the present day' expresses who we are by assigning us such enigmas. We will certainly also agree with Socrates' judgement, which he is supposed to have left behind on the text of Heraclitus[10]: 'What I have understood is excellent; I am convinced that even what I have not understood is equally excellent. Admittedly, it requires a masterful diver to bring what is precious from the depths to the light of day'.

9

Hegel and the Historical Spirit (1939)

[384] I found myself confronted with the question of the topic with which I should introduce myself as professor of philosophy in this University of Leipzig: whether with a topic from my particular area of work, ancient philosophy, on the basis of which the whole of philosophy and its history had revealed itself to me, or with a topic closer to the general consciousness. The task then presented itself to me as if from itself: to speak about Hegel and the historical spirit. For nothing can be closer to the general consciousness and the general knowledge of philosophy today than the question which expresses itself and conceals itself in the form of this assignment. Also, for a century, nothing has been more obvious to the consciousness of philosophical research if it wants to give an account of the turn of its gaze backwards towards the past forms of philosophy, beginning with the philosophy of the Greeks. Hegel and the historical spirit, this is no random item of research in the history of philosophy, not even a chapter of its history which is particularly alive for contemporary philosophy. What vividly grips us from the vantage point of this topic is the question of the being and the possibility of philosophy in general. It is a question which is present to philosophical consciousness since this consciousness has also become a historical consciousness. This means: since Hegel. The spirit knows of itself that it is historical, that is to say, prejudiced by its time and helplessly obsolete, as every present is before its future. This is a knowledge that threatens the spirit in its freedom. If philosophizing means knowing the eternal, being capable of glimpsing eternity, then, under the burden of historical consciousness even the question of such truth appears to grow weak.

It could be tempting to ascribe this self-destructive turn of philosophical consciousness to the weary force of an overripe spirit and to wish to endure in the regained innocence of oblivion. It is only that this turn of philosophy against itself has demonstrated the harshness of a fact which knows how to assert itself. This turn revealed itself in a twofold direction. On the one side, in the triumph of 'historicism' in philosophy itself. The concept of truth became suspect and seemed to succumb to relativism. Correspondingly, the research in the history of

---

'Hegel und der geschichtliche Geist' was Gadamer's inaugural lecture at the University of Leipzig on 8 July 1939. It was first published in *Zeitschrift fur die gesamte Staatswissenschaft* 100 (1939): pp. 25–37. It is also in *Kleine Schriften* III, pp. 118–28. It is now in *Gesammelte Werke*, vol. 4. Tübingen: J. C. B. Mohr (Paul Siebeck), 1987, pp. 384–94.

philosophy arrogated to itself [385] a privileged place within philosophy. Indeed it constantly threatened to dissolve philosophy in general into a discipline of the general historical sciences. Above all, this teaches us that philosophy has been dethroned and has ceased since then to be the imperial leader of science and life. Therein we see the powerlessness of merely wanting to forget the threat which philosophy is to itself, that philosophy itself began to lead a forgotten existence in the whole of historical reality. As Rudolf Haym could already assert in 1857: Hegel's philosophy 'created the last great system that was accompanied by universal recognition'. Since then, philosophy is no longer a theory of truth of world historical scope and import, but either an academic shadow world of recurring spirits (which are then called 'Kantianism', 'Hegelianism', among others) or world-stirring exceptional existences in a new sense, as in Kierkegaard and Nietzsche.

Thus, philosophical research can no longer avoid the problem of its historicity. Only where it lives in the consciousness of this risk to its own self, does the history of philosophy also become for philosophical research the presence of a philosophical endeavour. It has no other truth anymore either for the sciences or for the life of human beings in readiness than the truth of this question of its own existence directed at itself. But it is Hegel who can teach us that this unique and ultimate truth is the whole truth or more correctly: it can become the whole truth and all of the truth. It is in this sense that we pose the question concerning Hegel and the historical spirit (provided that this is possible in just about an hour), aware of the fact that we are thereby also questioning the philosophical sense of our own work in the field of the history of philosophy.

What constitutes his most essential uniqueness and gives him a decisive weight for our question is that Hegel had undertaken to give philosophy a historical grounding. He did not do this by way of a historical introduction to his own philosophy, giving a critical account of his predecessors, as had become customary since the days of Hegel and was already cherished by Aristotle. He rather did it by way of a comprehensive interpenetration of the history and the systematic aspect of philosophy. Hegel pointedly characterized this task as the idea of a new science. The *Phenomenology of Spirit* is this new science, as the 'science of the becoming of knowledge'. In this most profound work by Hegel, the comprehensive meaning at the core of philosophical knowledge and its history finds its scientific expression. 'The true is the whole, the whole, however, is only the essence which completes itself through its development'. This means that for philosophical knowledge and the truth of the spirit in general, to have a history is not a mere exteriority. It does not mean having put history behind and forgotten it. The spirit is really only what it [386] has become, what it has made out of itself. To be sure, consciousness in the present, in each case, intends to know the true. But it must always have the experience that its truth becomes stale. To grasp the course of its experience with itself not as the unfortunate destiny of all that is finite, but as the way to its completion, the way to itself, on which it is only what it is at all, this is the achievement of the *Phenomenology*, this 'system of the experience of the spirit'. One sees that the historicity of the spirit is Hegel's fundamental insight. He recognized that the history of the spirit belongs to the essence of its manifestation and that there is only a historical manifestation of the spirit.

It is easy to understand that Hegel became the founder of the research into the history of philosophy on the basis of this insight and, one has to say, the creator of the only philosophical history of philosophy there is until today. He grasps the history of philosophy as a whole, as the way of the spirit to itself. He downright calls it the inmost part of world history. 'That the spirit wanted this in its history', this 'clear insight' is the history of philosophy. Hegel purposely modifies a famous verse from Virgil: *tantae molis erat se ipsam cognoscere mentem* ('so much effort did it cost the spirit to know itself') and transfers the weighty, acquired pride of the mythical historical consciousness of the Augustan Rome onto the historical self-consciousness of the spirit.

If in this way the philosophizing consciousness of the present might indeed recognize itself in its most essential concerns in Hegel, then the recognition of Hegel's achievement, of the historical grounding of philosophy, is confronted with the resistance of the critique of Hegel which has been tested for a century. Has this historical saturation of philosophy not led to a philosophical and speculative violence to history (to say nothing of the violence to the truth of the natural sciences)? Is what Hegel formulated as dialectic supposed to be the truth of the historicity of the spirit, that is to say, this universal schema of grasping [*Begreifen*] which leaves for no shape of the spirit, whether of nature or of history, its right to individuality, but rather from the very outset limits each of them through their contradiction? Does Hegel do justice at all to history? And does he not place himself, as the one grasping and completing history, beyond any admission of his own historicity?

In fact, it is still the mildest objection to say that Hegel did violence to the experience of history through his speculation. We have to acknowledge the kind of fruitfulness which Hegel's effort to conceive of the world history in thought has evinced even for empirical historical research. From the distance of a century, the old [387] hostility between Hegel and the historical school, which at the time never allowed for admitting Hegel into the Berlin Academy, will appear quite petty[1]. We find so much genuine historical intuition in Hegel; so much concealed metaphysics in the spirit of Hegel is at work in the great researchers of the historical school (I am thinking here of the doctrine of the world-historical ideas, of the idea of the spirit of a people, etc.).

Whether this conceptual history of Hegel is still history in the authentic sense has been asked again and again, and not without reason, since Schelling critically confined Hegel's accomplishment to a merely 'negative philosophy'. According to Hegel, the content of world history, as is well-known, is the 'progress in the consciousness of freedom' or, put more generally, 'the rational and necessary course of the world spirit'. But the spirit is free 'in itself' and the course of world history consists precisely in this that the spirit presses through towards knowing itself to be free, not only 'in itself' but also 'for itself'. In the three stages comprising the world of the East, the Greco-Roman world and the Christian-Germanic world, Hegel sees the world-historical course of the spirit realizing itself. In the world of the East, there was only one who was free (the despot), in Greece and Rome some were free (at the cost of others, the slaves), in the Germanic age the human being is free as a human being, in the 'self-consciousness and self-assurance of the essence of spirituality' – a schema of truly impressive historical force. Yet, if we think through with Hegel the concept of development underlying this schema and lay out the consequences of this thinking through, it in fact becomes questionable as to whether this can still be called 'history'. 'Development' is in itself a category of organic life. What develops is already all laid out in the seed or in the bud. Hegel himself says: 'The principle of development includes what comes after, that there is an underlying inner determination, a presupposition available in itself, which brings itself into existence'. 'This is how the organic individual produces itself: it makes itself into that which it is in itself. In the same way, the spirit is only that into which it makes itself and it makes itself into that which it itself is'. Hegel is thus well aware of the difference between organic development and spiritual-historical development. He emphasizes over and over again how the development, which as such 'in the case of the organic is a calm coming out, is, in the case of spirit, a hard, endless struggle within the individual against itself'.

Nevertheless, it is no coincidence when Hegel so eagerly draws on the analogy of organic development. The necessity, which Hegel attributes to such a development and claims to conceptualize, is indeed appropriate to organic life, but not to history, in which action and creative freedom constantly know how to engender the inconceivably new. This objection to Hegel crosses over into the [388] general consciousness at that point where Hegel characterizes the role of the agent, the role of the great individuals in world history. They are for him, as we know, nothing but the 'representatives in charge' of the world spirit. In following the passion for their will and their thirst for action, they realize the goals of the cunning reason which uses them. It is clear that the creative freedom of the human being who creates something new is accordingly an illusion. This too is certainly an assertation which has a kernel of truth. The historical self-interpretation of the acting present amends itself constantly before the forum of world history. From the standpoint of history, no one has the significance they have for themselves. Yet, from the standpoint of world-historical providence, from which Hegel describes things, Hegel himself had to be what he deemed to know himself to be. He is himself factually an unhistorical possibility of the spirit. He stands at the end of history. For this reason, the critique of Hegel had not only to defend the creative freedom of human beings; it also had to defend the historical and creative freedom of God against Hegel's interpretation of history in the style of antiquity (bending the understanding of history to the categories of organic life).

Here again we have a well-known problem, in which this critique of Hegel finds its sharpest philosophical formulation: the problem of the end of history. Hegel has been accused over and over again of understanding himself in fantastic *hubris* as completing the return of the spirit to itself in world history. There was thus no sense of history left for the ensuing period or better: no genuine sense in history anymore. Hegel has also often been defended against this alleged arrogance and one could appeal to Hegel himself, who strongly derided any philosophy that deemed to be beyond the horizon of its times. Nevertheless, this discussion is significant in and of itself. The attempt which Hegel undertook to conceptualize history brings history to a standstill. At the very least, such a conceptualizing knowledge of history frees itself, it seems, from the world of those historical possibilities that only action can reveal. It is a history that deems to have shut itself off from its future.

It is not possible here to establish the connection of these objections to Hegel's conception of history (which are also all our objections) with the other philosophical critiques of Hegel. Hegel had to provoke everyone to object, whether they saw in him, with Schelling, the logicization of the world of free action or with Kierkegaard, the speculative volatilization of the existing thinker or with the political liberals, the sanction of the power of what prevails, or with the protestant orthodoxy, a pantheistic-Christian gnosis. Even for us, who know ourselves to be exposed to the historicity of philosophy, this speculative dialectic of history has to be a disappointment.

[389] However, this critical depiction of Hegel has since then begun to undergo a critical demise. This is the point at which our hopes in Hegel may be rekindled. For thirty years our knowledge of Hegel has expanded in an important direction. Wilhelm Dilthey published 'The Early History of Hegel' in the Berlin Academy in 1905. In 1907 his student Nohl edited the so-called early theological writings of Hegel, to which still numerous manuscripts from the Jena period were added later. A new portrait of Hegel gradually began to emerge in the consciousness of philosophical research. One is even tempted to play the young Hegel against the accomplished Hegel. Obviously, to misjudge the unity and sameness of the essential issues which moved Hegel would be, it seems to me, a dubious underestimation of the inner unity of a life, which called itself a life dedicated to science[2]. As such, Hegel the theologian was as little a surprise for Hegel scholarship as Hegel the young politician and educator of the people. Nevertheless, we needed the youthful language of these documents in order to learn how to see the younger and more lively Hegel. Above all, the *Phenomenology of Spirit* can be read fruitfully when one no longer takes one's departure in the ordered dialectical systematization of the *Logic*, the *Encyclopaedia* and the Berlin lectures, but in the uninhibited foray, beyond the Kantian-Fichtean philosophy of subjectivity, into the uncharted territory of the historical spirit, which the attempts by the young Hegel presented. Even in Hegel the reader, we have a confirmation of what he himself taught, namely that the true is the whole, the essence completing itself through its development. It is a matter of taking seriously Hegel's own insight, if we want to understand Hegel fruitfully. The foundation of philosophy in the history of the spirit has not happened and is not in the past, if science unfolds itself on the basis of the absolute standpoint. The *Phenomenology* is indeed itself the science of this becoming of absolute knowledge. It is thus itself science and absolute knowledge is only what it is because it is what it was and became. The *Logic* is nothing without the *Phenomenology*.

It is not a matter of whether the world history of the spirit or at least its inmost core, the history of philosophy, is accessible or closed off to conceptualization. It is rather a matter of grasping what the spirit is [390] and that it produces itself only from its active becoming. The *Phenomenology* can teach us this right away, after we have learnt to see it. The experience of the spirit, the way of its externalization and alienation give it a content in the first place, and to maintain itself in this content, this alone is the spirit. The spirit is absolutely not already beyond every opposition of consciousness, as it could in formal reflection, for the precise reason that it is very well able to think every contradiction. This is how it is in Hegel, but this is only correct if we already know what the spirit and thus the thinking of the spirit are for Hegel. It is not in already knowing about its superiority as the infinite capacity of reconciliation that the spirit is spirit. This is the unending misunderstanding of Hegelianism in the liberal age. Only through itself having the experience of the opposites does it constantly gain the infinity of its force anew. However, this experience does not complete itself within the limits of theoretical reason. Only in action – Hegel's *Phenomenology* teaches us that – does being reveal itself. Only in the unity of being and action so elaborated – in the form of morality as the morality of the spirit of the people – does Hegel recognize the immediacy of the spirit, which is then elevated to a moral, religious and finally philosophical awareness.

The writings of the young Hegel can teach us how to comprehend this movement of the spirit towards itself and thereby the historicity of the spirit in its concrete fulfilment. With the boldness which comes with a first breaking through to oneself, these writings lay before us the whole, also of its ultimate truth in the spirit of *love*.

In the young Hegel, love is at one time called an analogue of reason. 'Just as reason recognizes itself in every rational being, as a fellow citizen in an intelligible world' (at the time, Hegel still loved to talk like Kant), in the same way, love finds itself in another individual. Lovers forget themselves, place themselves out of their existence, living, as it were, in others. With these early expressions, Hegel hits upon his ownmost theme for the first time. For in this analogy of reason with love, we find both accord and discord. The universality of love is not the universality of reason. Hegel is not Kant. In love there is, even when giving oneself over to the other, an I and a you. Love is the overcoming of the estrangement between I and you, an estrangement which is always there, and must be there for love to be alive. In reason, by contrast, I and you are exchangeable and representable as the same. Further: precisely for this reason, love is not an abstract but a concrete universality; it is not what all are (as rational beings) but what I and you are, and in such a way that it is neither I nor you: God, who manifests himself, is love: the common spirit which is more than the knowledge of the I and the knowledge of the you.

[391] We have fundamentally the whole of Hegel here, even if still undeveloped, without the proof of a philosophical method. In later writings of his youth too, Hegel develops his views only on the occasion of particular individual questions. This is how he develops the essence of love more precisely in relation to the theme found in the exegesis of Saint John of the forgiveness of sins and the concept of spirit in relation to the theme of Jesus being the son of God and all Christians being the children of God. The whole of his endeavours is governed through and

through by the explicit opposition to what he calls 'positivity': the statute, which is opposed to the living as a dead, rigid, hostile givenness. I cannot present in detail this first elaboration of what Hegel later calls 'spirit'. I will only single out one thing that makes the task clear of how first to learn what lies in the Hegelian concept of spirit.

It is a fundamental determination of life as a spiritual and historical accomplishment that it can reconcile itself with destiny. All injury to life – Hegel makes this clear in a profound analysis of crime and punishment – manages to heal, as the living organism is capable of doing. The return to life, to love – Hegel once says: 'to the general friendship of life' – is not limited to the dogmatic problem of the forgiveness of sins. It is simply the fundamental universal constitution of human life or, as we would say with the late Hegel, of the historical spirit. For the historical spirit is only in the return to itself. In this context, Hegel turns explicitly against the complaint about the innocence which suffers. He dares the provocative statement: 'Never has innocence suffered, every suffering is guilt'. By this, Hegel means that suffering is never the passive incurrence of a wrong from outside. Through the way in which people receive and react to the act coming from outside, thus whether they defend themselves or endure it, everything becomes their guilt, their destiny. It is a profound thought, which Hegel never forsook. Only his interpreters have not correctly heeded it in its later incarnation. From the *Phenomenology* we have the famous line: 'Healing the wounds of the spirit without leaving a scar'. These are not images with which Hegel embellishes his thoughts, but what speaks from such expressions is the content which Hegel deems to be in the concept of spirit. The spirit appears as the all-powerful force of the unification, the reconciliation of all contradictions and the way to its freedom is that of tenaciously, persistently working away at all that is alien, until the spirit is fully reconciled with itself, until all reality is found in the rational. If this is so, this is in no way that speculative volatilization of the wilful mastery of destiny; it is not that powerless spiritual affirmation of what prevails, which political liberalism derides. The reconciliation with itself is rather the concrete life of the spirit, what lets it be free at all in the first place, free for [392] the claim of the moment, free for forcefully bringing about the future. Hegel's vision here is profound. Already the offence we cannot get over deprives us of freedom by keeping us bound to ourselves in vindictive powerlessness. Only those who take over their lot as destiny win themselves back from everything. Endless self-mediation in fact characterizes the spirit in its concrete life. Letting something stand unmediated, not getting over something, not being able to pass over something, this is that same positivity of the alien to which Hegel's critique of Christian and Jewish orthodoxy already refers. This positivity is the death of the spirit. It is a magnificent vision in which Hegel here saw love at once, as the constant overcoming of the alien in the you and the force of the spirit overcoming destiny.

What unites love and spirit is not only the overcoming of that which is alien. Love is indeed the kind of elimination and overcoming [*Aufhebung*] of all separations, in which the separated become continually 'richer'. Hegel himself quotes from Shakespeare's *Romeo and Juliet*: 'The more I give, the more I have'.

This is the decisive determination of the historical spirit: to multiply oneself in oneself in this way, to comprehend oneself and in this way to rise continually to a higher form of oneself. Hegel explicitly contrasts this being of the spirit as an increment accruing to oneself with the being of nature, to which belongs the form of the recurrence of the same.

Again, in connection with theological questions, following the trinitarian doctrine in the Gospel of St. John, Hegel finally develops the essence of the community of love, as it exists between father and son as a living relation of spirit to spirit, in which there is no rift of objectivity any more. It is a whole in which every part can be the whole. It is here, for the first time, that the word and concept of spirit appear, initially in the context of this mysticism of love. But already here Hegel sees in this living substance of the people the same actuality of the spirit. His theory of the 'objective spirit' only gives shape to this thought of the spirit beyond the subjectivity of the spirit knowing itself.

With this, a final point also becomes clear. It seems insufficient to take one's point of departure in the phenomenon of love, which fuses an I and a you into a living whole, this whole tolerating nothing dead in itself, no being-for-itself anymore (for example, no separate property, indeed not even the separated being of the body without the pain of shame). This mere opposition of the living concreteness of love to the positivity of the given seems insufficient as soon we are dealing with the power of reality, which simply demands stepping out of such an intimacy of feeling and interiority of thought. Nevertheless, Hegel does not preach love, like Jesus. He even said this in the famous study on the spirit of Christianity and its destiny: love as Jesus proclaimed it and left it to his disciples has led to an exclusionary [393] confinement to oneself, to the flight from all forms, 'even if the spirit of love was living in them'. 'This distance from all destiny is precisely its greatest destiny'. Jesus' passive relation to the kingdom of this world, to the state means according to Hegel, a 'loss of freedom, a limitation of life'. In opposition to this, he himself sees in love – with an eye on classical antiquity – also the force to spiritualize reality by appropriating it. This is the love, which as he says 'robs what opposes it of all its alien character'. The magical power of the spirit, which tarries in the negative and, in this way, turns it back into being, is in no way a rise over reality in the sense of a mere reconciliation in thought; it is no 'restoration of the life passing into emptiness in ideality'. Hegel explains it rather with the statement: 'Only the life that endures death and maintains itself in it is the life of the spirit'. This is no metaphor but the rigorous sense and content of this experience of the spirit that the *Phenomenology* presents. Initially, the spirit comes to its existence in the objective spirit, in the form of the morality of the spirit of a people. To gain existence, to step out of the inhibition of consciousness in itself into actual existence is what Hegel indicates in the manifestation of love, and not the closed interiority of feeling. The love which becomes actual, which surpasses the I and the you, teaches us to measure the concept of spirit in its consequences.

Thus, as I hope to have made clear, the theological speculation of the young Hegel about love has not really taught us something new. It has only helped us to give Hegel's concept of spirit the concrete historical fullness which it fundamentally possesses but is in the constant danger of losing in the speculative effortlessness of the dialectical performance. No other work in the history of philosophy is constantly threatened by the loss of its substance as the work of Hegel is. To maintain it in the fullness from which his thoughtful experience arose is the task of all philosophical efforts dealing with Hegel. Thus, to take over Hegel's task – if not his solution – becomes fruitful especially also for the most contemporary tasks of philosophy, as I hope to have made palpable.

I thus summarize the results:

First, Hegel may not relieve us from answering the question of questions, that of the historicity of philosophy, but he teaches us that the historicity of the spirit is not so much a threat to its freedom as the grounding of its own possibility.

Further, Hegel's concept of the spirit must be understood from the experience of its history. But what the spirit is at all, this we have to learn from what the young Hegel sees in the concept of love.

But this means that the historical spirit is first determined through [394] the overcoming of what is alien. It is the work in which the alien becomes its own, in which what is in opposition is reconciled into a unity.

The historical spirit is secondly determined by becoming free for its future. Only the spirit which has become one with its past is capable of the freedom for the future.

The historical spirit is thirdly determined by being rooted and being fulfilled in the moral substance of the people. In light of the great themes of people, state and society, all attempts to overcome the subjectivist approach of modern thinking take us close to Hegel and the insight of his metaphysics of love.

If we want to draw out a lasting feature from all of this, it is that of acquiring continuity with oneself. The being of the spirit consists in merging into itself. The spirit has its content in the explicit appropriation of its history, just because it merges history with its own future. The deduction of world history or the history of philosophy from the height of the absolute concept is not the concretely living teaching which Hegel gives us. It is rather the task of merging with one's history, which always presents itself anew in the historical life of the individual as in that of the whole. Only in such a merging with oneself do individuals gain their vocation in the whole and the strength to fulfil it. Only in such merging with oneself does a historical people have its honour and the courage for its future. Philosophy has lost the unprejudiced way of questioning the truth – even more, the allegiance of those who would accept the answers to such questioning – and has turned to working through its history. But philosophy has for this reason in no way abandoned its great task. It is the first in the merging of historical existence with itself and precisely for this not the last in shaping the future.

10
Hegel and Heidelberg Romanticism (1961)

[395] Hegel's philosophy was very controversial in Germany, especially in the second half of the nineteenth century. Nevertheless, it remained dominant over that whole period and what was true of Germany as a whole applies especially to Heidelberg. If one considers the role played by philosophy in the Heidelberg of the last hundred years and if one thinks of the big names associated with Heidelberg, of Eduard Zeller, Kuno Fischer, who was influential here for more than fifty years, of Wilhelm Windelband, Heinrich Rickert, and Karl Jaspers: these individuals have given the university of Heidelberg a particular resonance as a site of philosophical studies. There is especially the fact that it is from Heidelberg that the revival of the study of Hegel in Germany originates, beginning with the famous academic address by Wilhelm Windelband in 1910. It was a group of young people who had gathered here, whose names for the most part are known to us today in a significant way. I am singling out the most important of these names: Emil Lask, Paul Hensel, Julius Ebbinghaus, Richard Kroner, Ernst Hoffmann, Ernst Bloch, Eugen Herrigel, Fjodor Stepun and Georg von Lukács. All of these names point back eventually to a single name, which, as it says in the appointment letter of the rector at the time, the theologian Daub, would bring about for the first time a real defence of philosophy in Heidelberg, after the appointment of Spinoza in the eighteenth century had not met with success. This name is that of Hegel. It was for only two years that Hegel taught in Heidelberg before accepting an invitation to go to Berlin. But these were important years for him. They signified for him a reconnection with his former academic teaching activity and resignation from the post of secondary school principal in Nürnberg. These were thus the years in which the man who found himself in the middle of his scientific development reconnected with the academic teaching position, simultaneously bringing in the harvest of the rich didactic experiences he had garnered as a secondary school teacher. The fruit

---

'Hegel und die Heidelberger Romantik' was a lecture given at the occasion of the 575th anniversary of the Ruprecht-Karl University of Heidelberg in 1961. It was first published in *Ruperto-Carola* 30 (1961): pp. 97–103. It was also published in *Hegels Dialektik. 5 hermeneutischen Studien*. Tübingen 1971 (second augmented edition 1980.). Tübingen: J. C. B. Mohr (Paul Siebeck), 1971. It is now in *Gesammelte Werke*, vol. 4. Tübingen: J. C. B. Mohr (Paul Siebeck), 1987, pp. 395–405.

of the experience acquired and of the maturity gained was the so-called *Heidelberg Encyclopaedia of the Philosophical Sciences*, a work which in its first draft described and elaborated the fundamental contours of the Hegelian system. [396] It was the early form of that system which as the last and most brilliant creation of the great times of German idealism radiated out from the philosopher's activities in Berlin into the whole wide world. Yet, what came about through Hegel's appointment in Heidelberg was more than the mere return to an academic teaching position. This appointment meant, as Hegel himself was aware, entering into a space filled with the muses. Here we are at the birthplace of the collection of folk songs 'The Boy's Magic Horn', here in closest proximity to the famous collection of paintings by Boisserée.[1] This was the first great German collection of old German and Flemish masters which, as a consequence of the secularization process of those years, was put together through private initiative and housed in Heidelberg for a time before passing into the possession of the Alte Pinakothek in Munich.

It was a unique constellation into which Hegel entered here. His Heidelberg years meant his renewed encounter with romanticism, which had put him on the defensive in Jena and which he now encountered in a transformed state, shaped by the romantic spirit and romantic landscape of Heidelberg. Let us consider the paradox of this situation: to think of the simple and awkward Hegel – as a contemporary had characterized him, certainly in a well-meaning manner – in a place and a climate positively echoing of poetry through the fiery Görres, through Achim von Arnim and Clemens Brentano, through Josef von Eichendorff and Friedrich Creuzer. The years of Hegel's activities in Heidelberg also coincided with the famous visit of Jean Paul, which was a true triumphal procession. The whole city lay at the feet of this incarnation of its poetic ideal. At Hegel's suggestion, Jean Paul was granted the title of honorary doctor of the philosophy department of Heidelberg. And yet, how particularly poorly did Hegel fit into this Heidelberg, whose proper mission and achievement were the discovery of folk poetry, fairy tales, popular books, folk songs, all of which must have appeared to Hegel's eyes more like a babbling of the soul of the people than a language of the spirit. One may readily believe, as Hegel himself wrote later after the move to Berlin, that the romantic landscape of Heidelberg was not as suited for his philosophy as the Berlin sand.

However, it is interesting and worthwhile to wonder whether the two Heidelberg years were not of epoch-making significance in Hegel's life. Not only did he make a lot of friends here and found a great appeal among the students. Also, conversely, his scientific work has retained in itself the enduring trace of these few years. Above all, the personal friendship, which brought him close to the philologist Friedrich Creuzer, stimulated him into working out his aesthetic ideas. We know today, through a letter known to us for not too long, how highly Hegel [397] valued the merit of Creuzer and of his main work on the symbolism of the ancient world for the formation of his own ideas. We have also known all along from the editing of Hegel's lectures on aesthetics the explicitly appreciative reference to Friedrich Creuzer's work. We are thus justified in posing the question, to the discussion of which this essay is dedicated, of how the Heidelberg years and the influence of Heidelberg romanticism are reflected within the formation of Hegel's intuition of art. This question has its own methodological difficulty. It casts a light on the particular research task which has to be dealt with especially today, when Hegel scholarship again stands on the verge of the establishment of a great critical edition. The most efficacious form in which Hegel's work was able to exert an influence on posterity was indeed not in the form of the works which Hegel had published. The access to those works was blocked to the normal consciousness of the reader by a thicket of the most bizarre esotericism. In fact, the proper influence of Hegel comes from his captivating lectures, which were edited by his students shortly after his death and published in the complete works. Hegel's aesthetics belongs to the cycle of these lectures. Indeed, they were repeated particularly often and with particular fondness by Hegel[2]. Unfortunately, the original version of this aesthetics conceived in Heidelberg is no longer available. We must resort to many very complicated and indirect ways of research if we want to get a picture of this first draft of the aesthetics and thereby also find an answer to the question of the contribution of Heidelberg's romantic spirit of art and nature to the conception of this great central lecture of Hegel.

The appearance of art had already been distinguished in Hegel's *Phenomenology of Spirit* of 1807 as an important form of the spirit. There it was called the religion of art. What is of particular importance for our findings is that it still functions in a similar way in the *Encyclopaedia of the Philosophical Sciences*, which first came out in print in Heidelberg. The question is thus about how the late form of his understanding of art, of which we are familiar in the form of the edited lectures on aesthetics and the later editions of the *Encyclopaedia of the Philosophical Sciences*, sets itself apart from the earlier form. In other words, how was that later form of Hegel's philosophy of art supposed to have developed from this early form, that later form which was to have turned aesthetics into a history of worldviews, of the ways of intuiting the world and shaping it artistically.

It has been rightly pointed out that the romantic movement [398] consisted of fairly different orientations and that particularly between Jena and Halle, on one side, and Heidelberg, on the other, a deep-seated spiritual difference held sway[3]. The romanticism of Jena was connected to classical Weimar, to Schiller's and Goethe's tyrannical education of the German public into an aesthetic state. Like all rivalry and innovation, this romanticism of Novalis and Tieck, of the Schlegel brothers and their numerous like-minded comrades, eventually remained subordinated to the aesthetic cosmos of that small Weimar republic. By contrast, the Heidelberg romanticism has a popular national and political character, if indeed it is the emerging awareness of one's own historical origin that first empowers the sovereign formation of peoples and nations. Undoubtedly, during the first decade of the nineteenth century, Heidelberg, in acquiring the deep dimension of history for the aesthetic character of early romanticism, belonged to the preparatory sites where that spirit was nurtured which was supposed to shake off the yoke of the Napoleonic occupation. Hegel's famous critique of Jena romanticism and its sentimental interiority, which does not dare the rigour of the concept and does not engage with the hardness of reality[4] cannot be easily transferred to the Heidelberg spirit of romanticism, which attains such a powerful historical and political influence in the wars of liberation. It might also have been through the favour of an intermediary that Hegel opened up to the romantic spirit of Heidelberg at all. Between him and Friedrich Creuzer there existed a special affinity, propitious for friendship. This man, world-famous through his tragic love story with Caroline von Günderode, was himself a mix of artistic, emotive sensitivity and erudite pedantry. We could hardly imagine that the real founder and inspirer of this Heidelberg romanticism, that Josef Görres, if he had still been in Heidelberg at the time, could have gotten along with Hegel. The kind of influence Görres had formerly exercised in Heidelberg in the first decade of the nineteenth century is attested by a well-known and much-cited depiction by the poet Eichendorff. He writes in his memoirs:

> It is unbelievable, the kind of influence this man, at the time still young and not famous, exercised in all aspects over all the youth who came into any kind of intellectual contact with him. And this mysterious power lay solely in the greatness of his character, in the truly burning love for the truth and an irrepressible feeling of freedom with which he relentlessly defended the truth once known, [399] as a matter of life and death, against open and closeted enemies as well as false friends. For all half-measures were mortally repugnant to him, indeed impossible. He wanted the whole truth. If God still graces individuals in our time with a prophetic gift, then Görres was a prophet, thinking in images, and prophesying, admonishing and chastening everywhere from the highest parapets of the turbulent times, also comparable to the prophets in that the words 'stone him!' were shouted out often enough about him. His completely free delivery was monotonous, almost like the distant roaring of the sea, rising and falling; yet, through this uniform murmur, there shone two wonderful eyes constantly flashing bolts of thought here and there; it was like a magnificent nightly tempest, suddenly revealing hidden abysses here, new unsuspected landscapes there, and everywhere powerfully awakening and rousing for the whole land.

We can imagine that Hegel would have never paid such tribute to this volcanic, ecstatic figure, as he did to the more methodical mind of the philologist Creuzer. And later Hegel really expressed his distance from Görres clearly enough in a review[5]. It was thus a fortunate turn of events, which allowed Hegel, this stolidly inconspicuous man, rather prosaic than ingenious, whose philosophical genius was averse to all sentimentality, to accept romanticism and the great fantasies of a Görres in its refraction through Creuzer[6]. Through the mediation of Creuzer, decisive impulses originating in Görres were passed on to Hegel. In particular, it was his *History of the Myths in the Asian World*[7], a surging, fantastic and gigantic portrayal, in which there was absolutely no discipline and method, and all the more fantasy, intuition, poetry and prophesy, which inspired Creuzer's investigations into the symbolism of ancient peoples[8].

Through the idea of his symbolism, Creuzer exerted a decisive influence on Hegel. In the language of Creuzer, which Hegel was still to retain, symbolism means that system of figurative wisdom and figurative religious transmission which underlay all religious cultures of the early period.

> The purest light of the clearest knowledge must first be refracted into a corporeal object so that it can fall upon the unclouded eye only in reflection and in a coloured, if also cloudy appearance. Only the imposing can awaken us from the slumber of half-animal dullness. But what is more imposing than the image? [9]

Creuzer himself formulates the task of symbolism as that of finding the laws of the higher language of images and grounds this task by the idea that [400] it is about seeking these laws at the point 'where human beings, after the inner world has dawned on them, pressed to express its sense and, despairing at the same time of the adequacy of writing and speech, opt out of the faltering of concepts, seek help under the wide space of intuition'. Creuzer's attempt at a symbolism is thus not a blind chasing after images but the investigation of the secret systematization in those half-colossal, half-grotesque sculptures and cult forms, which sets the East apart from the classical artistic form of the Greeks.

Since Winckelmann and Herder, it is a recognized truth that the classical world of the Greeks was itself no first beginning but that the Greeks picked up the spear at that point where other early peoples of the East had managed to hurl it. We learned this in part from the retrospective interpretations referring to Egyptian antiquity, which we found in Greek literature itself. In part, we read this out from religious poems, above all from Hesiod, those testimonies of a tremendous and productive early religious world, in which other religious powers reigned than those of the Olympians: the Titans, who still half-animal in form and half just formless cosmic powers, like light and night, determined the beginning of the Greek history of the gods. Even Hegel's first presentation of the forms of religious consciousness in the *Phenomenology of Spirit* shows a familiarity with such a pre-history of the Greek religion of art. Their wild creations often have something sublime, but not that beauty of the harmony between form and meaning, which constitutes the inimitable distinction of classical Greece and to which we owe the greatest flowering of the plastic arts the world has seen. Yet Hegel, just as Görres and basically everyone who looked in that direction before him, still misses the unifying concept.

One will ask: just one concept? In comparison to the tremendous richness of this intuition opening itself into the Asian religious world, what is this concept of the symbolic under which Hegel, following Creuzer, finally encapsulates the early period of the history of classical art? Yet, it appears to me to be no accident that the unification under this concept of the symbolic, which Hegel borrowed from Creuzer, first became possible when this early period had found its proper concrete form through the gigantic portrayal by Görres's *History of the Myths in the Asian World*. As far as I can see, the concept of the symbolic in the sense in which it is employed by Creuzer and taken over by Hegel was not used previously even in Hegel, at least not as a specific essential feature of the early religious world. For to be symbolic means, for the contemporaries, to be allegorical. And that means, in the visible appearance to point to something else, invisible and infinite. But this is for Hegel still a characteristic of art in general. Art is this contradiction [401] between finitude and infinity, which only finds its solution in the philosophical concept of speculative dialectic and in absolute knowledge. We read something like this in Hegel's manuscripts of the earlier Jena period and it remained so also in the Nürnberg period, which immediately precedes his Heidelberg years. Now, in the philosophical history of art developing out of the Heidelberg conception, which Hegel transmitted in his aesthetics lectures, this means that everything acquires a historical colouring. What now precedes the classical period of art as the art of the Eastern world[10] is called 'symbolic' because, through the incommensurability between appearance and meaning, by pointing beyond the visible, it possesses a formless sublime otherworldliness, constituting the great background for the luminous spirituality and perfect beauty of the Greek world of the gods. Hegel owes Creuzer and thus the Heidelberg romanticism his freedom from the abstract and polemical opposition between the classical and romantic sensibilities towards art, which dominated aesthetic discussion at the time – think of Schiller and Friedrich Schlegel. It is thanks to Creuzer and Heidelberg romanticism that Hegel could raise himself in the realm of the history of art first to the great triptych, which encapsulates the early world, the classical world and the romantic world into the unity of the historical course of the West.

Thus, the fruit of the Heidelberg years – the conception of the aesthetic lectures – is at the same time the decisive step through which the systematic construction of Hegel's dialectic is transformed into a philosophy of history. It is the step through which the dimension of history, the development of the spirit in time, began to unfold its own systematic right vis-à-vis the eternalizing view of philosophical dialectic. Görres had written:

> There is no more sacred principle that history has to defend and it has imposed no other with more blood and death against all individual restrictions than the principle of its own constant growth without being bound by boundless time. Religion in its finitude also participates in this growth. It is itself included in the circle of the transmigration of souls.

It was something of the greatness of Görres' historical vision that found reception in Hegel's organizing spirit.

This result of our analysis of the sources can also be confirmed by looking at the lectures on religion, which in Hegel's work like the one on aesthetics, have also been transmitted to us in a later version and in which the situation of its transmission is still more favourable to the extent that Hegel's main notebook from the Heidelberg period has still been partially preserved.

We see that in this earliest form of the lecture on religion, a conceptual articulation as tight as the one that became possible through the concept of symbolic art is not yet to be found.

[402] We can also mention a second instance of how the turn of events relating to Heidelberg was a significant piece of assistance for Hegel for the great achievement of his later conception of history. And even this piece of assistance, it seems to me, is owed in particular to the encounter with Friedrich Creuzer. It is the intensification of his interest in neo-Platonism. Creuzer had already emerged as a pioneer for this in the first decade of the century. If we page through the first volumes of the studies by Daub and Creuzer, which appeared in Heidelberg in 1805 and after, what we find here in addition to the first programmatic essays by Creuzer on his *Symbolism and Mythology* and many peculiar speculative theological essays by Daub, is mainly a series of studies and translations of writings by Plotinus, which stem from Creuzer's pen. At that time, Creuzer has first edited the text *On the Beautiful* and later he created the exemplary great edition, which was printed in Oxford. This is anything but a coincidence. For Creuzer had tried to legitimate the idea of his symbolism essentially by appealing to Plotinus and other neo-Platonic writers. In them he found, in their development of a Platonic motif, the recognition of the fact that the highest truths are those that escape writing and speech and for this reason can only be conveyed in the indirect form of figurative intuition. Creuzer knew well that the deliberately allegorical method, which was nurtured among the neo-Platonic writers to the point of abstruseness, did not fulfil the sense of the symbolism he was seeking, namely that of the secret grammar of the 'pantheism of the imagination'. But because he could not discover any older testimonies for the oldest truth of symbolism, he sought through these later witnesses the shimmers of the older truth, so to speak. As we know, Creuzer's investigations on mythology were quickly and definitively discredited very soon by the sharp critique of philological and historical scholarship, particularly by Lobeck[11]. Yet, from Hegel's defence of Creuzer's mythology in his later aesthetics lectures, we see that a moment of truth lurks in the idea of this research, which the increasingly sober historical critique of the nineteenth century did not quite recognize and which even Creuzer himself did not know how to bring out, as we can now substantiate with Hegel. Hegel writes:

> In fact, peoples, poets, priests did not have before themselves the universal thoughts underlying their mythological representations in this form of universality, such that they would have had first shrouded these thoughts intentionally in symbolic form. This is not even what Creuzer claims. If, however, the ancients did not [403] think in their mythology that which we now see in them, it still does not follow in any way that their representations are nevertheless not in themselves symbols. They must therefore be taken in such a way that the peoples in that time, when they composed their myths, were living in poetic states themselves and for this reason brought to consciousness what was innermost and deepest to them not in the form of thought, but in the forms of fantasy, without separating the universal abstract representations from the concrete images[12].

That this is really the case, we have here (Hegel means: in the aesthetics) 'to establish it essentially!'. We see how Hegel takes his point of departure in Creuzer and goes beyond Creuzer. Creuzer himself had never moved beyond the ideas cherished by the Enlightenment about religion, in particular about a secret knowledge of the priesthood, which masks and conceals its knowledge. Only the decisive placement of emphasis which Hegel brings into his idea of symbolism puts things right. Now it is clear that the form of thought and of the concept is not something that comes first but something which comes last, something to which the 'pantheism of the imagination' was not yet able to rise. Hegel first liberates Creuzer's thought of symbolism from its rationalist fetters. The figurative language of intuition, the imposing nature of the image does not take the form of a cover or of an instrument of a truth already known and conceptually fixed. It is rather the case that in the form of a figurative fantasy, something obscure and still without the consciousness of itself brings itself to expression, which must first still be elevated into the language of concepts.

The significance which the neo-Platonists acquired for Hegel and Creuzer otherwise exhibits characteristic differences, which we must examine in our context. We have in our possession an autobiographical document, a statement by Creuzer in his biography, in which he speaks of the common interest which linked him to Hegel in multiple ways. He sprinkles this instructive remark that Hegel was particularly interested in Proclus for whom he himself had little affinity. At that time, there was the prospect of a common edition of Plotinus, which Creuzer later brought out alone. Creuzer's statement shows how, when dealing with the same object, the artistically excitable and sensitive philologist Creuzer and Hegel, driven by an almost eerie demon of constructive thought, opposed each other in gentle tension. After the tremendous discovery of this thinker for the West, which was made by Marsilius Ficinus in the Florentine academy, Plotinus was nevertheless even in the days of Creuzer a daring philological discovery of a writer whose peculiarly unclassical formulation did not readily fit into the classicist and humanistic ideal of style. [404] The copy from the Heidelberg library which I used in those days contains a fairly significant marginal gloss of a modern hand at that place where Creuzer states that the Plotinian form and writing style obviously 'falls infinitely short' of the Platonic original. The marginal remark puts a question mark and manifestly finds this statement astounding and strange. So much has this author and the thinker of late antiquity gained in reputation now as someone genuinely classical and stylistically great. Creuzer did not yet have the full courage for his discovery, so to speak. But it was a discovery. By contrast, Proclus is one for whom Hegel opts, to whose work he warmed up so much that in his history of philosophy he believes to have recognized in Proclus the true completion and synthesis of the whole of Greek philosophy. This Proclus is still counted today – and rightly so – among those neo-Platonic commentators who, with diligence and astuteness, but also with pedantry and an obsession for the most abstruse constructions, systematized classical Greek philosophy syncretically and made it scholastic. An author who is an outright torture to read. Now, I do not want to say that it is his sojourn in Heidelberg and Creuzer's influence which drove Hegel to the study of Proclus. Presumably, it had already happened in Jena and Hegel received the first impetus to the particular form of his own philosophical method there, this most peculiar form of all dialectic, through which Hegel's own style of thinking is unmistakably distinguished from all the contemporary varieties of dialectic[13]. Yet, what in Heidelberg resulted from the influence of someone inspired by neo-Platonic philosophy was, as it seems, Hegel's application of the triadic schema to history and, above all, to the history of art. What a wonderful paradox: the didactic late-born child of ancient thinking as the inspirer of the last great systematician of Western metaphysics and as the initiator of this turn of philosophical thought to history, to which finally Hegelian philosophy itself, in the spirit of the historical century, the nineteenth, was to succumb. It seems to me that only in this way does Creuzer's influence, to which Hegel himself attests, become visible in its full systematic scope.

Hegel owes Creuzer not only the encapsulating concept which systematically subordinates the early world of Greek art to the world of fine art, integrating it into the context of a world history of art. The concept of the symbolic rather also expresses what [405] Hegel had always thought about the relationship between art, religion and philosophy. Now, however, this concept of the symbolic receives a historical colouring even in its universal application. Hegel had always thought the discrepancy between the finitude of appearance and the infinity of the spirit in the concept of the symbolic. This discrepancy, which is necessary where the infinite becomes visible in something finite, means for Hegel at the same time the insurmountable limit which has been erected for this form of truth. Now, Hegel tells us that even in this relation of concepts, there is truth in so far as it is historical. Art belongs as a whole to the past precisely because art as a whole is symbolic. It is no longer the highest manner of expressing the truth of the spirit, after Christianity and its speculative absorption through the philosophical concept have brought a new, more intimate form of truth into the world. The form of art remains the form of external representation and is, for this reason, as a whole something that, if not in its constant possibility to be further nurtured, has passed away. Hegel's theory of the pastnesss of art in general is one of those daring theses by way of which his system so peculiarly oscillates between conceptual despotism and genuine intuition. This theory has proven itself in that it is the foundation upon which the philosophy of art transforms itself into a genuine history of art. Not only does the early period before the Greeks escape the concept, to speak with Creuzer, and turns to intuition. The entire history of art is separated from the truth of the concept. Like all other historical forms of the spirit, the history of art belongs to the early forms of one unique spirit that is sure of itself and for Hegel completes itself in the philosophical concept. That there is truth in all these early forms, and that in Hegel's magnificent exalting of the claim made by the philosophical concept, nevertheless, a powerful legacy of acquired historical intuition is assimilated and transformed, in this too we see that the trace of Heidelberg in this despotic spirit of philosophy has not passed away.

Notes

Introduction

1. Kurt von Fritz, 'Die Rolle des *Noūs*', in *Um die Begriffswelt der Vorsokratiker*, ed. Hans-Georg Gadamer. Darmstadt: Wissenschaftlich Buchgesellschaft, 1968, pp. 246–363.
2. In 'Die Rolle des *Noūs*', p. 276.
3. 'Parmenides or Why Being Pertains to This World', in this volume, p. 54.
4. 'Die Rolle des *Noūs*', p. 266.
5. 'Die Rolle des *Noūs*', p. 269.
6. Jean-Paul Sartre, *Being and Nothingness: An Essay in Phenomenological Ontology*, trans. Hazel Barnes. New York: The Citadel Press, 1965, p. 235; *L'Être et le néant. Essai d'ontologie phénoménologique*. Paris: Gallimard, 1943, p. 305 (translation modified).
7. 'Parmenides or Why Being Pertains to This World', p. 57.
8. 'Parmenides or Why Being Pertains to This World', p. 59.
9. See 'Parmenides or Why Being Pertains to This World', p. 56.
10. 'Parmenides or Why Being Pertains to This World', p. 54.
11. 'Parmenides or Why Being Pertains to This World', p. 55. It is not accidental that this ancient understanding of 'mind' found some resonance in people like Sartre, quoted above, or Heidegger. For their 'philosophy of existence' in their different forms attempted to recover the articulating power of life itself. It is worth noting that a current trend in philosophy of mind, called 'enactivism', inspired by Husserl's phenomenology, mediated by Merleau-Ponty, attempts, from within a cognitivist approach, to reconnect the mind with the world and the body, so that the mind is envisaged as embodied and spread in the world, 'taking in' the world.
12. In Hans-Georg Gadamer, *Hermeneutics between History and Philosophy, The Selected Writings of Hans-Georg Gadamer*, vol. I, ed. and trans. Pol Vandevelde and Arun Iyer. London: Bloomsbury, 2016, pp. 179–206.
13. See 'Dialectic Is not What Sophists Do', in this volume, pp. 117, 125–6.
14. 'Parmenides or Why Being Pertains to This World', p. 55.
15. 'Dialectic Is not What Sophists Do', p. 125–6.
16. 'Dialectic Is not What Sophists Do', p. 126. Elsewhere Gadamer writes: 'In my *Platos dialektische Ethik* I worked out to what extent this investigation of reality as it is present in the *logoi* provides access to the truth of what is, and how it serves in uncovering the true order of the cosmos. I also showed that investigation of the *logoi* is the actual task which the whole tradition of early Greek philosophy set for itself, and how Plato, in building upon this tradition, approaches this task mythologically in the *Timaeus*' (*Dialogue and Dialectic: Eight Hermeneutical Studies on Plato*, trans. P. Christopher Smith. New Haven, CT: Yale University Press, 1980, p. 198).
17. Gadamer writes: 'I believe we have reasons to assume so, that it was Plato who was the first to have discovered the relativistic implications of the technical and political pragmatism of the older generation of sophists' ('Mathematics and Dialectic in Plato', in this volume, p. 88).

18 See 'Amicus Plato magis amica veritas (1968)', in *Gesammelte Werke*, vol. 6. Tübingen: Mohr (Paul Siebeck), 1985, [71–89], p. 74.
19 'Zur platonischen Erkenntnistheorie', in *Gesammelte Werke*, vol. 7. Tübingen: Mohr (Paul Siebeck), 1991, [328–37], p. 329.
20 'Amicus Plato magis amica veritas', p. 82.
21 Gregory Vlastos, *Socrates, Ironist and Moral Philosopher*. Ithaca, NY: Cornell University Press, 1991, p. 257.
22 'Dialectic und Sophistik im siebenten Brief', in *Gesammelte Werke*, vol. 6, p. 112.
23 'Dialectic Is not What Sophists Do', p. 105.
24 'Dialectic Is not What the Sophists Do', p. 120.
25 'Platos dialektische Ethik', in *Gesammelte Werke*, vol. 5. Tübingen: J. C. B. Mohr (Paul Siebeck), 1985, p. 100; *Plato's Dialectical Ethics: Phenomenological Interpretations Relating to the* Philebus, trans. Robert Wallace. New Haven, CT: Yale University Press, 1991, p. 139.
26 See the essay 'Aristotle's Protrepticus in Consideration of the Historical Development of Aristotle's Ethics', in *Ethics, Aesthetics and the Historical Dimension of Language, The Selected Writings of Hans-Georg Gadamer*, vol. II, ed. and trans. Pol Vandevelde and Arun Iyer. London: Bloomsbury, 2022, pp. 9–26.
27 'Amicus Plato magis amica veritas', p. 74.
28 'Amicus Plato magis amica veritas', p. 74.
29 'Amicus Plato magis amica veritas', p. 75.
30 'Dialectic Is not What the Sophists Do', p. 126.
31 'Amicus Plato magis amica veritas', p. 85.
32 Quoted by Gadamer in 'Oetinger as Philosopher', in this volume, p. 131.
33 'Oetinger as Philosopher', p. 138.
34 In 'Oetinger as Philosopher', p. 135.
35 'Herder and the Historical World', p. 144.
36 'Herder and the Historical World', p. 146.
37 'Herder and the Historical World', p. 146.
38 'Herder and the Historical World', p. 147.
39 'Herder and the Historical World', p. 150.
40 Quoted in 'Herder and the Historical World', p. 150.
41 'Die Kontinuität der Geschichte und der Augenblick der Existenz', in *Gesammelte Werke*, vol. 2. Tübingen: Mohr (Paul Siebeck), 1986, p. 142. He laments the fact that 'the accusation has often been made about [his] investigations that their language is too imprecise' and recognizes that this defect 'may often enough be the case' ('Nachwort zur 3. Auflage', in *Gesammelte Werke*, vol. 2, p. 461).
42 Gadamer has written on the connection between reading and hearing in many places, among them in 'Voice and Language (1981)', in *Ethics, Aesthetics and the Historical Dimension of Language*, p. 194 and 'Hearing – Seeing – Reading (1984)', in the same volume, p. 204.
43 This translation is justified because Dilthey was not interested in the effect or influence any single action or circumstance has, as if life or history would be a web or a nexus of singular mechanical effects and countereffects. Rather, for Dilthey, it is the nexus as a whole that has the efficacy and is thus not reducible to the sum of the individual effects in the nexus. Gadamer commented on this notion of nexus in an essay of 1943, writing: 'An epoch presents a unitary meaningful nexus [*Bedeutungszusammenhang*]. Dilthey calls this nexus the "structure" of the time' ('Das Problem der Geschichte in der neueren deutschen Philosophie', in *Gesammelte Werke*,

vol. 2, p. 31). This 'meaningful nexus' is qualified as a *Wirkungszusammenhang*, about which Gadamer says that it 'is not first configured in the understanding but exerts an effect at the same time as a nexus of forces [*als Zusammenhang von Kraften wirksam*]' ('Das Problem der Geschichte', p. 31). This productive nexus illustrates the fact that for Dilthey, as Gadamer says, 'history is always both meaning and force [*Bedeutung und Kraft*] at the same time' (p. 31).

44 *Wahrheit und Methode. Grundzüge einer philosophischen Hermeneutik*. Tübingen: J. C. B. Mohr (Paul Siebeck) [1960] 1990, p. 383.
45 *Wahrheit und Methode*, pp. 346–7.
46 *Wahrheit und Methode*, p. 382.
47 *Wahrheit und Methode*, p. 381.
48 'Begriffsgeschichte als Philosophie', in *Gesammelte Werke*, vol. 2, p. 82.
49 *Wahrheit und Methode*, p. 305.
50 *Truth and Method*, 2nd revised ed., trans. Joel Weinsheimer and Donald Marshall. New York: Continuum, 1998, p. 300.
51 *Wahrheit und Methode*, p. 305.
52 *Truth and Method*, p. 300.
53 *Wahrheit und Methode*, pp. 305–6.
54 'Vorwort zur 2. Auflage', in *Gesammelte Werke*, vol. 2, p. 441.
55 *Wahrheit und Methode*, p. 306.
56 *Wahrheit und Methode*, p. 306.
57 *Wahrheit und Methode*, p. 306.
58 'Die Kontinuität der Geschichte', p. 142.
59 *Wahrheit und Methode*, p. 380.
60 *Wahrheit und Methode*, p. 460.
61 Paul Ricoeur, *Temps et récit*, vol. 3. Paris: Éditions du Seuil, 1985, p. 391.
62 *Wahrheit und Methode*, p. 347.
63 *Wahrheit und Methode*, p. 347.
64 'Nachwort zur 3. Auflage', p. 475.
65 *Wahrheit und Methode*, p. 311.
66 'Reflections on My Philosophical Journey', in *The Philosophy of Hans-Georg Gadamer*, ed. Lewis Edwin Hahn. Chicago: Open Court, 1997, p. 41.
67 'Rhetorik, Hermeneutik und Ideologiekritik', in *Gesammelte Werke*, vol. 2, p. 247.
68 *Wahrheit und Methode*, p. 307.
69 *Wahrheit und Methode*, p. 352.
70 *Wahrheit und Methode*, p. 307.
71 *Wahrheit und Methode*, p. 226.
72 *Wahrheit und Methode*, p. 306.
73 *Wahrheit und Methode*, p. 306.
74 *Wahrheit und Methode*, p. 347.
75 *Wahrheit und Methode*, p. 346.
76 *Wahrheit und Methode*, p. 477.
77 'Die Kontinuität der Geschichte', p. 143.
78 In English in the text.
79 'Plato's Thinking in Utopias', in this volume, p. 71.
80 'Reflections on My Philosophical Journey', [2–63], p. 26. As he notes elsewhere, 'in my view, my studies in Greek philosophy are the part of my philosophical works which most stands on its own' ('Platos dialektische Ethik – Beim Wort genommen', in *Gesammelte Werke*, vol. 7. Tubingen: Mohr (Paul Siebeck), 1991, [121–7], p. 121).

81   'Hegel and the Historical Spirit', in this volume p. 175.
82   *Kakou mageirou tropō*, *Phaedrus* 265e (in *Lysis, Symposium, Phaedrus*, trans. Christopher Emlyn-Jones. The Loeb Classical Library. Cambridge, MA: Harvard University Press, 2022, p. 266).
83   *Wahrheit und Methode*, p. 381.
84   *Wahrheit und Methode*, p. 374.
85   *Hermeneutics between History and Philosophy*, p. 118.
86   *Wahrheit und Methode*, p. 392.
87   *Wahrheit und Methode*, p. 368.
88   *Wahrheit und Methode*, p. 3.
89   'Vom Zirkel des Verstehens', in *Gesammelte Werke*, vol. 2, p. 65.
90   *Wahrheit und Methode*, p. 387; *Truth and Method*, 383.
91   *Wahrheit und Methode*, p. 387.
92   *Wahrheit und Methode*, p. 310.
93   *Wahrheit und Methode*, p. 125.
94   *Wahrheit und Methode*, p. 477.
95   *Wahrheit und Methode*, p. 125.
96   *Wahrheit und Methode*, p. 172.
97   *Wahrheit und Methode*, p. 477.
98   *Wahrheit und Methode*, p. 364.
99   *Wahrheit und Methode*, p. 302.
100   Donald Davidson, who interacted with Gadamer and offered his own version of what interpretation is, defended such an atemporal and asubjective ascription of beliefs under the name of a radical interpretation. For a discussion of the interactions between Gadamer and Davidson and a comparison between their views, see Pol Vandevelde, *The Ethics of Interpretation: From the Principle of Charity to Love as a Hermeneutic Imperative*. New York: Routledge, 2023, pp. 25–31 and 69f.
101   'Text und Interpretation', in *Text und Interpretation*, ed. Philippe Forget. Munich: Wilhelm Fink Verlag, 1984, [24–55] p. 45.
102   'Seventh Letter' 344b, in Plato, *Epistles*, in *Timaeus. Critias. Cleitophon. Menexenus. Epistles*, trans. R. G. Bury. The Loeb Classical Library. Cambridge, MA: Harvard University Press, 1952, p. 541.
103   'Und dennoch: Macht des Guten Willens', in Philippe Forget *Text und Interpretation*, p. 59.
104   *Wahrheit und Methode*, p. 398.
105   *Hermeneutics between History and Philosophy*, p. 118.
106   Gadamer's habilitation is titled *Plato's Dialectical Ethics: Phenomenological Interpretations Relating to the* Philebus (trans. Robert Wallace. New Haven, CT: Yale University Press, 1991). About this kind of understanding of dialectic, Davidson writes: 'Gadamer views dialectic, not as a tool or method, but as establishing the ethical hierarchy directly through its relation to the phenomena. He therefore speaks, not of Plato's ethical theory as being dialectical, but of the dialectic being ethical' (*Plato's* Philebus, Harvard Dissertations in Philosophy. New York: Garland Publishing, 1990, p. 36).
107   *Wahrheit und Methode*, p. 373. This is clearly a principle of charity close to Davidson, although with another purpose. It is close to Davidson's because it attempts to maximize the meaning content of what is interpreted but it is very different because Davidson wants to bracket any mental intention of the author and replace such intention by the interpreters' own, who will substitute their beliefs to the author's

beliefs. If instead we want to do justice to the text in context and thus to the author, we have to heed Oetinger's maxim, which Gadamer paraphrases: 'Ultimately, is the principle which Oetinger opposes to his theological opponents not also *mutatis mutandis* the right principle for us? If interpreters do not recognize that the statements they want to interpret are the outpourings of the highest insight and cognition, then they are not seeking anything that is worthy of their investigative efforts' ('Oetinger as Philosopher', p. 139).
108 Friedrich Schleiermacher, *Hermeneutics and Criticism and Other Writings*, trans. and ed. Andrew Bowie. Cambridge: Cambridge University Press, 1998, p. 30.
109 *Hermeneutics and Criticism*, p. 44.
110 *Hermeneutics and Criticism*, p. 110.
111 Hans-Georg Gadamer, *Truth and Method*, translation revised Joel Weinsheimer and Donald G. Marshall. London: Bloomsbury Academic, 2013, p. 303.
112 *Truth and Method*, p. 282.
113 *Truth and Method*, p. 282.
114 *Truth and Method*, p. 307.
115 *Truth and Method*, p. 308.
116 *Truth and Method*, p. 489.
117 'Whether I grasp the age in observation, as an intellectual principle, as peculiar feeling of life, as sociological structure, as a particular economic order or form of governance, in each case I do not grasp any ultimate origin of the whole but only a possible perspective of orientating myself in it. *For, that from which I can in no sense get out, I cannot get an overview as if from the outside*' (Karl Jaspers, *Die geistige Situation der Zeit*. Berlin: Walter De Gruyter and Co., 1955, p. 26, translation mine).
118 In this volume, p. 175.
119 *Truth and Method*, p. 435.
120 Hans-Georg Gadamer, 'Dialectic and Sophism in Plato's Seventh Letter', in *Dialogue and Dialectic: Eight Hermeneutical Studies on Plato*, trans. P. Christopher Smith. New Haven and London: Yale University Press, 1980, pp. 93–123.
121 Hans-Georg Gadamer, 'Plato's Unwritten Dialectic', in *Dialogue and Dialectic*, pp. 124–55.
122 'Plato's Unwritten Dialectic', p. 153.
123 'Plato's Unwritten Dialectic', p. 153.
124 In this volume, p. 118.
125 In this volume, p. 123.
126 In this volume, p. 124.
127 In this volume, p. 63.
128 In this volume, p. 161.
129 In this volume, p. 161.
130 In this volume, p. 190.
131 In this volume, p. 144.
132 In this volume, p. 144.
133 In this volume, p. 147.
134 In this volume, p. 147.

1

1 Georg Andreas Gabler, *Kritik des Bewusstseins. Eine Vorschule zu Hegels Wissenschaft der Logik* [Critique of Consciousness: A Primer on Hegel's *Science of Logic*]. Erlangen: Palm, 1827; Leiden: A. H. Adriani 1901.

2 Wilhelm Purpus, *Zur Dialektik des Bewußtseins nach Hegel. Ein Beitrag zur Würdigung der Phänomenologie des Geistes* [On the Dialectic of Consciousness according to Hegel: A Contribution to the Assessment of the *Phenomenology of Spirit*]. Berlin: Trowitzsch, 1908.

3 *Parmenides' Lehrgedicht*, griechisch und Deutsch, ed. Hermann Diels. Berlin: Georg Reimer, 1897. The numbers of the fragments and of the verses in what follows are taken from the edition by Diels/Kranz, *Die Fragmente der Vorsokratiker* griechisch und Deutsch, ed. and trans. Hermann Diels, ninth edition by Walther Krantz. Berlin: Weidmannsche Verlagsbuchhandlung, 1959. Abbreviated as VS.

4 Diels, *Parmenides' Lehrgedicht*, p. 21.

5 E. R. Dodds, *The Greeks and the Irrational*. Berkeley, CA: University of California Press, 1951. Uvo Hölscher, *Anfängliches Fragen. Studien zur frühen griechischen Philosophie* [Inceptual Questions. Studies on Early Greek Philosophy]. Göttingen: Vandenhoeck & Ruprecht, 1968.

6 B. L. van der Waerden, *Erwachende Wissenschaft*. Basel/Stuttgart: Birkäuser, 1956 [English translation: *Science Awakening*, trans. Arnold Dresden. New York: Oxford University Press, 1961]; *Die Pythagoreer. Religiöse Bruderschaft und Schule der Wissenschaft* [The Pythagoreans: Religious Brotherhood and School of Science]. Zurich/Munich: Artemis, 1979. In this regard, see my review in *Gesammelte Werke*, vol. 6, pp. 312–18.

7 Translators' Note: In this essay we translate *Ansicht*, which Gadamer uses for *doxa*, by 'point of view'. Gadamer's choice of *Ansicht* is in deliberate contrast to the regular German words *Meinung* or *Vorstellung*, both of which correspond to the English 'opinion' commonly used to translate *doxa*. Gadamer is doing so in order to emphasize the reference to the visual present. He does the same when using *Augenschein* in reference to the Greek *phainomenon*, which we translate as 'what appears to the eye'. The term *Augenschein* explains what defines human existence in Parmenides, namely, the fact that we human beings are guided by what appears to our eyes and as a result of which we come to hold many *doxai* or 'points of view'.

8 When this text was in press, I realized that W. R. Chalmers in his critical overview of the state of research at the time (*Phronesis* 5, 1960, pp. 5–22) reached the same conclusion on this point.

9 *Metaphysics* A.5, 986b31: *anankazomenos d'akolouthein tois phainomenois …* ['being compelled to follow the phenomena'] (*Metaphysics*, trans. Hugh Tredennick. The Loeb Classical Library. Cambridge, MA: Harvard University Press, 1990 [1935]).

10 See Hermann Fränkel, *Wege und Formen frühgriechischen Denkens. Literarische und philosophiegeschichtliche Studien* [Ways and Forms of Early Greek Thinking: Studies in Literature and History of Philosophy]. Munich: Beck, 1955, p. 188. Hölscher simply, and quite rightly translates *chrēn* as 'correct'.

11 Hans Schwabl, 'Sein und Doxa bei Parmenides' [Being and *Doxa* in Parmenides], *Wiener Studien* 66 (1953): pp. 50–75. Reprinted in Hans-Georg Gadamer (ed.), *Um die Begriffswelt der Vorsokratiker* [On the Conceptual World of the Pre-Socratics]. Darmstadt: Wissenschaftliche Buchgesellschaft, 1968, [pp. 391–422], p. 393ff.

12 Translators' Note: In her French translation and commentary, Magali Année translates verse 8, 54 as: 'dont l'une n'est pas nécessairement "est"' ['one of which is not necessarily "is"'] (Parménide, *Fragments Poème*, trans. Magali Année. Paris: Vrin, 2012, p. 173).

13 Translators' Note: Fragment B57 (D25) runs as follows: 'The teacher of the most people is Hesiod; they are certain (*epistasthai*) that it is he who knows (*eidenai*) the most things – he who did not understand (*gignōskein*) day and night, for they

are one' (Heraclitus, *Testimonia*, Part 2: *Doctrine*, in *Early Greek Philosophy*, vol. III *Early Ionian Thinkers*, trans. André Laks and Glenn Most. Loeb Classical Library. Cambridge, MA: Harvard University Press, 2016, p. 151. Online edition).

14 Translators' Note: The fragment B40 (D20) runs as follows: 'Much learning does not teach intelligence: for otherwise it would have taught it to Hesiod and Pythagoras' (Heraclitus, *Testimonia*, p. 147. Online edition).

15 This is also the sense in which Jeanne Croissant and Jaap Mansfeld have understood its meaning.

16 *Glōtta* ['tongue'] has here, in this context, a cognitive sense like *akoē* ['hearing'] and *opsis* ['sight'], which, since Hesiod, must obviously have meant only the tongue which speaks and not the tongue which tastes.

17 Hermann Langerberk, *Doxis epirhusmiē. Studien zu Demokrits Ethik und Erkenntnislehre* [Opinion is a rhythmic Afflux. Studies on Democritus' Ethics and Epistemology]. Berlin: Weidmann, 1935 (Neue Philologische Untersuchungen, vol. 10). See my review in *Gesammelte Werke*, vol. 5. Tübingen: J. C. B. Mohr (Paul Siebeck), 1985, pp. 341ff.

18 Heidegger's lecture course on the *Theaetetus* in 1931 (in *Gesamtausgabe*, vol. 34 [*Vom Wesen der Wahrheit. Zu Platons Höhlengleichnis und Theätet*, ed. Hermann Mörchen. Frankfurt am Main: Klostermann, 1988]) was not yet available to me at the time of writing my essay.

19 Rudolf Carnap, 'Überwindung der Metaphysik durch logische Analyse der Sprache', *Erkenntnis* 2 (1931): pp. 219–41. Here, p. 229ff. [English translation: 'The Elimination of Metaphysics through Logical Analysis of Language', in *Logical Positivism*, ed. A. J. Ayer. Glencoe, IL: The Free Press, 1959, pp. 60–81].

20 Translators' Note: *Vergehen* in German can mean 'to go by', 'to wear off' or 'to pass away'.

21 See Theophrastus, *De sensu* (in Diels/Krantz, *Die Fragmente der Vorsokratiker*, VS 28 A 46).

22 Now in *Um die Begriffswelt der Vorsokratiker* [About the Conceptual World of the Pre-Socratics]. Dasrmstadt: Wissenschaftliche Buchgesellschaft, 1968, pp. 246–363.

23 Walter Bröcker, *Die Geschichte der Philosophie vor Sokrates* [The History of Philosophy before Socrates]. Frankfurt: Klostermann, 1965, p. 60.

24 See Hermann Diels, *Parmenides Lehrgedicht*, p. 23ff. and my 'Retraktationen', in *Gesammelte Werke*, vol. 6, pp. 44f.

25 Parmenides, *Vom Wesen des Seienden. Die Fragmente, griechisch und Deutsch* [On the Essence of Beings: The Fragments: Greek and German], ed., trans. and explained by Uvo Hölscher. Frankfurt am Main: Suhrkamp, 1969.

26 Agostino Marsoner, 'La struttura del proemio di Parmenide' [The structure of the Proemium of Parmenides], *Annali dell' lstituto Italiano per gli Studi Storici* [Annals of the Italian Institute of Historical Studies] V (1976/1978): p. 175 A. 290.

27 Jürgen Wiesner, 'Überlegungen zu Parmenides B 8, 34' [Reflections on Parmenides B 8, 34], in *Études sur Parménide*, ed. Pierre Aubenque. Paris: Vrin, 1987, pp. 170–90.

28 Translators' Note: Gadamer writes '*heterousthai*'. Melissus' text in the Loeb Classical Library says '*heteroiousthai*', from *heteroiō*: to become different (Melissus, *Testimonia*, Part II *Doctrine*, D11 (B8) 559, in *Early Greek Philosophy*, vol. V, ed. and trans. André Laks and Glenn Most. The Classical Loeb Library. Cambridge, MA: Harvard University Press, 2016, p. 250. Online version).

29 Translators' Note: Gadamer is referring to *Parmenides* 131b1–6. In responding to Parmenides, Socrates says about the idea, 'No,' he replied, 'for it might be like

day, which is one and the same, is in many places at once, and yet is not separated from itself; so each idea, though one and the same, might be in all its participants at once' (*Parmenides, in Cratylus, Parmenides, Greater Hippias, Lesser Hippias*, trans. H. N. Fowler. The Loeb Classical Library. Cambridge, MA: Harvard University Press, 1996 [1926], p. 215).

30 Translators' Note: Gadamer is referring here to Socrates' reply to Parmenides asking Socrates whether his metaphor of the day for the idea is equivalent to another metaphor, that of a sail. Socrates does not reply with a confident 'yes', but with an uncertain 'perhaps' (131c1), suggesting to us readers that the exchange of metaphors on the part of Parmenides is not all that sound.

31 Jacob Bernays, 'Heraklitische Studien' [Heraclitean Studies], *Rheinisches Museum für Philologie* 7 (1850): pp. 90–116.

32 If one notes that Plato's text says *oudamē* ['nowhere'] and absolutely not what is currently prevalent in the text *damē* ['subjugate'], then one will immediately have to see that it was not a spelling mistake or a lapse in memory on Plato's part. For Plato, of his own initiative, inserts the *verbum* which was missing, completely in opposition to the verse: *phēsin*, 'he says'. At any rate, it is not fortunately a matter of interpretation. [Translators' Note: We reconstruct Gadamer's brief remark in the following manner. The first verse of Fragment 7 in the manuscript usually used in edition and translation is taken from Simplicius' transcription and says: 'For no, never will it be subjugated [*damē*] that the things that are would not be'. *Damē* is a subjective aorist third person singular with the possible sense of an imperative. In the *Sophist* Plato quotes this verse and inserts *phēsin* after *damē*. This insertion indicates to Gadamer that we should follow another manuscript that says *oudamē* ['nowhere'] so that Parmenides' verse should read: 'No, never and nowhere, he says, [is it the case that] the things that are not are' (237a)].

33 For example in Peter Szondi, *Schriften I*. Frankfurt am Main: Suhrkamp, 1978, pp. 280ff.

34 Here I must correct Hölscher's otherwise excellent translation. The expression [27] cannot mean 'harshly contentious refutation'. It must rather mean: 'the point of contention which is always engendering controversy'. We are otherwise not familiar with the word *poludēris*. But the context leaves no doubt that we are also dealing here again with what is repeated, that is to say, the always-needed refutation. Going astray is an ever-recurring danger.

35 The relevant works by Heidegger are primarily the texts from the 1950s: in *Holzwege*, (GA 5, ed. Friedrich-Wilhelm von Herrmann. Frankfurt am Main: Klostermann, 1978) 'Der Spruch des Anaximander' [English translation: 'Anaximander's Saying (1946)', in *Of the Beaten Track*, ed. and trans. Julian Young and Kenneth Haynes. Cambridge, UK: Cambridge University Press, 2002, pp. 242–81] as well as in *Vorträge und Aufsätze* (GA 7, ed. Friedrich-Wilhelm von Herrmann. Frankfurt am Main: Suhrkamp, 2000) 'Logos (Heraklit)' [English translation: 'Logos (Heraclitus, Fragment B50)', in *Early Greek Thinking*, trans. David Farrell Krell and Frank Capuzzi. New York: Harper and Row, 1985, pp. 59–78] and 'Moira (Parmenides)' [English translation: 'Moira, Parmenides VIII, 34–41)', in *Early Greek Thinking*, pp. 79–101].

36 This was indeed already emphasized by Wilhelm von Humboldt and Teichmüller!

37 Translators' Note: In the *Parmenides* Plato writes at the beginning that it was the first time that Zeno's writing was introduced to Athens. Later on in the dialogue, Zeno explains that he composed the work in his youth but that it was stolen from him (128d).

38 See *Gesammelte Werke*, vol. 6. Tübingen: J. C. B. Mohr (Siebeck), 1985, index.
39 On this, see the studies on Plato: 'Socrates' Frömmigkeit des Nichtwissens', in *Gesammelte Werke*, vol. 7, pp. 83–117 [English translation: 'Religion and Religiosity in Socrates', *Proceedings of the Boston Area Colloquium in Ancient Philosophy* 1 (1986): pp. 53–75], 'Plato als Porträtist' [English translation: 'Plato as Portraitist', *Continental Philosophy Review* 33/3 (2000): pp. 245–74], 'Die Idee des Guten zwischen Plato und Aristoteles' [English translation: *The Idea of the Good in Platonic-Aristotelian Philosophy*, trans. P. Christopher Smith. New Haven, CT: Yale University Press, 1986] and the studies on the Eleatic dialogues of Plato in *Gesammelte Werke*, vol. 7 and in this volume.

2

1 Translators' Note: The book is *The Open Society and Its Enemies*, published in two volumes, the first one being originally titled *The Age of Plato* in the first edition by Caxton Press in 1945 and renamed *The Spell of Plato* in the second edition (London: Routledge, 1947).
2 See, for example, 'Hegel und die antike Dialektik', in *Gesammelte Werke*, vol. 3. Tübingen: J. C. B. Mohr (Siebeck), 1987, pp. 3–28. [English translation: 'Hegel and the Dialectic of the Ancient Philosophers', in Hans-Georg Gadamer, *Hegel's Dialectic: Five Hermeneutical Studies*, trans. C. Christopher Smith. New Haven, CT: Yale University Press, 1976, pp. 5–34].
3 Werner Jaeger, *Studien zur Entstehungsgeschichte der Metaphysik des Aristoteles* [Studies on the History of the Emergence of Aristotle's Metaphysics]. Berlin: Weidmann, 1912.
4 'Der aristotelische "Protreptikos" und die entwicklungsgeschichtliche Betrachtung der aristotelischen Ethik', now in *Gesammelte Werke*, vol. 5. Tübingen: J. C. B. Mohr (Siebeck), pp. 164–86. [English translation: 'Aristotle's *Protrepticus* in Consideration of the Historical Development of Aristotle's Ethics (1928)', in *The Selected Writings of Hans-Georg Gadamer*, vol. II *Ethics, Aesthetics and the Historical Dimension of Language*, ed. and trans. Pol Vandevelde and Arun Iyer. London: Bloomsbury, 2022, pp. 9–25].
5 See my contribution 'Stefan George (1868–1933)', in *Die Wirkung Stefan Georges auf die Wissenschaft* ['Stefan George's Influence on Science'], ed. Hans-Joachim Zimmermann, *Proceedings of the Heidelberg Academy of Sciences*, Philological-historical Class. Supplement vol. 4. Heidelberg: Carl Winter Universitätsverlag, 1984, pp. 39–49. Now, under the title 'Die Wirkung Stefan Georges auf die Wissenschaft (1983)', in *Gesammelte Werke*, vol. 9. Tübingen: J. C. B. Mohr (Siebeck), 1993, pp. 258–70.
6 On this, see my study 'Logos und Ergon im platonischen *Lysis* (1972)', in *Gesammelte Werke*, vol. 6. Tübingen: J. C. B. Mohr (Siebeck), 1985, pp. 171–86. [English translation: '"Logos" and "Ergon" in Plato's Lysis', in Hans-Georg Gadamer, *Dialogue and Dialectic: Eight Hermeneutical Studies on Plato*, ed. and trans. P. Christopher Smith. New Haven, CT: Yale University Press, 1980, pp. 1–20].
7 Translators' Note: in English in the text.
8 See my contribution 'Platos ungeschriebene Dialektik', in *Gesammelte Werke*, vol. 6, pp. 129–53. [English translation: 'Plato's Unwritten Dialectic', in Hans-Georg Gadamer, *Dialogue and Dialectic: Eight Hermeneutical Studies on Plato*, 124–54].

9 'Plato und die Dichter', in *Gesammelte Werke*, vol. 5. Tübingen: J. C. B. Mohr (Siebeck), 1985, pp. 187–211 [English translation: 'Plato and the Poets', in Hans-Georg Gadamer, *Dialogue and Dialectic: Eight Hermeneutical Studies on Plato*, pp. 39–72].
10 'Platos Staat der Erziehung (1942)', in *Gesammelte Werke*, vol. 5, pp. 249–62. [English translation: 'Plato's Educational State', in Hans-Georg Gadamer, *Dialogue and Dialectic: Eight Hermeneutical Studies on Plato*, pp. 73–92].
11 'Die Idee des Guten zwischen Plato und Aristoteles (1978)', in *Gesammelte Werke*, vol. 7, pp. 128–227. [English translation: *The Idea of the Good in Platonic-Aristotelian Philosophy*, trans. P. Christopher Smith. New Haven, CT: Yale University Press, 1986].
12 Translators' Note: *Prolegomena zu Platons Staat und der platonischen und aristotelischen Staatslehre* [Prolegomena to Plato's State and the Platonic and Aristotelian Theory of the State]. Basel: I. Reinhardt, Universitäts-Buchdruckerei, 1891.
13 On this point, Emilio Lledó reminded me of the Phaeacian romanticism of the *Odyssey*.
14 Aristotle, *Politics* B7 1266a39ff, trans. H. Rackham. The Loeb Classical Library. Cambridge, MA: Harvard University Press, 1932.
15 Plato, *Republic* IX, 592b, trans. Paul Shorey. The Loeb Classical Library. Cambridge, MA: Harvard University Press, 1988.
16 See Edgard Salin, *Plato und die griechische Utopie* [Plato and Greek Utopia]. Munich/Leipzig: Duncker & Humblot, 1921.
17 Gerhard Müller, *Platons Dialog vom Staat. Kunstform und Lehrgehalt* [Plato's Dialogue on the State: Artistic Form and Doctrinal Content]. Wiesbaden: Steiner, 1981.
18 See 'Dialektik und Sophistik im siebten platonishen Brief', *Gesammelte Werke*, vol. 6, pp. 90–115. [English translation: 'Dialectic and Sophism in Plato's "Seventh Letter"', in Hans-Georg Gadamer, *Dialogue and Dialectic: Eight Hermeneutical Studies on Plato*, pp. 93–123].
19 On this, see my detailed engagement with N. P. White's interpretation of Plato in 'Zur platonischen "Erkenntnistheorie" (1988)', in *Gesammelte Werke*, vol. 7, pp. 328–37.
20 Ludwig Edelstein, *Plato's Seventh Letter*, vol. XIV. Leiden: Brill, Philosophia Antiqua, 1966.
21 Kurt von Fritz, *Platon in Sizilien und das Problem der Philosophenherrschaft* [Plato in Sicily and the Problem of the Rule of the Philosophers]. Berlin: De Gruyter, 1968.
22 On this, see above all 'Die Idee des Guten zwischen Palto und Aristoteles', in *Gesammelte Werke*, vol. 7, pp. 215ff. [English translation: *The Idea of the Good in Platonic-Aristotelian Philosophy*].
23 Erwin Wolff, *Platos 'Apologie'* [Plato's *Apology*]. Berlin: Weidmann, 1929. See on this my review in *Gesammelte Werke*, volume 5, pp. 316–22.
24 Xenophon, *Memorabilia*, Delta 4, 5ff. [English translation: *Memorabilia*, in *Memorabilia, Oeconomicus, Symposium, Apology*, trans. E. C. Marchant and O. J. Todd. The Loeb Classical Library. Cambridge, MA: Harvard University Press, 2014].
25 Besides the passage mentioned in note 15 above, see also *Republic* V, 472dff.
26 Translators' Note: These are wisdom, temperance, courage and justice.
27 *Republic* VII 523a-537d.
28 See *Gesammelte Werke*, volume 5, pp. 187–211 [English translation: 'Plato and the Poets', in Hans-Georg Gadamer, *Dialogue and Dialectic: Eight Hermeneutical Studies on Plato*, pp. 39–72].
29 *Republic* VIII, 546b4.

30 Now, in *Gesammelte Werke*, volume 6, pp. 242–70. [English translation: 'Idea and Reality in Plato's *Timaeus*', in *Dialogue and Dialectic: Eight Hermeneutical Studies on Plato*, pp. 156–92].
31 Now, in *Gesammelte Werke*, volume 7, pp. 191ff (on the *Philebus*) [English translation in *The Idea of the Good in Platonic-Aristotelian Philosophy*].
32 See Salin, *Plato und die griechische Utopie*.
33 Hans Herter, 'Platons Staatsideal in zweierlei Gestalt' [Plato Political Ideal in Two-fold Form], in *Der Mensch und die Künste (Festschrift für Heinrich Lützeler)* [The Human Being and the Arts (Festschrift for Heinrich Lützeler)]. Düsseldorf: L. Schwann, 1962.

3

1 See my study 'Idee und Wirklichkeit in Plato's *Timaeus*', *Gesammelte Werke*, vol. 6. Tübingen: J. C. B. Mohr (Siebeck), 1985, pp. 242–70 [English translation: 'Idea and Reality in Plato's *Timaeus*', in *Dialogue and Dialectic: Eight Hermeneutical Studies on Plato*, trans. P. Christopher Smith. New Haven, CT: Yale University Press, 1980, pp. 156–92].
2 Translators' Note: We translate *Zahl* as number and *Anzahl* as 'numerical count'. The number six, for example, which for us is an abstraction is for Socrates a set of six units, each of which is a 'monad', with the set itself being what we translate as a 'numerical count'. 'Six' is thus the name of the set but the components of the set, the 'ones', do not share 'six' among themselves.
3 Aristotle alludes to this repeatedly: *Nicomachean Ethics*, Alpha 4 1096a18 [*Nicomachean Ethics*, trans. H. Rackham. The Loeb Classical Library. Cambridge, MA: Harvard University Press, 1934 [1926]]; *Eudemian Ethics* A8 1218a2 [*Eudemian Ethics*, in *The Athenian Constitution, The Eudemian Ethics, On Virtues and Vices*, trans. H. Rackham. The Loeb Classical Library. Cambridge, MA: Harvard University Press, 1971 1925]; *Metaphysics* Bēta 3 999a6 [*Metaphysics*, trans. Hugh Tredennick. The Loeb Classical Library. Cambridge, MA: Harvard University Press, 1990 (1935)].
4 Paul Friedländer, Kurt Hildebrandt, Leo Strauss, Jacob Klein, and my own works are to be mentioned here.
5 Hermann Langerbeck, *Doxis epirhusmiē, Studien zu Demokrits Ethik und Erkenntnislehre* [Opinion is a Rhytmic Afflux: Studies on Democritus' Ethics and Epistemology], *Neue philologische Untersuchungen* [New Philological Investigations], vol. 10. Berlin: Weidmann, 1935. See also the recent dissertation of Karl-Martin Dietz (1976), which relies on my own works and the unpublished dissertation of Ruprecht Pflaumer (1956). Detailed proofs are provided there.
6 'Die Rolle des *noûs*', now in *Um die Befgriffswelt der Vorsokratiker* [On the Conceptual World of the Pre-Socratics], ed. Hans-Georg Gadamer. Darmstadt: Wissenschaftliche Buchgesellschaft, 1968.
7 Werner Jaeger (*Paideia* II, p. 29) sees in *aisthēsis* a medical expression for 'diagnosis' ('thorough measure'). This too fits with the 'broad' sense of *aisthēsis*, which resonates as far as Aristotle, for example in *Physics* Alpha 1 (*to gar holon kata tēn aisthēsin gnōrimōteron* ['the whole is indeed better known by perception') and especially when applied to mathematics in the *Nicomachean Ethics* Zēta 9 1142a27; *aisthēsis* [...] *oia aisthanometha hoti to en tois mathēmatikois eschaton trigōnon stēsetai gar kakei* ['perception [...], the sort in which we perceive that the ultimate among the

mathematical objects is a triangle; for it will come to a stop here too']. See also Karl-Martin Dietz's dissertation mentioned above, especially pp. 86–92.
8   On this, see Dietz's dissertation, p. 16f.
9   In 'Die Idee des Guten zwischen Plato und Aristoteles' (now in *Gesammelte Werke*, vol. 7, pp. 128–227) [English translation: *The Idea of the Good*, trans. P. Christopher Smith. New Haven, CT: Yale University Press, 1986], I have said something about this, which goes beyond 'Platos dialektische Ethik' (in *Gesammelte Werke*, vol. 5. Tübingen: J. C. B. Mohr (Paul Siebeck), 1985, pp. 3–163 [English translation: *Plato's Dialectical Ethics: Phenomenological Interpretations Relating to the* Philebus, trans. Robert Wallace. New Haven, CT: Yale University Press, 1991]).
10 See 'Dialektik und Sophistik im siebten platonischen Brief', *Gesammelte Werke*, vol. 6, pp. 90–115 [English translation: 'Dialectic and Sophism in Plato's Seventh Letter', in Hans-Georg Gadamer, *Dialogue and Dialectic: Eight Hermeneutical Studies on Plato*].
11 F. M. Cornford, *Principium sapientiae: The Origins of Greek Philosophical Thought*, ed. W. K. C. Guthrie. Cambridge: Cambridge University Press, 1952, p. 48.
12 Here *aisthēsis* naturally has the narrow sense of 'sense perception'.
13 Translators' Note: Gadamer is referring to *Theaetetus* 185d3 where Theaetetus says: 'But it appears to me that the soul views by itself directly what all things have in common' (in *Theaetetus, Sophist*, trans. Harold North Fowler. The Classical Loeb Library. Cambridge, MA: Harvard University Press, 2002 [1921], p. 163).
14 The problematic of this study on 'mathematics and dialectic' leaves out a central part of the *Theaetetus*. When I wrote this essay in 1982, Heidegger's lecture course, now published as volume 34 of his *Complete Works*, which interprets this part, was not yet available to me [*Vom Wesen der Wahrheit. Zu Platons Höhlengleichnis und Theätet*, ed. Hermann Mörchen. GA 34. Frankfurt am Main: Klostermann, 1988; English translation, *The Essence of Truth: On Plato's Cave Allegory and Theaetatus*, GA 34, trans Ted Sadler. London: Continuum, 2002].
15 I also have my doubts whether (in this vague recollection!) the expression *epistēta* ['knowable'] with *houtōsi kai onomazōn* ['naming in this way'] is really meant as a new word. The fact that *onomazein* ['to name'] appears here in connection with *logos* (*hōn mē esti logos* ['those of which there is no account']) makes it implausible that it is only to be understood functionally and to be linked to the word *epistēta*. From the substance of what is said, one would rather surmise that we are dealing with a brief explanatory remark which describes the mere showing – through *houtōsi* ['in this way'] – and the mere naming – through *onomazōn* ['naming'] – as the *alētheuein* ['to tell the truth'] (see *onomazesthai monon* ['they can only be named'] 202b2).
16 See Kurt von Fritz, 'Zur anthisthenischen Erkenntnistheorie und Logik' [Towards an Antisthenesian Epistemology and Logic], in Kurt von Fritz, *Schriften zur griechischen Logik* [Writings on Greek Logic], vol. I. Stuttgart: Frommann-Holzboog, 1978, pp. 126ff.
17 The meticulous studies in conceptual history, which Wilhelm Schwabe has presented (*Archiv für Begriffsgeschichte*, supplement vol. 3, 1980) seem to me plausible. Someone like Antisthenes must have brought the two motifs together and connected the concept of *stoicheion* ['letter'] in grammar to the theory of elements of an atomistic character. At any rate, it is clear that Socrates in the *Theaetetus* refers back to the original grammatical sense of *stoicheion* for the purposes of this refutation.
18 The dialectic of whole and part often plays an important role in Plato: *Parmenides* 144e, 157c; *Sophist* 244d; *Statesman* 262a, 265a; *Philebus* 12e, 14e.
19 The fact that two expressions are used here, both of which mean 'indivisible' in German, sounds like a conscious linguistic composition. In Aristotle, *atmēton*

apparently gives far more way to *atomon*. Following Konrad Gaiser, Hans Joachim Krämer even discerns an 'elementary' theory from Aristotle's *Topics* and the treatise on the *Categories*; in fact, those texts talk of a being here and now as *atomon* ['indivisible'] and *arithmō hen* ['one in number']. What does 'indivisible' mean here? Like the triangle, which cannot be divided into biangles? So eidetic. And precisely for this reason (occasionally) we have the addition of *arithmō hen*, which designates real individuality within what is eidetically indivisible. This individuality is also involved in mathematical essentialities like the triangle, for example, in the equality of triangles. The individuality here still remains mathematical and eidetic! *Enuparchei en tō eidei* ['it is present in the essence']!

20 See *Metaphysics* Delta 25 (*meros* ['part']), Delta 26 (*holon* ['the whole']), Delta 27 (*kolobon* ['mutilated']).
21 See most recently Konrad Gaiser, *Platons ungeschriebene Lehre. Studien zur systematischen und geschichtlichen Begründung der Wissenschaften in der Platonischen Schule* [Plato's Unwritten Doctrine: Studies on the Systematic and Historical Foundation of the Sciences in the Platonic School]. Stuttgart: Klett Cotta, 1962, p. 168, p. 378 A 144. The famous news of Eudemos (Simplicius, *On Aristotle's Physics* 7, 10ff Diels) should directly trace back to our passage in *Theaetetus*.
22 See Johannes Lohmann, Musikē *und* logos. *Aufsätze zur griechischen Philosophie und Musiktheorie* [*Musikē* and *logos*: Essays on Greek Philosophy and Music Theory]. Stuttgart: Musikwissenschaftliche Verlags-Gesellschaft, 1970, pp. 4ff.
23 See my essay 'Antike Atomtheorie', now in *Gesammelte Werke*, vol. 5, pp. 263–79. [English translation: 'Ancient Atomic Theory', in *The Beginning of Knowledge*, trans. Rod Coltman. New York: Continuum, 2002, pp. 82–101].

4

1 Translators' Note: The passage in the *Republic* reads: 'And do you not also give the name dialectician to the man who is able to exact an account of the essence of each thing? […] And is not this true of the good likewise – that the man who is unable to define in his discourse and distinguish and abstract from all other things the aspect or the idea of the good […] does not really know the good itself or any particular good [?]' (*The Republic*, trans. Paul Shorey. The Loeb Classical Library. Cambridge, MA: Harvard University Press, 1988, p. 207).
2 This has certainly been controversial and has provoked criticism. This comes to the fore in the *Clitophon* under the name of Plato and perhaps conceding to Plato's spirit, which delights in playfulness, we should accept Plato as its real author. As a prelude to the *Republic,* it is certainly not unworthy of Plato.
3 'Plato als Porträtist', in *Gesammelte Werke*, volume 7, pp. 228–57. [English translation: 'Plato as Portraitist', trans. Jamey Findling and Snezhina Gabova, *Continental Philosophy Review* 33/3 (2000): pp. 245–74. This conference was given at the occasion of the acquisition of effigies of Plato for the sculpture gallery in Munich in 1988].
4 See my contribution 'Platos ungeschriebene Dialektik', in *Gesammelte Schriften*, vol. 6. Tübingen: J. C. B. Mohr (Paul Siebeck), 1985, pp. 129–53. [English translation: 'Plato's Unwritten Dialectic', in Hans-Georg Gadamer, *Dialogue and Dialectic: Eight Hermeneutical Studies on Plato*, trans. P. Christopher Smith. New Haven, CT: Yale University Press, 1980, pp. 124–54].

5 *Prior Analytics*, A 31 [*Prior Analytics*, in *The Categories, On interpretation, Prior Analytics*, trans. Hugh Tredennick. The Loeb Classical Library. Cambridge, MA: Harvard University Press, 1983 [1938]]; see also *Posterior Analytics* B5 [*Posterior Analytics*, in *Posterior Analytics, Topica*, trans. Hugh Tredennick. The Loeb Classical Library. Cambridge, MA: Harvard University Press, 1966].
6 *Meno* 81cd: *tēs phuseōs hapasēs suggenous ousēs* ['all of nature is akin'] [*Meno*, in *Laches, Protagoras, Meno, Euthydemus*, trans. W. R. M. Lamb. The Loeb Classical Library. London: William Heinemann, 1924, p. 303].
7 Hermann Cohen, *Platos Ideenlehre und die Mathematik*. Marburg: C. L. Pfeil, 1878.
8 Johannes Kepler, *Mysterium Cosmographicum*, 1596, Ch. 1, in *Gesammelte Werke*, vol. 1. Munich: C. H. Beck, 1938, pp. 14ff.
9 I do not mention here the contributions of the historical school (from Schleiermacher to Wilamowitz) [343] nor the corresponding scholarship from abroad, and refer to the compilation made by Ernst Moritz Manasse, 'Bücher über Plato' [Books on Plato] (Supplement 1 (1957), 2 [1961] and 7 [1976] of the *Philosophische Rundschau*).
10 Translators' Note: In the passage referred to by Gadamer, the Greek word is *katakekermatismenēn*, feminine participle which, in the sentence, is predicated of *phusis* ['nature'].
11 *Platos Logik des Seins* [Plato's Logic of Being]. Giessen: Töpelmann, 1909, which Natorp explicitly cites in the second edition of his *Platos Ideenlehre. Eine Einführung in den Idealismus*. [Plato's Theory of Ideas: An Introduction to Idealism]. Leipzig: Felix Meiner, 1921.
12 Translators' Note: Gadamer does not cite the work. It seems to be a reference to Stenzel's book *Studien zur Entwicklung der platonischen Dialektik von Sokrates zu Aristotles. Arete und Diairesis* (published in 1917 in Breslau by Trewendt and Granier), whose fifth chapter is on 'The "atomic" form'. English translation: *Plato's Method of Dialectic*, trans. D. J. Allan. New York: Arno Press, 1973.
13 Translators' Note: Gadamer is referring to *Sophist* 216a5-b6, where Socrates, addressing Theodorus, who has brought with him the stranger from Elea, says: 'Are you not unwittingly bringing, as Homer says, some god, and no mere stranger, Theodorus? He says that the gods, and especially the god of strangers, enter into companionship with men who have a share of due reverence and that they behold the deeds, both violent and righteous, of mankind. So perhaps this companion of yours may be one of the higher powers, who comes to watch over and refute us because we are worthless in argument – a kind of god of refutation' (in *Theaetetus, Sophist*, trans. Harold North Fowler. The Classical Loeb Library. Cambridge, MA: Harvard University Press, 2002 [1921], p. 265).
14 A new contribution by C. D. C. Reeve (['Socrates Meets Thrasymachus'], *Archiv für Geschichte der Philosophie* 67, 1985) gives a good insight into the recent state of research. The obstinate emphasis on the exclusive opposition between *kinēsis* ['movement'] and *stasis* ['rest'], and the way it is loosened up, which already began in the confrontation between the materialists and the friends of the ideas, does not appear in this meticulous analysis as the great achievement through which Plato, by using the mouth of an Eleatic stranger, leads someone to the understanding of dialectic. It rather appears as a 'trap' and the play between identification and predication on Plato's part appears as his own confusion. This is how philosophy looks when it is assessed by its results like a science, which it is not.

15 Meanwhile the dialogical process has also been taken seriously for the *Sophist*, as we see in Seth Benardete, *The Being of the Beautiful*. Chicago: University of Chicago Press, 1984, which obviously takes not Theaetetus but Socrates as its focus.
16 See the contributions collected under the title 'Das Lehrgedicht des Parmenides', in *Gesammelte Werke*, vol. 6, pp. 30–57, as well as 'Parmenides oder das Diesseits des Seins', in *Gesammelte Werke*, vol. 7, pp. 3–31 [English translation: 'Parmenides or Why Being Pertains to This World', in this volume, pp. 43–66].
17 On this, see 'Plato und die Vorsokratiker', in *Gesammelte Werke*, vol. 6, pp. 68ff [English translation: 'Plato and Presocratic Cosmology', in Hans-Georg Gadamer, *Beginning of Knowledge*. New York: Continuum, 2002, pp. 102–18], as well as 'Der platonische "Parmenides" und seine Nachwirkung', in *Gesammelte Werke*, vol. 7, pp. 319ff [English translation: 'Plato's *Parmenides* and Its Influence', *Dionysius* 7 (1983): pp. 3–16].
18 238b: *prospherein* ['to transfer'; 'to attribute']; 250b10: *proseipein* ['to address']; 245d5: *prosagoreuein* ['to declare']; as well as 238c: *prostithenai* ['to add'], *prosarmottein* ['to adapt']; 238a7: *prosgignesthai* ['to be added']. In sum, the question is constantly about the *pros ti* ['towards which'], as Aristotle will call it later.
19 The analysis of the essence of the 'what' (*ti ēn einai* ['what is being']) proceeds exactly in the same way in Aristotle, *Metaphysics* Z 5 [*Metaphysics*, trans. Hugh Tredennick. The Loeb Classical Library. Cambridge, MA: Harvard University Press, 1990 [1935]].
20 On the connections between the *Timaeus* and the *Sophist*, see my study 'Idee und Wirklichkeit in Platos "Timaios"', *Gesammelte Werke*, vol. 6, pp. 249ff. [English translation: 'Idea and Reality in Plato's *Timaeus*', in *Dialogue and Dialectic: Eight Hermeneutical Studies on Plato*, pp. 156–92].
21 The theme of *methexis* appears many times in my studies of Plato since 1930. For example, recently in 'Plato as Portraitist', *Gesammelte Werke*, vol. 7, pp. 245ff. [English translation: 'Plato as Portraitist', trans. Jamey Findling and Snezhina Gabova, *Continental Philosophy Review* 33/3 (2000): pp. 245–74].
22 See Ernst Hoffmann, 'Methexis und Metaxy bei Plato' [*Methexis* and *Metaxy* in Plato] (1918), in *Drei Schriften zur griechischen Philosophie* [Three Texts on Greek Philosophy]. Heidelberg: Carl Winter, 1964, pp. 29–51.
23 Translators' Note: The German word *Zeitwort*, which means 'verb', literally says 'temporal word'.
24 I recall numerous incisive works on the 'flying Theaetetus' (some examples are mentioned in 'Platos ungeschriebene Dialektik', in *Gesammelte Werke*, vol. 6, pp. 147f, n. 24) [English translation: 'Plato's Unwritten Dialectic', in *Dialogue and Dialectic: Eight Hermeneutical Studies on Plato*. The note 24 to which Gadamer refers has not been included in the English translation, which was based on the German text published in *Kleine Schriften*]. One may want to test my 'simple' solution.
25 As far I can see, Whitehead had something similar in mind when he understood relation as perception – a 'footnote to Plato'.
26 Translators' Note: Aristotle ends Book Lambda of the *Metaphysics* by saying that 'those who maintain that mathematical number is the primary reality', like Speusippus, 'make the substance of the universe incoherent […] and give us a great many governing principles. But the world must not be governed badly: "the rule of the many is not good; let one be the ruler"' (*Metaphysics* Lambda, X14. trans. Hugh Tredennick. The Loeb Classical Library. Cambridge, MA: Harvard University Press, 1990 [1935], p. 175).
27 On this, see 'Die Idee des Guten zwischen Plato und Aristoteles", in *Gesammelte Werke*, vol. 6, pp. 216f. [English translation: *The Idea of the Good*, trans. P. Christopher Smith. New Haven, CT: Yale University Press, 1986].

5

1. Robert Schneider, *Schellings und Hegels schwäbische Geistesahnen* [Schelling's and Hegel's Swabian Intellectual Predecessors]. Würzburg: Triltsch, 1938; Ernst Benz, *Christliche Kabbala* [Christian Kabbalah]. Zürich: Rhein Verlag, 1958.
2. See note above.
3. *Inquisitio in sensum communen et rationem*, p. 269; *Brevissima theoriae musicae analysis*, p. 37 [Translators' Note: this second treatise has been published in the same volume as the *Inquisitio* (see reference above) and following it with its own pagination. See online version: Inquisitio in sensum communem et rationem. Faksimile-Neudruck der Ausgabe Tübingen, 1753: Oetinger, Friedrich Christoph, 1702–1782: Internet Archive. Accessed 8/3/2023].

6

1. Friedrich Meinecke, *Die Enstehung des Historismus*. München/Berlin: R. Oldenbourg, 1936 [English translation: *Historicism: The Rise of a New Historical Outlook*, trans. J. E. Anderson. London: Routledge & Kegan Paul, 1972].
2. Karl Hinrichs, *Ranke und die Geschichtstheologie der Goethe-Zeit* [Ranke and the Theology of History in the Era of Goethe]. Göttingen/Frankfurt/Berlin: Musterschmidt Wissenschaftlicher Verlag, 1954.
3. Isaak Iselin, *Philosophische Mutmaßungen über die Geschichte der Menschheit* [Philosophical Conjectures on the History of Humanity]. Frankfurt am Main: Harscher, 1764.
4. Voltaire, *Siècle de Louis XIV*; see also 'Essai sur les moeurs et l'esprit des nations et sur les principaux faits de l'histoire depuis Charlemagne jusqu'à Louis XIII', in *Siècle de Louis XV*, *Oeuvres*, vol. 16–22. Basel: Jean-Jacques Tourneisen, 1784.
5. Charles Perrault, *Parallèle des Anciens et des Modernes*, with an introduction by Hans Robert Jauß. Munich-Allach: Eidos Verlag, 1965.
6. See 'Oetinger als Philosoph (1964)', in *Gesammelte Werke*, vol. 4, pp. 306–17 [English translation: 'Oetinger as a Philosopher (1964)', in this volume pp. 129–39].
7. Translators' Note: 'Adrastea' is the name of a Goddess in ancient Greece, sometimes associated with Nemesis as the goddess of what is inescapable. Herder wrote a work titled 'Adrastea', as mentioned later in the essay.

7

1. 325cff. [*Epistles*, in *Timaeus, Critias, Menexenus, Epistles*, trans. R. G. Bury. The Loeb Classical Library. Cambridge, MA: Harvard University Press, 1952].
2. Xenokrates, Fragment 1, in Xenokrates, *Darstellung der Lehre und Sammlung der Fragmente*, ed. Richard Heinze. Leipzig: Teubner, 1892.
3. 'Grundlinien der Kritik der bisherigen Sittenlehre', in *Sämtliche Werke*. Berlin: Reimer, 1834, p. 35.
4. *Dialektik*, in *Sämtliche Werke*. Berlin: Reimer, 1839, p. 568.
5. Translators' Note: In the French original, the word which Gadamer translates as *Kunstlehre* is 'méthode': 'la philosophie s'y présente davantage comme une méthode' ('Schleiermacher platonicien', p. 34).

6   *Dialektik*, p. 8.
7   *Geschichte der Philosophie*, in *Sämtliche Werke*. Berlin: Reimer, 1839, p. 102.
8   *Meno* 81cd [*Meno*, in *Laches, Protagoras, Meno, Euthydemus*, trans. W. R. M. Lamb. The Loeb Classical Library. London: William Heinemann, 1924].
9   *Geschichte der Philosophie*, p. 103.
10 Translators' Note: We corrected the reference, which is not 86c, as Gadamer writes, but 86a, as correctly stated in the French original ('Schleiermacher platonicien', p. 35). There Socrates asks: 'So if in both of these periods – when he was and was not a human being – he has had true opinions in him which have only to be awakened by questioning to become knowledge, his soul must have had this cognizance throughout all time?' (in *Laches, Protagoras, Meno, Euthydemus*, p. 321).
11 Translators' Note: Gadamer wrote '*erōtēsesin egertheisai*', which we restored as in the French original and the text in the Loeb Classical Library.
12 *Geschichte der Philosophie*, p. 98.
13 *Sophist* 258e6ff [*Sophist*, in *Theaetetus, Sophist*, trans. Harold North Fowler. The Loeb Classical Library. Cambridge, MA: Harvard University Press, 2002 (1921)].
14 *Geschichte der Philosophie*, p. 102.
15 See the essays of Philip Merlan, *From Platonism to Neo-Platonism*. The Hague: Martinus Nijhoff, 1968; Willy Theiler, *Forschungen zum Neuplatonismus* [Research on Neo-Platonism]. Berlin: De Gruyter, 1966; Hans Joachim Krämer, *Der Ursprung der Geistmetaphysik. Untersuchungen zur Geschichte des Platonismus zwischen Platon und Plotin* [The Origin of Spiritual Metaphysics. Investigations into the History of Platonism between Plato and Plotinus]. Amsterdam: Schippers, 1964.
16 *Geschichte der Philosophie*, p. 105. (See the essay 'Gibt es die Materie?', in *Gesammelte Werke*, vol. 6. Tübingen: J. C. B. Mohr (Paul Siebeck), 1985, pp. 201ff.).
17 *Geschichte der Philosophie*, p. 105.

8

1   Unless otherwise noted, the quotations from Hegel are taken from the chapter on Heraclitus in the *Lectures on the History of Philosophy*. Heraclitus' fragments are quoted according to the numbering of Diels/Kranz, *Die Fragmente der Vorsokratiker Griechisch und Deutsch*, vol. 1. Berlin: Weidmannsche Buchhandlung, 1906. Abbreviated in the text as VS.
2   *Enzyklopädie*, par. 386 [*Encyclopaedia of the Philosophical Sciences in Basic Outline*, vol. 1, trans. Klaus Brinkmann and Daniel O. Dahlstrom. Cambridge: Cambridge University Press, 2010].
3   *Vorlesungen über die Philosophie der Weltgeschichte* [Lectures on the Philosophy of World History], *Werke*, vol. I, ed. Johannes Hoffmeister. Hamburg: Meiner, 1955, p. 153.
4   For example, in *Philebus* 14e [*Philebus*, in *The Statesman, Philebus*, trans. W. R. M. Lamb. The Loeb Classical Library. Cambridge, MA: Harvard University Press, 2001 (1925)].
5   Translators' Note: *Wortschatz* literally means 'treasure of words'.
6   Translators' Note: In the fragment, there are several possible sources of ambiguities. The first one is that the verb *haptetai* can mean to touch, to tie or to light or ignite

something. Gadamer translates the first occurrence with *anzündet* ['kindles'] and the second with *rührt* ['touches' or 'comes in contact']. He does not translate the word *eudōn*, 'sleeping' in the phrase which Diels renders as 'living he touches the dead in sleep', which Gadamer only translates as 'living, they come in contact with the dead'. The second possible source of ambiguity is about two additions in the fragment, which some translators accept and others do not. The first addition is the word *apothanōn*, 'dying', after the first phrase 'in the night human beings kindle a light for themselves', which creates a tension with the word *zōn*, 'living', which occurs two words afterward. In his edition of *Die Fragmente der Vorsokratiker* (9th ed. by Walther Kranz, vol. 1. Berlin: Weidmannsche Verlagsbuchhandlung, 1960, p. 156), Diels considers it a gloss and did not translate it (Gadamer follows him). The second addition is the repetition of 'when light of their eyes has been extinguished' after the phrase 'they come in contact with the dead'. Wilamowitz considers this second occurrence as a dittography or erroneous repetition. Neither Diels nor Gadamer translates it. Now, when translators keep some of those alleged additions or all of them, the translations sound quite different. Here, for example, is the version of André Laks and Glenn Most. We mark the addition in italics: 'A human being, in the night, lights [*haptesthai*] a lamp for himself, *dead*, his eyes extinguished; living, he touches on [*haptesthai*] a dead man when sleeping; when awake, he touches on [*haptesthai*] a sleeping man' (*Testimonia*, Part 2: *Doctrine* (D), in *Early Greek Philosophy*, vol. III, ed. and trans. André Laks and Glenn Most. The Loeb Classical Library, p. 173. Online version, accessed 5/31/2023). In an online publication, William Harris translates all the additions, which we mark in italics: 'As in the nighttime a man kindles for himself (*haptetai*) a light, so when *a living man* lies down in death with his vision extinguished, he attaches himself (*haptetai*) to the state of death; even as one who has been awake lies down *with his vision extinguished* and attaches himself to the state of sleep' (*Greek Philosophy and Heraclitus (archive-it.org)*. Accessed 5/31/2023).

7   See on this, my essay 'Vorgestalten der Reflexion', in *Gesammelte Werke*, vol. 6. Tubingen: J. C. B. Mohr (Pasul Siebeck), 1985, pp. 116–28.
8   Translators' Note: The fragment says: 'He who travels on every road would not find out the limits of the soul in the course of walking: so deep is its measure [*logon*]' (*Early Greek Philosophy*, vol. III, Early Ionian Thinkers, Part 2. The Classical Loeb Library, ed. and trans. André Laks and Glenn Most, p. 189, translation modified. Online version, accessed 7/25/2022).
9   Translators' Note: the Greek says: *athanatoi thnētoi, thnētoi athanatoi, zōntes ton ekeinōn thanaton, ton de ekeinōn bion tethneōntes*. The last word is a participle, 'being dead', which Gadamer translates as 'dead'. We use the present participle to keep the symmetry, as in the Loeb translation, which says: 'Immortals mortals, mortals immortals, living the death of these, dying the life of those' (*Early Greek Philosophy*, p. 173).
10 VS 22 A4.

9

1   Translators' Note: Friedrich Schleiermacher was instrumental in rejecting Hegel, with whom he had philosophical but also political disagreements. When Hegel founded his own scholarly circle, he threatened to resign from it when there was a suggestion

to admit Schleiermacher. See Richard Crouter, *Friedrich Schleiermacher: Between Enlightenment and Romanticism*. Cambridge, UK: Cambridge University Press, 2005, pp. 87–9. E-book.

2 Serious tasks await us here of investigating what the formation of the dialectical method means, what the translation of his project into the conceptual language of antiquity means, thus what the *Logic* above all means for Hegel's philosophy. All of this should not be covered over by elaborating this essential consistency of Hegel with himself. I hope to be able myself to present some of my own contributions to these tasks soon. (See in the meantime *Gesammelte Werke*, vol. 3. Tübingen: J. C. B. Mohr (Siebeck), 1987, pp. 3ff and 65ff). [Translators Note: These essays are: 'Hegel und die antike Dialektik (1961)', pp. 3–28; English translation: 'Hegel and the Dialectic of the Ancient Philosophers', in *Hegel's Dialectic: Five Hermeneutical Studies*, trans. P. Christopher Smith. New Haven, CT: Yale University Press, 1976, pp. 5–34; and 'Die Idee der Hegelschen Logik (1971)', pp. 65–86; English translation: 'The Ideal of Hegel's Logic', in *Hegel's Dialectic: Five Hermeneutical Studies*, pp. 75–98].

10

1 Translators' Note: Melchior Boisserée (1786–1851) was an art collector and cataloguer with his brother Sulpiz Boisserée (1783–1854). Influenced greatly by the Romantic vision of Friedrich Schlegel, they became collectors of medieval art in an effort to save it from destruction. They were responsible for kindling interest in medieval art through their collection which was first exhibited to the public in 1810 in a baroque palace at Karl's Square, Heidelberg. In 1827, their collection was purchased by Ludwig I of Bavaria for 240000 Gulden, who made it part of his museum building in Munich. In 1835, this museum along with the Melchior collection was opened as the Alte Pinakothek (Old Picture Gallery]. Source: Sorensen, Lee, ed., 'Boisserée, Melchior', *Dictionary of Art Historians (website)*. https://arthistorians.info/boissereem).

2 See my essay 'Die Stellung der Poesie im System der Hegelschen Ästhetik', *Hegel-Studien* 27 (1986): pp. 213–23. [English translation: 'The Place of Poetry in the System of Hegelian Aesthetics and the Question of the Pastness of Art (1986)', in *Ethics, Aesthetics and the Dimension of Language, The Selected Writings of Hans-Georg Gadamer*, vol. II, ed. and trans. Pol Vandevelde and Arun Iyer. London: Bloomsbury, 2022, pp. 77–86.]

3 See Alfred Baeumler in his introduction to J. J. Bachofen's work, *Der Mythus von Orient und Occident. Eine Metaphysik der alten Welt* [Myths from the East and the West: A Metaphysics of the Ancient World]. Munich: Beck, 1926.

4 See Otto Pöggeler, *Hegel und die Romantik*. Bonn: Bouvier, 1956.

5 *Jahrbücher für wissenschaftliche Kritik* (ed. Societät für wissenschaftliche Kritik, Berlin) September (1831): pp. 438-463.

6 See the repeated references to Creuzer in Hegel.

7 Translators' Note: The original title of Joseph von Görres is *Mythengeschichte der asiatischen Welt*. Heidelberg: Mohr and Zimmer, 1810.

8 Translators' Note: Creuzer's work is titled *Symbolik und Mythologie der alten Völker, besonders der Griechen* [Symbolism and Mythology of the Ancients, Especially the Greeks], published in four volumes from 1810 to 1812 by C. W. Leske in Leipzig in 1880.

9 *Der Kampf um Creuzers Symbolik* [The Battle over Creuzer's Symbolism], ed. Ernst Howald. Tübingen: Mohr, 1926, p. 48.
10 Translators' Note: Gadamer uses the rare poetic word *Morgenland*, which can be literally translated as 'land of the morning', just as the more common German *Abendland* for designating the west can be literally translated as 'land of the evening'.
11 See *Der Kampt um Creuzers Symbolik*.
12 Hegel, *Äesthetik*, vol. 1. ed. Bassenge. Frankfurt am Main: Europäische Verlagsanstalt, 1955, p. 306f.
13 In the meantime, we owe a philosophical interpretation of Proclus to Werner Beierwaltes: *Proklos. Grundzüge seiner Metaphysik* [Proclus: Fundamental Traits of his Metaphsyics]. Frankfurt am Main: Klostermann, 1965. On the history of the effects of neo-Platonism, see by the same author: *Platonismus und Idealismus* [Platonism and Idealism]. Frankfurt am Main: Klostermann, 1972 and *Identität und Differenz* [Identity and Difference]. Frankfurt am Main: Klostermann, 1980. [Translation note: We corrected the title, which Gadamer lists as *Identität in der Differenz*].

Appendix: Glossary of German Terms

Abbild: image
Abwesende, das: what is absent
Anschein: impression
Ansicht: opinion, point of view
anwesend: present
Anwesenheit: presence
Anwesenheit des Anwesenden: presence of what is present
Anzahl: numerical count
Arten: kinds
Aufhebung: overcoming
Aufzählung: enumeration
Ausgleichskultur: culture of evening out
Enstehen: coming to be
Erkennen: to know, to recognize
Erkenntnis: knowledge
Erscheinung: appearance
Gefüge: arrangement
Gespräch: dialogue, discussion
Gestalt: form
Gewesene, das: that which was
Inbegriff: comprehensiveness, inclusion, paragon
kennen: to be aware
Kennen: awareness
Können: ability
lebendig: vivid
Lebendigkeit: liveliness
leibhaft: in person
Logistik: mathematical logic
Meinungen: opinions
Schein: semblance, seeming
Scheinbild: semblance of an image
Scheinen: seeming
seiend: existing
Seiende, das: a being, a specific being, that which is
Seinshaftigkeit: ontological quality
Seinwerdende, das: that which becomes being
Ungedanke, der: vacuous thought
Unwesen, das: corrupted essence
Urworte: primordial words
Vergehen: passing away
Vernehmen: taking in

Verwindung: transformation
Vorliegende, das: what is available
Weile, die: the while
Wesende, das: that which unfolds
wirklich: actual, real
Wirklichkeit: reality, what is actual
Wirkungsgeschichte: history of effects, historical efficacy
Wissen: knowing
Zusammengriff: grasping together

Glossary of Ancient Greek Terms and Expressions

(in accordance with Gadamer's translation of these terms in German)

adiairheton: undivided
adikia: injustice
adoleschia: gibberish
agathon: the good
agenēton: not born
agnoēsantes: unknowingly
aidōs: shame
aisthēsis: perception
aitia: cause
alētheia: truth
alēthēs doxa: true opinion
alēthēs doxa meta logou: true opinion with an account (with an explanation)
alētheuein: to tell the truth
allelois: with each other
allo parex tou eontos: something else besides this being
allote allōs: different at different times
alogon: without an account, without an explanation
analogizesthai: to calculate
anamnēsis: recollection
anankazomenos d'akolouthein tois phainomenois: being compelled to follow the phenomena
anankē: necessity
anepistēmosunē: non-science, ignorance
anepistēton: unknowable
anō – katō: upside down
anōlethron: imperishable
anōnumon: unameable
anthrōpos: human being
aretē: excellence, virtue
arithmō hen: one in number
arithmos: number
arithmos teleios: perfect number
asumblētoi monades: non-combinable units
athanatoi: the immortals
athroisma: aggregate, sum
atmēton eidos: indivisible essence
atomon: uncut, indivisible
atomon eidos: indivisible essence
atopon: strange

au: conversely
brotoi: mortals
chōrismos: separation
chrēn: it is necessary, it is to be considered necessary
dektikon tou eidous: receptive of the form
dēlounta: revealing
diairesis: division, separation
diaireta: separated
diakosmos: arrangement
dia pantos panta perōnta: all going through all things
diaphorai: differences
dia tēn ouk ek kalou thean: through a view that is not favourable
dikaoisunē: justice, righteousness
dikē: justice
doxa: opinion
dunamis: potentiality
dunamis koinōnias: capacity of being together
eidōla legomena: spoken images
eidos: essence, form, idea
eidē: forms, ideas
einai: to be
einai te kai ouchi: being and not being
emoi: for me
en de tē pros allēla homilia: in the mutual interaction
energeia: actuality
en hō: in which
en soi: in you
en tē paideia: in education
enuparchai en tō eidei: it is present in the essence
eon, to: being
    See *on*
epagōgē: leading to, induction
epakolouthēsōmen: let us follow
epistēmē: knowledge
ēremoun: being at rest
ergon: work
erōtēsei epegertheisai: awakened by questioning
esti: is
esti einai: being is
esti noein: knowing is
ēthos: habit, character, mores
euboulia: good judgment
genē: genera
genesis eis ousian: coming to being
genos: genus
gigantomachia: battle of giants
heteran, heteron: another, the other
heteroiousthai: to become different
heterotēs: difference

holon: the whole
hōn mē esti logos: those of which there is no account
hoper on: this determinate being
ho skoteinos: the obscure
ho sos logos: your statement
houtōsi kai onomazōn: naming in this way
hupokeimenon: substance
hupothesis: supposition
husteron: next
kairos: the right moment
kolobon, to: what has been damaged, mutilated
kalon: beautiful
kata ton auton logon: in the same sense
katholou: for all
kata genē: by genera
kata genē diaireisthai: to divide by genera
katakekermatismenon: fragmented
kat' exochēn: par excellence
kathaper epistēmē: like knowledge
kath' auto: by itself
kinēsis: movement
koina: that which is common
ktistēs: founder
legein te kai noein: the voicing and the taking in
lēthē: concealment, sheltering
logos: discourse, reason, explanation
logoi: arguments
mathemata: knowledge
mēdeis ageōmetrētos eisitō: let no one ignorant of geometry enter
mē eon, to: non-being
melē: members
meros: part
mērē te kai melē: parts and members
meta logou: with an account, with an explanation
methexis: participation
mia: one
mia idea: one idea
mimēsis: imitation
mixis: mixture
moira: destiny
monoeides: the singular
morphas duo: two forms
muthos: word, story, myth
noein: knowing
noēsis: thought
nomothetein: legislation
noūs: mind, reason
oikeios logos: germane argument
ois to pelein te kai ouk einai tauton nenomistai kou tauton: those for whom it has become customary that being and not being are the same

on, to: being
    See *eon*
onoma: name
onomata: names
onomazesthai monon: they can only be named
ontōs on: what is most being in being
ontōs ousia: really being
orthoepeia: correct diction
orthotēs: correctness
ouk emathon: I do not understand
ouk epistēta einai: are not knowable
ousia: being, essence, substance
palaia diaphora: age-old quarrel
palintropos: turning backward
panapeuthea atarpon: a narrow path on which there is ignorance everywhere
pantē diatetamenēn […] *diaisthanetai*: sees clearly […] maintained everywhere
para kairon: against the time
parousia: presence
phantastikē: art of illusion
phortikos: coarse
phronēsis: practical wisdom
phusei onta: natural beings
phusis: nature
phusis kruptesthai philei: nature likes to conceal itself
poion: which one
polis: city state
politika: affairs of the city
politikē technē: political ability
poludēris elegchos: the much disputed refutation
polupragmosunē: being a busybody
pōs: roughly
poson: how much
prosagoreuein: to declare
prosarmottein: to adapt
proseipein: to address
prosgignesthai: to be added
prosgignomenos: supplementary
prospherein: to transfer
pros ti: in relation to something, towards which
prostithenai: to add
prōton: first
protreptikos: exhortatory
pseudos: false
psuchē: soul
pur phronimon: fire of the soul
rhēma: verb
schēmati: shape
sēmata: signs
skoteinos: obscure
sophos: wise

sōphrosunē: prudence, moderation
stasis: rest
stoicheion: letter, element
sugkatathesis: approval
sullabē: syllable
sullogismos: thinking
sumblētai monades: combinable units
sumphōnei ē diaphōnei: is in accord or in disaccord
suneches: continuous
suneidēsis: conscience
sunoran eis hen eidos: sees together in the unity of what is meant
talla: the other things
ta onta: beings
ta polla: the many
tauton: the same
tauton t' en tautō: the same and in the same
tautotēs: identity
taxei: order
te kai: and also
teleuta eis eidē: ends in ideas
telos: the end
tēs phuseōs hapasēs suggenous ousēs: the whole of nature is akin
thanatos: death
thateron: the other, the different
thesei: position
thigganein: to touch
ti: what
ti ēn einai: what is being
to auto, tauto: the same
to gar auto noein estin te kai einai: knowing and being are the same
to heteron: the other
tōn mian ou chreōn estin – en hō peplanēmenoi eisin: one of them is not correct – in this they are in error
to pantelōs on: being par excellence
tou biou tē proairesei: in the choice of life

Glossary of Other Foreign Terms and Expressions

(in accordance with Gadamer's translation of these terms in German)

ad absurdum (Lat): to absurdity
ad hominem (Lat): directed at the person
aggregatio virium simplicium infinita (Lat): the infinite combination of simple forces
amor fati (Lat): love of one's fate
anima naturaliter christiana (Lat): a naturally Christian soul
ars inveniendi (Lat): art of invention
audax temperarius (Lat): temperate bold individual
civitas (Lat): citizenship
cogitatio (Lat): thought
cogito (Lat): I think
composita (Lat): things composed
coniectura (Lat): conjecture
conscientia (Lat): consciousness
definiendum (Lat): what is to be defined
demonstratio (Lat): demonstration
docta ignorantia (Lat): learned ignorance
entia rationis (Lat): beings of reason
esprit de finesse (Fr): refined spirit
esprit géométrique (Fr): geometrical spirit
excellentia vitae (Lat): the excellence of life
ex centro vel corde (Lat): from the centre or the heart
facultas transformationis (Lat): faculty of transformation
formam certe fixam non habet, et nullam quoque non habet (Lat): it certainly has no fixed form and does not even have any
forma substantialis (Lat): substantial form
gravitas (Lat): gravity
gustus (Lat): taste
homo-mensura (Lat): the human being as the measure
humanitas (Lat): human nature
hypotheses non fingo (Lat): I do not invent hypotheses
idealiter (Lat): ideally
idola fori (Lat): idols of the market place
in ipsa individuatione rei (Lat): in the very individuation of the thing
in unum vitae circulum (Lat): into a circle of life
Magna Graecia (Lat): the greater Greece
materialitas (Lat): materiality
materialiter (Lat): materially
maximum compositum in simplicitate maxima (Lat): most composed in the greatest simplicity

participatio (Lat): participation
primae sensationes (Lat.): original perceptions (sensations)
querelle des anciens et des modernes (Fr): quarrel between the ancients and the moderns
quod hodie pretiosa experimenta nimis aestimantur, quod communia negligantur (Lat): that today valuable experiments are overestimated because common things are neglected
radicatae tendentiae (Lat): original tendencies
ratio (Lat): reason
res cogitans (Lat): thinking thing
res extensa (Lat): extended thing
residua simulacra imaginis Divinae in anima (Lat): the residual images of the divine imprint in the soul
sapientia practica (sive politica) (Lat): practical (or political) wisdom
sensatio (Lat): sensation
sensus communis (Lat): common sense
sensus communis totius antiquitatis (Lat): the common sense of the totality of antiquity
sensus interior (Lat): inner sense
sensus naturam imitatur, ratio artem (Lat): sense imitates nature, reason imitates art
simplex (Lat): simple
simplificatae (Lat): simplified
simplificat in unum (Lat): simplifies into one
simplificatio (Lat): simplification
species (Lat): species
spiritualitas (Lat): spirituality
spiritus rectores vitae (Lat): the spirits governing life
subiectum (Lat.): what is available
sub specie aeternitatis (Lat): under the aspect of eternity
superioritas (Lat): superiority
supermechanica vis (Lat): super-mechanical force
supra me (Lat): above me
tactus (Lat): touch
tantae molis erat se ipsam cognoscere mentem (Lat): so much effort did it cost the spirit to know itself
theologia de idea vitae deducta (Lat): a theology deduced from the idea of life
transformatio (Lat): transformation
una instantia negativa (Lat): a negative instance
ut linea viva cum praesentia Dei unita (Lat): like a living line united with the presence of God
verbum (Lat): word
vere sint instrumenta (Lat): are really tools
vinculum (Lat): unifying bond
virtus (Lat): virtue
vis (Lat): force
vis attractionis (Lat): force of attraction
vis repraesentativa (Lat): representational force

Works Cited by Gadamer

Aristotle. *Eudemian Ethics*, in *The Athenian Constitution, The Eudemian Ethics, On Virtues and Vices*, trans. H. Rackham. The Loeb Classical Library. Cambridge, MA: Harvard University Press, 1971 [1925].
Aristotle. *Metaphysics*, trans. Hugh Tredennick. The Loeb Classical Library. Cambridge, MA: Harvard University Press, 1990 [1935].
Aristotle. *Nicomachean Ethics*, trans. H. Rackham. The Loeb Classical Library. Cambridge, MA: Harvard University Press, 1934 [1926].
Aristotle. *Politics*, trans. H. Rackham. The Loeb Classical Library. Cambridge, MA: Harvard University Press, 1932.
Aristotle. *Posterior Analytics*, in *Posterior Analytics, Topica*, trans. Hugh Tredennick. The Loeb Classical Library. Cambridge, MA: Harvard University Press, 1966.
Aristotle. *Prior Analytics*, in *The Categories, On Interpretation, Prior Analytics*, trans. Hugh Tredennick. The Loeb Classical Library. Cambridge, MA: Harvard University Press, 1983 [1938].
Aristotle. *Topica*, in *Posterior Analytics, Topica*, trans. Hugh Tredennick. The Loeb Classical Library. Cambridge, MA: Harvard University Press, 1966.
Bachofen, J. J. *Der Mythus von Orient und Occident. Eine Metaphysik der alten Welt*. Munich: Beck, 1926.
Beierwaltes, Werner. *Identität und Differenz*. Frankfurt am Main: Klostermann, 1980.
Beierwaltes, Werner. *Platonismus und Idealismus*. Frankfurt am Main: Klostermann, 1972.
Beierwaltes, Werner. *Proklos. Grundzüge seiner Metaphysik*. Frankfurt am Main: Klostermann, 1965.
Benardete, Seth. *The Being of the Beautiful*. Chicago: University of Chicago Press, 1984.
Benz, Ernst. *Christliche Kabbala*. Zürich: Rhein Verlag, 1958.
Bernays, Jacob. 'Heraklitische Studien', *Rheinisches Museum für Philologie* 7 (1850): pp. 90–116.
Bröcker, Walter. *Die Geschichte der Philosophie vor Sokrates*. Frankfurt am Main: Klostermann, 1965.
Carnap, Rudolf. 'Überwindung der Metaphysik durch logische Analyse der Sprache', *Erkenntnis* 2 (1931): pp. 219–41; English translation: 'The Elimination of Metaphysics through Logical Analysis of Language', in *Logical Positivism*, ed. A. J. Ayer. Glencoe, IL: The Free Press, 1959, pp. 60–81.
Cohen, Hermann. *Platos Ideenlehre und die Mathematik*. Marburg: C. L. Pfeil, 1878.
Cornford, F. M. *Principium sapientiae: The Origins of Greek Philosophical Thought*, ed. W. K. C. Guthrie. Cambridge: Cambridge University Press, 1952.
Creuzer, Friedrich. *Der Kampf um Creuzers Symbolik*, ed. Ernst Howald. Tübingen: Mohr, 1926.
Creuzer, Friedrich. *Symbolik und Mythologie der alten Völker, besonders der Griechen*, four vol. Leipzig: C. W. Leske, 1880.
Diels, Hermann (ed.). *Parmenides Lehrgedicht*, griechisch und Deutsch, ed. Hermann Diels. Berlin: Georg Reimer, 1897; English translation: in *Testimonia*, Part 2: *Doctrine*

(D), in *Early Greek Philosophy*, vol. III, ed. and trans. André Laks and Glenn Most. The Loeb Classical Library, p. 173. Online version.

Diels, Hermann and Walther Kranz. *Die Fragmente der Vorsokratiker*, griechisch und Deutsch, ed. and trans. Hermann Diels, ninth edition by Walther Krantz. Berlin: Weidmannsche Verlagsbuchhandlung, 1959.

Dodds, E. R. *The Greeks and the Irrational*. Berkeley, CA: University of California Press, 1951.

Dümmler, Ferdinand. *Prolegomena zu Platons Staat und der platonischen und aristotelischen Staatslehre*. Basel: I. Reinhardt, Universitäts-Buchdruckerei, 1891.

Edelstein, Ludwig. *Plato's Seventh Letter*, vol. XIV. Leiden: Brill, Philosophia Antiqua, 1966.

Fränkel, Hermann. *Wege und Formen frühgriechischen Denkens. Literarische und philosophiegeschichtliche Studien*. Munich: Beck, 1955.

Gabler, Georg Andreas. *Kritik des Bewusstseins. Eine Vorschule zu Hegels Wissenschaft der Logik*. Erlangen: Palm, 1827; Leiden: A. H. Adriani, 1901.

Gadamer, Hans-Georg (ed.). *Um die Begriffswelt der Vorsokratiker*. Darmstadt: Wissenschaftliche Buchgesellschaft, 1968.

Gadamer, Hans-Georg. 'Antike Atomtheorie', in *Gesammelte Werke*, vol. 5. Tübingen: J. C. B. Mohr (Siebeck), 1985, pp. 263–79; English translation: 'Ancient Atomic Theory', in *The Beginning of Knowledge*, trans. Rod Coltman. New York: Continuum, 2002, pp. 82–101.

Gadamer, Hans-Georg. 'Der aristotelische "Protreptikos" und die entwicklungsgeschichtliche Betrachtung der aristotelischen Ethik', in *Gesammelte Werke*, vol. 5, pp. 164–86; English translation: 'Aristotle's *Protrepticus* in Consideration of the Historical Development of Aristotle's Ethics (1928)', in *The Selected Writings of Hans-Georg Gadamer*, vol. II *Ethics, Aesthetics and the Historical Dimension of Language*, ed. and trans. Pol Vandevelde and Arun Iyer. London: Bloomsbury, 2022, pp. 9–25.

Gadamer, Hans-Georg. 'Dialektik und Sophistik im siebten platonishen Brief', in *Gesammelte Werke*, vol. 6. Tübingen: J. C. B. Mohr (Siebeck), 1985, pp. 90–115; English translation: 'Dialectic and Sophism in Plato's "Seventh Letter"', in Hans-Georg Gadamer, *Dialogue and Dialectic: Eight Hermeneutical Studies on Plato*, ed. and trans. P. Christopher Smith. New Haven, CT: Yale University Press, 1980, pp. 93–123.

Gadamer, Hans-Georg. 'Gibt es die Materie?', in *Gesammelte Werke*, vol. 6, pp. 201–17.

Gadamer, Hans-Georg. 'Hegel und die antike Dialektik', in *Gesammelte Werke*, vol. 3. Tübingen: J. C. B. Mohr (Siebeck), 1987, pp. 3–28; English translation: 'Hegel and the Dialectic of the Ancient Philosophers', in Hans-Georg Gadamer, *Hegel's Dialectic: Five Hermeneutical Studies*, trans. C. Christopher Smith. New Haven, CT: Yale University Press, 1976, pp. 5–34.

Gadamer, Hans-Georg. 'Die Idee des Guten zwischen Plato und Aristoteles', in *Gesammelte Werke*, vol. 7. Tübingen: J. C. B. Mohr (Siebeck), 1991, pp. 128–227; English translation: *The Idea of the Good in Platonic-Aristotelian Philosophy*, trans. P. Christopher Smith. New Haven, CT: Yale University Press, 1986.

Gadamer, Hans-Georg. 'Die Idee der Hegelschen Logik (1971)', vol. 3, pp. 65–86; English translation: 'The Ideal of Hegel's Logic', in *Hegel's Dialectic: Five Hermeneutical Studies*, pp. 75–98.

Gadamer, Hans-Georg. 'Idee und Wirklichkeit in Platos "Timaios"', in *Gesammelte Werke*, vol. 6, pp. 242–70; English translation: 'Idea and Reality in Plato's *Timaeus*', in *Dialogue and Dialectic: Eight Hermeneutical Studies on Plato*, pp. 156–92.

Gadamer, Hans-Georg. 'Das Lehrgedicht des Parmenides', in *Gesammelte Werke*, vol. 6, pp. 30–57.
Gadamer, Hans-Georg. 'Logos und Ergon im platonischen *Lysis* (1972)', in *Gesammelte Werke*, vol. 6, pp. 171–86; English translation: '"Logos" and "Ergon" in Plato's Lysis', in Hans-Georg Gadamer, *Dialogue and Dialectic: Eight Hermeneutical Studies on Plato*, pp. 1–20.
Gadamer, Hans-Georg. 'Plato als Porträtist', in *Gesammelte Werke*, vol. 7, pp. 228–57; English translation: 'Plato as Portratist', trans. Jamey Findling and Snezhina Gabova, *Continental Philosophy Review* 33/3 (2000): pp. 245–74.
Gadamer, Hans-Georg. 'Der platonische "Parmenides" und seine Nachwirkung', in *Gesammelte Werke*, vol. 7, pp. 313–27; English translation: 'Plato's Parmenides and Its Influence', *Dionysius* 7 (1983): pp. 3–16.
Gadamer, Hans-Georg. 'Platos dialektische Ethik', in *Gesammelte Werke*, vol. 5, pp. 3–163. English translation: *Plato's Dialectical Ethics: Phenomenological Interpretations Relating to the Philebus*, trans. Robert Wallace. New Haven, CT: Yale University Press, 1991.
Gadamer, Hans-Georg. 'Platos Staat der Erziehung (1942)', in *Gesammelte Werke*, vol. 5, pp. 249–62; English translation: 'Plato's Educational State', in Hans-Georg Gadamer, *Dialogue and Dialectic: Eight Hermeneutical Studies on Plato*, pp. 73–92.
Gadamer, Hans-Georg. 'Platos ungeschriebene Dialektik', in *Gesammelter Werke*, vol. 6, pp. 129–53; English translation: 'Plato's Unwritten Dialectic', in Hans-Georg Gadamer, *Dialogue and Dialectic: Eight Hermeneutical Studies on Plato*, pp. 124–54.
Gadamer, Hans-Georg. 'Plato und die Dichter', in *Gesammelte Werke*, vol. 5, pp. 187–211; English translation: 'Plato and the Poets', in Hans-Georg Gadamer, *Dialogue and Dialectic: Eight Hermeneutical Studies on Plato*, pp. 39–72.
Gadamer, Hans-Georg. 'Plato und die Vorsokratiker', in *Gesammelte Werke*, vol. 6, pp. 58–70; English translation: 'Plato and Presocratic Cosmology', in Hans-Georg Gadamer, *Beginning of Knowledge*, pp. 102–18.
Gadamer, Hans-Georg. 'Retraktationen', in *Gesammelte Werke*, vol. 6, pp. 39–49.
Gadamer, Hans-Georg. 'Socrates' Frömmigkeit des Nichtwissens', in *Gesammelte Werke*, vol. 7, pp. 83–117; English translation: 'Religion and Religiosity in Socrates', *Proceedings of the Boston Area Colloquium in Ancient Philosophy* 1 (1986): pp. 53–75.
Gadamer, Hans-Georg. 'Die Stellung der Poesie im System der Hegelschen Ästhetik', *Hegel-Studien* 27 (1986): pp. 213–23; English translation: 'The Place of Poetry in the System of Hegelian Aesthetics and the Question of the Pastness of Art (1986)', in *Ethics, Aesthetics and the Dimension of Language, The Selected Writings of Hans-Georg Gadamer*, vol. II, ed. and trans. Pol Vandevelde and Arun Iyer. London: Bloomsbury, 2022, pp. 77–86.
Gadamer, Hans-Georg. 'Vorgestalten der Reflexion', in *Gesammelte Werke*, vol. 6. Tubingen: J. C. B. Mohr (Paul Siebeck), 1985, pp. 116–28.
Gadamer, Hans-Georg. 'Die Wirkung Stefan Georges auf die Wissenschaft (1983)', in *Gesammelte Werke*, vol. 9. Tübingen: J. C. B. Mohr (Siebeck), 1993, pp. 258–70.
Gadamer, Hans-Georg. 'Zur platonischen "Erkenntnistheorie" (1988)', in *Gesammelte Werke*, vol. 7, pp. 328–37.
Gaiser, Konrad. *Platons ungeschriebene Lehre. Studien zur systematischen und geschichtlichen Begründung der Wissenschaften in der Platonischen Schule*. Stuttgart: Klett Cotta, 1962.
Goerres, Joseph von. *Mythengeschichte der asiatischen Welt*. Heidelberg: Mohr and Zimmer, 1810.
Harris, William. *Greek Philosophy and Heraclitus* (archive-it.org).
Hartmann, Nicolai. *Platos Logik des Seins*. Giessen: Töpelmann, 1909.

Hegel, Georg Wilhelm Friedrich. *Ästhetik*, ed. Friedrich Bassenge. Frankfurt am Main: Europäische Verlagsanstalt, 1955.
Hegel, Georg Wilhelm Friedrich. *Encyclopaedia of the Philosophical Sciences in Basic Outline*, vol. 1, trans. Klaus Brinkmann and Daniel O. Dahlstrom. Cambridge: Cambridge University Press, 2010.
Hegel, Georg Wilhelm Friedrich. *Vorlesungen über die Philosophie der Weltgeschichte*, vol. 1, ed. Johannes Hoffmeister. Hamburg: Meiner, 1955.
Heidegger, Martin. *The Essence of Truth: On Plato's Cave Allegory and Theaetatus*, trans Ted Sadler. London: Continuum, 2002.
Heidegger, Martin. *Holzwege*, GA 5, ed. Friedrich-Wilhelm von Herrmann. Frankfurt am Main: Klostermann, 1978.
Heidegger, Martin. 'Logos (Heraklit)', in *Vorträge und Aufsätze*, GA 7, ed. Friedrich-wilhelm von Herrmann. Frankfurt am Main: Suhrkamp, 2000; English translation: 'Logos (Heraclitus, Fragment B50)', in *Early Greek Thinking*, trans. David Farrell Krell and Frank Capuzzi. New York: Harper and Row, 1985, pp. 59–78.
Heidegger, Martin. 'Moira (Parmenides)', in *Vorträge und Aufsätze*; English translation: 'Moira, Parmenides VIII, 34–41', in *Early Greek Thinking*, pp. 79–101.
Heidegger, Martin. 'Der Spruch des Anaximander', in *Holzwege*, GA 5, ed. Friedrich-Wilhelm von Herrmann. Frankfurt am Main: Klostermann, 1977; English translation: 'Anaximander's Saying (1946)', in *Of the Beaten Track*, ed. and trans. Julian Young and Kenneth Haynes. Cambridge, UK: Cambridge University Press, 2002, pp. 242–81.
Heidegger, Martin. *Vom Wesen der Wahrheit. Zu Platons Höhlengleichnis und Theätet*, ed. Hermann Mörchen. GA 34. Frankfurt am Main: Klostermann, 1988.
Heraclitus. *Early Greek Philosophy*, vol. III, *Early Ionian Thinkers*, Part 2, ed. and trans. André Laks and Glenn Most. The Classical Loeb Library. Cambridge, MA: Harvard University Press, 2016. Online version.
Herter, Hans. 'Platons Staatsideal in zweierlei Gestalt', in *Der Mensch und die Künste. Festschrift für Heinrich Lützeler*. Düsseldorf: L. Schwann, 1962, pp. 177–95.
Hinrichs, Karl. *Ranke und die Geschichtstheologie der Goethe-Zeit*. Göttingen/Frankfurt/Berlin: Musterschmidt Wissenschaftlicher Verlag, 1954.
Hoffmann, Ernst. 'Methexis und Metaxy bei Plato', in Ernst Hoffmann, *Drei Schriften zur griechischen Philosophie*. Heidelberg: Carl Winter, 1964, pp. 29–51.
Hölscher, Uvo. *Anfängliches Fragen. Studien zur frühen griechischen Philosophie*. Göttingen: Vandenhoeck & Ruprecht, 1968.
Hölscher, Uvo (ed.). *Parmenides, Vom Wesen des Seienden. Die Fragmente, griechisch und Deutsch*. Frankfurt am Main: Suhrkamp, 1969.
Iselin, Isaak. *Philosophische Mutmaßungen über die Geschichte der Menschheit*. Frankfurt am Main: Harscher, 1764.
Jaeger, Werner. *Studien zur Entstehungsgeschichte der Metaphysik des Aristoteles*. Berlin: Weidmann, 1912.
Kant, Immanuel. *De Mundi sensibilis atque intelligibilis forma et principiis – Von der Form der Sinnen- und Verstandeswelt und ihren Gründen*, in *Schriften zur Metaphysik und Logik. Werke in sechs Bände*, vol. III, ed. Wilhelm Weischedel. Darmstadt: Wissenschaftliche Buchgesellschaft, 1958; English translation: 'On the Form and Principles of the Sensible and Intelligible World [Inaugural Dissertation] (1770)', in Immanuel Kant, *Theoretical Philosophy, 1755–1770*, ed. and trans. David Walford. Cambridge/New York: Cambridge University Press, 1992.
Kepler, Johannes. '*Mysterium Cosmographicum*', in *Gesammelte Werke*, vol. 1. Munich: C. H. Beck, 1938.

Krämer, Hans Joachim. *Der Ursprung der Geistmetaphysik. Untersuchungen zur Geschichte des Platonismus zwischen Platon und Plotin*. Amsterdam: Schippers, 1964.

Langerberk, Hermann. *Doxis epirhusmiē. Studien zu Demokrits Ethik und Erkenntnislehre*. Neue Philologische Untersuchungen, vol. 10. Berlin: Weidmann, 1935.

Lohmann, Johannes. Musikē *und* logos. *Aufsätze zur griechischen Philosophie und Musiktheorie*. Stuttgart: Musikwissenschaftliche Verlags-Gesellschaft, 1970.

Manasse, Ernst Moritz. 'Bücher über Plato', *Philosophische Rundschau*, Supplement 1, 1957; 2, 1961; 7, 1976.

Marsoner, Agostino. 'La struttura del proemio di Parmenide', *Annali dell' lstituto Italiano per gli Studi Storici* V (1976/1978): pp. 127–82.

Meinecke, Friedrich. *Die Enstehung des Historismus*. Munchen/Berlin: R. Oldenbourg, 1936.

Merlan, Philip. *From Platonism to Neo-Platonism*. The Hague: Martinus Nijhoff, 1968.

Müller, Gerhard. *Platons Dialog vom Staat. Kunstform und Lehrgehalt*. Wiesbaden: Steiner, 1981.

Natorp, Paul. *Platos Ideenlehre. Eine Einführung in den Idealismus*. Leipzig: Felix Meiner, 1921.

Oetinger, Friedrich Christoph. '*Brevissima theoriae musicae analysis*', in *Inquisitio in sensum communen et rationem*, facsimile reprint of the Tübingen edition of 1753. Stuttgart: Friedrich Fromann, 1964.

Oetinger, Friedrich Christoph. *Inquisitio in sensum commune et rationem*, facsimile reprint of the Tübingen edition of 1753. Stuttgart: Friedrich Fromann, 1964.

Parmenides. *Parmenides' Lehrgedicht*, griechisch und Deutsch, ed. Hermann Diels. Berlin: Georg Reimer, 1897; English translation: in *Testimonia*, Part 2: *Doctrine* (D), in *Early Greek Philosophy*, vol. III, ed. and trans. André Laks and Glenn Most. The Loeb Classical Library, p. 173. Online version.

Parmenides. *Vom Wesen des Seienden. Die Fragmente, griechisch und Deutsch*, ed., trans. and explained by Uvo Hölscher. Frankfurt am Main: Suhrkamp, 1969.

Perrault, Charles. *Parallèle des Anciens et des Modernes*, introduction by Hans Robert Jauß. Munich-Allach: Eidos Verlag, 1965.

Plato. *Cleitophon*, in *Timaeus, Critias, Menexenus, Epistles*, trans. R. G. Bury. The Loeb Classical Library. Cambridge, MA: Harvard University Press, 1952.

Plato. *Epistles*, in *Timaeus, Critias, Menexenus, Epistles*, trans. R. G. Bury. The Loeb Classical Library. Cambridge, MA: Harvard University Press, 1952.

Plato. *Greater Hippias*, in *Cratylus, Parmenides, Greater Hippias, Lesser Hippias*, trans. H. N. Fowler. The Loeb Classical Library. Cambridge, MA: Harvard University Press, 1996 [1926].

Plato. *Meno*, in *Laches, Protagoras, Meno, Euthydemus*, trans. W. R. M. Lamb. The Loeb Classical Library. London: William Heinemann, 1924.

Plato. *Parmenides*, in *Cratylus, Parmenides, Greater Hippias, Lesser Hippias*, trans. H. N. Fowler. The Loeb Classical Library. Cambridge, MA: Harvard University Press, 1996 [1926].

Plato. *Philebus*, in *The Statesman, Philebus*, trans. W. R. M. Lamb. The Loeb Classical Library. Cambridge, MA: Harvard University Press, 2001 [1925].

Plato. *The Republic*, trans. Paul Shorey. The Loeb Classical Library. Cambridge, MA: Harvard University Press, 1988.

Plato. *Sophist*, in *Theaetetus, Sophist*, trans. Harold North Fowler. The Loeb Classical Library. Cambridge, MA: Harvard University Press, 2002 [1921].

Plato. *Statesman*, in *The Statesman, Philebus*, trans. W. R. M. Lamb. The Loeb Classical Library. Cambridge, MA: Harvard University Press, 2001 [1925].

Plato. *Theaetetus*, in *Theaetetus, Sophist*, trans. Harold North Fowler. The Loeb Classical Library. Cambridge, MA: Harvard University Press, 2002 [1921].

Plato. *Timaeus*, in *Timaeus, Critias, Menexenus, Epistles*, trans. R. G. Bury. The Loeb Classical Library. Cambridge, MA: Harvard University Press, 1952.

Pöggeler, Otto. *Hegel und die Romantik*. Bonn: Bouvier, 1956.

Popper, Karl. *The Open Society and Its Enemies*. London: Routledge, 1947.

Purpus, Wilhelm. *Zur Dialektik des Bewußtseins nach Hegel. Ein Beitrag zur Würdigung der Phänomenologie des Geistes*. Berlin: Trowitzsch, 1908.

Reeve, C. D. C. 'Socrates Meets Thrasymachus', *Archiv für Geschichte der Philosophie* 67 (1985): pp. 246–65.

Salin, Edgard. *Plato und die griechische Utopie*. Munich/Leipzig: Duncker & Humblot, 1921.

Schleiermacher, Friedrich. *Dialektik*, in *Sämtliche Werke*. Berlin: Reimer, 1839.

Schleiermacher, Friedrich. *Geschichte der Philosophie*, in *Sämtliche Werke*. Berlin: Reimer, 1839.

Schleiermacher, Friedrich. *Grundlinien einer Kritik der bisherigen Sittenlehre*, in *Sämtliche Werke*. Berlin: Reimer, 1834.

Schneider, Robert. *Schellings und Hegels schwäbische Geistesahnen*. Würzburg: Triltsch, 1938.

Schwabl, Hans. 'Sein und Doxa bei Parmenides', *Wiener Studien* 66 (1953): pp. 50–75.

Simplicius. *On Aristotle's Physics* 7, in Diels/Kranz, *Die Fragmente der Vorsokratiker*.

Stenzel, Julius. *Studien zur Entwicklung der platonischen Dialektik von Sokrates zu Aristotles. Arete und diairesis*. Breslau: Trewendt & Granier, 1917; English translation: *Plato's Method of Dialectic*, trans. D. J. Allan. New York: Arno Press, 1973.

Szondi, Peter. *Schriften I*. Frankfurt am Main: Suhrkamp, 1978.

Theiler, Willy. *Forschungen zum Neuplatonismus*. Berlin: De Gruyter, 1966.

Theophrastus. *De sensu*, in Diels/Kranz, *Die Fragmente der Vorsokratiker*.

van der Waerden, B. L. *Erwachende Wissenschaft*. Basel/Stuttgart: Birkäuser, 1956; English translation: *Science Awakening*, trans. Arnold Dresden. New York: Oxford University Press, 1961.

van der Waerden, B. L. *Die Pythagoreer. Religiöse Bruderschaft und Schule der Wissenschaft*. Zurich/Munich: Artemis, 1979.

Voltaire. 'Essai sur les moeurs et l'esprit des nations et sur les principaux faits de l'histoire depuis Charlemagne jusqu'à Louis XIII', in *Siècle de Louis XV, Oeuvres*, vol. 16–22. Basel: Jean-Jacques Tourneisen, 1784.

von Fritz, Kurt. *Platon in Sizilien und das Problem der Philosophenherrschaft*. Berlin: De Gruyter, 1968.

von Fritz, Kurt. 'Die Rolle des *Noūs*', in *Um die Begriffswelt der Vorsokratiker*, ed. Hans-Georg Gadamer. Darmstadt: Wissenschaftliche Buchgesellschaft, 1968, pp. 246–363.

von Fritz, Kurt. 'Zur anthisthenischn Erkenntnistheorie und Logik', in Kurt von Fritz, *Schriften zur griechischen Logik*, vol. I. Stuttgart: Frommann-Holzboog, 1978.

Wiesner, Jürgen. 'Überlegungen zu Parmenides B8, 34', in *Études sur Parménide*, II, ed. Pierre Aubenque. Paris: Vrin, 1987, pp. 170–90.

Wolff, Erwin. *Platos 'Apologie'*. Berlin: Weidmann, 1929.

Xenokrates. *Darstellung der Lehre und Sammlung der Fragmente*, ed. Richard Heinze. Leipzig: Teubner, 1892.

Xenophon. *Memorabilia*, in *Memorabilia, Oeconomicus, Symposium, Apology*, trans. E. C. Marchant and O. J. Todd. The Loeb Classical Library. Cambridge, MA: Harvard University Press, 2014.

Index of Names

Anaxagoras 4, 54, 55, 58
Anaximander 44, 45, 48, 51, 64, 65, 124, 169, 170
Aristophanes 71, 72
Aristotle 4, 11, 54, 65, 69, 89, 95, 96, 103, 115, 136, 162, 166, 176, 203n14, 204n3, 204n7, 205n19, 206n19, 208n18, 208n19, 208n26
    Aristotelian 28, 44, 53, 70, 75, 118, 124, 126, 144, 162, 164, 168, 169, 170
    Aristotelianism *See* Index of Subjects
    and categories 43, 88, 109, 126
    and Heidegger 62
    and mathematics 91, 99, 123
    and metaphysics 72, 75, 124–5
    and physics 96, 125, 161
    and Plato 14, 18, 27, 29, 30, 52, 66, 67, 70, 71–3, 81, 83–4, 106–7, 165, 169, 171
    and politics 71, 73, 78
    and the pre-Socratics 33, 45–7, 49, 53, 58, 106, 113, 116, 168
    and substance ontology 20
    and the theory of forms or ideas 6, 7–8, 63, 72, 105
Augustine 66, 70, 172

Bacon, Francis 104, 131, 133
Bernays, Jacob 61, 201n31
Boisserée, Melchior and Sulpiz 186, 212n1
Bröcker, Walter 55, 200n23

Carnap, Rudolf 53, 200n19
Cohen, Hermann 69, 104, 207n7
Cornford, F. M. 91, 205n11
Creuzer, Friedrich 37, 186, 188–93, 212n6, 212n8

Daub 185, 191
Democritus 4, 54, 68, 96, 98
Descartes, René 34, 131
    Cartesian 20, 21, 32, 131, 136, 149

Diels, Hermann 44, 45, 49, 62, 199n3, 199n4, 200n21, 200n24, 206n21, 210n1, 211n6
Dilthey, Wilhelm 10, 13, 32, 35, 36, 44, 157, 158, 164, 179, 195n43, 196n43
    Diltheyan 10
Dodds, E. R. 45, 199n5
Dümmler, Ferdinand 71, 72

Edelstein, Ludwig 74, 203n20
Eichendorff, Josef von 186, 188
Euripides 71, 72

Fichte 36, 44, 104, 161, 162
    Fichtean 179
Friedländer, Paul 63, 70, 109, 204n4

Gabler 43, 198n1
Gaiser, Konrad 71, 206n19
George, Stefan 70, 202n5
Görres, Josef von 186, 188, 189, 190, 212n7

Hartmann, Nicolai 102, 105
Hegel 113, 115, 124, 137, 149, 152, 155, 161, 165–73, 175–83, 185–93, 210n1, 211n1, 212n2, 212n6, 213n12, 205n14
Heidegger, Martin 4, 20, 22, 26, 27, 39, 58, 62–5, 69–70, 75, 117, 124–5, 166, 170–2, 194n11, 200n18, 201n35, 205n14
    and being 9, 44
    Heideggerean 4, 9
    and truth 53
Heraclitus 33, 43–4, 46, 50–1, 61, 64, 88, 124, 165–73, 210n1
    and Hegel 33
    Heraclitean 61, 88, 96, 116, 165–73
Herder, Johann Gottfried 1, 9, 38, 39, 141–55, 189, 209n7
Herter, Hans 81, 204n33

Hesiod 45, 46, 47, 50, 99, 117, 189, 199n13, 200n14, 200n16
Hoffmann, Ernst 185, 208n22
Hölscher, Uvo 44, 45, 56, 57, 199n5, 199n10
Homer 3, 45, 46, 47, 145, 207n13
  Homeric 4, 34, 45, 64, 80, 88, 115

Iselin, Isaak 142, 209n3

Jaeger, Werner 8, 70, 79, 106, 202n3, 204n7
Jaspers, Karl 22, 23, 185, 198n117

Kant, Immanuel 36, 44, 52, 69, 103, 105, 129, 161, 169, 180
  Kantian 20, 34, 69, 103, 104, 105, 143
  Kantianism *See* Index of Subjects
Kepler, Johannes 104, 207n8
Kierkegaard, Soeren 176, 179
Krämer, Hans Joachim 71, 206n19, 210n15

Langerbeck, Hermann 53, 87, 200n17, 204n5
Leibniz 130, 131, 132, 134, 149, 150, 151, 163
  Leibnizian 34, 130, 132, 134
Lohmann, Johannes 97, 206n22

Marsoner, Agostino 56, 200n26
Maupertuis 133, 137, 138
Meinecke, Friedrich 141, 142, 209n1
Melissus 57, 58, 65, 200n28
Montesquieu 153, 154
Müller, Gerhard 73, 74, 76, 203n17

Natorp, Paul 69, 86, 102, 103–5, 159, 207n11
Newton 8, 9, 34, 38, 131, 132, 134, 135, 144, 145, 151
  Newtonian 34, 38, 130, 134, 144
Nietzsche, Friedrich 44, 67, 124, 147, 166, 170, 176
  Nietzschean 44

Oetinger, Friedrich Christoph 1, 8, 34, 35, 38, 129–39, 144, 198n107, 209n3

Parmenides 1, 4, 5, 30, 31, 38, 43–65, 101, 105, 108, 112–16, 121, 124, 160, 162, 163, 167, 170, 199n7, 200n25, 200n29, 201n30, 201n32
Peter the Great 144, 153
Plotinus 56, 70, 106, 191, 192, 210n15
  Plotinian 192
Plato 30, 31, 35, 36, 43, 46, 52–5, 57, 58, 60, 62, 64–6, 67–81, 83–113, 115–18, 120–6, 157–64, 165, 167–9, 171–2, 194n16, 194n17, 197n102, 197n106, 201n32, 201n37, 202n39, 203n15, 203n19, 206n2, 206n3, 207n14, 208n21, 208n25
  and Aristotle *See* Aristotle and Plato
  and dialectic 96, 101, 105, 107, 111
  and dialogue 34, 35
  neo-Platonic 137, 149, 159, 191–2
  neo-Platonism *See* Index of Subjects
  neo-Platonist 192
  Platonic 36, 43, 49, 52, 53, 58, 60, 63, 66, 67–75, 77–9, 81, 83, 85–93, 96, 100–5, 107–8, 113, 115–16, 118, 120, 123–5, 157–64, 167–8, 191–3
  Platonism *See* Index of Subjects
  Platonist 35, 69, 106, 157
  and Pythagoreanism 45, 46
Popper, Karl 67–9, 74–5, 77, 79, 80
Proclus 56, 192, 213n13
Protagoras 6, 28, 45, 53, 76, 86–93, 108, 114, 122
Purpus, Wilhelm 44, 199n2
Pythagoras 46, 50, 170, 200n14
  Pythagorean *See* Index of Subjects
  Pythagoreanism *See* Index of Subjects

Ranke, Leopold 141, 142
Reinhardt, Karl 44, 49, 203n12

Schelling 104, 171, 177, 179
Schiller, Friedrich 187, 190
Schlegel, Friedrich 70, 157, 159, 160, 190, 212n1
  brothers 187
Schleiermacher, Friedrich 1, 19, 20, 21, 32, 33, 35, 36, 43, 44, 70, 157–64, 165, 198n108, 207n9, 211n1, 212n1
Schwabl, Hans 49, 199n11

Shaftesbury 34, 134
Shakespeare, William 74, 181
Simplicius 46, 52, 56, 58, 61, 201n32, 206n21
Socrates 8, 15, 18, 49, 60, 64, 70, 73–4, 76–7, 81, 84–95, 98–9, 101–5, 107–11, 117, 122–3, 139, 160, 171–3, 200n29, 201n30, 204n2, 205n17, 207n13, 208n15, 210n10
 pre-Socratic *See* Index of Subjects
 Socratic 18, 43, 59, 60, 68, 74, 77, 78, 79, 86–8, 92, 93, 96, 100, 101, 103, 107, 109, 160
Solomon 34, 130, 136
Speusippus 126, 208n26
Spinoza, Baruch 36, 149, 161, 163, 185
Stenzel, Julius 69, 102, 106, 207n12
Szondi, Peter 62, 201n33

Thales 45, 65
Theodorus 84, 85, 87, 89, 90, 93, 95, 108, 207n13

Theophrastus 45, 115, 126, 200n21
Thucydides 67, 76

van der Waerden 45, 199n6
Voltaire 142, 209n4
von Fritz, Kurt 2, 3, 4, 54, 74, 89, 194n1, 203n21, 205n16

Wiesner, Jürgen 57, 200n27
Wilamowitz 71, 78, 207n9, 211n6
Winckelmann 147, 189
Wolff, Christian 130, 131
Wolff, Erwin 76, 203n23

Xenocrates 107, 209n2
Xenophanes 46, 47, 50, 51
Xenophon 73, 76, 203n24

Zeno 58, 64, 72, 96, 101, 108, 201n37

Index of Subjects

aesthetics 37
   aesthetic 52, 91, 112, 143, 186-7, 190
   Hegel's 186-7, 190-1
   See art
aisthēsis 52, 56, 80, 89, 93, 95, 96, 204n7, 205n12
   See perception
alētheia 47-9, 55, 60-3, 65-6, 70, 89, 124-5 *See* truth
anamnēsis 93, 102, 106-7, 110
appearance 30, 48, 50-1, 96, 113, 115, 122, 133, 187, 189, 190, 193
   of being 59
   false 27, 109, 153
   and the ideas 105
Aristotelianism 69, 126
art 37, 109, 111, 123, 125, 133, 168, 187, 189, 190, 212n1
   appearance of, of illusion 122, 187
   argumentative 112
   and dialogue, discussion, disputation, oration, persuasion 87, 92, 101, 102, 104, 108
   of flattery 108, 124
   Greek 193
   history of 37, 190, 193
   and midwifery 86
   musical 99
   and nature 137
   philosophy of 189, 193
   of reading 39
   religion of 187, 189, 193
   and rhapsody 47
   of the sophists 112, 123
   spirit of 187
   and symbolism 37, 190
   of thinking 18
   work of 15, 19, 115, 173
   of writing 98
   See aesthetics

becoming 4, 9, 51, 63, 77, 90, 116, 117, 120, 164, 166, 167, 169, 176, 179, 180
   and being 119, 3
   nothing and 43, 168
   and passing away 85
being 3-4, 6-8, 11, 13, 22, 25, 26, 28-32, 43, 49-66, 69, 75, 83, 85, 93, 94, 98, 101, 106, 110, 115-21, 123, 125-6, 131, 134-6, 145, 149, 161, 164, 169-72, 180, 182, 206n19
   and *alētheia*, truth 47, 48, 50, 53, 66, 167
   and becoming 3, 43, 85, 167-8 *See* coming-into-being
   a being, beings 6-7, 14, 62, 65, 66, 98, 112
   coming into 2-4, 13, 15, 64, 90, 118, 167 *See* becoming
   doctrine of 30, 48, 69
   event of 39, 170
   highest 69, 75, 126
   historical 13, 25
   history of 9, 20
   interpretation of, understanding of 9, 135
   of language 26
   meaning of, question of, sense of 2, 4, 29, 44, 53, 69, 115, 117, 125, 175
   and non-being, nothing 4, 25, 29, 30-2, 49, 50, 53, 55, 57, 59, 60, 61, 64, 100, 112, 113-17, 119-21, 162, 167-70
   oblivion of 167
   reality of 69
   and seeming, semblance 49, 115, 119, 124
   sphere of 49, 55, 59
   and spirit 182, 183
   thinking of, and thought 1, 4, 8, 35, 50, 55, 57, 126, 161
   in-the-world 22
   See non-being, ontology

Index of Subjects

body 3, 130, 134–6, 154, 182, 194n11
    essence of 132
    lived 136
    and soul 35–6, 136, 164
    world- 36

category, categories 8, 29, 43, 53, 88, 126, 142, 178
    doctrine of, theory of 43, 53, 118, 167
    schema of 8
common sense 8, 34, 84, 129, 133, 167
    as *sensus communis* 34, 129–33, 135–9
concept 2, 8, 12, 15, 17, 18, 22, 26, 31, 36–8, 44, 46–7, 52, 54–5, 57–8, 60, 63, 65–6, 69–70, 74, 79, 81, 86–7, 90, 93, 95–7, 100, 103–7, 109–10, 113, 115–21, 123, 125–6, 134–5, 137–8, 145, 149–52, 155, 161–2, 164, 166–9, 175, 178, 180–3, 187, 189–90, 192–3, 205n17
    conceptual 2, 5, 12, 15, 18, 33, 37–8, 44, 52, 54–5, 65, 69–70, 75, 90, 97, 102, 103, 107, 109–10, 144, 149–50, 168–70, 190, 205n17
    conceptuality 90
    conceptualization 2, 12, 33, 179
    to conceptualize 33, 154, 178, 179
    formal 85
    formation of 9, 57, 62
    and history 177
    and language 33, 192, 212n2
    non- 3, 33
    reflective 115
    universal 84
consciousness 10, 13, 15, 20–2, 68, 86, 109, 114, 131, 135, 141–3, 151, 176–80, 182, 187, 191–2
    absolute 33–4, 36
    Cartesian 136
    dialectic of 43
    general 175, 178
    and hermeneutics 20
    historical, and history 12–13, 18, 22, 24, 31–4, 36, 38, 68, 130, 141, 175, 177
    individual 149
    inner 137
    philosophical, philosophizing 67, 175, 177
    religious 189
    of self, self- 69, 86, 131, 136, 142–3, 145, 155, 163, 168–70, 172, 177–8
    of the world 172
    See unconscious
culture 18, 141, 143, 147
    religious, spiritual 144, 189
    world 141

demiurge 75, 126
diairesis 64, 102–3, 106, 110, 119
    diaireta 96
dialectic 5, 27, 36, 43, 47, 52, 64, 65, 68, 80, 83, 85–6, 96, 100–3, 105–8, 111, 115–17, 119, 122–5, 139, 159, 160–4, 167–70, 177, 190, 193, 197n106, 205n18, 207n14
    dialectical 43, 86, 101, 108, 125, 160–1, 163, 168–9, 179, 183, 212n2
    dialectician 29, 102, 104, 108, 109, 111, 114, 120, 123, 163, 197n106, 206n1
    and dialogue 35, 68, 125, 101, 158, 160
    and ethics 18
    of forces 149
    Hegel's 44, 190
    of history 141, 179
    method 5
    of the one and the many 58
    Socratic 86–7
    and the sophists
dialogue 5, 15, 18, 25, 27, 32, 35, 64, 87, 107, 110, 113, 114, 161
    and dialectic *See* dialectic
    dialogical 15, 29, 70, 73, 83, 87, 90, 103, 115, 157–9, 162, 208n15
    early 86, 160
    Eleatic 5, 46, 101–3, 106, 202n39
    form 116, 162, 164
    late 64, 86, 101
    logic of the 64
    See dialectic
difference 3, 6, 17–18, 31, 35, 37, 52, 56, 58, 61, 65, 70, 84, 92, 93, 97, 100, 111–2, 118, 121, 137, 143, 163, 164, 172, 178, 187

between being and beings 62, 66
characteristic, specific 84, 192
and identity, and sameness 115, 120–1, 163
ontological 62
between philosophers and sophists 27, 29, 108, 109, 111, 123
discourse 52, 57, 59, 61, 108, 119, 130, 206n1
and *logos* 5, 158
mythical 5, 50, 55
doxa, doxai 116
and *logos* 121 *See logos*
as opinion 5, 76
as point of view 199n7
true 94, 95
See opinion
dunamis 117–19, 171
concept of 8, 126, 149
and *energeia* 8, 126

eidos 6, 60, 84, 98, 105, 107, 125
eidetic 100
and essence 5, 96, 100, 106
and *genos* 100
hypothesis of 85, 103, 107
and idea, form 5, 72, 160
and *logos* 86
See genos, idea
Eleatics 53, 58, 64, 107
Eleatic 5, 47, 52, 53, 66, 96, 101, 103, 114–16, 120
Eleatic dialogue 5, 46, 101–3, 106, 107, 202n39
Eleatic doctrine, thesis 96, 116, 120, 167
Eleatic philosophy 46, 114
Eleatic school 46
Eleatic stranger 27, 102, 110–16, 118, 120, 123
energeia 8, 126
enlightenment 37, 38, 39, 68, 79, 129, 142, 146, 148, 152, 192
enumeration *See* number
eon 51, 53, 57–9, 63–5
mē eon 53, 60 *See* non-being
and *noein* 31
essence 11, 39, 43, 56, 57, 73, 84, 118–20, 131, 135–7, 163–4, 169, 176–9, 206n19, 206n1, 208n19

of dialectic 161
of *dunamis* 171 *See dumanis*
and *eidos, idea* 5, 26, 72
of history 147, 149
of human beings, of the human race 67, 150, 151
indivisible 96, 100, 106
of knowledge 28, 86, 87, 98
of language 25, 107
of the *logos, logoi* 108, 118 *See logos*
of love 180, 182
and *ousia* 28
quintessence 9, 146
of the state 153, 154
unity of 162, 163
See eidos
essentialism 69, 70, 74, 107
ethics 70
ethical 16, 17, 18, 39, 197n106
Eudemian 103, 204n3
Nicomachean 103, 204n3, 204n7
and physics 36, 161–4
existence 3, 22, 25, 26, 28, 34, 35, 37, 67, 72, 83–4, 91, 119, 120, 131, 148, 165, 168, 176, 180, 199
co- 5, 55
existential, existentially 29, 39
existentialists 3
factual 103
of God 132
heroic 172
historical 151, 183
of ideas 160
philosophy of 194
pre- 162
of the spirit 182
experience 2, 9, 13, 16, 19, 25, 33–5, 39, 48, 50, 62, 65, 90, 95, 103–4, 106–8, 110–11, 113, 131, 139, 145, 171, 176, 180, 183, 185–6
authentic 69
concept of 105
of the divine, religious 135, 170, 173
of force 149, 151
Greek 171, 173
hermeneutic 15, 34
of history 33, 145, 177
and the life-world 122
living 146

pre-predicative 138
primordial 63
of reality 117, 144, 154
scientific 34, 104, 130
of the spirit 176, 180, 182
of the world 34, 145, 171

finitude 39, 147, 190
   and history, and historicity 32, 34, 35, 37, 38, 39
   human, of the human being 33, 35, 38
   of human reason 27, 31
   and infinity 190, 193
force, forces 8, 18, 34, 50, 124, 131–2, 134–6, 142, 145–7, 149–51, 154, 165, 170, 175, 180–2
   of attraction 9, 134, 145, 196n43
   balance of 38
   central 34, 134, 135
   efficacy of 9, 150
   historical, of history 9, 150, 154, 178
   immaterial 134, 135
   interaction of, relation of 144, 151
   living 151, 152
   mechanical 134, 135
   natural, of nature 149, 151
   persuasive, of conviction 113, 159
   play of 38, 149
form 5, 10, 12, 15, 19, 20, 30, 69, 72, 73, 76, 78, 80, 81, 98, 110, 117, 122, 124, 131, 135, 136, 141, 144, 153, 154, 160, 162, 165, 168, 175, 180, 182, 186, 187, 189–93, 194n11, 198n117
   in the Aristotelian sense 51, 64
   dialogue, dialogical, of discourse, discursive, of exposition, literary 5, 53, 59, 73, 75, 76, 81, 116, 162, 164
   of knowledge 79, 87, 161, 162
   of life 141, 146, 164
   mythical 75, 106
   in the Platonic sense 6, 7, 72, 84, 97, 99, 118 *See* idea
   of the spirit 166, 187, 193
   of thought, of thinking 14, 72, 191, 192
   verse 5, 55
freedom 19, 36, 146, 175, 178, 181–3, 188, 190
   consciousness of 177
   exercise of 134

individual, of the individual 19, 37
problem of 11

genos 84, 85, 100 *See eidos*, genus
genre, literary 31, 71–3, 75
genus 84, 96, 121 *See genos*
geometry 83, 84, 91, 139
   geometrical 84, 130
good, the 66, 71, 84, 93, 172, 206n1
   ascent to 102
   goodness 151
   idea of 206n1
   question of 101
goodwill 108, 110

hermeneutics 1, 11, 20
   hermeneutic, hermeneutical 11, 20, 23, 70, 71, 74, 76
   hermeneutic consciousness 12
   hermeneutic experience 15, 34
   hermeneutic situation 13
   hermeneutic tradition 71
   hermeneutic turn 70
   philosophical 14
   romantic 21
historicism 1, 8–9, 75, 141–3, 148, 155, 175
historicity 23, 32–8, 176, 177, 179–80, 183 *See* history
history 1, 8–15, 17, 21, 23, 33, 37, 38, 44, 54, 72, 73, 78, 81, 86, 97, 129, 141–3, 145–53, 161, 166, 177–9, 183, 187, 190–3, 195n43, 196n43
   of art 37, 189, 190, 193
   of being 9, 20
   of concepts, conceptual 54, 55, 205n17
   consciousness affected by 12, 21, 151
   cultural 39, 153
   dialectic of 141
   dimension of 32, 43, 187, 190
   efficacy of, effective, history of effects [*Wirkungsgeshichte*] 1, 9–14, 18, 21, 23, 29, 30, 36, 52, 68, 213n13
   end of 36, 39, 178
   Greek 71, 73, 189
   of the human soul 143, 144
   of humanity 145
   intellectual 44
   life 145

of mathematics 86
of metaphysics 44, 125
of modern thought 130
of philosophy 1, 8, 39, 43, 45, 48, 129, 142, 150, 158, 162, 163, 167, 170, 175–7, 179, 183, 192
philosophy of 148, 152–3, 190
pre- 71, 72, 125
of the problem 1, 10, 44, 143
of religion 44
of the spirit 137, 177, 179
theology of 141, 142
universal 144
Western, of Western thought 20, 81
world 9, 13, 145, 148, 149–51, 167, 177–9, 183, 193
See historicity
horizon(s) 9, 10, 15, 23–5, 53, 117, 119, 145–7, 38, 125, 145
fusion of 12–13, 21, 24–5
historical 12, 24
of time 44, 170, 179
humanism 68, 165, 170
anti-humanism 20
humanistic 9, 20, 192
hypothesis 69, 73, 103–4, 134–5, 145, 160
concept of 103–4
of the *eidos* 85, 103, 107

idea(s) 1, 10, 20–2, 25–9, 35, 38, 59–60, 68–9, 70, 72, 76, 78–9, 81, 110, 131, 141, 143–4, 147, 150, 154–5, 158–61, 163–4, 166–7, 176–7, 186, 189, 191–2
as *eidos*, idea 5, 84, 160, 163
friends of the 116, 117, 119, 120, 207n14
of the good 102, 206n1
of life 130, 134, 135, 137
and number 84–5, 99, 116
in Plato's sense, theory of 6–8, 27–9, 35, 65, 70, 72, 74–5, 86, 102–3, 105–7, 120–2, 124–6, 160, 165, 200n29, 201n29, 201n30
of *sensus communis* 133 See *sensus communis*
See form
ideal 7, 21, 77, 79, 83, 144, 147, 150, 151, 162
city, state 74, 76–7, 78, 80, 123
mathematical 38

poetic 186
political 153
idealism 69, 70, 107, 134, 137, 164
German 44, 57, 69, 104, 129, 186
Hegel's 167
idealist, idealistic 6, 8, 131
objective 164
Platonic 69, 101
post-Kantian 105
subjective 164, 172
transcendental 104
ideality 90, 182
identity 11, 57, 163, 164
of being 58, 167
concept of 58
and difference 115
philosophy of 57
self- 1, 17
imagination 144, 191, 192
interpretation 1, 13–18, 34–6, 68, 69, 71, 72, 74–5, 79, 81, 85, 104, 109, 124, 132, 134–5, 139, 157, 159, 161–2, 164, 169, 178, 181, 197n100, 201n32, 203n19
allegorical 108
Bible 133
false, misinterpretation 74
philosophical 48, 70, 102, 104, 213
re- 79, 103, 149, 163
retrospective 189
self- 178
task of 164
interpreter, interpreters 1, 12–13, 15–18, 22, 35, 62, 75, 108, 139, 198n107
Ionian(s) 46, 51
Ionian 30, 46, 51, 170
Ionian naturalist philosophers, physics, physiologists 48, 50, 30, 116, 170
Ionian school 45
Ionian science 47, 51

Kantianism 176
neo-Kantianism 44, 69, 103, 105
knowledge 4, 7, 21–2, 28, 34–5, 50, 54, 80–1, 83–4, 86–9, 93–5, 97–100, 105, 107–9, 111–2, 114, 119, 121–4, 130–4, 137–9, 145, 159, 171, 175, 180, 189, 192, 210n10
absolute 25, 36, 179, 190

and being 164
conceptual 33
divine 49, 115
foreknowledge 110
forms of 79, 87, 161, 162
of history 179
and mathematics 5, 28, 95, 108, 112
philosophical 176
pseudo-knowledge 111, 114, 131
real 45, 99, 162
self- 13
theory of 131–2
and virtue, *aretē* 76, 78

language 2, 9, 14, 19, 25–7, 29, 45, 47, 57, 63–5, 76, 92, 101, 107, 119, 121, 124, 137–9, 145, 153, 157, 168, 171, 173, 179, 189, 192, 195n26
of concepts 33, 192
conceptual 44, 52, 212n2
dimension of 26
living 5, 55
and music 97, 99
and speech 105, 110
of the spirit 186
theory of 26
of thought 14
and writing 97 *See* writing
life 8, 19, 25–6, 32, 34, 39, 47, 68, 75, 78, 85, 92–3, 95, 101, 110–1, 117, 119, 123, 129, 131, 134–5, 143–8, 150, 153–4, 170–3, 176, 179, 181, 186, 195n43, 198n117
concept of 44, 137
and death 170–3, 188, 211n9
expression of 21
form of 164, 141, 146
historical 183
idea of 130, 134–5, 137, 144
organic 178
philosophy of 44, 133
political 108, 137, 155
power of 194n11
psychological 138
and soul 102, 106, 119
of the spirit 181, 182
-world 107, 122
of the work 16–17

light 119, 171, 182, 189, 211n6
and darkness, and night 30, 48–51, 54, 59, 170–1, 189
and day 173
logos 5–8, 25–30, 52–3, 60, 64, 90, 94–7, 99, 101–2, 112–13, 115–18, 121–3, 125–6, 136, 158, 162, 165–6, 170–1, 194n16, 205n15, 211n8
concept of 63, 95, 117
and *eidos* 86
and *ergon* 70, 87
and *ethos* 18
flight into the *logoi* 8, 90
and knowledge 84
logoi 6, 106–10, 112–15, 119, 122–3, 194n16
and *mūthos* 6, 55, 158
and opinion 86, 94, 99–100
See mūthos

many, the 35, 53, 58, 64, 84, 105, 107, 114–16, 118, 137, 160, 162, 208n26
Marburg school 69, 104
mathematics 28, 46, 75, 83–7, 89–91, 93, 103–5, 108, 118, 123, 204n7, 205n14, 206n19
Euclidean 85
mathematical 4, 9, 38, 45, 54, 80, 84–5, 87, 90–3, 95, 98, 112, 117, 130, 144, 151, 206n19, 208n26
mathematical cosmogony, world 81, 90, 114
mathematical hypothesis 104
mathematical knowledge 28, 95, 108, 112
mathematical method 134
mathematical object 83, 105, 205n7
mathematical science 83, 89–90, 131
mathematician 5, 27, 28–9, 83–4, 86–96, 98, 100, 108, 110–2, 114–15, 117–18, 123, 137
mathematization 105
meta- 75
pure 80
metaphysics 36, 44, 53, 69, 75, 104, 126, 132, 137, 163, 170, 177
Aristotelian 72, 75, 125
critique of 138
history of, tradition of 44, 52

and logic 161
  of love 183
  metaphysical 34, 52, 70, 131, 136, 138,
    148, 149, 151–2
  and ontotheology 75 See ontotheology
  overcoming of, transformation of 65, 124
  and physics 130
  of presence 4
  substance 69
  Western 193
  See ontology
method 1, 11, 19, 29, 32, 39, 44, 76, 104,
    159, 162, 172, 188, 197n106, 209n5
  allegorical 191
  of *diairesis* 102 See *diairesis*
  dialectic, dialectical 5, 212n2
  elenctic 5
  ideal of 38
  mathematical 134, 144
  philosophical 180, 192
  and science 110
mimēsis 65, 70, 81
  mimetic 70, 87
mind 2–5, 14, 22, 45, 103, 172, 194n11
  Christian 132
  methodical 188
  as *noûs* 5, 89, 119
  scientific 130
  See *noûs*
music 19, 46, 97–8, 119
  musical 99, 118
muthos 2, 5–6, 55, 115, 158
  See *logos*, myth
myth 5, 37, 47, 73, 77, 93, 115–16, 158, 191
  cosmological 84
  Homeric 34
  mythic, mythical 5, 6, 50, 52, 55, 75, 85,
    91, 101, 105–6, 117, 162, 172, 177
  Orphic 45
  See *mūthos*, mythology
mythology 191, 146
  mythological 47, 151
  See myth

nature 6, 32, 38, 47, 102, 113, 126, 143,
    145, 148–52, 161–2, 165, 170, 177,
    207n6, 207n10
  and art 137, 187 See art
  being of 182

course of, cycle of 144, 172
  force of 151 See force
  and history 143, 152
  human 136, 141, 144, 150
  knowledge of, theory of, vision of 130,
    137, 143, 149
  law of 103, 154
  mechanical 151, 154
  as *phusis* 46, 170 See *phusis*
  understanding of 9
neo-Kantianism See Kantianism
neo-Platonism See Platonism
night 171, 211n6
  and day 50–1, 59, 199n13
  and light 30, 48–51, 54, 59, 189
noēsis 26, 30, 52 See knowledge
non-being 25, 29–32, 49, 50, 59, 63–4,
    100, 112–17, 119–21, 162, 168–70
  as *mē on* 53, 60–1, 162
  See being, nothing
nothing, the 48, 51–5, 57, 59–60, 62–3, 69,
    113, 124, 167–8
  and being 4, 43, 50, 59, 168
  nothingness 29, 124, 167
  thought of 48, 50, 51, 55
  See non-being
noûs 2, 4–5, 54–5, 89, 119, 126 See mind
number 80, 84, 85, 89–90, 93, 95,
    97–9, 103, 113–14, 116, 120–1, 131,
    204n2, 206n19, 208n26
  enumeration 54, 55, 84, 86, 87, 97–9,
    100
  and idea 84–5, 116
  ideal 72, 99
  numerical count 84–5, 98–100, 204n2
  perfect 81
  relation between 27–8, 84, 98–9
  world of 102

one, the 50, 52, 96, 100, 105, 114, 116, 118,
    120, 135, 169–70
  doctrine of 167
  and the many 35, 58, 84, 105, 160, 162
onoma 26, 28, 54, 59, 63, 96
  and *rhēma* 121–2
ontology 2, 20, 27, 72, 126
  anthropological-ontological 136
  Aristotelian 124
  and epistemology 14

formal-ontological 85, 120
  ontological 1–3, 6, 8, 22, 27, 63–4, 75, 80, 90–2, 116, 121, 131, 134, 149
  ontological difference 62, 66
  spiritualistic 137
  substance 8, 20
  See metaphysics, ontotheology
ontotheology 69, 75, 125 *See* ontology, theology
opinion 5, 32, 49, 76, 86, 93–4, 99, 110, 113, 115–16, 162, 199n7
  correct, right, true 86, 93–5, 99–100, 210n10
  and perception 122
  See doxa

participation 7, 16, 22, 27–8, 65, 74, 84–5, 105, 120, 122
  concept of 121
  problem of 106
particular(s), the 6, 27, 35, 69, 126
perception 2, 133, 204n7, 208n25
  as *aisthēsis* 52, 56, 80
  mental 3
  and opinion 122
  self- 171
  sensible, sense 28, 80, 87–9, 138, 205n12
philology 44, 67, 168, 169
phusis 46, 48, 170, 207n10 *See* nature
physics 53, 58, 105, 116, 144
  Aristotelian 45–6, 125
  of the earth 9, 144
  and ethics 36, 161–3
  of heavenly bodies 9, 144
  Ionian 30, 48
  and mathematics 118
  mechanistic 131
  and metaphysics 130
  Newton's 8
  Platonic 164
  universal 88
Platonism 66, 69, 70, 126, 157, 158, 162
  Christian 66, 68
  neo-Platonism 157, 191, 213n13
politics 78–9
  Aristotle's 71–2
  Athenian 77
  Plato's 74

political *ēthos* 76
political interpretation 71
political life 108, 137, 155
political utopia *See* utopia
political virtue 79
political writings 68, 73, 81
politician 85, 90, 108–9, 179
presence 7, 17, 37, 44, 106, 110, 121, 134, 173, 176
  as *Anwesenheit* 4, 7, 59
  coming to, entering into 4, 64–5
  God's 139
  metaphysics of 4
  as *parousia* 85
  universal 7, 105
pre-Socratic(s) 2, 8, 43–5, 64, 124
  pre-Socratic 33, 46, 124
proposition 5, 26, 33, 53, 86, 138, 168
  non-propositional 3
  propositional
  scientific 22
psuchē 53, 75, 77, 120 *See* soul
psychology 21, 79, 138
  psychological 19, 138
Pythagorean(s) 83, 105
  Pythagorean 45, 46, 58, 84, 91, 97, 98, 103, 116
  Pythagoreanism 46

ratio 130, 133, 135–7 *See* rationality, reason
rationalism 45, 69, 129
  rationalist 192
rationality 26, 30–2, 72, 80–1, 170
  irrationality 26, 27, 31–2
  logical 47
  political 31
  See ratio, reason
realism 69, 77
  realist 6
reality 5, 12, 15, 31, 36, 38, 49, 55, 73–4, 80–1, 88, 93, 104–6, 133, 145, 154, 164, 170–1, 181–2, 188, 194n16, 208n26
  of being 69
  experience of 111, 117, 144, 154
  external 134
  historical 32, 33, 149, 176
  of history 11, 33, 150–1

living 70
mathematization of 105
otherworldly 77
structure of 26
theory of 9
reason 5, 36, 48, 83, 110, 119, 129–30, 139, 148, 151–2, 166, 180
   consistency of 48, 49
   cunning 178
   and history 166
   human, mortal 27, 30–2, 48
   as *logos* 158
   as *ratio* 130, 136, 137
   sufficient 34, 134
   system of 26
   theoretical 180
   and unreason 166
   See ratio
relativism 21, 28, 92, 175
   and conventionalism 88
   pragmatic 91, 108
   Protagoras' 28
   relativist 92
   relativistic 6, 86, 87, 88, 143, 194n17
rhetoric 76, 92, 108, 124
   Gorgias' 108
   political 88
   rhetorical practice 90
   rhetorician(s) 67
   teacher(s) of 88, 89
romanticism 37, 44, 185–8, 190, 203n13
   Egyptian 73
   German 20, 70, 143, 155
   Heidelberg 37
   Phaeacian 73
   romantic 21, 142, 143, 154, 155, 160, 186–8, 190, 212n1
   romantic hermeneutics 21
   romantics 37

science(s) 9, 13, 29, 35, 83, 87, 95, 108, 110, 117, 119, 121, 124, 131, 138, 161, 179, 207n14
   eidetic 90
   empirical 103–6, 165
   historian of 86
   and history 38, 39, 150, 152, 176
   human 10–1

Ionian 47, 51
   of language 153 *See* language
   mathematical, of mathematics 83, 89–90, 93
   method of 110
   modern 8, 20, 34, 104, 106–7, 130, 132
   natural 32–3, 106, 129–31
   new 47, 130, 176
   Newtonian 38, 144
   non-science 94
   philosophical 161, 165
   political 78
   speculative 177
   theory of 161
   universal 130
sophists 1, 26–7, 64, 67, 87–8, 92, 102, 109–15, 119–20, 121–4, 162, 194n17
   and the dialectician, and the philosopher 6, 29, 102, 108–9, 114, 119, 122–4
   and Socrates 76
   sophistry 115
soul(s) 35, 77, 79, 93, 126, 136–7, 143–4, 147, 149, 172, 186, 205n13, 210n10, 211n8
   and the body 35–6, 134, 136, 164
   Christian 68
   communion of 20
   and death 102
   essence of 137
   fire of 46
   human, individual 78, 143–4
   immortality of 172
   and life 102, 106, 119
   as *psuchē* 53, 75 *See psuchē*
   transmigration of 45, 190
   and world 66, 119, 164 *See* world
spirit 9, 44, 130–1, 136–8, 143–4, 146, 154, 166–7, 176–83, 187, 190, 193, 206n2
   absolute 167
   concept of 36
   as force 136, 181
   historical, historicity of, history of 36–7, 43, 137, 175–83
   human 153, 165
   language of 186

living, life of the 153, 182
objective 182
of a people 9, 155, 180
reform of the 8, 138
romantic, of romanticism 186–8
spirituality 134
unitary 135
world 177–8
spirituality *See* spirit
stoicheion 96, 97, 205n17
Stoic(s) 149, 169
  Stoic 34, 57, 72
subjectivity 22, 32, 69, 137, 179, 182
substance 28, 35, 43, 53, 125, 131, 138, 164, 169, 170, 208n26
  as *hupokeimenon* 118
  living 182
  material 33
  metaphysics 69
  ontology *See* ontology
  as *ousia* 118
  primary and secondary 65
symbol 37, 53, 99, 191
  symbolic 37, 97, 189–91, 193
  See symbolism
symbolism 37, 186, 188
  Creuzer's 37, 189, 191–2
  See symbol

theology 75, 130, 133, 137, 141
  Christian 11
  of history 141–2
  philosophical 164
  theologian 34, 129, 138–9, 179, 185
  theological 36, 129–30, 133, 139, 152, 179, 182, 191, 198n107
  See ontotheology
thinking 1–10, 13–15, 18, 34–5, 37–8, 50, 54, 59, 62–5, 67–9, 71–7, 81, 83, 87, 90, 93, 97, 100, 104, 107, 120, 126, 133, 139, 143, 145–6, 154, 157, 161, 163–4, 166, 167–9, 171–3, 178
  ancient, Greek 45–6, 53, 63, 124, 193
  and being, of being 55, 57, 114
  Christian 66
  conceptual 37–8
  as an event 170
  historical, and history 1, 9, 13, 44, 65

  in images 188
  inceptual 52, 55, 124
  law of 58
  and life 117, 168
  modern 183
  nature of 14
  as *noūs See noūs*
  Platonic 68, 72, 83, 87, 167
  scientific 107, 115
  and speaking 110
  of the spirit 180
  style of 193
  as taking in 2–4
  thing 131, 149
tradition 8, 43, 61, 63, 68, 73, 76, 79, 87, 115, 130, 139, 141–2, 151, 194n16
  Greek 88
  hermeneutic 71
  literary 19
  medieval 69
  metaphysical, of metaphysics 52
  of myth 47
  oral 62
  peripatetic 67
  Platonic 81, 103, 161
  Pythagorean 46, 58
transcendence 26, 66, 85, 142, 143, 173
  transcendental 43, 104
truth 8, 16, 22–5, 27, 29, 33, 47–50, 52–3, 55, 57, 60, 63–4, 69–70, 83, 91, 93–4, 104, 108–9, 123–5, 129–30, 132–4, 136–8, 145, 152, 155, 165–8, 175–8, 183, 188–9, 191–3, 194n16
  absolute 22
  as *alētheia* 47, 70, 124–5
  and being 53
  and certainty 172
  claim to 21, 25, 77
  concept of 25, 175
  historical 9, 77, 150
  idea of 21
  mathematical 85
  and opinion 32
  theory of 176
  true, the 77
  ultimate 180
  and untruth 166

understanding 2, 8, 9, 11–14, 16, 18–26, 38, 44, 48, 74, 76, 86, 95, 98, 107, 114, 136, 146, 159, 162, 164–5, 170, 178, 194n11, 196n43, 197n106, 207n14
   better 90
   concept of 104
   difference in 3
   mis- 132, 180
   natural 131
   philosophical 104
   pre- 68, 110
   principle of 139
   rules for 139
   self- 68, 90, 91, 93, 144
   See interpretation
universality 5, 36, 100, 120, 130, 154, 181, 191
   abstract 36
   concrete 36, 180
   logical 8
   of love 180
   of reason 180
   universal(s), the 6, 27, 35, 36, 69, 84, 85, 105, 153, 160, 164
utopia 31, 67, 71–7, 81
   counter- 78
   as literary genre 71–2
   utopian 71–3, 76–7, 81

verb 5, 28, 65, 121, 125, 208n23
   verbal 10
verbum 25, 64, 138, 139, 201n32 See word
virtue(s) 79, 102, 136, 145–6, 150–1
   as *aretē* 76, 78–9, 89, 109, 159, 161
   four, cardinal, Platonic 35, 78–9
   knowledge of, teachability of 78, 159
   political 79
   as *virtus* 136

word 5, 8, 13–16, 19, 26, 30–1, 38, 56, 63, 97–8, 107, 110, 120–1, 124, 138–9, 145, 147, 165, 168, 171, 210n5
   and concept 38, 44, 119, 182
   of God 129, 134, 139
   history of 44, 54
   and image 38
   and language 55
   living 129
   and picture 38

primordial 171
temporal 28, 208n23
See onoma
world(s) 2, 4–8, 14, 22, 31, 35–8, 43, 47–51, 55, 66, 75, 80, 92, 97, 104, 107–8, 124, 130–1, 141, 144–6, 154, 163, 169–72, 176, 179, 182, 186–7, 193, 208n26
   ancient 186
   animal 135
   Asian 188–9
   being-in-the 22
   -body 36, 164
   Christian 177
   classical 189–90
   cultural, and culture 68, 141
   early religious 188–90, 193
   Eastern 45, 177, 190
   experience of 9, 34, 145, 171
   First World War 44
   Greco-Roman 177
   historical 141, 144–5
   history, and history 9, 13, 148–51, 167, 176–9, 183, 193
   of ideas 117
   inner 189
   intelligible 7, 52, 69, 157, 159, 164, 180
   layout of, order, ordering of 2, 5, 17, 48, 51, 75
   life- 107, 122
   material, physical 75, 135
   mathematical, of numbers 90, 102, 114
   mind and 4, 194n11
   otherworldly, otherwordliness 31, 38, 77, 148–9, 151–2, 190
   picture 48–51
   pre-classical 37
   real 164
   romantic 190
   sensible 7, 52, 69
   -soul 36, 119, 119, 164
   spirit 177–8
   view(s), view of the 30, 164, 187
   and wisdom 131, 133
   See experience, history, life
writing (as human activity) 63, 97, 98, 99, 119, 166, 189, 191